Britain as a military power,
1688–1815

Also by Jeremy Black and published by UCL Press

European warfare, 1660–1815
America or Europe? British foreign policy, 1739–63

Britain as a military power, 1688–1815

Jeremy Black

© Jeremy Black, 1999

This book is copyright under the Berne Convention.
No reproduction without permission.
All rights reserved.

Published in the UK in 1999 by UCL Press

UCL Press Limited
Taylor & Francis Group
1 Gunpowder Square
London EC4A 3DE

and

325 Chestnut Street, 8th Floor
Philadelphia
PA 19106
USA

The name of University College London (UCL) is a registered trade mark
used by UCL Press with the consent of the owner.

ISBN: 1-85728-772-X HB

British Cataloguing-in-Publication Data
A catalogue record for this book is available from the British Library.

Library of Congress Cataloging-in-Publication Data are available

Typeset by Graphicraft Limited, Hong Kong
Printed and bound by T. J. International Ltd, Padstow

Contents

Preface		vii
Maps		ix
1	Introduction	1
2	The suppression of rebellion	11
3	Conflict in Europe 1688–1763	45
4	Naval triumph, 1688–1763	79
5	The conquest of Empire, 1688–1763	115
6	Rebellion successful: the American War of Independence	155
7	Conflict in Europe, 1793–1815	193
8	Naval success, 1793–1815	221
9	Britain the world power, 1783–1815	241
10	Conclusion: Britain as a military power	267
	Notes	295
	Index	321

For Kim

Preface

Between the "Glorious Revolution" of 1688–9 and the defeat of Napoleon at Waterloo in 1815, Britain became the strongest military power in the world, arguably the strongest at any time till then, and also the strongest in relative and absolute terms until the American century of the present age. This book is an attempt to explain this process. It concentrates on the military dimension, because it is all too easy to respond to understandable scholarly interest in themes such as state-building by losing sight of the course of conflict. In place of an emphasis on domestic political and economic factors at the expense of military ones, I have stressed the importance for Britain of armed force directly applied. We have to look at more than just institutional and resource reasons for Britain's "greatness".

Another important aspect of this work is its comprehensive nature. Britain's military history for this period is usually considered in separate compartments: Europe, North America, the West Indies. Land and sea power are also placed in their own compartments. This book is unusual in that it combines land and sea, European and extra-European effectiveness and war. The entire spectrum of roles played by armed force in Britain's rise to great-power status is synthesized.

The approach is not deterministic; instead, discussion of "structural" aspects of British strength is matched with consideration of the contingent nature of challenge and success. Intensive archival work leads to an emphasis on contingency and provides a sense of exceptions – of the singularity and malleability of events. Britain's armed forces operated in unpredictable situations and particular circumstances. It is necessary to understand the alternate possibilities in given cases, and to provide a counterpoint to general works that seek similarities and congruences.

With more space, it would have been possible to include much that has unfortunately had to be omitted. Despite the temptation to remove much of the discussion of events, I have left this in because all too few people are aware of them. Similarly, despite pressures of space, I have retained some of the accounts by participants: they offer a valuable perspective that counters the tendency to provide clear-cut descriptions of past engagements. They also serve as a reminder of the brutality and carnage of war. Major Skerry of the 52nd Regiment recorded after the victory of 15 May 1791 over the Indian ruler Tipu Sultan of Mysore, "The night of the 15th we lay on the field of action, amidst hundreds of mutilated carcasses, and shocked with the cries of such as had the misfortune to survive their wounds". Another British participant noted

> some of the poor fellows had ghastly wounds – you might easily distinguish the handywork of the 15th Regiment Dragoons who are very powerful men. Some wretches had half their faces cut off some their hands lying by their sides; and two bodies I particularly marked which had their heads severed clean off by a single stroke, and lay at a distance from the trunks.[1]

I am grateful for the opportunity to develop views provided by giving lectures at the Consortium on Revolutionary Europe conference at Baton Rouge, the Newport Preservation Society conference on Trade and Empire, the Wellington conference at Southampton, the Triangle Institute for Security Studies, the Institute of Historical Research, and the Universities of Bristol, Cambridge, Exeter, Massachusetts – Boston, North Carolina – Asheville, Oxford, Richmond, Southeastern Louisiana, SUNY-Prospect, Texas – Dallas and Texas – San Antonio, at Adelphi, Appalachian State, James Madison, Lamar, Ohio State, Southern Methodist and Stephen F. Austin Universities, at the Virginia Military Institute, and at Assumption College and Mary Washington College. I am grateful to Enid Case for granting access to the Hill papers. I have benefited from the comments of Keith Bartlett, Huw Bowen, Gerry Bryant, John Derry, David Gates, Jan Glete, Richard Harding, Tony Hayter, Peter Marshall, Richard Middleton, Roger Morriss, Murray Pittock, Nicholas Rodger, Armstrong Starkey, Ian Steele, Philip Woodfine and three anonymous readers on earlier drafts of sections of the book. The book is dedicated to my brother-in-law with much appreciation for his friendship.

Maps

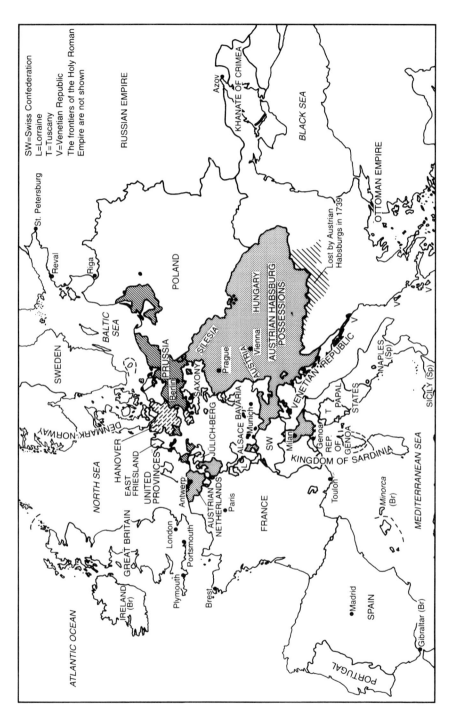

Europe in 1739

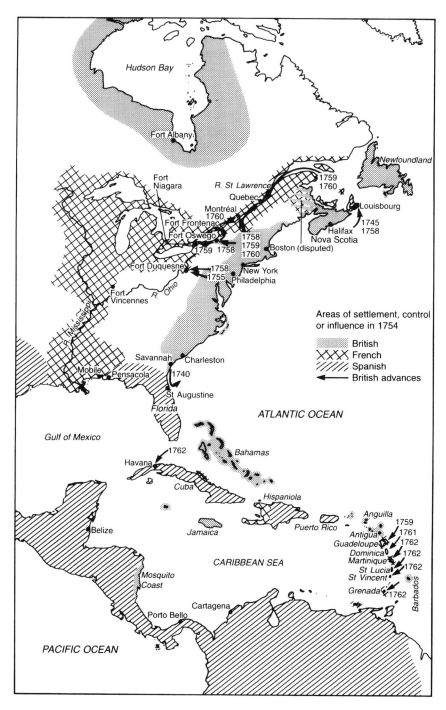

North America and the Caribbean

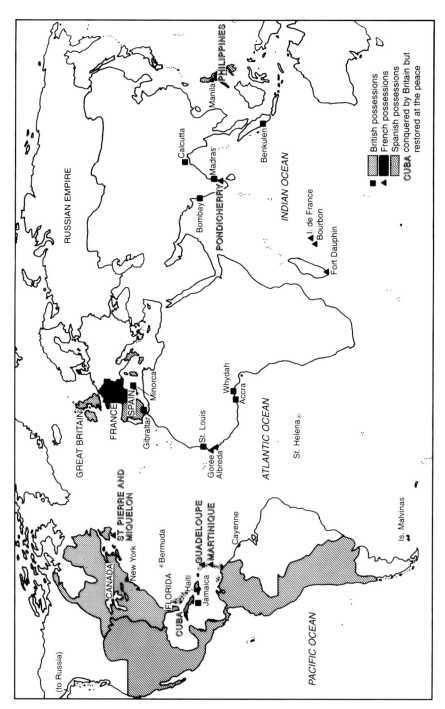

RUSSIAN EMPIRE

GREAT BRITAIN
FRANCE
SPAIN
Gibraltar
Minorca

PHILIPPINES
Manila

Calcutta
Madras
Bombay
PONDICHERRY
Benkulen

INDIAN OCEAN

I. de France
Bourbon
Fort Dauphin

Whydah
Accra
St. Louis
Gorée
Albreda

ATLANTIC OCEAN

St. Helena

(to Russia)

ST PIERRE AND
MIQUELON
CANADA
New York
Bermuda
FLORIDA
Haiti
CUBA
Jamaica
GUADELOUPE
MARTINIQUE
Cayenne

PACIFIC OCEAN

Is. Malvinas

British possessions
French possessions
Spanish possessions
CUBA conquered by Britain but
restored at the peace

The world in 1763

CHAPTER ONE

Introduction

A parliamentary-based system

Between 1688 and 1815 Britain fought its way to being the strongest power in the world. This involved her forces in conflict across the globe, from the waters of the Pacific, where Anson captured the treasure-filled Manila Galleon, to the rocky reaches of the Breton coast, where warships sought signs of French opponents seeking to leave their blockaded bases. Redcoated soldiers served on every continent bar Antarctica, and braved disease and terrain without the technological aids their modern counterparts benefit from. Today, there is scant sympathy for imperial power and colonial rule, and indeed for war, especially if aggressive. There is also a risk that this lack of sympathy may lead to a failure to understand the nature of the British military achievement and its importance both for Britain and for other countries and peoples.

The current orthodoxy in explaining Britain's rise to great power status focuses on domestic political, rather than military, factors. It is based on the interpretation offered by John Brewer in his study *The sinews of power. war, money and the English state, 1688–1783* (1989). Brewer emphasizes the inherent strength and the political culture of Britain, specifically the system of parliamentary-backed public finance that raised substantial sums of money at a lower rate of interest than that paid by rivals, particularly France, the state that for most of the period opposed Britain in Europe, on the oceans and elsewhere in the world. This system is traced to the "Glorious Revolution" of 1688–9, in which James II was replaced by William III of Orange. It was followed by a process of constitutional, political and financial settlement, which ensured that by 1695 William was obliged to meet Parliament every year, that Parliament was elected at least every three years, and that public finance focused on a Bank of England and a national debt guaranteed by Parliament.

Furthermore, Parliament served to incorporate the powerful social groups and political interests in the country, and to ensure that the government, answerable to them in Parliament, was in some way theirs. This was more a process of combination of interests and views than simply a matter of political consent. Such a process was particularly important because of the possibility that differences in the social structure, specifically between land and trade, would lead to political division. Instead, an important aspect of the success of the House of Commons was its openness to the new emergent mercantile and industrial interests of the period: both in membership and in the House's consideration of commercial views. Commercial growth did not lead to serious social tension or political problems. An appreciable number of the businessmen in the Commons came from elite families, and the heavy representation of boroughs in the Commons increased the urban, and thus often the commercial, presence in the House. Furthermore, commercial pressure groups played a major role in the Commons. Parliament provided an opportunity for commercial groups to exert influence and to seek to define public support for commerce, greater than any forum available in France.

Parliament therefore can be presented as a crucial nexus of political, social and economic relationships that helped to create as well as define and reflect British power. This has been seen as fundamental to Britain's military power because of the central role of military expenditure in government finances. Thanks to Parliament, it was possible to obtain national public support for the government's fiscal needs, both through borrowing and through taxation. Parliament both validated existing taxes and made possible new ones. Thus, an income tax was introduced when wartime needs in the French Revolutionary War called for far more than customary wartime financial resources.

This analysis, an essentially domestic explanation of Britain's rise to greatness, is problematic for two reasons. First, it neglects or underplays the problems created by Parliament's position. Secondly, it suggests that warfare is primarily a matter of resources and domestic political circumstances.

The first is readily apparent, and is so for a number of reasons. First, it was by no means the case that Parliament accepted what the government felt to be necessary. Sir Robert Walpole's proposals to extend excise regulations to wine and tobacco in 1733, the centrepiece of his financial strategy, provoked a furious political row, and the ministry had to abandon the scheme. Although the Walpole government was opposed anyway to taking an active role in the War of the Polish Succession (1733–5), the failure of its financial plans and the evidence of a loss of control over Parliament were also important in preventing participation in the conflict, and thus in resisting France and Spain as they regained influence in Europe.

More generally, the absence of a reliable party unity on which governments could rest left ministers feeling vulnerable to attack, and this caused particular problems in wartime. Despite devoting so much of their time to electoral patronage and parliamentary management, first ministers, such as Walpole and the Duke of Newcastle, knew that it was difficult to maintain the impression of governmental control of the Commons. In 1744 and 1746, during the War of the Austrian Succession, Lord Carteret was weakened by his inability to secure the management of the Commons. During the Seven Years' War (1756–63) the approach of the parliamentary session in 1756 destroyed the Newcastle ministry, and in the subsequent political crisis the creation of a viable leadership in the Commons was the key issue. Furthermore, the large proportion of government expenditure met by borrowing, rather than taxation, can be presented in part as a response to the known reluctance of Parliament to raise taxation.

Secondly, even if Parliament did support government proposals, that did not necessarily imply that popular consent was gained. Despite parliamentary backing in 1738 for a pacific policy towards Spain, public agitation helped to create a political crisis that led to war the following year. After the Seven Years' War the government sought to ease the burden of its debts. This was believed to be necessary in its own right and also a vital preliminary to any future conflict. However, the Cider Excise of 1763, a tax upon cider and perry made in Britain, encountered considerable opposition and was repealed in 1766, as were the Stamp Act duties imposed on the American colonies in 1765. Indeed, the danger of a parliamentary system, whether democratic, quasi-democratic or neither, was clearly reflected in this episode, because those who cannot prevail in the assembly or who feel unrepresented in it will not necessarily accept its injunctions.

Parliament sat for less than half the year and, in particular, was in recess during the summer and autumn, the campaigning seasons. Thus, it was not in session during Marlborough's very costly victory at Malplaquet (1709), or when George II and Carteret mishandled the victory at Dettingen (1743), or during the 1779 panic about a possible Bourbon invasion, or when the Revolutionary French overran the Austrian Netherlands (Belgium) in November 1792. At other times, Parliament could be the occasion of unwelcome criticism and pressure, as when William Pitt the Elder attacked the government during the Jacobite rising of 1745, and again over the feared French invasion of 1756.

The role of parliamentary opposition can be seen in two ways. Pitt can be presented as a cynical opportunist, needlessly threatening political and governmental stability at a time of national crisis. Alternatively, it can be argued that the existing government could not cope, that war accentuated a central feature of the political system, namely that successful parliamentary management required competent leadership and acceptable policies, as well as patronage, and that such policies had to take note of the wider political world, especially in periods of real and apparent crisis. Furthermore, the difficulty of managing Parliament could lead to the rise of a more competent leadership.

Thus the existence of Parliament caused serious difficulties, as well as the advantages that are generally stressed in schematic accounts. The same was true of the other representative bodies within the British empire, for this was an imperial system in which consent was institutionalized. Colonel Dudley, the Governor of Massachusetts, complained in 1703 about a lack of support:

> the neighbour charter colonies of Rhode Island and Connecticut sit still covered with our forces, and will not allow me a man nor a penny towards the charge after all possible application made to them, but on the contrary in Rhode Island they hide the deserters both from the sea and land service and no regulation of trade nor observation of the Acts of Parliament are to be hoped for there.

Dudley noted that the General Assembly of Massachusetts had refused to rebuild the fort at Pemaquid, while as the Council of the colony was "of the people's choice . . . I am fully doubtful they are more careful of their election than of the Queen's service and satisfaction, in so much that I have only power to deny anything offered me that is amiss in the assembly, but no assistance to bring to pass what is necessary for the service, which will be in a great measure altered when Her Majesty will please to assume her just power to name her own Council here as in all the other governments in America".[1]

It is unclear how much weight should be placed on these problems, either with the Westminster Parliament or with other bodies. Much clearly depended and depends on an obviously subjective response to the issues of stability, continuity and order. This mirrors the role of debates over Britain's foreign policy, strategic needs and military capability. Once it came to be necessary to translate rhetoric into policy, there was little sense of generally agreed steps, more particularly of how to respond to adversity and difficult circumstances.

In an age of competitive international relations, the Westminster Parliament was unusual in being a representative institution that survived. Thus the parliamentary system became more part of British exceptionalism. However, the very different fate of other states with such systems, such as Poland and the United Provinces (Dutch), suggests caution about placing too great an explanatory weight upon them.

Resources and war

If the existence of Parliament itself may not have been crucial to British military success, that is not a counter to the argument that the nature of British public finances was important. They were crucial to the resources available for the pursuit of security and gain. Resources were particularly important to the ability of Britain to take part in sustained warfare, and also permitted the state and country to recover between conflicts. The success of British public finances lay in their permanence and their acceptability, allowing the shifts from war to peace and from peace to war to be made, in fiscal terms, quite effectively. As so many contemporaries acknowledged, access to funds lay at the heart of Britain's success.

However, the notion that power is a product of resources, is indeed the use of resources, has to be qualified. There are many instances of states being defeated by rivals that possessed fewer resources – most obviously, in this period, of the survival of Prussia during the Seven Years' War. More generally, any consideration of resources has to be within a number of contexts. First, political, specifically the nature and number of external and internal commitments, and the dynamics of the international system, not least the exigencies of alliance relationships. Secondly, the conversion of resources – men, *matériel* and money – into military units is and was not an automatic or uncomplicated process, but rather one that reflects and reflected different conventions and administrative practices and possibilities. Thirdly, the effectiveness and use of units and weaponry were, and are, not simply a matter of the quantity of resources, but of tactics, strategy, morale and social–military characteristics such as discipline and leadership. The notion of resources has to include non-quantifiable ones such as political skill. Two crucial issues were how much "quality" in resources could offset a lack of "quantity", and the flexibility of the response to demands and crises. Even then, as the Duke of Cumberland pointed out in 1757, "no mortal can answer for success in military affairs".[2] Later that year he was to be defeated and disgraced.

Multiple capability

It was not the availability of resources *per se* that was crucial to the character of the British military system, certainly to the character of its system on land. Instead, this system was most impressive because of its multiple capability, one of the major themes of this book and the basis of its organization. As a military power, the British state operated in four spheres, although it did not possess a strategic theory to that effect.

The first was in opposition to public disorder and rebellion, both in the British Isles and in British overseas possessions. The most prominent instance of the latter was in opposition to the American War of Independence, but there were other, less well-known episodes, for example the campaigns against escaped slaves in Jamaica. The gap in military strength between army and insurgents was far less than would be the case in Britain today. The state did not monopolize firearms as it now seeks to do, its firearms were less powerful than the modern counterparts, and there were important traditions of military practice in parts of the imperial system.

The second sphere was as a land power fighting other land powers in Europe. Most of this conflict took place outside the British Isles, but there were exceptions caused by Bourbon intervention on behalf of the Jacobites, as in Ireland in 1690–1 and Scotland in 1719, and Revolutionary French invasions linked to opponents of the British state. British forces fought on the Continent in the Nine Years' War (1689–97), the War of the Spanish Succession (1702–13), the War of the Austrian Succession (1740–8), the Seven Years' War (1756–63), and the French Revolutionary and Napoleonic Wars (1792–1815), although these dates are somewhat misleading as British armies were not engaged, or even present, throughout. Thus, in the Seven Years' War, British forces campaigned on the Continent in 1758–62 and fought from 1759. British armies were mostly deployed in Western Europe, although in 1704 they advanced to Blenheim on the Danube, and in the Napoleonic War forces were sent to the Baltic, Sicily and the eastern Mediterranean. The small size and limited training of the peacetime British army made the transition to coping with the demands of continental warfare particularly difficult. The problem was exacerbated by Britain's "late" entry into Continental campaigning in a number of wars, including the Nine Years', Austrian Succession, Seven Years' and French Revolutionary Wars. Furthermore, the British were opposed to France, then at the height of its military power. Whereas Russian armies primarily operated against weakening military powers, especially Poland and, from the 1730s, the Turks, the British fought France, particularly in an area, the Low Countries, where the latter was best able to deploy its force.

The third sphere was naval. It is difficult to appreciate the constraints of eighteenth-century naval warfare, because conditions were very different to those today. This was true of the seaworthiness of sailing vessels, which, by modern standards, lacked deep keels, as well as of the rudimentary nature of charts and lighthouses. The operational problems of working ships for combat were very different to those of steam-powered vessels. The optimal conditions for combat were to come from windward in a force 4–6 wind across a sea that was relatively flat; it was more difficult to range guns in a swell. Limitations on manoeuvrability ensured that ships were deployed in line in order to maximize their firepower. The skill in handling ships entailed getting wind behind the topsails. As battles arose from chance encounters, much had to be left to the discretion of commanders. The period is commonly remembered in terms of naval triumphs, from Barfleur (1692) to Trafalgar (1805), but there were also many checks and disappointments. It was difficult both to achieve battle and to obtain victory.

The fourth sphere of operation was trans-oceanic land conflict. This can in turn be divided into two categories: warfare with European land forces, as against the French in North America, the West Indies, West Africa and India, the Spaniards in Cuba, the Philippines and the Plate Estuary, and the Dutch in South Africa, Surinam and the West Indies; and warfare with

English Privateers engaging, by Samuel Scott, c.1750. Privateers were smaller and less heavily-gunned than ships of the line, but they were more manoeuvrable and of shallower draft, and thus more appropriate for commerce raiding. The major role of privateers and of light warships – frigates, sloops, ketches etc. – is a reminder of the danger of concentrating on ships of the line and major engagements in any account of naval history. French bases, especially St. Malo and Dunkirk, proved difficult to contain and the British suffered greatly from the *guerre de course*. Higher insurance premiums, danger money for sailors, and the need to resort to convoys and other defensive measures pushed up the cost of trade. Largely thanks to the British, nearly 1,800 ships and barges insured at Marseilles were captured in the Spanish Succession War. *National Maritime Museum, London.*

non-European forces. The last was by far the most varied category of British military activity. The formal nature of hostilities varied greatly – whether, for example, the British were formally at war or not, or whether they were engaged as the auxiliaries of other powers or in their own right. Operational circumstances and possibilities also varied greatly. Fighting in India, for example, was very different to conflict with Native Americans in North America, and each was in turn very varied.

Such a multiple capability was not unique to Britain. Indeed, it was true of all the Atlantic European powers – Britain, the United Provinces, France, Spain and Portugal. A different multiple capability was also true of Austria and Russia. Austria did not engage in trans-oceanic military activities, and neither did Russia, with the minor exception of fighting in the Aleutian Islands and Alaska, unless Siberia is considered as a land ocean. However, in the case of Austria the Turks, and in Russia the Turks, Persians and various Caucasian and Central Asian people and briefly the Chinese, ensured that both powers had extensive experience in fighting non-Europeans on land.

Lastly, multiple military capability was not itself restricted to European powers. In the seventeenth century the Mughal empire of India fought in a number of very different spheres and against different opponents, including the Ahom in the forested valley of the Brahmaputra, Kangra and Garhwab in the Himalayas, the Islamic Sultanates in the Deccan, the Uzbeks beyond the Hindu Kush, the Persians around Kandahar, the forested chiefdom of Palamu, and the mobile light cavalry of the Marathas in western India. Manchu China also displayed great range. Between 1680 and 1795 the Chinese conquered Taiwan, drove the Russians from the Amur Valley, conquered Mongolia, Tibet and Xinkiang, suppressed a number of risings and invaded Myanmar (Burma), Tongking (Vietnam) and Nepal.

Thus, multiple capability was not restricted either to the Europeans or to the British. However, it can still be argued that Britain was the most successful of the European and global powers in developing and utilizing such a capability. This was related to the considerable military resources and forces beyond the direct control of government and Parliament, especially, by the 1780s, the enormous army of the East India Company, and the colonial militias. Such forces were not always effective, but at times they played a decisive role, as with the capture of Louisbourg in 1745 and the battle of Buxar in 1764. No other European powers had such a number and range of quasi-official forces at their disposal on a regular basis, and these forces were not supported by domestic revenues. Instead, to a considerable extent, these forces were "self-supporting" and not a burden on British taxpayers. The peculiar nature of the British state allowed for these forces to be deployed in the interests of Britain, but in a way that saw them removed from direct control and supervision. This was an important extra dimension of the multiple capability of the British state.

British skill in alliance warfare was also important, in Europe, India and North America. Although they frequently encountered serious difficulties in all three areas, the British were experienced, and increasingly so, in the politics of alliances and in the handling of multinational armies. This was particularly apparent in the Fourth Mysore War in India in 1799 and in Wellington's campaigns in Portugal and Spain. In contrast, in Europe the French tended to dominate their military alliances both numerically and politically. The British did not do so, except at sea.

The range of British military capability reflected, in part, British skill and success in naval and trans-oceanic operations and, in part, the cultural, political and geographical factors that led British governments not to place as great a premium on warfare on the Continent as their European opponents.[3] There was, however, nothing inevitable about this process and, indeed, in the 1740s it was far from clear that Britain would be more effective than France either in this multiple capability or, indeed, in any aspect of it.

Military challenges

The British state was not involved in an inexorable process of world conquest. Nor did it face a stable international situation. Instead, British military activity arose in response to particular circumstances, most of which were unpredictable and to which the necessary response was both unclear and controversial. This was true not only of the European situation, but also of those in India and North America. Thus, alongside any stress on resources and capability, it is necessary to consider challenge, not least because the perception of challenge was important both to strategic decisions and to the willingness of ministers to devote resources to particular ends and their ability to obtain political support for so doing.

A sense of threat was apparent from the outset of the period, when the French-backed James II sought to regain the thrones from which he had been driven in 1688–9, until its close, when Napoleon strove for the destruction of British power. Even after Nelson's victory at Trafalgar in 1805 invasion fears only relaxed periodically. The Walcheren expedition of 1809, which was aimed at the French-controlled dockyard of Antwerp, indicated continued unease about the possibility of another armada appearing and threatening either the British homeland or one of the overseas possessions. There were even concerns about Canada in this regard, as well as more obvious targets such as British-garrisoned Sicily. Indeed, the proportion of the British army absorbed by the perceived need to guard each and every weak spot was immense, leaving relatively few troops available for offensive operations. Even the navy was committed to an essentially defensive role. While the British were able to devote a sizeable force to expeditions whenever the threat eased, the type of operations they mounted is revealing. They committed roughly as many men to Walcheren as they did to the Peninsula in 1809 and, given the limitations of naval transport in the age of sail, were generally reluctant to send their disposable forces too far from home; short, sudden coups with relatively small forces against vulnerable targets which were not too distant was the preferred option, as underscored by their general strategy in the Anglo-American conflict of 1812–15.

Challenges came from European and non-European opponents, but only the former had the capability to threaten the British Isles; the Americans lacked an effective fleet, their privateers did not present such a threat and, in military terms anyway, the Americans were seen as European. However, the fact that non-Europeans did not threaten the British Isles does not mean that they did not challenge British interests. Haidar Ali and Tipu Sultan of Mysore seriously threatened the British position in the Carnatic (south east India) in the last third of the eighteenth century. It would, therefore, be misleading to present a simple contrast of European opponents taking part in a struggle with Britain for mastery while the military role of their non-European counterparts was restricted to resistance, more or less unsuccessful, to British advance.

Before turning to consider the individual spheres of British military activity, it is as well to reiterate its importance. It is a central thesis of this book that Britain's rise in and to power was not inevitable, and that it had to be fought for. Furthermore, war, preparation for it, and its consequences, were major aspects of British government and society in this period. Compared to the period 1816–1913, Britain was heavily involved in wars that were not distant and relatively limited, as many Victorian imperial conflicts were, but were, instead, both arduous and crucial to the trajectory of British politics. These wars are therefore central to British history in the period, just as they are important to specialists in military history.

CHAPTER TWO

The suppression of rebellion

Warfare within the British Isles from 1688 principally involved the suppression of rebellion. The expanded power and pretensions of the British state ensured that a characteristic feature of earlier warfare in the British Isles, namely conflict between the forces of independent kingdoms or similar bodies, was no longer the issue. Indeed, although hostility within Scotland to the Union of 1707 played a role in encouraging support for Jacobitism, the cause of the exiled Stuarts, the Jacobite risings were essentially struggles to control one imperial state, not the product of, for example, warfare between Scotland and England or attempts to increase English power in Ireland.

Conflict within the British Isles had been frequent and serious in the sixteenth and mid-seventeenth century. However, mid-seventeenth-century warfare in particular was very different from what was to follow, because the reality and possibility of foreign intervention played a major role from 1688, whereas the British civil wars of 1639–52 had been conducted with limited intervention due to the major warfare between France and Spain from 1635 until 1659. Indeed, the willingness and ability of rebels to look for foreign support were an essential feature of rebellion from 1688. This owed much to foreign support for the exiled Stuarts, but also to the growth in the size and effectiveness of the royal army under James II and his successors. It was increasingly less likely that the army could be defeated by rebels, and, indeed, this was part of a general European shift towards a greater gap in military capability between armies and actual or potential rebellions. This gap reflected the increased specialization, professionalism and size of military forces, and the extent to which the personal arms of the population were of declining military value.

William III's invasion

The role of foreign intervention in Britain was clearly demonstrated in 1688. Although this was seen by its apologists as a "Glorious Revolution", and there were, indeed, a number of risings in England, for example at Derby, Durham, Hull, Nottingham and York, they were small scale. The removal of James II (1685–8) was dependent upon an invasion by his nephew and son-in-law, William III of Orange, since 1672 the effective ruler of the Netherlands. He was motivated by a wish to use British resources in what he foresaw as an impending struggle with his bitter rival, Louis XIV of France (1643–1715). Mistakes by James and Louis enabled William to build up the powerful diplomatic and military support without which he would not have invaded. Unwilling to commit himself fully to Louis, a course that he feared would encourage other powers to help William, and unaware of the seriousness of William's schemes, James responded in an equivocal fashion to Louis' offer of naval assistance. A positive response would have justified accusations of joint Anglo-French schemes against the Dutch, which were in fact necessary if hopes of invasion were to be thwarted.

William's first invasion attempt in mid-October 1688 was defeated by storms at sea, with the loss of many supplies, including over a thousand horses, which were crucial to the mobility of any invasion force. Horses were especially liable to break their legs in storms because ships were not stabilized. However, William's second attempt was more successful, and England was invaded despite its possession of a large and undefeated navy and a substantial army. A strong north-easterly wind prevented the English fleet, then lying at the Gunfleet off Harwich, from leaving their anchorage, and this allowed William to sail into the Channel. By the time the fleet's commander, George, Lord Dartmouth finally sailed on 3 November, the main Dutch fleet was already passing Dover.

William landed at Brixham in Devon on 5 November at a time that the pursuing fleet was no nearer than Beachy Head. Even so, a successful attack would have weakened William, but, at a Council of War on 5 November, the English captains decided not to attack what they believed would be a larger Dutch force and, thereafter, first storms and then bad weather prevented the English fleet from acting until it surrendered to William's authority on 13 December. This was the most ignominious naval campaign in English naval history, a campaign that was flawed from the outset by a defensive, reactive mentality that owed something to England being formally at peace and much to division and discontent among the captains.[1]

The position on land was no better. William was outnumbered by James, who blocked the route to London with a force of 30,000 men on Salisbury Plain. However, indecision, ill-health, and the desertion of his younger daughter, Anne, led James to abandon his army on 24 November, weakening his troops' morale. It had already been hit by dissension and conspiracy among the officer corps, not least the Association of Protestant Officers, which had been formed in 1688 in order to resist a possible purge of Protestant officers. Although only a handful of officers deserted to William soon after he landed, and they took few troops with them, these desertions wrecked James' confidence in the army. William seized the initiative without provoking a direct clash, which might have rallied support to James had he been successful. He marched on London and benefited from the power vacuum created by the disintegration of James' authority and power, a disintegration in which the army shared. It retreated before William's advance, losing large numbers of deserters, and was finally disbanded on James' orders.[2]

Scotland 1689–91

Scotland and Ireland did not fall so easily. On 11 April 1689, William and his wife Mary were proclaimed joint rulers of Scotland by the Convention of the Scottish Estates, but it lacked the legitimacy of the English parliamentary settlement, and five days later, the most active of James' Scottish supporters, John Graham of Claverhouse, Viscount Dundee, a Lowland Scot who had experience of counter-insurgency against the Covenanters in south-west Scotland, raised James' standard outside Dundee. Dundee had been appointed Commander-in-Chief of the army in Scotland by James in December 1688; in 1689 the separate existence of the army was abolished by the new regime.

Although Dundee captured Perth on 10 May, he was initially very short of men: on 8 May he commanded only about 200. The ineffective George, 1st Duke of Gordon surrendered Edinburgh Castle to William's supporters on 13 June: his small garrison had been affected by desertion and blockade. Dundee had meanwhile retired into the Highlands to obtain recruits, pursued by the royal army under Hugh Mackay of Scourie. The two clashed at the Pass of Killiecrankie while seeking to control Blair Castle in Perthshire which commanded, as it still does, a crucial north–south route through the Highlands.

Dundee had only 2,000 men, Mackay twice as many, but, on the evening of 27 July 1689, Dundee had the advantage of advancing from higher ground, while his opponents lacked the effective artillery that was to help the Duke of Cumberland at Culloden in 1746. Furthermore, unlike on the latter occasion, the firepower of the government forces was lessened both by their use of matchlocks rather than flintlocks, and by their employment of plug rather than socket bayonets: muskets could not be fired with these bayonets in place. After an inconsequential exchange of fire, the Highlanders threw down their guns and charged with their broadswords in a Highland charge. Mackay's static line collapsed at once under the charge, but, at the close of the battle, Dundee was shot dead and the victory had cost nearly

1,000 casualties; their opponents lost about 2,000 dead and 500 prisoners.[3] The high casualties on both sides reflected the willingness of both to fight hand-to-hand, which was extremely dangerous.

Victory led the doubtful clans to rally to James' cause. Dundee's successor, Colonel Alexander Cannon, who had brought 300 infantry from Ireland to reinforce the army, found himself in command of 5,000 men. However, swift moves by Mackay and Cannon's indecisiveness kept the Jacobites out of Perth and Aberdeen. The dynamic of success, so crucial in any rebellion that seeks rapidly to take over a state (as opposed to mounting a long drawn-out resistance), had been lost. A Lowland Scot, who lacked experience of Highland warfare, Cannon refused to engage Mackay and, instead, attacked an apparently vulnerable garrison of untrained Cameronian Covenanters at Dunkeld. He was, however, repulsed in bitter streetfighting on 21 August and retreated to Mull, while the Highlanders dispersed to their homes. The Cameronian commander, Lieutenant-Colonel William Cleland, died, like Dundee, as victory was obtained: battle was hazardous for officers as well as men.

Cannon was replaced by Major-General Thomas Buchan, but he was surprised and defeated on 1 May 1690 by Mackay's cavalry on the Haughs of Cromdale. The Jacobites had, therefore, lost the ability to secure victory, so crucial to their supporters' morale, as well as the initiative. Reinforced by clansmen, Buchan entered Aberdeenshire after his defeat, but he proved unwilling to attack Aberdeen. Loss of support and Mackay's advance led Buchan to retreat into the mountains in Lochaber. There his forces dwindled, an instructive example against the claim that Charles Edward Stuart could have fought on successfully in 1746 after Culloden.

The Jacobite army fell to fewer than 1,000 men and they posed no major threat to the Williamite position. Most of the Highland chiefs swore allegiance to William in late 1691, a process facilitated by indemnity, bribes and being allowed to obtain the permission of James. The surrender of the Bass Rock fortress in June 1694 marked the end of the war in Scotland.[4]

Ireland

The decisive battles were fought in Ireland. Support for James was stronger and French intervention easier than in Scotland. The Presbyterians who provided William with backing in Scotland were less important in Ireland and mostly confined to Ulster. Scotland was further from the major French naval base of Brest, and the route from the base at Dunkirk to Scotland was subject to the degree to which Anglo-Dutch naval power could be more readily brought to bear in the North Sea.

James II left France for Ireland in March 1689, landing at Kinsale on 12 March and arriving in Dublin on 24 March. Although he brought no more than 5,000 men, James received the support of most of the island. He was more popular there than William had been in England when he invaded it. Irish backing for James played a major role in persuading the Westminster Parliament to declare war on Louis XIV, thus securing William's geopolitical objective in invading Britain.

William's position was improved by the degree to which Ireland represented military potential, rather than strength. The army there was weak and poorly trained. About one-third of its 1688 strength had been lost in a poorly-managed attempt to challenge William's invasion of England. In 1689 a large new army was raised for James in Ireland, but it lacked adequate equipment, especially muskets and powder, and the largely agrarian Irish economy was not able to sustain the numbers envisaged. The Jacobites suffered from a serious shortage of funds, which led to the issue of a depreciated coinage. Warrants for raising 40,000 new troops had been issued in January 1689, but the size of the total army probably never exceeded 36,000; although that was a large force. These numbers were vitiated by poor training, which affected the battlefield capability of the infantry, especially its ability to manoeuvre under sustained fire. The artillery was also poor, although the cavalry was effective, in both battle and skirmish.

The Dublin Protestants were disarmed by the Jacobites in February 1689, but Ulster resisted. In March, Richard Duke of Tyrconnel's Jacobite forces overran most of Ulster, winning a battle at Dromore (14 March) and capturing Coleraine, but Enniskillen and Londonderry held out. Londonderry, fearing massacre by the Catholics, resisted a siege in which the Jacobites had few cannon and men, and was relieved by the English fleet on 28 July after the boom across the River Foyle blocking the harbour had been broken. Naval power thus offered William military flexibility and denied James overall control. Although able to land men and supplies at Kinsale and Bantry Bay in 1689, holding off the attempt by the English fleet to intervene in the indecisive battle of Bantry Bay (1 May), the French failed to challenge William's control of the Irish Sea. Thanks to this control, William was able to overcome the logistical problems of supplying a large force in Ireland, problems that were exacerbated after the Jacobites resorted to scorched-earth tactics from the autumn of 1689. The fleet thus enabled the British state to concentrate its resources, providing not just mobility, but also a local concentration of strength sufficient to achieve military goals.

On 13 August 1689, 10,000 of William's troops, many Huguenots (emigré French Protestants) and Dutch, landed near Bangor, County Down. They were no longer required to overawe England, and William felt that Ireland was more important than Scotland: it was certainly more so in the struggle with France. His Irish army was under the command of Marshal Herman von Schomberg, a Protestant general who had left the service of Louis XIV when that monarch revoked the Edict of Nantes in 1685. Having landed, Schomberg dispatched some troops to occupy Belfast successfully, while he led most of his army on an advance on Carrickfergus, a fortified port the rapid fall of which demonstrated the potential effectiveness of warfare in this period. It surrendered on 27 August, after a two-day bombardment by warships and shore batteries.

In general, as in the civil conflicts of 1639–52, the poorly fortified nature of most British towns and fortresses ensured that they fell more rapidly than positions in regions where the British fought on the Continent, such as the Low Countries. This had important implications in terms of the timetable and logistics of campaigns; they were faster moving than their counterparts in the Low Countries. However, it would be misleading to suggest that all positions within the British Isles fell rapidly or that sieges were generally short. This was not the case with Londonderry in 1689, Limerick in 1690, or Edinburgh and Stirling castles in 1745–6. Limerick had lacked modern fortifications, but its castellated walls were much improved in the weeks before the siege.

Having captured Carrickfergus, Schomberg then marched south to Dundalk, his advance handicapped by a shortage of supplies. At Dundalk he assembled his army in a good defensive position with secure maritime links across the Irish Sea to England, but the marshy character of the encampment was to prove fatal. The poorly trained and equipped Jacobite forces under James II moved north, but Schomberg refused to march out to fight them, and both armies then retired to winter quarters. Schomberg lost up to half of his troops that winter due to disease, especially dysentry and typhus.

Just as seriously, his failure to advance gave James II an opportunity to consolidate his position in Ireland. In dealing with rebellions, it was necessary to move rapidly in order to prevent such consolidation, a point appreciated by George II's forces when pressing Charles Edward Stuart in the winter of 1745–6. This necessity was a major aspect of the military requirement produced by a political context – the suppression of rebellion – that clearly differed from conflict on the Continent against other regular forces. To a considerable extent, however, the war in Ireland in 1689–91 differed from a rebellion of the type of the Irish rising of 1798 in that both sides engaged in position warfare and fielded forces of a regular character.

Nevertheless, for William in 1689–91, as for George II in 1745–6 and the government in 1798, speed was also of the essence, because it was considered necessary to free troops both for Continental operations and to act against any French invasion in support of the rebellion. Critical of Schomberg for having failed to force a battle, William decided that he would have to take command in the 1690 campaign, a decision that would he hoped lend added urgency to the task.

James' army had also been badly affected by disease, and he lost the strategic initiative. He was unable to challenge William's control of Ulster. The campaigning season in early 1690 was taken up by Schomberg's siege of Charlemont, on the Armagh–Tyrone border. Although successful, the time taken indicated the danger of piecemeal advances accomplished without the defeat of the opposing field army.

Meanwhile, William had been building up his forces in Ireland. He hired 7,000 Danish troops and fresh Huguenot units, and brought over another 6,000 English recruits. The new forces were well armed, with flintlock muskets, and the Dutch and Danes had bayonets as well. By the start of the 1690 campaign, William's effective strength was about 35,000 men. William also improved the supply situation, awarding the contract to supply bread to his troops in Ireland to an effective Jewish victualling partnership based in The Hague. Louis XIV also sent reinforcements to James, but they were far fewer than those joining his opponents.

William landed near Carrickfergus on 14 June and marched south. Ignoring French advice that he should abandon Dublin and retreat beyond the Shannon to western Ireland, James, in turn, marched north to Dundalk. After a skirmish at Moyry Pass, between Dundalk and Newry, the outnumbered James, who was a poor commander, withdrew to take up a defensive position covering Dublin behind the river Boyne, the sole defensible barrier, although one that was fordable.

This position was attacked by William on 1 July: he outnumbered James by about 36,000 to 24,000. William first launched a diversion, under Schomberg's son Count Meinhard, that outflanked the Jacobite left. James thought this force was the main Williamite body and dispatched the bulk of his army to counter it. Then William's infantry crossed the river at Oldbridge, while William, at the head of another force, crossed the river by a ford downstream (to the east). William's infantry, thanks in part to their bayonets, fought off Irish infantry and, particularly, cavalry attacks for two hours. Finally, the Irish cavalry were attacked on their right flank by the Williamite cavalry that had crossed further downstream. Under heavy pressure and concerned about the dangers of being surrounded, the Jacobites retreated. The retreat rapidly deteriorated into a confused flight with only the disciplined French infantry successfully delaying the pursuit. A demoralized James fled to Kinsale and then France, never to return. Yet his army had only lost about 1,000 men (William lost about 500) and, although Dublin was abandoned, the Jacobites were able to regroup at Limerick. The battle of the Boyne is an example of the error of assuming that warfare in this period was indecisive.

Having entered Dublin on 6 July 1690, part of William's army advanced west on Athlone, a major bridging point over the Shannon, but it was thwarted when the bridge there was broken. The nature of military engineering in the period was such that it was very difficult to build a bridge rapidly while on campaign, and the usual expedient, bridges of boats, had many disadvantages, not least the difficulty of securing sufficient boats. After capturing Waterford, and thus improving his maritime communications, William then turned on Limerick, the major port in west Ireland,

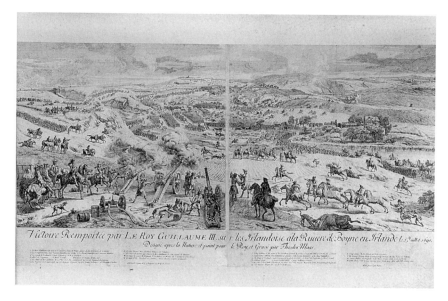

The Victory of William III at the Battle of the Boyne, 1 July 1690. Etching by Dirck Maas. Like many seventeenth-century battles, this was won by the larger force, but both the battle and the conflict in Ireland also demonstrated that, far from war being won by planned action, it was frequently the side that was less handicapped by deficiencies that was successful: coping with problems was the major skill of command. In battle, the launching of attacks and the retention and use of reserves amidst the fog of war was often crucial. Reproduction of Battle of the Boyne by Dick Maas *courtesy of the National Gallery of Ireland.*

although his siege train was badly damaged on route after it had been intercepted at Ballyneety by Patrick Sarsfield on 12 August. Partly as a result of the serious loss of gunpowder, the fortifications were still largely intact, despite a breach, when William unsuccessfully tried to storm Limerick on 27 August. The breach was only 40 yards wide and the attacking force suffered heavy losses from cannon fire from the walls. The overconfident William suffered over 2,300 casualties, a major loss of trained manpower. Short of shot and powder and affected by his heavy casualties and by very wet weather, William raised the siege on 29 August. His troops pulled back from the line of the Shannon and went into winter quarters. Although the Boyne had proved decisive for the war in eastern Ireland, the Irish war effort had not collapsed after the battle.

A separate expedition under John Churchill, Earl of Marlborough, launched against the major ports on the south coast and supported by the navy, was more successful. Cork surrendered on 27 September after its fortifications were breached by a bombardment from higher ground, and the Jacobite outworks were overrun. James Fort and Charles Fort, which dominated the harbour at Kinsale, followed in October. These successes improved the British naval position in Irish waters and made French reinforcement of the Irish more difficult. It was at Kinsale that Spanish troops had landed in 1601 in order to challenge the Elizabethan/Jacobean conquest of Ireland.

Nevertheless, thanks to their naval victory off Beachy Head in 1690, the French maintained their communications with Ireland: from Brest to the west coast of Ireland. This did not always work to James' advantage. Indeed, the French brigade was evacuated through Galway on 12 September 1690, considerably weakening the Jacobites and reflecting Louis XIV's far greater concern with the Low Countries.

In 1691 William concentrated on the war in the Spanish Netherlands, and his army in Ireland was commanded by a Dutch general, Godard van Reede van Ginkel. Athlone fell on 30 June, after hard fighting and a very heavy bombardment, with more than 12,000 cannonballs and 600 mortar bombs fired by 36 cannon and six mortars: the ability to fire so many reflected the industrial and logistical strengths of the English military system. The fall of Athlone opened the route across the Shannon towards Galway and the west coast and ensured that the Irish would have to fight to prevent such an advance. Sarsfield suggested that the Jacobites avoid battle, hold their major positions of Galway and Limerick, and harass their opponent's supply areas and lines, but he was overruled by the Marquis de St Ruth, a commander sent, without troops, by Louis.

On 12 July 1691 the two armies, each about 20,000 strong, met at Aughrim, a position prepared by St Ruth. After a bitter struggle in which the Irish made good use of field boundaries as breastworks, driving the English back on several occasions, St Ruth was killed by a chance cannon shot and the demoralized cavalry on the Irish left, pressed hard by the English cavalry, retreated. This collapsed the Irish position: the leaderless centre came under intense pressure and much of the infantry was killed in the retreat. The Irish lost possibly 7,000 killed, their opponents about 2,000 dead and wounded.

Aughrim was even more decisive than the Boyne. Galway, attacked on 19 July, surrendered on 21 July when favourable terms were offered. Sligo followed on 14 September. Twenty-three thousand Jacobite troops remained in Limerick, but they were badly equipped and led, and morale was poor. Ginkel arrived on 25 August, opened fire with his major battery on 8 September, firing over 10,000 cannon rounds in five days, hitting the defenders' morale and stamina, and on 15–16 September built a pontoon bridge across the Shannon. The town was surrounded as a naval squadron at the mouth of the Shannon blocked the planned French reinforcements. On 22 September Limerick was invested on all sides and on 23 September the demoralized Jacobites asked for a cease-fire. This led to the Treaty of Limerick, signed on 3 October, under which the Jacobites surrendered and those who wished, 19,000 "Wild Geese", sailed to France to fight for

James and Louis on the Continent. The war in Ireland had been brought to a close.[5]

The strategic initiative grasped by William in 1690 had been decisive. His forces displayed a strategic and tactical boldness and mobility that were not always so apparent in contemporary fighting in the Low Countries. As in the 1640s, conflict in Ireland was far from static. Bold generalship and success in battle were far more important than the holding of fortified positions. Although Derry, Athlone and Limerick successfully resisted attack, at least initially, the Boyne had given William an undefended Dublin, and Aughrim was followed by the fall of Galway. Both of the major engagements had been clearly won, and with fewer casualties, by the attacking force, and in each case tactical considerations relating to the terrain and to the ability to take advantage of developments had been crucial. The vulnerability of defending armies to flanking attacks by opponents that retained the initiative had been clearly demonstrated. William III also saw more clearly than Louis XIV the importance of control of Ireland for the use of British strength in the war on the Continent.

The conquest of Ireland was the third since the late sixteenth century. It was more difficult than the Cromwellian conquest in 1649–52: first, because James' forces had foreign support; and, secondly, because Cromwell started in 1649 with the advantage of control over Dublin and with a well-honed army. William, in contrast, had to break out of Ulster and had to face French intervention on an unpredictable scale. William's was the last conquest of Ireland. As with the Elizabethan/Jacobean and Cromwell's conquests, it was followed by a policy of appropriation that consolidated control of power and property in the hands of those who looked to London. The Catholics had held 22 per cent of the land in 1688; but only 14 per cent by 1703. Furthermore, whereas the two former episodes had been followed by a lack of continuity in government, particularly as a consequence of James II's Catholicism, there was to be no such opportunity for new alignments after 1691.

The '08

James II died in 1701, an exile in France. He was succeeded as the Jacobite claimant to the throne by the "warming-pan baby", "James III", whose claim was recognized by Louis XIV. This helped to embitter Anglo-French relations, and was a factor in the outbreak of hostilities between the two powers in 1702, Britain's entry into the War of the Spanish Succession. During this conflict the French planned an invasion of Britain in support of James. Louis had already planned invasions of England in 1692 and 1696. Both were designed to be large-scale affairs, but each was blocked by British naval power: victory at Barfleur in 1692 and the assembly of a large fleet off Dunkirk in 1696. Vigilance was maintained during the brief period of peace that followed the negotiation of the Peace of Rijswijk in 1697. In 1699 Vice-Admiral Thomas Hopsonn commanded a squadron of observation in the Channel.

In 1708 Louis decided to strike at Scotland. He no longer had a large fleet sufficient to battle for control of the Channel and, instead, sought a surprise landing, but this time in Scotland. The Union of England and Scotland in 1707 had raised great discontent in Scotland and hopes of an insurrection there, while Louis needed a diversion to reduce British military pressure in the Low Countries and enable France to invade the Spanish Netherlands.

The loss of secrecy led the British to anchor a squadron under Sir George Byng off Dunkirk, and the French naval commander, Forbin, sought to abandon the planned expedition. James, however, persuaded Louis to order Forbin to sail and he was able to avoid Byng in a mist: in-shore blockade was far from easy. Nevertheless, due to error, the initial landfall was not, as intended, the Firth of Forth, but 100 miles further north. By the time Forbin was in a position to land the troops, he was deterred by the proximity of Byng's pursuing fleet. However, he was able to evade them and to return safely to Dunkirk.[6] Having withdrawn ten regiments from Flanders to England, thus demonstrating the value to France of its strategy, the British returned them in time to take part in the campaign there.

Might-have-beens are important in military history. They were relevant to contemporaries and played a major role in attempts to assess relative capability. The '08 demonstrated, 20 years after the Glorious Revolution, that it was possible to out-manoeuvre a superior defending fleet, but it also showed that it was not possible to stage a landing in the face of a superior fleet. By its very nature, an invasion represented taking the initiative, and this was important. However, the Jacobite attempts in 1715, 1719 and 1745 were to reveal that the initiative was not enough.

The '15

Britain and France negotiated peace in 1713, and the agreement included a French undertaking to recognize Anne as queen and the Protestant succession in the House of Hanover. George I, the first Hanoverian ruler of Britain, succeeded peacefully in 1714, but, by turning against the Tories and denying them favour, he encouraged support for another Jacobite attempt. Unlike 1708, however, it would have to be without foreign support because, despite Jacobite hopes to the contrary, the French refused to provide troops.

In 1715 the Jacobites planned three risings. James was to copy William III, and the Duke of Monmouth in 1685, by landing in the south-west of England. This was to be the centre of a rebellion that was to result in a march on London. There were also to be rebellions in the Scottish Highlands and in the Border counties. Although there would be no foreign support, the Jacobites would benefit from the post-war demobilization of much of the British army (and navy), the principal advantage of attacking in peacetime, and one the Americans were also to benefit from in 1775.

However, co-ordination between the areas of Jacobite activity was inadequate, and the rising in the south-west was nipped in the bud due to poor leadership, indecision and effective government intelligence. James did not land and a muster of Jacobites near Bath lacked leadership. James' proclamation in Cornwall did not set the county afire, and the government arrested the leading conspirators in the West Country, including Lord Lansdowne and Sir William Wyndham.

In the Scottish Highlands on 6 September, John Erskine, Earl of Mar, who had been Secretary of State until 1714, raised the Stuart standard at Braemar, a long way from Edinburgh, let alone London. Mar failed to combine his operations sufficiently with those of the Jacobites in England. Nevertheless, the Jacobite cause was initially successful. James was proclaimed in Inverness on 13 September, Perth was captured on 14 September, and Aberdeen on the 22nd. The royal forces in Scotland under John, 2nd Duke of Argyll were outnumbered. Thanks in large part to hostility to the Union, the Scots who rose for the Stuarts in 1715 were more numerous than those who had served under Montrose in the 1640s and under Dundee in 1689. Nationalism was a crucial factor. Argyll was in no doubt of the unpopularity of the Hanoverian cause north of the Firth of Forth. Jacobite support was not restricted to the Highlands. Many Lowlanders also rallied to the cause. Indeed, in some respects the '15 looked back to Anglo-Scottish conflicts prior to the Union of the Crowns in 1603. In 1715 Campbell power under Argyll was crucial to the stalling of a near-general rising. Similarly, in the Wars of Independence, and in the fifteenth and sixteenth centuries, magnates could and did ally with the English crown.

However, Mar was a poor leader, lacking in the dynamism necessary for a rebellious situation, while Argyll was an experienced general who had served in the War of Spanish Succession, including at the battles of Ramillies, Oudenaarde and Malplaquet. Mar should have attacked Argyll rapidly in order to make Scotland a base for operations in England and to distract government troops there, especially in northern England, from attacking the English Jacobites.

Instead, the indecisive Mar did not march on Edinburgh until November. He had been affected by Argyll's firm action. Leaving London on 9 September, Argyll had seen to the defences of Edinburgh before concentrating his troops at the crucial bridging point of Stirling.

Argyll moved forward to block Mar's advance on high ground at Sheriffmuir, north of Stirling, on 13 November. Unaware of the other's dispositions, each general drew up his forces so that his right wing overlapped the other's left. This was instrumental in the defeat of the left wings of both armies, but Mar failed to exploit his numerical superiority: initially maybe about two to one, and probably far more after the defeat of Argyll's left. Mar did not use his reserves. Argyll was left in possession of the battlefield. The indecisive nature of the battle was to Argyll's advantage as Mar did not continue his advance, and needed a victory to keep his army united and to maintain the momentum of success.

The Jacobites had also risen in Northumberland and the Scottish Borders. Many Scottish Lowlanders rose as well as Highlanders. The Northumbrian Jacobites were far less numerous and far less formidable as a military force than the Scots, but this was consistent with their role as the light forces for the Jacobite army, designed to prepare the ground for more heavily armed French and Scottish forces. However, they were poorly commanded. Lindisfarne, captured on 10 October, was lost the following day due to a failure to send reinforcements. As a result, two French ships that appeared off Lindisfarne, did not lend support. James was proclaimed in Alnwick, Morpeth and Hexham, but little effort was made to seize Newcastle, and thus gain a port that would provide a vital gateway for possible foreign assistance. Instead, Newcastle was reinforced by the British army, and the Northumbrians retreated to Scotland, joining a Lowland force at Kelso on 22 October.[7]

From there they could have sought to co-ordinate operations with Mar, marching north as he moved south, and thus threatening Argyll's rear, but such coordination was generally difficult in early-modern rebellions, most of which lacked central direction and an authoritarian practice. Furthermore, the Jacobites were affected by the advance to Wooler of a government force under the determined Lieutenant-General George Carpenter, a veteran of the War of the Spanish Succession. The more numerous Jacobites did not attack Carpenter, but, instead, against the wishes of the Scots present, decided to invade Lancashire, an area with many Catholics whom they hoped to raise: the search for manpower was to determine strategy.

The army, fewer than 3,000 strong, crossed the border on 1 November. Carlisle was judged too strong to attack, as Dumfries had earlier been, but the march south was initially successful. The Cumberland and Westmorland militia offered no resistance, and on 9 November the Jacobites entered Preston. This, however, was to prove as unfortunate for them as it had been for the invading Scots under the Duke of Hamilton at the hands of Cromwell in August 1648. The Jacobite commander, Thomas Forster, proved a poor leader, unable to respond to a crisis. He failed to take adequate steps to learn of his opponent's moves, and to defend the line of the River Ribble against the government troops under generals Carpenter and Wills, the latter another veteran of the recent war. Although a government assault on the town, which the Jacobites had hastily fortified with barricades, failed on 12 November, instead of attacking them or trying to fight their way out, the Jacobites allowed their enemies to surround the town, and Forster unconditionally surrendered on 14 November.

Preston marked the end for the '15 in England, but the same was not true of Sheriffmuir and Scotland. After the battle, Mar fell back on Perth. On 22 December 1715 James arrived at Peterhead, but he had failed to bring any French support. Nevertheless, James was warmly welcomed, making state entries to Dundee on 6 January and to Perth three days later. He moved on to Scone where his coronation was planned.

However, freed of concern about England, Argyll had now been provided with a far larger army, including 6,000 Dutch troops under Lieutenant-General William Cadogan. Despite the bitterness of the winter and a Jacobite scorched-earth policy, Argyll marched on Perth on 21 January. Unable to confront Argyll in the field, and unwilling and unprepared for guerrilla warfare, the Jacobites had lost the initiative and their army suffered badly from low morale and desertion. James abandoned Perth on 31 January, throwing his artillery into the Tay. The army retreated to Montrose, pursued by the inexorable Argyll. Rather than defending the position or making a fighting retreat along the coast, James and Mar sailed for France and their force dispersed. Argyll pursued the remaining Jacobites, but without the vigour and violence that was to follow the '45. As in Ireland, physical geography, particularly climate and terrrain, greatly influenced campaigning, not least due to its impact on logistics, and did so to a greater extent than in the Low Countries, but the British army was able to adapt successfully.

In some respects the '15 was the Jacobites' best chance. The Hanoverian dynasty was only recently established in Britain, and Jacobite support in Scotland was at a higher pitch than during the '45. However, the '15 indicated that rebellion could only achieve limited success without good leadership and foreign support. The existence or prospect of such support was to play a major role in the '19 and the '45.

The '19

In 1719 Britain and Spain were at war as a result of Philip V of Spain's attempt to reverse the provisions of the 1713 peace settlement insofar as they affected Italy. A diversionary attack on the British Isles appeared an obvious ploy to the Spanish first minister, Cardinal Alberoni. Indeed, the ability of Spain to mount such an attack a year after a Spanish fleet had been decisively beaten by the British off Cape Passaro in Sicily was an instructive lesson in the problems facing British naval power.

An expeditionary force under the leading Jacobite general, James, 2nd Duke of Ormonde, sailed from Cadiz in March 1719, but a violent storm off Cape Finisterre at the end of the month damaged and dispersed the fleet. This was to be no second Armada, threatening British home waters.

Two separate frigates reached Stornoway in the Western Isles, carrying a diversionary force of 300 Spanish troops under another Jacobite leader,

George Keith, the Earl Marischal. It was intended to tie down British troops in Scotland at the same time as Ormonde invaded England. This small force moved to the mainland, but its main magazine, stored in Eilean Donan castle, was destroyed by British frigates on 10 May. The penetration of the land mass by sea lochs and the narrow nature of the coastal strip made western Scotland particularly vulnerable to British naval power.

The Earl Marischal advanced on Inverness, but the failure of Ormonde's expedition discouraged much of the Highlands from supporting him, and the government forces acted rapidly and decisively. The Earl Marischal's army, swollen to 1,850 strong by Highland support, met 1,100 government troops under Major-General Wightman in Glenshiel on 10 June 1719. There was no Highland redoubt: the British army was capable of operating in the Highlands.

The Jacobites did not charge at Glenshiel, remaining instead in a good defensive position that gave them the potential to mount a charge. However, Jacobite morale was low, and Wightman, assisted by mortar fire, took the initiative, and successfully attacked the Jacobite flanks. The Spaniards tried to retreat and the Jacobite army disintegrated, the Highlanders retiring to their homes and the Spaniards surrendering. The battle is instructive, given the frequent stress on the invincibility of the Highland charge prior to Culloden. Glenshiel, however, was not simply an example of the successful use of firepower. It also indicated the importance of leadership and morale, especially in what were comparatively small-scale operations.

The '19 was the last invasion/rising prior to the '45. In the intervening period, a Jacobite revanche appeared an increasingly unlikely prospect. Firm action by the government, including the deployment of troops in London, thwarted the Atterbury Plot in 1722. Five years later, George II succeeded his father without any insurrection.

The '44

British and French forces next began hostilities – in Germany – in 1743, and went to war in 1744. The intervening period, first of Anglo-French alliance (1716–31) and then at least of an absence of hostilities (1731–42), was crucial to the consolidation of the Hanoverian regime in Britain; without the prospect of French invasion, Jacobite hopes were slim. In order to strike at the heart of British power in 1744, the French planned an invasion of southern England on behalf of the Jacobites. The French plan was to send the Brest fleet under de Roquefeuil to cruise off the Isle of Wight in order to prevent the British from leaving Spithead or, if they did, to engage them in the western Channel. Five of the Brest ships were to sail to Dunkirk and escort Maurice of Saxe's invasion force to the Thames. The plan was wrecked by storms, but it indicated the potential vulnerability of southern Britain to invasion and, more generally, of Britain's European position to the threat of invasion at home. Both themes were to be present during the '45.

The '45

Disappointed with French reluctance to back a second attempt in 1744, James' eldest son, Charles Edward Stuart, came to support the idea of a Scottish rising and of his going it alone without French assistance. He planned to exploit continued Scottish hostility to the Union and hoped that the French could be encouraged to intervene militarily if a rising had already broken out. This ignored the argument of the Scottish Jacobites that the prince should come only if accompanied by a substantial force: 6,000 men and the funds to pay them.

No such force accompanied Charles Edward when he landed in July 1745, and he was also very short of money. Charles Edward had set sail with two ships, but one, carrying much of the supplies, had to turn back after it was intercepted by a British warship. Nevertheless, his arrival was followed by a rising. The "Seven Men of Moidart" who landed at Eriskay on 23 July had swelled to 1,300 when Charles Edward raised his standard at Glenfinnan on 19 August. The British army in Scotland, part of a military establishment weakened by the need to send most of its troops to resist the French in the Austrian Netherlands, was outmanoeuvred, and Charles Edward successfully captured Perth on 4 September and Edinburgh on 17 September. To its east, at Prestonpans, he then attacked the government army in Scotland, under Lieutenant-General Sir John Cope, on 21 September. Cope was a long-serving officer who had commanded the second line of cavalry at the battle of Dettingen in 1743, but he had no experience of command against irregular forces.

In conventional military terms, Cope had a more balanced force than Charles Edward, with dragoons and six cannon, whereas the prince had no cannon and only 40 horsemen. However, neither arm was of much use to Cope in a battle that developed much faster than he had anticipated. The nautical gunners fled and their inexperienced army replacements did little damage before they were overrun, while most of the dragoons refused to charge. Some attempted to do so, but they were met by Highlanders slashing at their mounts. A Highland charge, the formation unbroken by the fire of Cope's infantry, led the latter to flee in panic a few minutes after the first impact of the charge. Cope's men had little opportunity to use their equipment: the royal forces only fired one round of ammunition per man and apparently not one bayonet was stained with blood. In contrast, Jacobite broadswords caused most of the casualties. The Jacobites lost about 25 men, Cope about 300, but Cope's army was destroyed, with at least 1,500 men taken prisoner. Most of the casualties occurred during the retreat, for infantry formations that lost their order in retreat were particularly vulnerable to pursuing troops. Charles Edward gained a useful £3,000 from Cope's war chest.

Although cleared by a court martial, Cope never commanded troops in action again. While he had served in the War of the Spanish Succession, his rise had been due to connections. The Jacobite advance at Prestonpans would have tested most British commanders, but Cope was not up to a challenge.

Prestonpans indicated that defensive firepower alone was insufficient to secure victory and that the British army lacked a reliable counter to the Jacobites. It was a dangerous omen for the start of the campaign. The battle was more decisive than Sheriffmuir and, unlike Killiecrankie, was followed by a retention of the strategic initiative by the Jacobites.

After Prestonpans, Charles Edward consolidated his position around Edinburgh while his opponents assembled an army under the elderly Field Marshal George Wade (1673–1748) at Newcastle. Wade was familiar with northern Britain, but his combat experience was on the Continent, most recently in 1744, and he proved too slow moving to cope with Charles Edward. The latter avoided Wade by invading England via Carlisle, which fell after a short siege (10–15 November). The defences were not impressive, but, even had they been, the defending force was insufficient in number and it lacked civilian support. Wade's slow attempt to march via Hexham to Carlisle's relief, was hampered by the winter weather, and the Jacobites advanced unopposed through Penrith, Lancaster, Preston and Manchester, en route towards London. Their advance was more similar to that of the Scots in the Second Civil War in 1648 than the Jacobites in 1715, but, unlike on both the former occasions, the advancing force outmarched its opponents. The ability of armies to respond differently to similar strategic parameters, and the role of leadership in doing so, were amply demonstrated in these three advances.

Aside from that under Wade, another army was assembled to confront the Jacobites. The government was not short of money: substantial sums were voted by Parliament in November 1745. Built up in the West Midlands and commanded by George II's younger son, William, Duke of Cumberland, this force, however, was out-manoeuvred, misled by deliberately circulated reports that the Jacobites intended to advance on Chester and North Wales. Cumberland moved to block such an advance and, therefore, failed to stop a Jacobite advance on Derby, which they entered unopposed on 4 December.

At that point, the Jacobites held the strategic initiative and were also in a central position while their opponent's forces were divided. Wade's army was still in Yorkshire and Cumberland's was exhausted by its marches. The government was assembling a new army on Finchley Common to protect London, but it was a relatively small force.

Nevertheless, the Highland chiefs were disappointed by the lack of the support promised them by Charles Edward: both assistance from English

Jacobites and the absence of a French landing in southern England. After bitter debates, the chiefs forced Charles Edward to turn back and he began his retreat north on 6 December.

Government troops sought to block the retreat, but were unsuccessful. Once back in Scotland, a Highland charge was again decisive in giving the Jacobites victory at Falkirk (17 January 1746), although a defensive volley was important in breaking the advance of the government troops. The latter were hindered by fighting uphill, by growing darkness, and by the heavy rain wetting their powder. Indifferent leadership and a lack of fighting spirit also played a role.

Falkirk, however, was to be the last Jacobite victory. Charles Edward was short of money and the dynamic of Jacobite success had been lost. The inexorable nature of the deployment of resources by the British state, once its cohesion was not challenged by losing the initiative, was readily apparent in the preparations made by Cumberland. A large army was built up at Aberdeen, and Cumberland then advanced on Charles Edward's base at Inverness. Charles Edward failed to use the terrain to his advantage. Cumberland's crossing of the Spey was not contested and Charles Edward took no steps until, with an underfed and underpaid army, he attempted a night attack on Cumberland's camp, an advance that was mishandled and then abandoned before any attack could be mounted.

At Culloden, the terrain suited Cumberland's defensive position. Cumberland also outnumbered his opponent, 9,000 to 5,000, and the Jacobites were outgunned. The circumstances were not suitable for a Highland charge, not least because Cumberland's numbers permitted defence in depth. Any gaps in the front line could be filled. His artillery, firing canister shot, and infantry so thinned the numbers of the advancing clansmen that those who reached the royal troops were driven back by bayonet. The artillery were far more effective than at Prestonpans. Controversy surrounds the effectiveness of Cumberland's bayonet tactics, specifically the instruction to thrust forward and to the side, and thus rely on the next soldier for cover. However, the effectiveness of these tactics was not called into real question because of the role of firepower. The general rate of fire was increased by the level ground and the absence of any serious disruptive fire from the Jacobites, while the flanking position of the royal units forward from the left of the front line made Culloden even more of a killing field. Many factors led to confusion amongst the Jacobites: the slant of their line, the nature of the terrain, which was partly waterlogged, the difficulty of seeing what was happening in the smoke produced by the guns, and the independent nature of each unit's advance. John Maclean, a Jacobite officer, recorded,

> When all that pleased or was able to follow ther Collours marched out and was Drawn in order of Battel about 2 muskets shot from the Enemy they was waiting us in very good order with their

Artilary befor them and the wind and snow in ther Backs. After a short stay and all the Disadvantages an Army could meete with as to ther numbers they Doubled or tripled ours and all advantages of Ground and wind and weather our Canon began to play upon them and they upon us. After we stayed about 10 minutes we wer ordered to march hastily to the Enemy which we did Boldly. They began a smart fire of their Small Guns and Grape Shots from there Cannons till we wer Beat Back with Great Losses our Right wing was flanked and surrounded by the horse which did Great Execution.

The results of Culloden, not least the heavy Jacobite casualties, marked the military end of Jacobitism as a serious force. Charles Edward's idiosyncratic and undisciplined behaviour in the following years greatly lessened foreign support, so that the Jacobite movement ceased to be of major importance in diplomacy or international relations. Charles Edward's conversion to the Church of England on a secret visit to London in 1750 did not lead to any rallying to the Jacobite cause, and the Elibank Plot of 1751–3, a scheme for a *coup d'état* in London involving the kidnapping of George II, was betrayed.[8]

Jacobitism: the military challenge

Modernization is a central theme of historical studies, and a major, if not the major, way of approaching and presenting the crucial topic of change; not least because cyclical methods of understanding history are no longer in fashion. Modernization is a particularly popular way of treating the eighteenth century because it offers a way in which the period can be incorporated in, and made significant to, modern concerns: the past can be appropriated to the present. Thus the prominence given to, and treatment of, topics such as economic change, the rise of the novel, gentility, enlightenment, and constitutional change establish an agenda and frame a discourse of period. In such an analysis, Jacobitism can be seen and presented as anachronistic and obsolete, and scholars who seek to demonstrate the "modernity" of Jacobite views on, for example, marriage or estate management, contribute to this discourse by implicitly or explicitly accepting its assumptions.

There is a military dimension to this approach and it is of considerable importance, not simply as it is indicative of the general trend, but also because an apparent demonstration of the military bankruptcy of Jacobitism, not simply its flaws but also its commitment to an outdated trajectory of military activity, would seem to guarantee the more general failure of the movement. It is possible to present Jacobite military methods as the last gasp of a Celtic system that had been made redundant by the development of hand-held gunpowder weapons and, more generally, by the so-called

Military Revolution. Culloden can be seen as a defeat for an army emphasizing speed, mobility and primal shock-power by a force reliant on the concentrated firepower of disciplined infantry and their supporting artillery. That, indeed, is how the battle has been depicted, and visual force is lent by the contrast between disciplined rows of British troops with their standard weaponry and the more fluid, but also archaic individualism of their opponents, who are generally, but misleadingly, presented as without guns. The mental picture created is somewhat similar to the modern film *Zulu*, and it is made clear that the two sides are starkly different and that one represents order and other characteristics commonly associated with military activity and progress. Although the Zulu charge was at times effective, it was only so at the cost of heavy casualties, and British firepower generally defeated it. Thus the Jacobites can be seen as representatives of an earlier form of warfare that was bound to fail because it was redundant for tactical and technological reasons. It can be compared to other eighteenth-century forces using non-western tactics, for example the Cossacks and the Tatars, and they can be seen as examples of barbarian warfare, rather as Edward Gibbon presented the Tatars, or at the very least as dated by the March of Modernity, as an Ossianic fragment of times past, primitive virtue and prowess, that might be impressive on an individual basis, but was unsuccessful as an organized, i.e. social, means of waging war.

Another dimension can be added by noting the success of the British state in dealing with its military opponents in the British Isles from the 1640s. The New Model Army was successful under Oliver Cromwell against both Irish and Scots, so that for the first time all of the British Isles was under effective control from London. In 1685 James II defeated the Duke of Monmouth's rising, and in 1688 he would have destroyed any domestic risings had it not been for the invasion of a regular army under William of Orange. William's forces suppressed opposition in both Scotland and Ireland, Jacobite risings in 1715–16, 1719 and 1745–6 were defeated, and in 1798 the Irish rising was crushed. Within the British world only the American colonists were successful in rebelling, but the American War of Revolution is commonly seen as different, and treated in both its military and political aspects as a harbinger of a new world, an aspect of the Modernity of the period. The apparent differences with the Jacobite risings thus help to underline the necessary failure of the latter. Such an approach can, however, be challenged. It can be suggested both that Jacobite warfare was not anachronistic and that the Jacobites came near to success in 1745. The entire set of assumptions underlying the supposed context and chronology of military modernity can be queried.

It is in fact misleading to separate Jacobite from Western European warfare, although there were clearly differences. However, most of the Jacobite infantry relied on muskets, not broadswords, and the Jacobites were not without artillery: they employed it to attack Fort William. Other armies, as well as the Jacobites, relied on the strategic offensive and the tactical attack. This can be seen clearly if the '45 is placed in the context of the conflict it was in some respects part of, the War of the Austrian Succession (1740–8). The classic image of that conflict is the apparently parade-ground battle of Fontenoy, also in 1745, and the battles of the '45 – Prestonpans, Falkirk and Culloden – seem very different. Strategically, the '45 has an "all-or-nothing" character that seems out of keeping with contemporary Continental warfare, which is generally presented as limited, if not decisive.

Yet 1745 also saw the Second Silesian War (1744–5) between Prussia on the one hand and Austria and Saxony on the other. Frederick the Great of Prussia was a bold general. His trops fought in tight formations and he had scant interest in light infantry tactics, but Frederick favoured rapidly moving advances, as in his invasions of Silesia in 1740–1, Bohemia in 1744 and Saxony in 1756, and the tactical offensive. In 1745 Prussian infantry attacks brought victory at Hohenfriedberg, Soor and Kesseldorf: linear tactics were adapted and made more flexible and offensive in order to permit the so-called oblique attack. Prussian victories appeared to vindicate the commitment to cold steel that in 1741 had led Frederick to order his infantry to have their bayonets permanently fixed when they were on duty. Frederick did not alter his tactics until Austrian firepower produced heavy casualties in 1757.

Marshal Saxe, the leading French general of the mid-1740s, was also an exponent of the strategic offensive, close-quarter tactics and cold steel. The rapidity of his campaigns in Flanders in the summer of 1745 and in Brabant in early 1746 can be compared with the speed of the Jacobite advance, although the logistical situation was different and the Jacobites advanced further in late 1745. It is also possible to stress the rapidity of the Franco-Bavarian advance into the Habsburg dominions in 1741, of the Russians in Finland in 1742 and of the Franco-Spanish forces in northern Italy in late 1745.

The notion of Continental warfare as indecisive and limited is flawed. Casualty rates in battle were very high, generals fought to win and major political changes were effected through violence: both territorial changes, such as the Russian gain of a Baltic coastline in 1710, and important shifts in the relationship of states within the international system. Sieges are often seen as indicative of limited warfare. They are presented as slow, a substitute for battle and generally of limited consequence. This thesis, however, should be advanced with care. Sieges could be very bloody, as with the British capture of Lille in 1708, and could serve to obtain and secure territorial gains, as with the Russian capture of Riga in 1710 and the French gain of Antwerp in 1746. Continental armies could also seize strongly fortified positions by a surprise storming, not an example of modern "industrial warfare" as conventionally understood. This Bavarian, Saxon and French forces did at Prague in 1741, and the French at Charleroi in 1746 and

Bergen-op-Zoom in 1747, the last the best-fortified position in the Low Countries. The British used storming frequently in India.

It would not have been impossible for the Jacobites to seize fortified positions by the same means. They were anyway helped by the unfortified nature of most of the British Isles. The major fortified British positions were naval dockyards or overseas bases, such as Gibraltar and Fort Philip on Minorca. There was no system of citadels protecting major domestic centres of government, especially in England. Not only did this ensure that the Jacobites did not have to fight their way through a series of positions, losing time and manpower as they did so, but it also meant that the British army lacked a network of bases that could provide shelter and replenish supplies. After Charles Edward captured poorly fortified Carlisle he faced no fortified positions on his chosen route to London and, had he chosen instead to invade north Wales, as was feared for a while, he would have been able to bypass Chester.

The Jacobites were, of course, different in several major respects. They lacked a navy and were, therefore, unable to challenge the maritime strength of the British state, a strength that was crucial in a number of respects in the '45, especially because it covered the movement of British troops back from the Low Countries in 1745 and the supply of advancing British forces on the eastern seaboard of Scotland in 1746. The Jacobite army was also a volunteer and non-regular force with non-bureaucratic supply and recruitment systems, and this necessarily affected its *modus operandi*, not least in matters of control and command, and logistics.

In his *Decline and fall of the Roman Empire*, Gibbon raised the question of whether "barbarian" invasions of Europe could recur, and came to th comforting conclusion that advances in military technology, specifically the development of artillery and fortifications, made this highly unlikely. Thus progress, in the form of science, allowed advanced and settled societies to employ a military technology that multiplied the impact of their soldiery. Gibbon saw this as crucial in enabling such societies to restrict military service to specialized forces and thus free the rest of society for productive activity and civilized pursuits. Progress therefore secured and benefited from military modernity. The Jacobite forces, indeed Celtic warfare in general, was recognizably different in type, but the '45 proved Gibbon wrong. The more "advanced" society in conventional terms was nearly overthrown, and its eventual victory was far from inevitable. The Jacobites won two of the three battles they fought in 1745–6, and the projected night attack on Cumberland's forces at Culloden would probably also have been successful. Indeed, it is arguable that the Jacobites should have pressed on in their night attack at Culloden even when their advance had become disordered and they had lost the element of surprise. Poor visibility would still have affected British fire discipline and morale. However, in 1685 Monmouth's night attack with irregular forces at Sedgemoor had been defeated.

The Jacobites not only won at Prestonpans and Falkirk, but they also managed to advance through Scotland and into the heart of England, creating a military crisis that, for example, was greater than any faced by France during the century. The nearest comparison is probably the Prussian advance on Paris in 1792, but at Valmy the Revolutionary French were able to field a substantial, undefeated force to block them: the British had no equivalent in 1745. The Jacobite force was arguably more threatening than the Spanish thrust to Corbie near Paris in 1636. Possibly the nearest equivalent was the Franco-Bavarian advance towards Vienna in 1741, an advance that was diverted to Prague.

The Jacobites had another advantage. Unlike in 1715, France was then at war with Britain and planned to assist the Jacobites, and had indeed already attempted an invasion in 1744. France provided much that the Jacobites lacked militarily. It was the second leading naval power after Britain, and in 1745–6 the French navy was still undefeated. It was thus a potent force in being, a situation that lasted until the two defeats off Cape Finisterre in 1747. Until then the British lacked a clear margin of naval superiority and the French fleet in Brest retained the strategic initiative because the port could not be blockaded effectively. In the summer of 1746 the Duc d'Anville's Brest fleet was able to sail for Cape Breton: the British had feared that it would mount a landing on the west coast of Scotland.

The French also had an effective army, much of which was stationed near a series of ports from which they could sail to Britain: Boulogne, Calais, Dunkirk and, once it was captured from an Anglo-Dutch-Austrian garrison in the summer of 1745, Ostend. Charles Edward asked the Duke of Richelieu, commander of the projected invasion in 1745–6, to make a junction with him near London. Richelieu himself was to mount a successful amphibious attack on Minorca in 1756. French battlefield superiority over British and allied forces was shown at Fontenoy (1745), Roucoux (1746) and Lawfeldt (1747). Cumberland was the defeated commander at the first and the last, and was to be defeated again, at the head of Hanoverian and allied forces, at Hastenbeck in 1757. That battle was followed by the overrunning of the Electorate of Hanover and the capitulation of Cumberland's army, an interesting indication of the possibility of achieving total victory, overthrowing a state and forcing a Hanoverian capitulation.

The prospect of French intervention raises the comparison of the '45 and the American War of Independence. In the latter the British crucially lost control of the sea, most obviously off the Chesapeake in 1781, but also off New York in 1778 and Savannah in 1779. There was no such comparable loss during the '45, but no necessary reason for this difference. During the American war the French had no other military commitments bar war with Britain. Crucially, despite her Austrian alliance, France did not get involved in the War of the Bavarian Succession of 1778–9. In contrast, in 1745 France was also at war with Austria and the Kingdom of Sardinia

(Savoy-Piedmont) and fighting the Dutch. However, this did not weaken France appreciably at sea, and did not prevent the French from planning invasions in 1744 and in the winter of 1745–6.

Even without French intervention or its absence, the British had been badly handicapped in 1745 and 1775–83 by other factors that do not relate to the issue of whether the Americans had a progressive, and the Jacobites a regressive, military system. The Jacobites were more of a threat because they could readily threaten the centres of British power, but, equally, relative propinquity ensured that they could easily be attacked. This interacted with the issue of time. The British failure to crush the American rebellion in 1775 gave the Americans time to organize themselves politically and militarily, to extend the rebellion greatly and to weaken the Loyalists. The Jacobites lacked this margin, just as they lacked the wealth of the American economy. All these factors are military in the widest sense, but do not pertain to tactics and technology, the standard repertoire of military history and one in which it is inaccurate to claim that the Jacobites were doomed. A wider perspective casts light on the different results of the two conflicts, but does not ensure that the question of whether the Jacobites could have won should be answered in the negative. As is so often the case, a study of a conflict from both sides reveals the danger of making its course or result appear inevitable. The gravity of the Jacobite threat should be underlined and mistaken notions of military modernity and consequences should be challenged. A rewriting of the mid-eighteenth century British crisis can therefore be offered. The Union with Scotland nearly had as serious consequences for England as, in a very different fashion, that with Ireland was to do.

The '98

The Irish rebellion of 1798 drew on attitudes and roots that were partly different to those that had sustained Jacobitism. Ireland was governed with scant role for the views and interests of the bulk of the population, but the level of organized resistance that this encouraged was low. There were a number of reasons. First, the Irish economy grew during the century. As Ireland was drawn more fully into the market economy, its agricultural sector experienced growing diversification and commercialization. Textile production also developed markedly. Recent scholarship has emphasized that the Catholics of the period should be seen not as an amorphous mass of down-trodden victims, but as a more flexible group that came to play a more central role in politics and a more active role in society.

French invasion plans on behalf of the Jacobites, for example those of 1708, 1744–5, 1746 and 1759, concentrated on England and Scotland, not Ireland, and the same was true in 1779 during the War of American Independence. In 1760, during the Seven Years' War, Commodore François

Thurot, in command of three ships and 600 troops, sent in October 1759 to mount a diversionary attack in support of the planned French invasions of Scotland and England, attacked Carrickfergus. Its garrison, about 200 strong, supported by some of the local gentry, resisted both in the town and at the castle until, their ammunition exhausted, they surrendered. A large force was ordered to retake Carrickfergus, but, before it could arrive, Thurot abandoned both town and castle, only for his expedition to be smashed by three British frigates under John Elliot: the three French ships surrendered after an engagement off the Isle of Man. There was no Irish rising to coincide with Thurot's expedition, which, indeed, was the only part of the invasion plan to come to fruition.

If a combination of social stresses and agrarian discontents led to outbreaks of organized violence in certain parts of Ireland in the later eighteenth century – the Whiteboys of 1761–5 and 1769–76, the Oakboys of 1763, the Steelboys of 1769–72 and the Rightboys of 1785–8 – these outbreaks were sporadic, although troops were used against them. In addition, arson, cattle-maiming and attacks on agents, while very unsettling to local landowners, were not a serious military threat to the state. They were not part of a guerrilla resistance determined to seize control of the countryside as part of a revolutionary strategy.

It was, therefore, possible for the government in London to regard such violence as a minor military priority, although the use of the army for "civil" duties was a major reason for maintaining a separate "Irish Establishment". The army in Ireland was relatively small, more so at moments of international tension when troops were transferred elsewhere: in early 1778 there were only 8,500 troops. Fortifications were poorly maintained. In 1760 Carrickfergus Castle had a 50 foot breach in the wall, while the cannon were dismounted and unable to respond to the French attack. There was no effective, planned system of military organization in Ireland, until George, 4th Viscount Townshend, who became Lord Lieutenant in 1767, introduced one based on well-constructed barracks and magazines. Townshend also supported the recruitment of Catholics to the army. This began in 1771 and was aided by the replacement of the religious test by an oath of allegiance in 1774.

However, the French Revolution radicalized Irish discontent, weakened patterns of social control and provided the possibility of foreign support for a rebellion. It also increased governmental sensitivity to any sign of discontent, and provided a pattern for rebellious activity. Government concessions on Catholic rights, and the loyalty of the Irish Catholic Church concerned about the hostility to the Catholic Church, and indeed to Christianity, of the French revolutionaries, both failed to prevent the rise of radicalism. The United Irishmen, founded in Dublin in 1791, largely as a Presbyterian Ulster movement pressing for political reform, was banned in 1794, but it reformed as a secret society that was openly republican and increasingly Catholic, and began to plot revolution. Its leader, Wolfe Tone, sought support in America and France. He managed to persuade the French to mount a major invasion attempt in 1796, but, although the French fleet evaded its British counterpart, it was thwarted by adverse winds. When the French fleet reached Bantry Bay that December, it failed to land any of the 14,500 strong force it carried. A violent storm, one of the worst of the century, dispersed the French, which was just as well as the British army's response to the threatened invasion reflected an absence of adequate preparations.

The French intervention in Wales the following February was also unsuccessful, although it was on a far smaller scale. Colonel William Tate's poorly disciplined 1,400 strong *Légion Noire* (named after their dark-brown coats, captured from the British at Quiberon Bay and dyed) landed at Carreg Wastad in Pembrokeshire on 22 February. Once landed, the French seized food and alcohol, while the Fishguard Fencibles, only 190 strong, retreated. However, the defence was rallied by Lord Cawdor, the local aristocrat, who assembled a 600-strong force and advanced with determination. Intimidated by this advance and affected by a collapse of confidence, Tate surrendered on 24 February. The French had planned to win the support of the local poor and disaffected and to press on to attack and burn Bristol.[9] Much of the force was composed of jail-sweepings (although it included two troops of grenadiers), and its American commander was not up to the task.

Ireland had not initially been seen as a source and site of vulnerability. In light of twentieth-century nationalist notions of an oppressed land this might appear surprising, but in fact it matched the pattern of eighteenth-century Irish activity: Ireland had been quiet in both the '15 and the '45. Furthermore, Ireland had become increasingly important as a source of troops for the British army and such military service had indeed become increasingly important for Ireland as its population rose. Initially, there was scant fear of rebellion. All of the regular battalions and half of the regiments of cavalry serving in Ireland in 1793 had gone abroad by mid-1795: cavalry was more difficult to transport overseas and more appropriate for patrolling the distances of Ireland. The troops sent to Ireland were less high-grade. The Irish militia was embodied in 1793.

The situation changed in 1796 because of growing British concern about French schemes and because of the adoption of a pro-active policy towards possible internal discontent, including an Insurrection Act that decreed harsh penalties for administering and taking illegal oaths, and also authorized curfews and searches for concealed weapons. Habeas Corpus was suspended, and a largely Protestant Irish Yeomanry, an armed constabulary nearly 20,000 strong by the end of 1796, was established. This essentially sectarian policy alienated Catholic support. Calling on the army to disarm potential opponents helped to militarize the situation. The United Irishmen developed a military organization from 1795, but the British army violently disarmed and terrified its Ulster network in 1797. As the United Irishmen increasingly sought to win Catholic backing, they alienated Protestant support.

The military situation was eased for the government by the ready availability of troops from Britain in 1798, so that a peak strength of 70,000 men was attained, and by the presence of warships to transport them. Having been driven from the Low Countries, the army was largely concentrated in the British Isles, although many units had also been sent to the West Indies. Furthermore, the government controlled the major towns, and in 1798 the insurgents had far less success in seizing towns than had the Jacobites in England and Scotland in 1745. Lord Edward Fitzgerald, a discontented ex-Major had planned an insurrection in Dublin, which might have been difficult to suppress, to be followed by co-ordinated risings elsewhere, but the scheme was nipped in the bud: Fitzgerald was seized on 19 May, four days before the projected rising, the Yeomanry occupied key positions in the city, and there was no rising in Dublin. Controlling the major towns, the government controlled the communication foci, and this helped them retain the initiative.

Rising sectarian violence and harsh repression by the army culminated in rebellion in 1798. The arrest of the Leinster provincial committee of the United Irishmen in March and of the organizers of the projected uprising in Dublin gravely handicapped the rebels, who were only able to mount a serious military challenge in County Wexford where the local garrison was weak. The rising in County Wexford began on the evening of 26 May, the blazing heather highlighting the meeting points. The rebels won a victory at Oulart Hill (27 May) over a detachment of overconfident North Cork Militia whom they drew into an ambush: only five of the original 110 strong Militia force returned to the town of Wexford; their opponents lost six men. The United Irishmen pressed on to overrun most of the county. They captured the town of Wexford on 30 May, establishing the Wexford Republic. This was politically significant, but strategically mistaken. New Ross, the alternative target, offered a link to the counties of Carlow and Kilkenny. The morale of the rebels was hit by the failure of the Dublin rising and, after the fall of Wexford, instead of concentrating on attacking one target, their army was divided into three units on 31 May, each with a different objective. They were defeated when they attacked Arklow, Newtonbarry and New Ross, the last, on 5 June, an especially close battle in which brave advancing Irish pikemen were finally beaten back by cannon. The rebels then advanced on Dublin, but were checked by a far smaller force at Arklow (9 June).

Meanwhile, the United Irishmen had also risen in Ulster on 6 June, although they were badly prepared and led. They captured the town of Antrim, but were then driven out by a force equipped with effective cannon, and the other attacks they mounted proved ineffective. Their colleagues in north Down were defeated at Ballynahinch (12–13 June). On 25 May, 460 United Irishmen had died in an unsuccessful attack on Carlow.

In Wexford, the poorly led rebels concentrated at Vinegar Hill, losing the strategic initiative and allowing the British to land reinforcements near Waterford from 16 June. Lieutenant-General Gerard Lake was able to concentrate an army of 20,000 men and a large artillery train against Vinegar Hill. He attacked his 9,000 opponents on 21 June, using his artillery to devastate them. The rebels fought for two hours, suffering heavy casualties, and finally retreated when their ammunition ran out. Many of the camp followers were killed in cold blood by the victors. Their cohesion lost and many returning home, the rebels suffered heavy losses in government punitive operations over the following weeks. Wexford Town was recaptured by the crown forces on 21 June.

The French landed, but they did so on 22 August, not earlier, near Killala in distant Connacht, not in Wexford, and only 1,100 troops, under the competent and determined General Jean Humbert, arrived. They advanced south through Ballina, and received local Irish reinforcement. Lake, with a force mostly of Irish militia, tried to stop Humbert at Castlebar (20 August). His artillery fire led the Irish in Humbert's force to flee, but the French regulars advanced rapidly and Lake's larger army fled at bayonet point.

Castlebar was too late. There was no insurrection to greet the French. Instead, the British deployed about 20,000 men to converge on Humbert from several directions. They were supported by warships instructed to prevent the arrival of any reinforcements. The French government delayed sending reinforcements until too late, and, when they sailed, they were captured by the British. Without fresh troops, Humbert at first tried to evade the trap, but soon surrendered at Ballinamuck to a far larger British force under the new Lord Lieutenant and Commander-in-Chief, Cornwallis (8 September), who had himself surrendered to George Washington at Yorktown in 1781.

Organized and effective resistance to British authority was now at an end, but in County Wicklow a band under Michael Dwyer continued to defy the government, successfully employing guerrilla tactics, until Dwyer surrendered in 1803 in the aftermath of Robert Emmet's unsuccessful rising in Dublin. Emmet (1778–1803), a United Irishman who had been in France during the 1798 uprising, visited Napoleon in 1802 and received a promise of support, but his preparations for a rising in Ireland were made without any anticipation of French backing. Having prepared a force of about 100 men, Emmet, in a green coat and white breeches, launched his rising on 23 July 1803 by marching on Dublin Castle, but his poorly organized men were dispersed by the garrison and the rising collapsed.

An Irish element was also prominent in Edward Despard's plot to seize the Tower and the Bank of England and kill George III on his way to open

Parliament in 1802. Betrayed by informants, the conspirators were arrested, tried and hanged. Napoleon himself formed an Irish Legion in 1803 as he planned an invasion of Ireland in support of a possible invasion of England. However, there was to be no invasion and in 1806 the Legion was sent from Brittany to Germany.

There were various reasons for the failure of the 1798 rebellion. There was a clear difference in weaponry between the two sides, demonstrated most obviously in the use of the pike by the insurgents. Pikemen were able to check charging cavalry, as British dragoons learned to their cost at Kilcullen (24 May) and Ballyellis (29 June), and they were successful at close quarters, but they were far less effective if shot at, by either cavalry or infantry, from outside pike range, as at Vinegar Hill. The insurgents were critically short of cannon and this proved serious in battles where their opponents could deploy their artillery. They were also short of muskets, ammunition and provisions. The insurgents also lacked the discipline, experience of heavy fire, and training necessary for success in any lengthy engagement, although they displayed both determination and cohesion. The British benefited from the failure of their opponents to concert their risings. Furthermore, as in 1745–6 in Scotland, there was no effective co-operation between the French and the insurgents.[10]

The insurgents also suffered from the divided nature of Irish political opinion. As in India, this was not the case of an imperial power suppressing a people, but, rather, a more complex and nuanced set of religious, social, political and economic relations that enabled the government to recruit a significant amount of support. This support was not restricted to the minority Anglican and Presbyterian communities (some of whom supported the insurgents), but included Catholics. Indeed Catholics formed the majority in the ranks of the regiments raised for the new militia embodied in 1793 for all the counties outside Ulster, although this led the United Irishmen to think that the militia could be suborned and encouraged government surveillance.

The failure of the Irish rebellion of 1798 stands as an obvious contrast to the success of Spanish opposition to Napoleonic occupation in 1808–13, and to the superficial eye might suggest that the British military was more effective than its French counterpart. This would be a misleading conclusion.[11] Although Spanish armies and irregulars were generally unsuccessful in battle and were repeatedly defeated by the French, who conquered large tracts, the Spanish forces, however poorly armed, supplied and trained, enjoyed several important advantages that the Irish lacked. Spain had a tradition of independence, and, although not without divisions, was far less divided than Ireland. The terrain and logistical situation were far more difficult for any invader, and Spain was larger than Ireland. The British provided the Spaniards with support, equipment and finance and had a nearby base in Portugal. Furthermore, although not without severe problems, the

Spaniards possessed a leadership structure that the Irish lacked. In Spain, France was attempting to subjugate a country and fight an offensive war, while in Ireland Britain was only seeking to maintain a status quo.

It is also important not to exaggerate the capability of guerrilla operations in this period. Although Spanish regular and guerrilla operations denied the French control over much of the countryside and, in particular, greatly harmed their communications and logistics, it is a distinct possibility that the French could have won but for the diversion of resources for the invasion of Russia in 1812. In Calabria in Southern Italy, where the terrain and logistics were also very difficult, the French in the same period, nevertheless, developed a counterinsurgency strategy that brought them success.[12]

Irish failure is no more proof of military redundancy than that of the Jacobites, although it did indicate the resources deployed by the British state because, unlike in 1715, Britain was fully engaged in other conflicts. Yet, as in 1745–6, the British benefited from their ability to keep these conflicts largely apart. They were helped by Napoleon's greater concern with Egypt in 1798. It was impossible, because of the naval threat posed by the alliance of France, Spain and the Dutch, and the British policy of open blockade, rather than the difficult close blockade pioneered by Admiral Edward Hawke in the 1750s, to prevent the French from reaching Bantry Bay in 1796 and from landing some troops in Wales (1797) and Ireland (1798), but they were relatively small forces unable to deliver a knockout blow. Furthermore, the British navy was more impressive and successful in the 1790s than it had been during the War of American Independence. Victory over the Dutch at Camperdown (1797) was especially important because the Dutch fleet had been preparing to invade Ireland.

Domestic duties

The British military was not only expected to suppress rebellion. It was also responsible for the maintenance of law and order. Local police forces either did not exist or were inadequate. In 1785 opposition from local interests and fears about the consequences for liberty led Parliament to reject a bill to create a single centrally controlled police force for London, in place of the existing local ward and vestry constables and watchmen. As a result, the army was the essential force used to check public disorder, and that in a society in which collective protests were common. However, the ability of the army to respond was affected by the anti-militaristic nature of British society and by the army's dependence on an often hesitant civil magistrature for its authority in civil policing. By 1820 the Duke of Wellington was sufficiently concerned about the possibility of disaffection among the Guards to recommend the formation of a special force, police or military, to control London. This was not, however, an issue earlier. The army was seen as a reliable support for government, although in the 1790s there was concern about United Irishmen in the ranks, as indeed there was in the navy and the marines.[13]

In the British Isles in 1688–1815, lawlessness was often endemic and large in scale. Smuggling, wrecking, and cattle-rustling were serious threats to law and order over much of the British Isles.[14] Troops were sent to Connacht in 1711–12 to stop cattle-maiming by the Houghers. Tax riots led to the use of the army, as in Glasgow in 1725 where they killed 19 rioters in response to rioting against the imposition of a new Malt Tax. Industrial disputes led to collective violence, as did hostility to turnpikes: new roads and their attendant charges. In 1763 an official reported from Dublin, "The Lords Justices have at the request of the Earl of Hillsborough ordered a company of foot to the town of Lisburn for the preservation of the public peace. His Lordship was insulted or ill treated by a mob of weavers in that town". Troops were deployed against the Cornish tinners in 1757 and in 1773, the tinners "rose in such numbers that it was not in the power of any civil police to quell them", and seized grain, leading to the use of troops to restore order. The army was also supposed to deal with a range of disturbances judged unacceptable by the civil authorities. In 1789, for example, an officer wrote from Dublin:

A very melancholy affair happened here last Thursday. The mob were baiting a bull in one of the streets and were ordered by the Sherriff to disperse but to no purpose. He was obliged to send for a party from the Castle Guard which unfortunately were the 64th. They were very ill used by the mob, and the Sherriff ordered them to fire over their heads, which they did, but, instead of alarming them, it had a very different effect. They swore they had only powder in their pieces and began pelting them with bricks and stones. The Sherriff ordered a part of the party to fire, which they did, and killed four, and wounded several more of them desperately. Their leader receiv'd a ball in his forehead, came out at the back part of his head. We are now call'd the bloody 64th.[15]

Food riots were a major cause of disturbance and the use of troops did not always overawe the rioters. At Dysart in Scotland in 1720 the rioters attacked the soldiers and seized their weapons. When, in response to rising prices, local people seized control of Bristol market in April 1801 and forced the sale of goods at customary prices, the troops in the garrison were called out and detachments stationed around the town.[16]

Most of the army's domestic responsibilities did not involve fighting, although the threat of force was important to its effectiveness. Guard functions were widespread. Troops escorted valuable loads, especially of bullion and coin. Others, for example, guarded prisoners en route to trial,

A British warship in the English Channel pursuing a pirate lugger flying the Jolly Roger at her mizzen mast, artist unknown. Action against smugglers and pirates was a considerable peacetime charge on the army and navy. It brought together their tasks of sustaining government authority and protecting the commercial state. Piracy and smuggling hit trade and revenues. *National Maritime Museum, London.*

jail and execution, and theatres. They thus acted to overawe and contain potentially troublesome public gatherings. In addition, tax collectors and revenue officers were given support. The small detachments of the army stationed in peacetime Wales, at Carmarthen, Aberystwyth and Aberdovey, were there mostly to support the customs and the excise. Under Wade, the army built roads in the Scottish Highlands, roads that, paradoxically, were to be used by Charles Edward in his rapid advance on Edinburgh in 1745.

Similarly, warships were used against smugglers, yet another aspect of the navy's need for numerous small ships. Thus, Charles Tyler, later a Vice-Admiral in the Napoleonic War, served on anti-smuggling duty as commander of *Trimmer* in 1784–9 and of *Tisiphone* in 1790. A substantial percentage of government revenue was lost by smuggling. Warships were also used against pirates, both in British and colonial waters. Piracy was particularly a problem during the first four decades of the period, not least in North American and Caribbean waters. Piracy was a threat to imperial commercial links and to law and order in particular colonies. The navy played the major role in limiting the challenge. This entailed not only extensive defensive duties – long weeks of fruitless patrolling – but also hard-fought actions. In 1718 Blackbeard, who had held Charleston to ransom earlier in the year, was trapped in the Ocracoke Inlet in North Carolina, by Lieutenant Robert Maynard of the *Pearl*, who had hired two shallow-draft sloops. Blackbeard boarded Maynard's sloop and went for the Lieutenant, only to die after a bitter struggle, his life foaming away with the blood from his slashed open throat. In 1722 the 50-gun *Swallow* under Captain Chaloner Ogle defeated the two ships of Bartholomew Roberts off West Africa, killing Roberts himself in the exchange of fire. The following year the *Greyhound* captured 26 pirates in North American waters.[17]

The effectiveness of the military in dealing with domestic challenges was necessarily reactive and, perforce, limited to those that were seen as major threats requiring a military response. In dealing with such disorders the army was handicapped by the restrictions imposed by the law, especially the lack of clarity over the position under the Riot Act of 1715, and by its limited numbers and by the absence of any equipment other than firearms. The last led to fatalities that could outrage local opinion, as when the Edinburgh town guard under Captain John Porteous responded to disturbances after Andrew Wilson, a popular smuggler, was executed in 1736, and again in the St George's Fields Massacre in London in 1768, and in the Boston Massacre of 1770. In 1736 Porteous' men fired on the crowd causing fatalities. He was tried, sentenced to death, reprieved and lynched. Military support to the civil power did not endear the army to the populace.

However, in general, major outbreaks of violence could be suppressed, as eventually with the anti-Catholic Gordon Riots in London in 1780. George III took a close interest in the suppression of the Riots and pressed for firm action, "for I am convinced till the magistrates have ordered some military execution on the rioters this town will not be restored to order".[18]

During the French Revolutionary and Napoleonic period, concern about civil order rose,[19] especially during the Luddite riots of 1812. This concern affected the condition and location of the army. In place of the traditional reliance in England on billeting troops in inns, and thus ensuring that they lived among the people, rather than on what was seen as the militaristic practice of barracks, in July 1792 the government began a policy of purchasing or erecting buildings for barracks.[20] Numerous attacks on knitting frames in Nottinghamshire in 1812 led the government to send 2,000 troops to the county, and more than 12,000 were deployed across the Midlands and the North to deal with popular unrest.[21] However, in the Napoleonic period the general military situation had changed to the benefit of the government as the larger army was supplemented by militia and Volunteer units. The number of militia rose to over 100,000 in the mid-1790s, and Volunteer numbers were comparable.[22] The poor response to the 1800–1 disturbances, however, meant that the Volunteers were trusted less and less. Militia were therefore used almost as regulars. After initial teething troubles, and certainly by 1812, the militia could be, and were, used in public order situations. More generally, the military revealed in its ability to respond to rebellion a notable degree of flexible capability.

Conclusions

In 1729 Wade wrote from Dalnacardok,

> though the Jacobites are more numerous here than in any other part of His Majesty's dominions, by the present disposition of the forces it seems to me impracticable for them to give any disturbance to the government unless supported by troops from abroad.[23]

This interaction of domestic and international spheres was important, both in the British Isles and in North America during the War of American Independence. Ultimately, the British imperial system rested on force, but it was an economy of force, a use of naval power in order to prevent external intervention in the domestic sphere. In 1747 the Earl of Albemarle, military commander in Scotland, pressed the need for warships off the west coast of Scotland.[24]

The essential nature of a political system can be revealed under pressure, and the role of force was readily apparent in the crises of the period. It was through force that James II had been driven from Britain and Jacobite plans subsequently thwarted. However, as also with the role of North American colonists and chartered companies such as the East India Company, the British military system depended on active and extensive co-operation. Thus, in the '45 the army was supplemented by allowing trusted loyal aristocrats to raise regiments, and selected Lord Lieutenants were empowered to form their own military units.[25]

There was to be no repetition of the overthrow of the government in 1688. This was primarily due to political factors, but it was also necessary on a number of occasions to use force to preserve the political system. The army proved up to the challenge in 1715 (in England but not Scotland), 1746 and 1798, but far less so in 1745. The advance of Charles Edward to Derby is a reminder of the folly of assuming any inevitable military trajectory.

CHAPTER THREE

Conflict in Europe, 1688–1763

Eighteenth-century Britain is generally seen as a maritime and imperial power. The standard visual image of its army's contribution is that of James Wolfe's men ascending the Heights of Abraham in 1759, in preparation for their attack on Québec. To a considerable extent, this is a realistic impression because the successful trans-oceanic deployment and use of British military resources was the distinctive characteristic of British military history in this period. Furthermore, the British army did not match the overwhelming concentration of activity on large-scale Continental conflict that characterized the leading European armies of the period, those of France and the Prussia of Frederick II, "the Great" (1740–86). Nor prior to 1763 were the British particularly associated with tactical advances in land warfare, such as Frederick's development of the oblique attack in the 1740s, although they were at the forefront of the development of light infantry and riflemen. However, any concentration on Britain as a trans-oceanic military power risks an underrating of her important role in land warfare on the continent of Europe.

There is a certain symmetry to British land warfare on the Continent. In three pairs of wars – Nine Years' and Spanish Succession, Austrian Succession and Seven Years', and French Revolutionary and Napoleonic – the British army in each case was more successful in the second of the two conflicts. In each case this owed much to the strength or, at least, resilience of the alliance system that Britain was part of and to the problems facing her principal opponent, which in every case was France. However, Britain was not France's major opponent on land in the third pair of wars. There is little sign of any major shift in Britain's resource position within each of the pairs, but there are signs of significant operational improvement. Generalship was clearly important, most obviously with Marlborough and Wellington and, to a lesser extent, Granby, who were more able, within their respective pairs, than William III, the Duke of York and the Duke of

Cumberland. The French, in contrast, had better generals in the earlier wars: Luxembourg was better than Tallard or Vendôme, Saxe than Broglie and Contades, Pichegru than Joseph Bonaparte or Masséna in the Peninsula, in specific circumstances. Other operational factors may be cited, but it is important to note that these differing results suggest the need for caution before any structural interpretations are advanced.

The Nine Years' War, 1688–97

Although England and Scotland did not enter the Nine Years' War until 1689, the most decisive stage of the conflict was William's successful invasion of England in 1688. William's triumph ensured that English resources would be employed against Louis XIV, and thus that Louis would be put under greater pressure than in his wars of 1667–8 and 1672–8. Initially, this benefit was lessened by the disintegration of James's army in England in 1688 and, in large part, was counteracted by commitments in Scotland and, more particularly, Ireland, but this became far less the case from 1691.

In the meantime, the French had gained the initiative in the Low Countries, the cockpit of Europe, advancing in the Spanish Netherlands in 1690 and 1691: the French successfully besieged Mons in 1691 and Namur in 1692. This owed much to the excellent generalship of the Duke of Luxembourg, to nearby supply sources and to a large army, the largest in Western Europe since the days of Imperial Rome. From 1692, however, William was able to deploy more troops in the Low Countries, in large part because Ireland had been subjugated. Nevertheless, he was still defeated at Steenkirk (1692) and, after a hard struggle, at Neerwinden (1693). William was outgeneralled and his forces out-fought, but they were engaged against the leading army in Western Europe at the peak of its capability.[1] After Neerwinden, the French pressed on to besiege Charleroi successfully, thus gaining control of the line of the Sambre. Such gains were not only important strategically. They also ensured that the French would have more to bargain with in subsequent peace negotiations. William's forces were not only unsuccessful in the Low Countries. Another British force, 8,000 strong under Lieutenant-General Thomas Talmash, failed in an expedition against the leading French naval base of Brest in 1694: the landing-assault at nearby Camaret Bay was badly mismanaged.[2]

However, the commitment of Anglo-Dutch strength in the war denied Louis decisive victory, and the loss of Namur to William in 1695 shook French prestige. In addition, the British proved capable of supporting a greater military commitment than hitherto. Their commitment was larger, more sustained and more expensive than any they had mounted hitherto, and this contrasted greatly with the situation during earlier seventeenth-century conflicts. The size of the British corps in the Spanish Netherlands rose from 10,972 in 1689 to 29,100, plus 27,209 foreign troops in British pay, in 1694–7. Whereas Charles II's army had cost £283,000 in 1684 and James II's £620,322 per annum, between 1691 and 1697 the army and the navy each cost an annual average of £2.5 million.[3] Having secured an Act declaring that its consent was necessary for a peacetime standing army, Parliament was willing to pay for a substantial war army.

This expenditure also produced results. The military position did not collapse, despite successive defeats. Huy was regained in 1694. Fresh forces were raised and William Blathwayt proved an effective Secretary at War. The recapture of Namur provided "the essential negotiating card needed for future peace-making",[4] and by the Treaty of Rijswijk of 1697 Louis restored many of his gains. Furthermore, the British played an active role in the great re-arming of the 1690s, when pikes were replaced by muskets equipped by socket bayonets, and matchlock muskets were replaced by flintlocks. Whereas with the earlier plug bayonets inserted in the barrel of the musket it had been necessary to remove the bayonet before firing the musket, the socket bayonet enabled firing with the bayonet in place. The Ordnance Office displayed flexibility in this rearming, using the capacity of the Birmingham gunsmiths and thus circumventing the monopoly of their London counterparts.[5] All the new regiments raised from 1689 were equipped with flintlocks.[6] The Land Pattern Musket could be fired at least twice a minute and weighed one pound less than the matchlock previously used.

However, as the French were re-equipping in a similar fashion, the British did not benefit from a capability gap. Certainly the weaponry available did not play a crucial role at Steenkirk or Neerwinden. In the former, the difficulty of mounting a successful frontal attack against a prepared defence was crucial. At Neerwinden, heavy French massed attacks eventually drove William from his poorly chosen position, but only at the cost of heavier casualties. The experience gained of campaigning on the Continent was to be important for the next conflict.

The introduction of the socket bayonet increased firepower, but it did not greatly encourage attacks because bayonet drills were for a long time based on pike drills, with the weapon held high and an emphasis on receiving advances. It was not until the 1750s that a new bayonet drill, with the weapon held waist-high, made it easier to mount attacks.

The War of the Spanish Succession

Marlborough's War

The death of the childless Charles II of Spain in 1700 and his will in favour of Philip, Duke of Anjou, brought Louis XIV's younger grandson to the Spanish throne, but he was challenged by a rival candidate: "Charles III", the younger son of the Austrian ruler, Leopold I.[7] Conflict between Austrian and French forces broke out in northern Italy in May 1701, and in May

1702 Britain, Austria and the Dutch simultaneously declared war on Louis. William III and Parliament had been provoked by a series of moves by Louis that suggested he would use Philip's position to advance French interests, including the replacement of the Dutch garrisons in the "Barrier" fortresses in the strategic Spanish Netherlands by French forces in February 1701. The following month French troops were moved towards the Dutch frontier. The French Guinea Company was given the *Asiento* contract to transport slaves from West Africa to Spanish America for ten years, suggesting that the protected trade of the Spanish empire would be thrown open to France while Britain remained excluded. When James II died in September 1701, Louis recognized his son as "James III".

These steps led Parliament to reverse the suspicion of William and its hostility to a peacetime army that had produced a substantial post-war demobilization from 1697. Parliament voted the funds for 31,254 "subject troops" (recruited from the British Isles) in 1702, 50,000 by 1706 and 75,000 by 1711. There were also large numbers of foreign troops that were paid, in whole or part, by Britain, so that by 1709 the British had in theory a total of about 150,000 troops available for campaigning.

The war was to mark a significant expansion in the military and international role both of the British state and of the British army. Indeed, in the war, the British took a greater proportional role in the conflict with Louis than they were to take in the French Revolutionary and Napoleonic Wars, and in World War Two after 1941. The naval dimension, in which Britain played the central role in resisting France, is dealt with in Chapter 4, but it cannot be completely divorced from the issue of land warfare. Thanks to naval dominance, Britain was able to deploy and support land forces, both in nearby parts of Europe and more distantly. Land capability depended on naval strength.

As in earlier conflicts, Louis rapidly took the initiative, but, on this occasion, thanks to his grandson's accession as Philip V to the Spanish throne, he already controlled the Spanish Netherlands, Spanish Italy (Naples, Milan, Sicily, Sardinia) and Spain itself. Thus, the strategic and geopolitical threat posed by France was greater than at the outset of the Dutch war in 1672 and of the Nine Years' War in 1688–9, or at least it was greater on the Continent, for in the British Isles Louis lacked the opportunities created in 1689 by the Jacobite presence in Scotland and Ireland.

In the War of the Spanish Succession, the bulk of the British military commitment was made in the traditional nearby region of military activity, the Low Countries, but there was also important activity in two regions, first the Holy Roman Empire (essentially Germany) and, secondly, Iberia. The first reflected the actions of the British army based in the Low Countries, but the second was an independent sphere of action.

In alliance with Elector Max Emmanuel of Bavaria, Louis invaded southern Germany, and, in 1703–4, a combination of the two with Hungarian rebels appeared about to extinguish Habsburg power, and thus to destroy the basis of Britain's alliance strategy: the use of Austrian strength to resist French expansion. The British response was organized by John Churchill, then 1st Earl of Marlborough (1650–1722). Churchill was one of the greatest of British generals. He rose under the Stuarts, serving in the English garrison in Tangier (1668–70) and in an English regiment in French service in 1672–5 during the Third Anglo-Dutch war. Churchill played a crucial role in Monmouth's defeat at Sedgemoor in 1685. His desertion of James II in 1688 led William III initially to use his services, but he regarded Churchill with some uncertainty and in 1692 he was dismissed from his posts: his criticism of William's Dutch and German officers was unwelcome and he was suspected of Jacobite sympathies. Nevertheless, Churchill, created Earl of Marlborough in 1689, was brought back to the centre of affairs from 1698. In 1701 William appointed him Captain-General of the English forces in the Netherlands, a post he held until dismissed by the pacific Tory ministry in 1711. William had been a warrior king, but his sister-in-law and successor, Anne (1702–14), could not act thus, and there was no male royal who could fulfil the role: her husband, Prince George, was certainly not up to it. Nevertheless, Marlborough was untried. He had served in only five Continental campaigns and had never commanded a large army or formulated the strategy for a Continental campaign. His sole independent command – in southern Ireland in 1690 – had been a force of under 6,000 men.

However, Marlborough was soon successful in gaining the initiative from France. He captured Venlo, Roermond and Liège in 1702 and Rijnberk, Bonn and Huy in 1703, thus driving the French back on the Meuse/Maas and Rhine; although Dutch caution thwarted opportunities for battle with the French, and the failure of the Dutch to provide sufficient cannon and support for sieges was also a problem.[8]

In 1704 the crisis threatening Austria was averted by Marlborough's bold 350-mile advance – at the head of an Anglo-German army – from Bedburg, between Ruremonde and Cologne, via Koblenz and Mainz, to Launsheim, where he joined the Margrave of Baden's Austrian army on 22–23 June, and by his subsequent victory, in co-operation with the leading Austrian general, Prince Eugene, at Blenheim. This was the most decisive British military move on the Continent until the twentieth century and, unlike the Waterloo campaign in 1815, was a combination of the strategic and the tactical offensive. Marlborough was skilful in holding the anti-French coalition together, and was expert in conducting mobile warfare.

The advance was a formidable logistical challenge: depots of supplies were established along the route, providing the troops with fresh boots as well as food. Such depots enabled the army to maintain cohesion and discipline instead of having to disperse to obtain supplies. The latter would have been politically unwelcome also, because the advance was largely through

allied territory. The presence of supplies en route reflected excellent organization and also the gold supplied to the contractors from Britain.

It was not only hunger that was overcome. The French were kept unsure
of Marlborough's march towards the Danube by feints. The campaign was
a great triumph for mobility and planning, both in strategy and on the
battlefield. Once arrived in Bavaria, the British stormed the Schellenberg
Heights north of Donauwörth, defeating the 14,000 strong Franco-Bavarian
force holding the position and winning a bridgehead over the Danube. The
Elector of Bavaria, however, was joined by the French under Tallard on
6 August. Although the Franco-Bavarian army was larger, Marlborough,
now joined by the Austrians under Prince Eugene, forced a battle at Blenheim on the north bank of the Danube, where Tallard had a strong defensive position covered by the Nebel stream.

The battle of Blenheim (13 August 1704) was hard fought, with over
30,000 casualties out of 108,000 combatants: about 13,000 dead and wounded
in the Allied army, and 18,000 in that of their opponents, who also lost
about 13,000 prisoners. Victory was largely due to Marlborough's tactical
flexibility; in particular, to his ability to retain control and manoeuvrability, an ability that contrasted with the failure of the opposing generals both
to co-ordinate operations and to respond to particular crises. The decisive
factors were mastery of the terrain, the retention and management of reserves, and the timing of the heavy strike. Having pinned down much of
the French infantry in defensive engagements in and around the villages
of Blenheim and Oberglau, into which the French fed their reserves,
Marlborough launched the substantial force he had kept unengaged in the
centre. He was able to achieve a local superiority in what he made a crucial
part of the battlefield. The initial British cavalry attack there was checked
by the French, who had assumed they would be able to drive back any
British advance in the centre, but British infantry and artillery support
blocked the advance of the French cavalry and it was then unable to resist
the second British cavalry attack. This led to the rout of the French cavalry,
to the retreat of the Franco-Bavarian left, and to the surrender of 10,000
French infantry in the village of Blenheim, their retreat cut off by British
infantry who had exploited the victory in the centre. Marlborough was
more successful than his opponents in integrating cavalry and infantry, his
cavalry were better trained for charging, and the artillery, under Colonel
Holcroft Blood, manoeuvred rapidly on the battlefield and was brought
forward to help support the breakthrough in the centre.

Blenheim was followed by the conquest of southern Germany as Bavaria
was "taken out". After both the battle and the subsequent retreat to the
Rhine, most of the Franco-Bavarian army was no longer effective. French
forces were not to campaign so far east again until 1741. The major fortresses of Ulm, Ingolstadt and Landau fell before the end of 1704, although
Landau put up a long resistance that cost many casualties, while in the

Moselle valley, an invasion route between France and Germany, Marlborough captured the key positions of Trier and Traben-Tarbach after forced marches across the difficult terrain of the Hunsrück mountains. Marlborough had destroyed the image of French military superiority, achieving far more than William III had managed. He also helped for a while to make land warfare popular in British opinion and, in the long term, made it less unpopular. With the exception of 1702 and 1711, expenditure on land forces during the War of the Spanish Succession was greater than that on the navy, and this reflected political commitment to war on the Continent. The short term was of particular benefit to Marlborough, for Parliament provided the funds with which in Oxfordshire he built a major palace named after his great victory, a reward not granted to previous generals.

Marlborough won other battles, but none had the dramatic impact of Blenheim, in part because that victory had ended the danger of the anti-French alliance collapsing. Marlborough also found that victory did not end the difficulty of obtaining co-operation among the Allied forces, and this, combined with differences in military and diplomatic strategy among the political leaders, especially Dutch caution, made his task very difficult. Marlborough's plan to invade France up the Moselle in 1705, and capture Thionville and Metz, had to be abandoned due to lack of German support and because Villars took up a strong blocking position at Sierck. Instead, Marlborough transferred his forces, to campaign skilfully, but without any great victory, in the Spanish Netherlands. Tricking and out-manoeuvring his opponents, he passed through the Lines of Brabant, the strong French system of field fortifications, near Tirlemont. Although he then won a cavalry engagement, in which he was nearly killed, at Elixheim (18 July), Marlborough was prevented from exploiting his success by Dutch caution, and on 18 August the Dutch refusal to fight prevented a major battle with Villeroi on the Yssche. This was one of the might-have-been battles that are so easily overlooked. Villeroi had been out-manoeuvred and was in a poor position. Had Marlborough been successful, he might have been able to start pressing on the French frontier defences the following year. The limitations of coalition warfare were clearly displayed.

Nevertheless, already in July 1705, Marlborough had regained Huy, lost the previous month. By gaining control of the Meuse below Namur, and, in 1702–3, the major fortified positions in the pivot between the Spanish Netherlands and Germany, Marlborough had won the Grand Alliance an important strategic advantage. The French would not be able to threaten the United Provinces from Germany, as they had done in 1672. From 1705, the Spanish Netherlands and the French borderlands were the centre of British military activity north of Spain. This move of emphasis from Germany also reflected the greater ease of obtaining supplies in the Low Countries, both from Britain and locally, although in 1706 Marlborough initially planned to march to Italy in order to support Eugene, a daring and, in some respects, foolhardy scheme.

The year 1706 brought great success. Intent on avenging Blenheim, underestimating British strength, and concerned to push Marlborough back, Louis XIV ordered Villeroi to advance, but the consequences were disastrous for France. On a spread-out battlefield at Ramillies (23 May), Marlborough again obtained a victory by breaking the French centre after it had been weakened in order to support action on the flanks. Attacks on both flanks tied down much of the French army, including the infantry on their right. A cavalry battle on the French centre-right was finally won by the Allies and, as the French right wing retreated, the British, their preparations concealed by dead ground, attacked through the French centre, leading to the flight of their opponents. The French lost all their cannon and suffered about 19,000 casualties (including prisoners), compared to 3,600 Allied casualties. This was the only one of Marlborough's major battles in which Eugene did not take part.

Thus, in a six-hour battle of roughly equal armies, Marlborough showed the characteristic features of his generalship. Cool and composed under fire, brave to the point of rashness, Marlborough was a master of the shape and the details of conflict. He kept control of his own forces and of the flow of the battle, and was able to move and commit his troops decisively at the most appropriate moment, moving troops from his right flank for the final breakthrough in the centre.

Ramillies indicated the value of destroying the opposing field army, especially early in the campaigning season. It was followed by the rapid fall of a number of positions including Ath, Antwerp, Bruges, Brussels, Dendermonde, Ghent, Louvain, Menin, Ostend and Oudenaarde: most offered little or no resistance, but it proved necessary to besiege Dendermonde, Ostend, Menin and Ath. The cohesion of Villeroi's army was largely destroyed by the battle. The regional and municipal authorities and Spanish garrisons in much of the Spanish Netherlands hastened to surrender, and the French were only able to organize resistance in a few fortresses. Ostend fell on 6 July, after a short siege in which an Anglo-Dutch squadron had bombarded the defences, Menin on 22 August, Dendermonde on 5 September, despite the French drowning much of the surrounding countryside, and Ath on 4 October. The new French commander, Vendôme, led a larger army, much of it transferred from the Rhine, but he was unwilling to attack Marlborough as he covered the sieges in the Spanish Netherlands. The capture of Ostend improved supply routes between Britain and her army in the Low Countries.

The following year (1707) was less successful, as a result of political differences, both in Britain and among the Allies. Furthermore, both the larger French force, under Vendôme, and the Dutch were reluctant to provoke a battle. Vendôme cautiously took the initiative and improved the French position in the Low Countries. In 1708, however, the French advanced boldly from their fortified positions, although their larger army suffered from a poorly co-ordinated divided command. The French regained Ghent and Bruges, but Marlborough crushed their attempt to reconquer the Spanish Netherlands when he and Eugene defeated Vendôme's army at Oudenaarde (11 July). After several hours fighting, during which both sides moved units into combat as they arrived on the battlefield and the French pressed the Allied right and right-centre very hard, the French position was nearly enveloped when Marlborough sent the cavalry on his left around the French right flank and into their rear, thus destroying his opponents' cohesion. However, the French successfully retreated under cover of the approaching night. Vendôme had been badly let down by his co-commander, Louis XIV's eldest grandson, the haughty Duke of Burgundy, and the French lost, not only, like the Allies, about 7,000 killed and wounded, but also about 7,000 prisoners and, more worryingly, their confidence.

Several British leaders would have preferred to exploit the victory by a bold invasion of France, but Eugene and the Dutch favoured a more cautious policy. Oudenaarde was followed by the lengthy and, ultimately, successful siege of Lille, the most important French fortified position near the frontier. It was well fortified, ably defended by a large garrison under Marshal Boufflers, and there was the prospect of Vendôme relieving the position. A poorly co-ordinated attack on too wide a front on 7 September, commanded by Eugene, left nearly 3,000 attackers dead or wounded. The Allies were only successful when they concentrated their artillery fire, making a number of large breaches, beat off French diversionary attacks, and prevented the French from cutting their supply lines, defeating one such attempt at Wijnendale on 28 September. The town surrendered on 23 October, and the siege of the citadel proved less costly. It finally capitulated on 19 December 1708, after a siege of 120 days that cost the besiegers 14,000 casualties.

Far from going into winter quarters, Marlborough then overran western Flanders and recaptured Ghent and Bruges. The French attempt to regain the initiative in a nearby region had thus been defeated, and Marlborough had sustained his reputation, and that of his army, for delivering victory and for successful siegecraft. However, Vendôme's replacement, Villars, plugged the gap in the French defences by constructing the Lines of Cambrin which blocked any advance south from Lille.

Marlborough's reputation received a serious blow the following year. He first besieged and captured Tournai, another important frontier fortification, but one whose loss did not breach the French defences. Most of the campaigning season was taken up by the siege. Well garrisoned, Tournai did not surrender until forced to do so by a shortage of food on 3 September. Marlborough moved on to besiege Mons, and attacked a French army, under the able Villars, entrenched nearby at Malplaquet, a position chosen so as to threaten the siege and provoke a British attack on terrain suited to the defence. The battle, on 11 September 1709, exemplified Marlborough's belief in the attack, but it also indicated the heavy casualties that could be caused by the sustained exchange of fire between nearby lines of closely packed troops.

As later with Frederick the Great and his Austrian opponents, Marlborough's tactics had become stereotyped, allowing the French to prepare an effective response. They held his attacks on their flanks and retained a substantial reserve to meet his final central push by nearly 30,000 cavalry. The French finally retreated in the face of eventually successful pressure on their left and centre, but their army had not been routed and they were able to retreat in good order. The casualties were very heavy on both sides, including 24,000 (8,000 of them British) of the 110,000 strong Anglo-Dutch-German force, although only about 12,000 of their opponents; indeed, the battle was the bloodiest in Europe prior to that of Borodino during Napoleon's invasion of Russia in 1812. As before, Marlborough's tactics were based on the acceptance of the likelihood of heavy casualties, but at Malplaquet these casualties did not serve to obtain mastery of the battlefield. The heavy casualties affected Marlborough, not only by increasing political criticism, but also by making him less ready to risk battle.

As with the battle of Sheriffmuir in 1715, it was the momentum of result that was crucial. Marlborough went on to capture Mons (20 October) and Ghent (30 December 1709), but hopes of breaching the French frontier defences and marching on Paris were misplaced. In particular, heavy casualties among their soldiers lessened Dutch support for the war.

In 1710 Marlborough showed his mastery of manoeuvre, penetrated the Lines of Cambrin, south of Lille, early in the campaigning season and then sought to enlarge the new gap in the French defensive system. He besieged and captured Douai (29 June), but then, instead of pressing south towards Paris, moved west along the French lines, besieging and capturing Béthune (29 August), Saint-Venant (30 September) and Aire (9 November). The siege of Douai, however, had taken longer than expected, and Villars then blocked Marlborough's route towards Arras in a strong position.

The following year, Marlborough decided to press south, but Villars had strengthened the French defences with the 160 mile long Lines of *Ne Plus Ultra* (no further) which stretched from Etaples via Arras and Mauberge to Namur. Marlborough succeeded in misleading the defenders, crossed the lines without casualties near Arleux (5 August), and, in a well-conducted siege, besieged and captured Bouchain (12 September), a strongly-garrisoned fortress protected by marshes as well as fortifications.

Such achievements among the French frontier positions were no longer sufficient. Marlborough could no longer deliver a major victory, and Bouchain was too little to show for a year's campaigning. In addition, support for a continuation of the costly war had eroded in Britain and the

Tory government that came to power in 1710 both dismissed Marlborough (31 December 1711) and, in 1713, abandoned Austria in order to negotiate, by the Treaty of Utrecht, a unilateral peace with France. The previous year, Marlborough's successor, the Tory Duke of Ormonde, under "restraining orders" that forbade him from taking part in a battle or siege, had failed to provide Eugene with support, and Eugene was defeated by Villars at Denain. Villars went on to recapture Douai and Bouchain.

By 1713 British military expenditure had fallen to a point where there were only about 23,500 subject troops. Under the Treaty of Utrecht, Louis regained Aire, Béthune, Lille and Saint-Venant. His fortification system, which had served him so well in the war, was largely restored, although he had to accept a number of permanent losses, including Tournai. Philip V was left in control of Spain, but "Charles III", now the Emperor Charles VI, gained Lombardy, Sardinia and the Austrian Netherlands. Thus, the Bourbons had been kept out of the Low Countries.

Under Marlborough, the British army reached a peak of success that it was not to repeat in Europe for another century. The combat effectiveness of British units, especially the fire discipline and bayonet skill of the infantry, and the ability of the cavalry to mount successful charges relying on cold steel, owed much to their extensive experience of campaigning and battles in the 1690s and 1700s. These also played a vital role in training the officers and in accustoming the troops to immediate manoeuvre and execution. This was the most battle-experienced British army since those of the Civil War, and the latter did not take place in battles that were as extensive or sieges of positions that were as well fortified as those that faced Marlborough's forces.

The cavalry composed about a quarter of the army. Like Gustavus Adolphus of Sweden in the Thirty Years' War (1618–48), Marlborough made his cavalry act like a shock force, charging fast, rather than as mounted infantry relying on pistol firepower. He used a massed cavalry charge at the climax of Blenheim, Ramillies and Malplaquet. The infantry, drawn up in three ranks, were organized into three firings, ensuring that continuous fire was maintained. British infantry fire was more effective than French fire, so that the pressure of battlefield conflict with the British was high. The inaccuracy of muskets was countered by the proximity of the opposing lines, and their close-packed nature. The artillery were handled in a capable fashion: they were both well positioned on the field of battle, and were resited and moved forward to affect its development. As Marlborough was Master-General of the Ordnance as well as Captain-General of the Army, he was able to direct the artillery. His view of the need for co-operation led him to be instrumental in the creation of the Royal Regiment of Artillery in 1722; the first two artillery companies had been created at Gibraltar in 1716. However, the British lacked sufficient expertise to mount major sieges on their own and had to turn to Dutch engineers; they were not noted for their celerity.[9]

Marlborough's battles were fought on a more extended front than those of the 1690s, let alone the 1650s, and thus placed a premium on mobility, planning and the ability of commanders to respond rapidly to developments over a wide front and to integrate and influence what might otherwise have been in practice a number of separate conflicts. Marlborough was particularly good at this and anticipated Napoleon's skilful and determined generalship in this respect. Marlborough was also successful in co-ordinating the deployment and use of infantry, cavalry and cannon on the battlefield. In strategy, he was more successful than other contemporary generals in surmounting the constraints created by the need to protect or capture fortresses: Marlborough turned an army and a system of operations developed for position warfare into a means to make war mobile.[10]

The war in Spain

British troops were also engaged in Iberia, supporting opposition to Philip V. By 1707 there were nearly 29,000 subject troops in Iberia: initial success had led to an increase in the British commitment. However, despite the intervention of British troops and warships and of German and Portuguese troops, and the support of Catalonia and Valencia, the attempt to establish Archduke Charles as Charles III failed. It proved far easier to intervene on the littoral than to control the interior. Amphibious forces failed at Cadiz in 1702, but captured Gibraltar in 1704, Barcelona in 1705, and Minorca in 1708, and the British navy helped to raise the French siege of Barcelona in 1706.

Nevertheless, Castile was the key. Madrid was occupied briefly in 1706 and 1710, but Castilian loyalty to Philip V, and Louis XIV's support for his neighbouring grandson, proved too strong. Philip's cause became identified with national independence, despite his heavy reliance on French troops who badly defeated the Allies under Henry, Earl of Galway at Almanza (15 April 1707). The Portuguese cavalry and infantry fought poorly and were driven from the field, leaving the British and Dutch infantry to be defeated by Marshal Berwick's far more numerous Franco-Spanish forces.

In 1710 James Stanhope defeated Philip at Almenara (28 July) and Saragossa (19 August), before occupying Madrid, but few Castilians rallied to Charles III, and his communications became hazardous. As a result, he withdrew from Madrid. At Brihuega (9 December), part of his retreating army, commanded by Stanhope, was attacked by a larger army under Vendôme and forced to surrender. On the following day, another section of the retreating force, under Guido von Starhemberg, fought off a French attack at Villaviciosa, but Charles had now lost Castile and his forces retreated into Catalonia. The British and Dutch withdrew their fleets from the Mediterranean in December 1712 and Charles left Spain the following December.[11]

The Spanish Succession War was one of several conflicts in the period 1688–1815 in which the British fought in Iberia, and the least successful. It is important to consider why, not least for the light that it throws on success in the Peninsula War. In 1762, when the Portuguese were helped to repel a French-supported Spanish invasion, and 1808–13, the British enjoyed the majority of local support in the areas within which they campaigned, not least because in 1762 there was no advance into Spain. Thus, the obvious contrast is provided by Castilian hostility during the War of the Spanish Succession. Catalan support in that conflict was insufficient, because Catalonia could not be protected effectively from Castile, as had been earlier demonstrated in 1648–52 when French support for Catalonia had proved inadequate to preserve its independence from Castile.

Yet, local opinion was not everything. The course of the conflict was itself important and, in that, the Allies lost a number of major battles, in part due to French intervention. Partly thanks to the ability of James, Duke of Berwick, illegitimate son of James II and Arabella Churchill, and therefore Marlborough's nephew, the French benefited from a level of generalship higher than that they had shown in the Low Countries, Germany and Italy. Berwick was especially effective in manoeuvre and had a fine grasp of logistics.

Furthermore, none of the British generals were as able as Marlborough, although the difficulties they faced with both logistics and obtaining co-operation between the Allies were greater than those he encountered. Claiming his opponent's army "much superior and in better condition than ours",[12] Galway was manoeuvred out of Madrid by Berwick in 1706 and defeated a year later at Almanza. Complaints about allies, especially the Portuguese, were frequent. Their artillery was seen as terrible,[13] but there was also a serious problem of trust. There was concern that the Portuguese would simply use British units as garrisons. Wightman, then a colonel, wrote in 1704,

> We have but an ill prospect of affairs. Our generals disagreeing, the army mouldering away and having to do with a proud, sense-less sort of people which have depended upon the revolt of the Spaniards without making any reasonable preparations against any accident that might happen to the contrary.[14]

In June 1711, with allied Spanish troops mutinying for lack of pay and his own forces short of cannon and powder, the Duke of Argyll, who four years later was to face Mar at Sheriffmuir, was obliged to write from Barcelona:

> having with greater difficulty than can be expressed found credit to keep the troops from starving in their quarters all this while, which for my part I do not see how we shall be able to do any longer, for

> the not paying the bills that were drawn from hence the last year,
> has entirely destroyed her Majesty's[15] credit in this place; but though
> the troops could be supplied in quarters, that will not now do the
> business, for the enemy is already in motion . . . so that if we re-
> main in quarters, we shall be destroyed en detaille, and to get
> together is not in nature till we have money, for the whole body of
> troops that were here last year are without all manner of necessarys,
> having both officers and soldiers lost all their tents, baggage and
> equipage at the battle of Villa Viciosa, besides that the contractors
> for the mules to draw the artillery and ammunition and carry the
> bread will by no means be persuaded to serve any more till we
> have money to pay them.[16]

Such problems underlined Wellington's achievement a century later. He
was more successful in maintaining cohesion among the allies, supplying
the army and winning battles.

Finance posed problems even for as wealthy a state as Britain and this
was far more serious in Spain than in the Low Countries, not only because
of the relative poverty and shortage of food of Spain, but also because the
British ally in the Low Countries (the Dutch) was far better able to support
its own forces and to pay a portion of the cost of financing allied troops.

Conclusions

Despite defeats and failure in Spain, the War of the Spanish Succession
offered an impressive display of the effectiveness of the British army, certainly in comparison with that provided by the Nine Years' War. Circumstances played a major role. The French army of the early 1690s under
Luxembourg was in a better shape than a decade later; indeed by the 1700s
the French army was appreciably smaller. Furthermore, pressure on French
resources increased in the 1700s, as the French were pushed back to fighting
on their own territory. Yet, the British success also owed much to international circumstances, in particular the ability to create and sustain an effective coalition against France. It would have been impossible to resist, still
more defeat, Louis on the Continent without Austrian, Dutch and German
forces. The availability of these forces owed something to British financial
aid, but more to the international situation. The Austrians were no longer
distracted by war with the Turks.

Even allowing for troops from allies, Marlborough's forces were still
outnumbered on many occasions. Yet, this did not prevent him from both
engaging and winning: Marlborough understood that generalship entailed
the application of resources, not their addition. Both strategically and tac-
tically, he sought to use the forces he controlled with great vigour. If he
became more cautious in 1710–11 this reflected not some shift in resources,

but rather the psychological, military and political impact of Malplaquet. It was increasingly unlikely that fighting on would achieve a decisive peace and there seemed little point to risking further Malplaquets. The Whigs were let off the hook by their loss of office in 1710; it is difficult to see how they could have negotiated an acceptable peace, especially as the death, without sons, of the childless Emperor Joseph I on 17 April 1711 left his brother Charles ruler of the Habsburg territories, as well as claimant to the Spanish inheritance, and such a concentration of strength was unwelcome to Britain and the Dutch.

The Whig policy of no peace without Spain (for the Habsburgs) thus seemed bankrupt in international terms at the same time that hostility to Marlborough, the army and war on the Continent rose in Britain. In his *The conduct of the Allies*, which appeared in November 1711, Jonathan Swift claimed "we have spent all our vigour in pursuing that part of the war which could least answer the end we proposed by beginning of it" and he ascribed the concentration on Continental campaigns to Marlborough's influence: "It was the Kingdom's misfortune, that the Sea was not the Duke of Marlborough's Element, otherwise the whole force of the war would infallibly have been bestowed there, infinitely to the Advantage of his Country".[17]

The debate over national interests was to affect attitudes to the army over the following decades. It also influenced the view of the recent war. It was all too easy to forget how well the army had done. Other armies, as well as the British, were successful, but none to the same extent. From 1700 Charles XII of Sweden enjoyed an astonishing run of success up to his defeat by Peter the Great at Poltava in 1709. Marlborough shared with Charles a commitment to rapid advances, but was more methodical in his approach to logistical support. Moreover, Charles, like Peter at Narva (1700) and Eugene at Staffarda (1690), Toulon (1707) and Denain (1712), lost a battle, while Marlborough never suffered a defeat, although several of his campaigns brought only disappointing results.

Aside from success in the field, the army also enabled the government to play a major role in what was a period in which the European world altered territorially to a greater extent than at any time in the eighteenth century prior to the Revolutionary crisis at its close. Both by stopping France and by showing that Britain possessed a land capability, the army ensured that Britain played a major role in this process. Not least, the activities and size of the army, and of the supporting subsidized troops, made it important for France to detach Britain from the opposing alliance in 1713 and, therefore, to accept British views in international relations. Indeed the Anglo-French alliance of 1716–31 was in part a testimony to the strength of Britain's military position.

In addition, the period was one of a rapid transition in infantry weaponry, with the spread of flintlocks and of bayonets. Combined with the departure of the pike, made redundant by the socket bayonet, this shift increased firepower and also greatly altered infantry tactics. Thus, Marlborough showed proficiency and his army effectiveness, in what was a rapidly changing period of infantry warfare. The British army was not to experience a comparable change in weaponry until the introduction of rifled guns in the nineteenth century.

Forgotten War, 1718–20

Britain was at war again before the decade was over. Opposition to Philip V's Italian ambitions led to an attack on the Spanish fleet off Sicily in 1718, and, the following year, Britain and France, now allies, attacked Spain. The bulk of the fighting was done by France. However, the British followed the pattern set in the War of the Spanish Succession by launching an amphibious attack on Spain. An expedition under Lieutenant-General Richard Temple, Viscount Cobham, who had served under Marlborough, was ordered to attack Corunna. Judging it too strong, Cobham, instead, attacked and captured Vigo without opposition on 29 September, destroying the shipping and military stores that had been accumulated there. Two Spanish warships at Ribadeo were destroyed and the shore batteries dismounted. On 12 October a force of 1,000 men from Vigo under Major-General George Wade captured Pontevedra. The garrison abandoned the position and the British destroyed the arsenal, barracks and stores, as well as blowing up a nearby castle at Marin. On 24 October Wade evacuated Pontevedra, the following day the cistern in Vigo Castle was destroyed and the British re-embarked, and on the 27th the fleet sailed.[18] This expedition was a clear response to Spanish support for the Jacobites. In 1720, a Spanish invasion of the Bahamas was beaten off and peace was negotiated.

British naval power had played a major role in the conflict, but it was a French army, under Berwick, that had invaded the Basque country and captured Fuentarabia and San Sebastian. The British army was simply too small for the task. It could play a role in amphibious operations, but the peacetime army was too small for campaigning on the Continent.

The Walpole years

Britain was next at war, with Spain, in 1739–48, but, with the exception of Spanish pressure on Gibraltar, fighting on land was restricted to the Caribbean. Britain was not involved in large-scale conflict on land again until 1743, when she became a combatant in the War of the Austrian Succession, although her formal entry into the war did not occur until the following year.

In the period since the War of the Spanish Succession, the effectiveness of the army had declined. Numbers had been cut, the British establishment standing at only 12,400 in 1721, and, generally, at less than 18,000 there-after, until 1738, although it is necessary to add the separate Irish establish-ment, paid for by Dublin but available to London for deployment and use. Far from training for battle, the army was divided into small units, and its command positions were generally deployed for political purposes. Hostil-ity on the part of the opposition to a large, or, in many cases, any army, combined with Sir Robert Walpole's desire to cut government expenditure and his reluctance to become embroiled in European power politics. As a result, little was spent on the army, and dedication and morale, among both officers and soldiers, were not high. Absenteeism, cronyism and the pursuit of the financial benefits of command occupied the time of most officers, a reflection both of the extent to which the army shared in the values of society and of its institutional character. Many of the officers of the Minorca garrison, which fell to the French in 1756, were absent when the attack came, the counterpart to Admiral Byng's failure to relieve the island, and this led to criticism of the army's commander, George II's second son the Duke of Cumberland, who had been appointed Captain-General in 1745: "His Royal Highness is not unjustly blamed for neglect-ing to constrain the absentee Colonel, the Lieutenant-Colonel and the 33 Subalterns, to repair to their duty the beginning of the year". Fortified positions were often in a poor state. In 1729 the commander of the Minorca garrison complained about a lack of supplies, especially gunpowder.[19]

Appointments to senior positions reflected family influence and royal favour. Thus Sir Charles Hotham (1693–1758), received his first commis-sion in 1706, when only 13, and was promoted to Lieutenant-Colonel in 1720, Colonel in 1731, and Colonel in the fashionable First Troop of Horse Grenadier Guards in 1735, thanks to his friendship with George II. Never-theless, both George I and George II promoted the principle of long service as the main way to advancement, and did their best to counter the purchase of commissions. George II used his formidable memory for names to good effect in keeping oversight of the leading members of the officer class. He personally signed military commissions. Although the desire of both George I and George II to end corrupt financial practices, and, in particular, officers' pecuniary perquisites, was only partially successful, the traditional charac-ter of proprietary soldiering at troop and company level was fundamentally changed, to the significant detriment of the incidental income of captains. Regimental entrepreneurship, however, largely escaped, and colonels main-tained their private financial position until the reign of Victoria. Until the 1750s regiments were known by the names of their colonels. When the King asked General Churchill what had become of his hautboys, the Gen-eral struck his hand on his breeches pocket, so as to make the money rattle, and answered "Here they are, please your majesty, don't you hear them".

This was not the best basis for an effective response to a larger French army that had recently gained success and combat efficiency in the War of the Polish Succession (1733–5). The British army was not at the cutting edge in tactical practice, let alone debate or innovation. Nor was it improved as a campaigning force. Administration remained under a number of discrete and often clashing departments and officials, including the Board of Ordnance, the Paymaster General, the Secretary at War, and the Secretaries of State. The artillery had begun to improve with the creation of a regimental structure and the Woolwich Arsenal in 1716, but such changes did not amount to a major programme of raised capability for the army as a whole. In 1743 the British army lacked both numbers and an elite effectiveness that could enable it to cope with this inferiority. It did not compare with the army of Prussia which was also, like that of its then ally Britain, heavily outnumbered in the Seven Years' War of 1756–63. When war began neither the fighting units nor the administrative departments were prepared for it.[20]

The War of the Austrian Succession

The War of the Austrian Succession had begun in 1740 when Frederick II, the Great, of Prussia (1740–86) invaded the Duchy of Silesia (now southwest Poland), part of the Austrian Habsburg inheritance. Britain was initially neutral, but French entry against Austria in 1741 altered the conflict from the British point of view. From 1742, Britain came to play a role in opposing France. That year, 16,000 British troops were sent to the Austrian Netherlands, although they did not then come to blows with the French. The latter did not invade the Austrian Netherlands, and, despite some discussion, the British did not attack Dunkirk and other targets in France.

In 1743, however, George II (1727–60) led an army into the Empire where French armies were operating. On 27 June he clashed with the French at Dettingen near Mainz, winning a victory that owed much to superior British musketry. The French had laid a trap for the less numerous British. One part of their army under the Duke of Grammont was deployed in a strong position behind the Dettingen stream, blocking the British route, while another part threatened the British rear. However, instead of holding his position, Grammont advanced, only to be driven back. A British participant reported:

> On the 16 of June[21] in the morning we left the Camp of Aschaffenburgh (provisions being prodigiously scarce) with an intent of coming to Hannau. The French who were encamped opposite to us, did the same, pass'd the river at Dettingen, and waited for us on the plains near that place. They play'd their cannon on us three hours before we could come up to them, and kill'd great numbers. Whole ranks were swept off by my side, but, God, be praised I was not in the least hurt; about 12 o'clock we came up

with them, when the first line of our army (which was composed in the following manner – on the right of all, two regiments of *Austrians*: on the right of the English Brigadier *Pulteneys: then Onslows, Cornwallis's, Welsh and Scotch fuzileers, Ducour's,* and on the left of all *Johnson's*) attacked the French with great fury, and after a terrible firing of near half an hour, the French ran away. Then they brought up their second line, which, after we had given them a huzza, we fell on and beat back in about half an hour. After this they presented us their third line in most beautiful order; when My Lord Stair came to the head of our regiment and commended the bravery of the whole line, and said he would himself see us make the third attack, upon which, after giving him three huzzas, the English march'd up with surprising resolution; but such a panick run thro' the French, at seeing our first line still able to oppose their third, that they turn'd about and retreated over the river with great expedition. We were ordered not to pursue, or we should have taken thousands. Between the first and second attack we breathed a little, while the English horse attack'd the French cavalry; but I am sorry to tell you, after the first line they all ran away, and broke through our foot, but however the foot rallied immediately, and received the French horse guards or Gendarmes (who were pursuing our horse) with the greatest bravery. The behaviour of the Gendarmes cannot be sufficiently admired. They rode up to us with a pistol in each hand, and their broadswords slung on their wrists. As soon as they had fired their pistols they flung 'em at our heads, clapt spurs and rode upon us sword in hand; the fury of their onset we could not withstand so they broke our ranks and got through; but our men immediately closed and turned about, and with assistance of a regiment of Hanoverians who were in our rear, the French horse being between both we killed them in heaps: and out of about five hundred of the finest troops in the world, not forty escaped.

This engagement with the cannonading, lasted from a little after nine in the morning till after four in the evening. The loss of the French is very great in comparison to ours. They call it but 2000, but by deserters we are told it is near six.

The English at the most, have not lost above 1000. Our regiment has suffered as much as any. I had my right and left hand men killed twice by my side, and was myself shot through the hat, which I thank God was all I suffered. The King came to the head of us after the battle, complimented our Brigadier on the behaviour of his regiment, and made us his body guards that night. Other particulars you'll have from the papers. General Clayton is killed, the Duke of Cumberland wounded.[22]

An account of the cavalry engagement that valuably provides an impression of the battle, was written by Cornet Philip Brown, and was reproduced in a letter by Barbara Andrews. It refers to the clash of his regiment, the 1st or King's Own Regiment of Horse, General Honeywood's Regiment, with the French Maison du Roi (Household Cavalry) early in the battle. The British cavalry behaved badly: Honeywood and Ligonier's regiments lost formation and made little impression on the French cavalry.[23]

> he says for eight hours his life was every minute very precarious from the constant fire of the enemy . . . I will only write you what he mentions of their own regiment,
>
> upon their advancing to attack General Honeywoods and General Ligoniers horse we marched forward to meet them sword in hand, at the same time their cannon ceased, and they flanked us on the left with their foot, then we engaged and not only received but returned their fire. The balls flew about like hail and then we cut into their ranks and they into ours. Major Carr whose lieutenant I am was on my right. His skull cap turned two musket balls, but he received two deep cuts by their sabres. Cornet Allcraft who was near me was killed and the standard which he bore was hacked but he saved it. Captain Merriden on the right of the major was killed. Captain Smith on the left was wounded with two balls. 3 men and 8 horses of our troop was killed and 8 men cut and shot but not yet dead. Our squadron suffered most we being upon the left. In the right squadron Captain Saurin was wounded and his lieutenant Mr Draper killed. In the centre squadron Captain Thomson was dismounted, trod under foot by the horses and his lieutenant shot through the thigh. I did not receive the least hurt, but my left hand and shirt sleeve was covered in blood which must fly from the wounded upon me. Providence was greatly my kind Protector for though I was in the midst of the battle I was not in the least hurt; had not the English foot come to relief[24] we had been all cut to pieces, the enemies arms being nine deep and we but three. Afterwards we rallied again and marched up to attack them again, but before we were ordered the enemy had retired and the English, Hanoverians and Austrians remained masters of the field. We then proceeded on our march and came to our ground at eight o clock, it pouring then with rain and continued so all night and not an officer had a tent the baggage not being come up, and we had nothing to eat or drink and we quenched our thirst by the rain that fell upon our hats and we had neither forage or water for our horses. We laid upon our arms that night as we did the night before, and got here last night at ten o clock, so that besides the engagement we had neither provision for men nor horse from

Wednesday night to Saturday morning. I am perfectly well and have got no cold but am a little fatigued. I had a good meal of cold beef today and if I am not disturbed this night's rest will recover me.

Brown's account captured the confusion of a cavalry engagement and also the need to co-ordinate cavalry and infantry successfully in battle. Lieutenant Leonard Robinson of the 3rd Hussars, who had seen the French "come over [the stream] in great numbers", wrote to his wife, "our regiment is cut to pieces".[25]

Dettingen was not followed up. Political and military indecision, and serious differences of opinion, combined with the effects of poor weather and disease, and the absence of an adequate artillery train, ensured that George II was unable to make an impact on France's well-fortified eastern frontier. There was nothing to match the determination and unity of command that Marlborough had offered, and his successful co-operation with Eugene was not repeated in the War of Austrian Succession. This led to dissension and disappointment. The Earl of Stair resigned his command, and George II was criticized for allegedly showing favour to his Hanoverian troops at the expense of the British. Nevertheless, as after Blenheim, the French had been driven from Germany.

In December 1743 Viscount Cobham, who had served under Marlborough, resigned his commission. He emphasized the strategic problems affecting British operations on the Continent and the need to consider the international context. Cobham wrote of

the extreme difficulty and hazard of supporting the Queen of Hungary by an English Army in upper Germany, or of attacking France in her almost impenetrable barrier of Alsace, Lorraine, or the Netherlands, without the concurrence of the Dutch upon the foot of the last war.[26]

Cobham was correct. It was far from easy for a British army to invade France from the Rhineland. Aside from French fortifications, there were serious logistical problems.

The opportunity of repeating Marlborough's War – a conflict in the Low Countries with Dutch support – was offered the following year. In 1744, having built up their forces near Dunkirk to prevent a possible British attack, the French attacked the hitherto unassaulted Austrian Netherlands, capturing Courtrai in May. This led to Dutch participation in the conflict and permitted the British to plan offensive operations from the Low Countries. However, serious divisions among the Allies, and poor and cautious generalship by the 71-year-old Field Marshal George Wade, ruined the prospect for offensive operations and for an adequate response to the French.

Instead, it was the French who made advances, capturing Dutch-garrisoned fortresses, such as Furnes, Menin and Ypres, which were in a poor condition after decades of neglect. Wade, who was in poor health, was mostly concerned to preserve his lines of communication, and was unwilling to risk defeat by moving to the aid of besieged positions. He reported in June,

> The surrender of Menin, 6 days after opening the trenches, is what we least expected. But, as none of our frontiers have above a third part of the garrison sufficient to make a vigorous defence, and ill provided with stores, I shall not be surprised if other towns that are besieged, surrender in the like manner . . . if we could have an opportunity of engaging them with an equal front, I think, we ought not to decline the combat. But to attack them at disadvantage, would be rash, since the loss of a battle would be attended with the loss of the country.[27]

When an Austrian advance across the Rhine led the French to divert troops to the defence of Alsace, Wade was unwilling to exploit rapidly or fully his improved position. Wade eventually advanced towards Lille, but, once nearby, did little bar bicker with the Austrians about the cost of moving his cumbersome siege artillery from Antwerp.

The following year, the British Captain General, the young Duke of Cumberland, adopted a more aggressive stance and sought to relieve Tournai, besieged by the French under Marshal Saxe. Cumberland's infantry assailed the hastily prepared French position at Fontenoy (11 May 1745), demonstrating anew their discipline and fire control. The British troops were less raw than at Dettingen, but the battle showed the strength of a defensive force relying on firepower and supported by a strong reserve: the French had about 50,000 troops, the Allies 46,000. The French had prepared a series of redoubts, and the British had failed to reconnoitre them adequately. After several unsuccessful frontal attacks, and in the presence of Louis XV, Cumberland was forced to retreat with casualties far heavier than his opponents.

In the last attack, Cumberland's troops advanced in a large rectangular formation, the Allied lines forming a kind of large column, breaking the first French line and defeating the French guards with heavy musket fire. However, the earlier failure to capture Fontenoy and the redoubts on the flanks led to the failure of this attack. Saxe deployed his reserves effectively. Although Cumberland's infantry beat off successive attacks by the French cavalry, the French infantry, not held down by flank attacks as on a Marlborough battlefield, redeployed to attack the flanks of Cumberland's column. Cannon were also fired into the Allied flanks. Attacked and under fire from three sides, the Allied troops began a fighting withdrawal under the pressure of the French attack.[28] Saxe's army included the Irish Brigade of Irish Jacobite exiles who played a major role in Cumberland's defeat.

They advanced with their drums playing the Stuart hymn, "the White Cockade", and the officers encouraging their men with the Gaelic cry *Cuimhnigidh ar Liumreck agus feall na Sassanach* (remember Limerick and Saxon perfidy).

As at Dettingen, where Cumberland had been wounded, the British fought well. Unlike the Jacobites at Culloden, they did not break in retreat. The different results of Dettingen and Fontenoy reflected, in part, better French generalship, Saxe proving more effective in responding to developments than Noailles, but also the degree to which British steadiness and firepower were more effective in defence. Philip Brown was also present at Fontenoy, writing that afternoon,

> I write this from a pass where our squadron with others are posted to protect and secure the regular and exact order in which our forces are retreating – it is about a mile from the field of blood and slaughter, where true English courage and bravery hath been exercised and displayed in as high a degree as is possible for mankind to act . . . His Highness the Duke was never excelled by any hero whatever. He exposed his person everywhere the same as the most private soldier . . . But success is not always to the valiant and brave – would intrepid, calm courage and resolution have carried our point we had not now been a retreating – but our brave and not to be excelled forces are retreating in as much order as they advanced. We wish for nothing more than that the enemy would advance from behind their batteries and if they should my life upon it we should destroy them all. I admire and adore that kind Providence who hath been my great protector and preserver of my life and limbs during such a cannonading of nine hours, as could not possibly be exceeded and which that at the battle of Dettingen was nothing to. There were batteries continually playing upon our front and both flanks at the same time during the whole attack which was made by the infantry and they supported by the cavalry.

Brown continued with a personal reflection that reflected the familial dimensions of the economics of war:

> we are now part of the body of force which are posted as the rear guard to cover the retreat of the whole army, so that it is very uncertain whether I may yet live to see out the day or the sun rising the next morning should the enemy determine to harass us in our retreat – it was great pleasure to me that my commission was not signed when we marched to the battle to think that if I fell the money deposited would be preserved to my dear relations and friends.[29]

Brown's letter is interesting for other reasons. The encomiums heaped on Cumberland's personal conduct at Fontenoy were indeed universal. Contemporary praise for his personal bravery can, however, be contrasted with strictures on his generalship. For, as Brown tacitly admits, the British cavalry were mere spectators at Fontenoy and were only used to cover the retreat: the service he was upon when he wrote his letter. The cavalry was to the rear of Cumberland's column. The Duke's handling of his cavalry has been criticized.[30] In effect, he relied not on manoeuvre, but on force. His was the strategy and tactics of the direct approach, but, at Fontenoy, it fell victim to Saxe's clever exploitation of the advantages of resting on the defensive. Nevertheless, poor British generalship was balanced by the dogged savage qualities of the men in the ranks.

Napoleon suggested that Fontenoy prolonged the *ancien régime* monarchy in France by thirty years. The victory was followed by a rapid French advance, as the less numerous and divided Allies were outmanoeuvred and lost the ability to mount a successful response. The fall of Tournai (19 June) was followed by that of Ghent (15 July), Oudenaarde, Bruges (19 July), Dendermonde, Ostend (23 August) and Nieuport (5 September). The loss of the last two was especially serious as they were ports from which attacks on Britain could be mounted. The interrelationship of the defence of the British Isles and conflict in the Low Countries was amply demonstrated. By gaining these ports, France acquired invasion bases east of Dunkirk and, thus, increased British vulnerability, because British squadrons based in Portsmouth or Plymouth were not well placed to thwart such a threat, while, once free in the North Sea, the French could choose where to land along Britain's long east coast.

In fact, the invasion of 1745 was a tiny affair – the landing of Charles Edward Stuart in western Scotland – and was mounted from Brest. Yet, it was followed up by a threatened French invasion from the Channel ports. In addition, the French used the early months of 1746, when most of the British army was engaged in confronting the Jacobites, to conquer much of the Austrian Netherlands. Brussels fell to Saxe on 20 February after a surprise advance. Trenches were opened before Antwerp on 24 May, the garrison surrendering after a week. The French then turned to clear the Meuse valley and south Brabant. Mons fell on 10 July after a month's siege. Charleroi followed on 2 August, Namur on 1 October. These repeated blows destroyed the strategic axis offered by the Austrian Netherlands, an axis linking Britain to Germany, and thus covering Hanover from French attack, and an area from which the British could attack France by land. Neither option was provided by the United Provinces (Dutch Republic).

Returning to the Low Countries after Culloden, Cumberland and his troops played a major role in challenging the French. However, at Roucoux (11 October 1746), Saxe defeated an Anglo-Dutch-German army under

Charles of Lorraine, in a battle that centred on the hard-fought storming of three entrenched villages by the experienced French infantry.

The following year, Cumberland found his plans affected by Dutch caution, had to move to protect Maastricht from a possible advance, and was outmanoeuvred by Saxe in a race to gain the best position between there and Tongres. Saxe defeated him at Lawfeldt (2 July). In the battle, the British infantry in defence of the village inflicted heavy losses on the attacking French, only surrendering their position on the fifth attack.[31] A massive cavalry combat on the flank was eventually won by the French with infantry support, but Saxe failed to exploit the victory, leading to accusations that he had deliberately spared his opponents so that they could fight another day,[32] although his options were limited by the orderly retreat of the outnumbered British and by Cumberland's ability to maintain the army as a whole near Maastricht.

Like Fontenoy, Lawfeldt gave the French the strategic advantage. It was followed by the siege and storming of the leading Dutch fortress, Bergen-op-Zoom (1747), and by the successful siege of Maastricht (1748). The beaten Cumberland failed to respond effectively to French plans. In 1747 he did not fully appreciate the danger to Bergen-op-Zoom, although the garrison was strengthened by British troops and engineers, including the ballistics specialist Benjamin Robin.[33]

The alliance in which the British played a major role was therefore far less successful than its earlier counterparts in the Nine Years' and Spanish Succession wars. This reflected a number of factors, including quality of generalship. Saxe, not Cumberland, was the heir of Marlborough; and indeed Saxe, an illegitimate son of Augustus II of Saxony, had served under Marlborough and Eugene in 1709. He displayed Marlborough's preference for bold manoeuvres, emphasis on gaining and retaining the initiative, ability to control large numbers effectively in battle, and stress on morale.

Cumberland was less effective, but it is important to note the difficulty of the task. He was up against the best army in Western Europe, and was part of a coalition force that found it difficult to grasp the initiative. The British could not match French manpower. In July 1747 Cumberland wrote to Henry Pelham, the First Lord of the Treasury, "when we think ourselves vastly extravagant by adding five battalions to our strength, France raises fifty".[34] Furthermore, the years since the War of the Spanish Succession had not provided opportunities to train the British troops. There was no equivalent to the War of the Polish Succession (1733–5), in which the French had gained considerable combat experience. In addition, the small size of the peacetime British army was a poor base for the rapid expansion necessary to fight a major Continental war.

The battles were complex affairs. The large number of men involved (200,000 at Roucoux, 215,000 at Lawfeldt), the fluidity of the fighting, and the extent to which each battle was a combination of a number of distinct but related struggles, anticipated aspects of Napoleonic warfare. The frontage at Roucoux was about 10,000 yards. These were also long engagements. Including preliminary cannonading, Dettingen and Fontenoy each lasted seven hours, Roucoux several, and at Lawfeldt the hard fighting for the village lasted four. In contrast, Culloden was a relatively short battle.

These problems of control and command were not the sole difficulties facing the British. They also suffered from the different nature of alliance politics compared to previous conflicts. The Dutch played a much smaller and less effective military role and, until William IV of Orange, George II's son-in-law, seized power in Holland and Zeeland in 1747, Dutch political support for the war was far less than in the two earlier conflicts. Despite British hopes, William proved unable to increase the Dutch military contribution appreciably. The Austrians were more concerned about Prussia than France, especially during the Second Silesian War (1744–5), while, unlike in the Nine Years and Spanish Succession Wars, the French were not distracted by commitments in Spain; instead, Spain was an ally of France and active in attacking Austria in Italy. The war in the Low Countries played a smaller role in military and international relations than was the case in 1689–1713, but this affected the anti-French alliance, particularly Austria, rather than France itself. Indeed, the French were from 1744, and especially after Fontenoy, able to apply their strength effectively in the Low Countries. This was both cause and consequence of the failure of British Continental interventionism.

Despite her successes, France returned her gains when peace was negotiated at Aix-la-Chapelle (Aachen) in 1748. Her foreign trade had been greatly harmed by the British navy, her economy by a poor harvest, and her finances by the costly war. The French were also concerned by the advance of a British-subsidized Russian army towards the Rhine.

The Seven Years' War 1756–63

In 1747–8 the British discovered that they were unable to defend the Dutch. This led to energetic post-war efforts to strengthen international interest in protecting the Low Countries. Diplomatic commitments were seen as their protection; the task was clearly beyond the British army alone. Instead, it was felt necessary to create a strong alliance system. The army was reduced to a nominal peacetime establishment of 18,995 men, with another 11,850 troops on the Irish establishment. When invasion threatened in 1756, it was necessary to bring Hanoverian and Hessian units to England.

The diplomatic system the British tried to construct fell apart in 1755–6 as the Prussian attack on Saxony and Austria in 1756 led to new diplomatic configurations. Austria and France allied in the "Diplomatic Revolution", as did Britain and Prussia.[35] Thus, British politicians and generals did not have to consider the defence of the Low Countries. There was neither need nor opportunity to send troops to the Low Countries. Despite British efforts, the Dutch remained neutral, while the Austro-French alliance of 1756 covered the Austrian Netherlands.

British forces were involved in three separate areas of campaigning in Europe during the Seven Years' War. The first, and most important, was in Germany, as an ally of Frederick the Great of Prussia, the second in mounting coastal attacks on France in 1757–61, and the third in helping Portugal resist invasion in 1762. The British were effective and reasonably successful in all three spheres, and their army operated more impressively than in the War of the Austrian Succession, although the greater impact made by Frederick the Great and the importance of the struggle in which he was involved ensured that British achievements were somewhat in the shadow both then subsequently.

War in Germany

Initially, in large part due to the political sensitivity of appearing to use British resources to assist the unpopular Electorate of Hanover, the British government refused to get involved in fighting in Germany. Instead, it was at the head of a force of Hanoverians and other Germans that Cumberland was defeated by the French at Hastenbeck near Hameln on 26 July 1757. He fell back across the Electorate and capitulated at Stade in the face of a energetic pursuit.[36] However, the danger that Frederick would be forced out of the war and the political acceptability of assisting him, rather than Hanover, was such that in April 1758 the government agreed to maintain an army of 55,000 men in Hanover in order to protect Frederick's flank against French attack. Aside from paying for Hanoverian and Hessian troops, the British were also to pay the equivalent of 19 per cent of Prussian war costs.

This led to British troops campaigning in an area that was new to them, and, unlike the Low Countries, but like Iberia, it was one that posed serious logistical problems. These are important, given the subsequent tendency of armchair strategists armed with maps to criticize and suggest alternatives. North-west Germany lacked the resource base of the Low Countries. Marching south from the landing port of Emden in 1758, the 7,000 strong British force, under the 3rd Duke of Marlborough, found East Frisia bare of supplies, the commissionary, Michael Hatton, complaining,

> No contractors, no regular magazines . . . a continued rain [therefore] the roads are become so bad . . . the major part of the baggage is behind . . . the bread for want of covered waggons is dissolved, though I bought the best coverings I could, as is the two days bread the men had in their knapsacks, and I am afraid there is

> not a dry cartridge in the army. We have bread at Coesfeld . . . but
> that can't be got to us, nor we can't get to that. There has not been
> a pot boiled these two days the rain put out the fires . . . there are
> potatoes . . . which the men will get if the waters fall a little.

When he reached Coesfeld, Hatton found the available supplies inadequate and too expensive.[37]

Germany also lacked the communications network of northern France and the Low Countries, and did not benefit from a turnpike revolution. Rivers were often crucial supply routes, but the movement of supplies along them was affected by drought, floods, ice and a shortage of draught animals, and was in any case slow, as the British discovered with the Weser in 1761.[38] The following year, in Westphalia, "the heavy rains had so spoilt the roads and the whole country that the artillery couldn't possibly get on".[39]

Such problems affected the ability of the British to manoeuvre speedily, but, as part of an army under Prince Ferdinand of Brunswick, a protégé of Frederick the Great, they nevertheless achieved their tasks of defending Frederick's western flank and of denying the French control of Hanover, which would otherwise have served as a bargaining counter of negotiations. They were less successful in keeping the French out of Hesse-Kassel.

Landing at Emden in August 1758, the British did not see action until the following year, by which time Marlborough had died and been replaced by his second-in-command, Major-General Lord Sackville, the unpopular and difficult son of the Duke of Dorset and an MP, who was also a veteran of Dettingen and Fontenoy. At Minden (1 August 1759) an Anglo-German army under Ferdinand defeated the French under Broglie and Contades, inflicting 7,000 casualties with the loss of 2,762. The courage and fire discipline of the British infantry won the battle, six battalions defeating 60 squadrons of French cavalry by misunderstanding orders, advancing across an open plain, and then repulsing two charges by French cavalry. Most of the cavalry casualties were caused by musket fire, but those who reached the British lines were bayoneted. These charges were followed by a French infantry advance that was stopped by British cannon fire, and then by another French cavalry attack, which concentrated on the flanks and rear of the British infantry, only to find the rear ranks turn about and fire their deadly muskets. Again the French charged home, but relatively few reached the British lines and they were stopped by the British bayonets. A subsequent infantry attack on the British stopped under cannon fire. The French did not fight well: their planning was poor and their artillery out-gunned, but the British cavalry failed to cement the victory by charging. This led to the court-martial of its commander, Sackville. In contrast, thanks in large part to the British contingent, Ferdinand's artillery out-numbered that of the French and their fire dominated the battlefield. Ferdinand gave the artillery's commander, William Phillips, 1,000 crowns.[40] Although the French were able to withdraw in the face of a weak pursuit, the British exploited the victory by rapidly capturing Minden and Kassel. Münster was successfully besieged.

Sackville was replaced as commander of the British contingent by his second-in-command, Lieutenant-General John Manners, Marquis of Granby, eldest son of the Duke of Rutland and an MP, a prime representative of the sporting tradition of British generalship. He had a more successful war than Sackville, acquiring a reputation for boldness, bravery and success. His leadership of a cavalry charge on the French flank was decisive in the defeat of the French cavalry at Warburg (31 July 1760). Granby was supported by the British artillery which Phillips brought up at the gallop. At Fellinghausen Granby fought off a French attack (15–16 July 1761). Further successes followed at Gravenstein (24 June 1762) and Wilhelmstahl (25 June 1762). Granby was a popular commander who was personally brave, determined in command and yet an effective subordinate to Ferdinand of Brunswick. He does not enjoy much current fame, not for example receiving an entry in either Trevor Dupuy's *Encyclopedia of military biography* (London, 1992) or John Keegan's *Who's who in military history* (London, 1996), but he was the most successful British general on the Continent between Marlborough and Wellington. In 1760 the number of British troops under his command was increased to 14,600.

Granby was fortunate in his opponents – neither Broglie nor Soubise was a Saxe – but also, like the 1st Duke of Marlborough, benefited from his determination to gain and retain the initiative. Granby was expert at co-ordinating infantry, cavalry and artillery, and out-manoeuvred the French on a number of occasions. He was unfortunate in that none of the battles was as dramatic as Minden, while, more generally, the fighting in Westphalia has been seen as less militarily significant and impressive than that involving Frederick the Great. Ferdinand was not always victorious and the French also enjoyed a number of successes. In 1760 the French regained Kassel and Ferdinand's advance on Wesel proved unsuccessful. The following spring Kassel resisted an Allied siege, and it only fell, on 1 November 1762, after a second siege in which the French conducted an able defence.[41] Furthermore, for the British, the conflict on the Continent was overshadowed by the drama and success of colonial campaigns, while, by 1761, hostility to the continuation of the war, especially in Germany, was rising in Britain.

Coastal expeditions

The British were also involved in amphibious attacks on the French coast, seen as a second front that would divert French forces from the war with Frederick; he himself was more concerned to see British troops in Germany. The failure of a poorly organized attack on Lorient in 1746 during the previous conflict, largely because it was not pushed home, did not prevent a repeat of the strategy.[42] In 1757 William Pitt the Elder supported the idea of an attack on the French Atlantic port of Rochefort as a means to employ forces that had to be retained in or near Britain for defensive purposes, as a way to resist pressure to send troops to Germany and yet reduce French pressure there, and as a demonstration that in joining the ministry he had not abandoned traditional "Patriot" views of hostility to Continental interventionism.

However, after the British force reached the approaches to Rochefort on 21 September 1757, a combination of poor intelligence, inadequate co-operation between naval and army commanders, and indifferent and hesitant generalship led to a failure to attack the port. The combination of accurate information and decisive action, both essential to successful amphibious operations, especially if benefit was to be taken of surprise before larger opposing forces were deployed, was missing.

The consequences reflected the politicization of strategy and generalship in this period, and the problems of fighting a war in the glare of newspaper publicity. Public disquiet led to the establishment of a Commission of Enquiry into the conduct of the generals and to the unsuccessful court martial of the army commander, Sir John Mordaunt. Pitt played an active role in the last, appearing in order to criticize the generals. In contrast, Cumberland, whose influence Pitt held responsible for failure at Rochefort, espoused their cause.[43]

The following year, the plan for an attack on St Malo was initially abandoned due to the apparent difficulty of the task. Instead, Cherbourg was successfully attacked on 8 August and its fortifications were destroyed. The following month, a force landed for an attempt on St Malo had to re-embark at St Cast, with the loss of 750 men, in the face of a larger French army.[44]

Belle Isle, an island off the Breton coast, was captured in 1761,[45] and held until the peace in 1763. Pitt was a keen supporter of the expedition. When Major-General Studholme Hodgson, who commanded the land forces on it, saw him before sailing, Pitt "recommended me not to stay for trifles if the wind was fair, nor confine myself to forms; and has promised to support me in all stretches of power whatever and against whomsoever". Short of cannon and engineers, Hodgson was furious with the Board of Ordnance, but considerable resources were in fact deployed.[46]

Even if successful, the effect of such operations was limited, and was certainly far less than anticipated by British supporters. Whereas Britain could be threatened by invasion with serious strategic consequences, France was far less vulnerable, thanks in part to the greater size of its armed forces. The Duke of Bedford wrote to George III's favourite, the 3rd Earl of Bute:

> Mr Pitt tells you, that by the conquest of Belleisle, you are enabled
> to spread the alarm so thoroughly over the whole coast of France,

which is on the [Atlantic] ocean, that the people won't be able to sleep quietly in their beds. But can we do more? Upon the continent of France, after they have had so long a time to guard against us in the material places, such as Bordeaux, Rochefort, Brest, L'Orient and St. Malo, I fear not, especially as it will be impossible to spare any more troops from hence or Ireland, without leaving your own coasts liable to be insulted, even by a handful of men. What then in our situation can be expected from our efforts during this summer from Belleisle? Why possibly the taking another island, or burning a few miserable villages on the continent.[47]

Practicality as well as policy was at issue. Amphibious operations were also greatly affected by bad weather and by the possibility of such weather. The 3rd Duke of Marlborough, the commander of the expedition, wrote from the Channel off Cherbourg in June 1758:

We had been excessively unlucky in our winds as I was prevented three days ago from landing on the coast of Normandy by a gale of wind . . . last night I had everything ready to attack the forts of this place, just before we stepped into the boats the wind blew so excessive hard that we were forced to desist, and have had great difficulty in preventing some of the transports from being blown on shore.

Three years later, Hodgson reported at one stage, "we could get nothing landed yesterday, it blew so excessively hard".[48]

War in Portugal

In 1762 an expeditionary force was sent to Portugal. This British ally appeared to the French and Spaniards to be a vulnerable target that could be conquered and exchanged in a general peace treaty for British gains elsewhere. Spanish successes in overrunning weak and poorly defended Portuguese fortresses, such as Miranda, Bragança and Chaves, led to urgent requests for British troops. After being delayed by contrary winds in the Channel in late June, these troops helped to turn the tide, although the Spanish failure to exploit their early successes by a march on Oporto was also crucial.

The complaints made by British commanders are instructive as indications of the problems of campaigning in this period. In July Brigadier Frederick provided a depressing account of the logistical problems he faced on the march to Santarem, which in part arose from the poverty of the region, and also suggested that there had been no improvement in the logistical situation since the War of the Spanish Succession. Arriving at

Oprto de Mugen, Frederick had found no beef or bread prepared for his troops and it proved impossible to obtain adequate supplies:

> all the bread that the magistrate said he could possibly get before they marched was two hundred small loaves which was so small a quantity it was impossible to divide amongst the men. I ordered the regiment to march the next morning at half an hour past three, but the carriages for the baggage not coming at the proper time it was past six before they began their march. It was late in the day before they got to Santarem when Colonel Biddulph reported to me that by the excessive heat and sandy roads that above half the regiment had dropped behind and was afraid many of the men would die, on which surgeons were sent to their assistance . . . at Santarem . . . the men were lying in the streets, the inhabitants had shut up their houses, and the magistrates had provided no quarters for them neither was there beef or bread for the men . . . they were fainting with the heat and want of food.

Clearly the pressure on the soldiers was acute: "nine men of the Buffs died on the march yesterday".[49] Frederick's letter lends vivid point to the complaints of British generals over deficiencies in the quantity and quality of Portuguese supplies, especially of horses, mules, bread, forage and firewood. There were other serious problems, especially with communications and in co-operating with the Portuguese. Captain Fraser Folliott found a supposed ford over the Tagus was five feet deep and the current very rapid, while the roads nearby were impassable for wheeled vehicles. Much of his company was ill, while it was difficult to gain information because he had no interpreter.[50] Lord Tyrawly, the British general, complained that the British troops had neither straw nor beds and that the shelter and bread supplied were inadequate.[51]

Nevertheless, despite these problems, the British army operated effectively, and Burgoyne successfully captured Valença d'Alcântara, and, on 5 October, in the last significant action in the campaign, stormed the entrenched Spanish camp of Villa Velha, inflicting heavy casualties. Facing the onset of the winter rains, the imminence of peace, and the strength of the British presence, the French and the Spanish retreated.

Conclusions

The British army during the Seven Years' War is usually discussed in terms of James Wolfe and the capture of Québec in 1759. The campaigns in Europe are also worthy of note. They indicate the multiple capability of the British army, a capability that was certainly far greater than its Prussian ally, for the latter did not have to mount amphibious operations nor operate in Portugal, an area where the British had to face logistical problems, the difficulties of campaigning in an unfamiliar land and the problems of co-operating with allies.

The British army was in part to be divided in subsequent decades between "Germans" and "Americans": officers who had predominantly served in one or another sphere during the Seven Years' War. There was less difference between their experiences than is sometimes imagined, not least because "woodcraft" and dispersed tactics were less important in North America and less absent in Germany than is sometimes appreciated. Furthermore, the notion of Continental warfare as hidebound, rigid and limited can be challenged.

During the 1740s and 1750s there were some reforms in the way in which the army operated, although less so than in the case of the Austrian and Russian armies in the 1750s. After the War of the Austrian Succession, Cumberland sought to improve the army's effectiveness and, already, in 1744, a visit by the Duke to the Academy at Woolwich had led to measures being adopted to reform the discipline and system of training of the cadets.[52] More generally, Cumberland pressed the importance of merit in promotions, and sought to create an effective fighting force. The Duke stressed the responsibilities of commanders. However, Cumberland's controversial political position, alleged political ambitions and reputation as a martinet limited his influence.

In terms of weaponry the British army was in an acceptable position, and its infantry and artillery firepower both proved more than satisfactory at Minden. If the army is not noted for tactical innovation, as was the army of Frederick the Great, it was, nevertheless, the case that the British faced a number of different battlefield scenarios and were able to cope with them. Strategy owed much to political pressures and the exigencies of alliance politics, as with coastal expeditions and campaigning in Germany, respectively. Yet it proved easier to combine effectively in the Anglo-German army under Ferdinand of Brunswick than in the Allied armies in the Low Countries in the 1740s.

Potentially most serious, was the absence of a united military command structure that would be able to devise and sustain coherent peacetime programmes of planning and improvement. This reflected the anti-military ethos of British politics, specific suspicions of Cumberland, the difficulties of enforcing discipline and diligence on aristocratic officers who owned their positions, and the more general absence of a bureaucratic ethos. As a consequence, the ability of the army to respond in a united and planned fashion to new developments was limited, and it had only limited success in improving its capability during the years of peace. This exacerbated the problems created by the small size of the peacetime army and, therefore, the need to expand it rapidly at the outset of each war.

However, such an expansion had been successfully undertaken during the Seven Years' War and the army had gained in effectiveness with experience. It had not had to undergo the heavy casualties of the 1st Duke of Marlborough's battlefields, and had not, therefore, lost a high percentage of its trained officers and men. The absence of any need to operate in the Low Countries close to French bases helped to protect the army from the pressures faced by that of Prussia, but fighting quality was also important. Thanks to the British infantry at Minden, the French in 1759 were not able to repeat their success of two years earlier in overrunning north-west Germany.

CHAPTER FOUR

Naval triumph, 1688–1763

B ritain became the leading naval power in Europe, and thus the world, in the period 1688–1815. As so often with British military power in the period, it is necessary to be aware of earlier developments and to trace there the roots of capability and success. The growth of English naval power in both the sixteenth and the seventeenth centuries had equipped England with an important navy and a tradition of maritime power that subsequently affected political assumptions and views about the necessary identity and desirable policies of Britain as a military power. She had already been one of the leading naval powers, and had shown her strength during the Interregnum (1649–60), and, specifically, in her ability to contest naval mastery with the Dutch, the foremost naval power, in the three Anglo-Dutch wars of 1650–2, 1665–7 and 1672–4, although there had been a relative decline in English naval power in the 1660s: thanks to French and Dutch shipbuilding, the English declined from leading to third most important naval power.[1]

The Nine Years' War, 1689–97

English naval strength greatly revived in the late 1670s thanks to a major shipbuilding programme in 1676–80, but the French navy remained larger in the 1680s and launched more warships than England in the early 1690s. However, the situation altered during the later 1690s: English naval power increased, not least relative to that of the other two leading naval states, France and the Dutch. Between 1689 and 1698 the English launched 61 capital ships. The situation was initially less promising in 1689–92, but, as a result of an Act of Parliament of 1691 sponsoring new construction, from 1695 the English had a definite lead in new launchings over both the Dutch and the French. By 1700 the English fleet was larger than that of France. Furthermore, there was a significant improvement in the logistical support to English naval power: a substantial expansion of Portsmouth dockyard in the 1690s and the creation of an entire new front-line operational yard at Plymouth. This permitted the stronger projection of English naval power into the English Channel and Western Approaches in the 1690s.[2]

The impact of improvements in British capability was accentuated by changed priorities affecting the French and Dutch navies. Having invaded England successfully in 1688, the Dutch navy was affected by a concentration of expenditure on the army. As a result, whereas in the abortive defensive treaty of 1678 the ratio of Dutch to English capital ships had been fixed at 3 to 4, in 1689 this was lowered to 3 to 5 and during the Spanish Succession War the Dutch were generally more than halfway below their quota, and, even then, the ships often arrived late. Furthermore, from 1694 the French concentrated on the army, and at sea on privateering.

Prior to that, there had been a short-lived, but intense, naval crisis that exacerbated the dangers posed by Jacobitism. After the indecisive battle of Bantry Bay (1 May 1689) in which Admiral Herbert and 22 ships of the line were unable to defeat a French fleet of 24 ships of the line under Château-Renault covering a landing of troops in Ireland, the English had to return to Portsmouth for repairs, because there was no dry docking in the Channel further west. This gave the French a major advantage as, from their bases at Brest and Rochefort, they could challenge the English in the Channel and in Irish waters, and also attack shipping routes. Two months later, the French threat was accentuated when the able Anne-Hilarion Count of Tourville evaded the English fleet off Brittany to lead much of the Toulon fleet into Brest, creating a threatening concentration of French strength.

In 1690 the French successfully escorted another force of troops to Ireland, and were victorious off Beachy Head (30 June). Tourville greatly outnumbered the Anglo-Dutch fleet, which was affected by the determination of Viscount Torrington (the ennobled Herbert) not to risk his English ships for fear that that would expose England to invasion. Torrington had been ordered to engage, in part to cover English trade. However, he hung back, possibly with good reason, but nevertheless ensuring that the Dutch in the van were badly pummelled. Tourville was also successful in the pursuit, and a number of Allied warships ran aground and were burnt.

The French failed to exploit their victory until 1692. They did not have an invasion force ready and Louis XIV was more concerned about the conflict in the Spanish Netherlands. In addition, the concentration of French troops there did not lend itself to an invasion, because French naval power was based further west, in Brest. It was not until 1692 that invasion forces were prepared, but secrecy was lost, delays in the invasion preparations hindered Tourville, and he was compromised by a failure to unite the French naval forces and by rigid instructions enforcing conflict even if outnumbered. A far larger Anglo-Dutch fleet under Admiral Edward Russell attacked the French on 29 May 1692 off Barfleur on the Cotentin peninsula.

Admiral Edward Russell by Sir Godfrey Kneller. The portrait included the battle of Barfleur (1692), a victory in which numbers as well as skill told. The essential resilience of wooden ships ensured that they were difficult to sink by gunfire (although they would sink if shot detonated the magazine), but cannon firing at short range could devastate rigging and masts and effectively incapacitate the ships. The French warships damaged in the battle were attacked and burned by small boats while sheltering in the Bay of La Hougue. *National Maritime Museum, London.*

81

Russell was able to gain the initiative, but the French fought well before withdrawing. Twenty-two of the French warships reached St Malo through the hazardous race of Alderney, but many of the damaged warships took shelter under the forts at St Vaast and Ile Tatihou in the bay of La Hougue on the east side of the peninsula. They were attacked and burned on 2 June by small boats sent in by Vice-Admiral Sir George Rooke, one of the most successful small-boat operations of the period, but one made possible by the division and demoralization among the French fleet caused by their earlier pummelling from the larger Anglo-Dutch fleet. Fifteen warships, and the transports, were destroyed.

This victory not only dashed French invasion prospects. It also helped lead to a major shift in European naval history. Although Tourville took large fleets to sea in 1693 and 1694, he achieved little: the war in Ireland was over and an invasion of England appeared a less promising prospect; in 1694 there was little for Tourville to achieve in the Mediterranean. Encouraged by the economic crisis of 1693–4, which hit government finances, and by the limited benefits of recent naval operations, the French re-focused their naval strategy from the *guerre d'escadre*, the war of squadrons in which they had sought battle, to the *guerre de course*, in which attacks on trade took top priority, particularly in the War of the Spanish Succession in the 1700s.[3]

These could be very damaging. French commerce raiding hit English trade hard and thus affected the economy and public finances, both helping to cause, and exacerbating, a major financial crisis in 1696. Three years earlier, over 80 merchantmen were lost when the Smyrna convoy were intercepted by the Brest fleet under Tourville off Lagos in Portugal. French privateers ranged further afield. The East India Company lost the *Samuel* off Cape Town in 1692 and the *Canterbury* in the Straits of Malacca in 1703. However, commerce raiding did not provide a serious challenge to English naval power, certainly not one as serious as that posed by the French fleet in 1690. Indeed the shift in French priorities interacted with a rise in English naval power and confidence, although it also created problems by ensuring that there was not a French battlefleet at sea to engage and defeat.

After Barfleur, the English were in firmer control of Irish waters, but already before that they had played a key role there in support of the army, relieving Londonderry, helping Marlborough take Cork and Kinsale, blockading Limerick and co-operating in the capture of Duncannon Castle. English naval capability increased with a rapid and expensive programme of dockyard construction. Portsmouth, which already had two dry docks that acted as a double dock, was expanded with the creation of two new dry docks and two wet docks. At Plymouth, where the naval facilities had hitherto been primitive, a new dockyard including a dry dock and a wet dock was constructed. Initially, in 1689, it was decided that the Plymouth dry dock should be capable of receiving up to third-rates, but in 1691 the dock contract was upgraded so as to be able to take the biggest ships of the line.[4] The expansion of facilities at Portsmouth and Plymouth supplemented the Restoration concentration of naval facilities on the Medway and the Thames, at Chatham, Sheerness, Deptford and Woolwich.

French weakness enabled the English to prepare for a projection of naval power, but it proved difficult to follow up Barfleur. Naval advice clashed with governmental optimism, leading to Russell's loss of command after the 1692 campaign. St Malo and Brest were attacked unsuccessfully in 1692 and 1694, respectively. Subsequently, a policy of bombarding French ports such as Calais (1696), St Malo (1693, 1695) and Dunkirk (1695) was found less costly. However, such attacks had only a limited impact and did not distract the French from their campaigns in the Spanish Netherlands. The dispatch of a large fleet under Russell to the Mediterranean in 1694 was followed by its wintering at the allied port of Cadiz, a new achievement.[5] The interests of Austria, France and Spain in the western Mediterranean ensured that it was the cockpit of European diplomacy, and in the half-century from 1694 it was to be a major sphere of British naval power, setting the pattern for public assumptions about this power. English war-ships had been to the area previously, especially under Robert Blake in the 1650s, and, thereafter, to protect trade against the Barbary pirates of North Africa, but from 1694 such naval deployment was more closely linked to strategic confrontations with other European states.

English naval forces ranged widely in the 1690s. In 1697 a small squadron under Vice-Admiral Neville was sent to the Caribbean, but disease claimed Neville, all his captains and half of the sailors. The effectiveness of these operations varied, but there was a common theme of gaining the initiative, mounting attacks, protecting English trade and attacking that of France. The range of English naval activity was maintained after peace was negotiated in 1697. A squadron was sent to Newfoundland to protect English trade. This new-found confidence led in 1700 to the dispatch of a joint Anglo-Dutch fleet under Rooke to the Sound. It helped to enforce a settlement of Dano-Swedish differences.

War of the Spanish Succession, 1702–13

English naval strength was barely contested by the French during the War of the Spanish Succession, in large part because their expenditure continued to be dominated by the army. This enabled the English to inhibit French invasion planning, to maintain control of maritime routes to the Low Countries,[6] the crucial axis of the alliance, and to project power, especially into the Mediterranean. But for the English navy, there would have been no war in Iberia, not least because the threat of naval action, underlined by the fleet's success at Vigo in 1702, led Portugal to abandon its French alliance in 1703. Thanks in part to the availability of a position at Lisbon, the English fleet under Sir Cloudesley Shovell entered the Mediterranean in 1703, encouraging Victor Amadeus II of Savoy to abandon Louis XIV. The French made one major attempt to contest English naval predominance when in 1704 they attempted to challenge the newly established English position at Gibraltar. This was checked at the battle of Malaga (13 August). No ships were sunk, casualties were heavy on both sides, and several English ships ran out of ammunition, but this battle, although operationally indecisive, was strategically decisive, because it helped limit major French fleet action in the region. It thus had the same effect as Barfleur.

After the fall of Gibraltar to the English, the French besieged it with naval support. The squadron under Vice-Admiral Sir John Leake that had been ordered to cover Gibraltar, was then taking on supplies in Lisbon. Leake sailed to Gibraltar Bay, where on 25 October 1704 he surprised a French squadron of three frigates and five smaller ships. They were all captured or destroyed. Leake then returned to Lisbon to convoy a fleet of troop transports for Gibraltar. Reinforced by English, Dutch and Portuguese warships, he arrived in Gibraltar Bay on 10 March 1705. Leake's 35 ships of the line easily outnumbered the five French ships of the line there and they were captured or destroyed. The remainder of the French fleet, then sheltering from a storm in Malaga Roads, retreated to Toulon before Leake could catch them. These naval blows led the French to abandon the siege.

In 1705 the English fleet supported the successful siege of Barcelona, landing cannon and seamen. The following year, the arrival of the fleet led the French to abandon their siege of Barcelona: the French fleet did not stay to fight the English. Thus the fleet greatly affected the war on land, leading to pressure for it to winter nearby.[7] In 1706, the fleet, under Leake, went on to assist in the capture of Alicante, Majorca and Ibiza.

In 1707 the Alliance was able to attack the French Mediterranean naval base at Toulon. The English fleet under Shovell supported the Austro-Savoyard army in its crossing of the River Var and later covered its retreat. Although Toulon was not captured, the French destroyed most of their warships in the harbour and thus further improved the English naval position.[8] In addition, from 1709 the French built no more ships of the line during the war. Although poor weather led to the abandonment of a planned attack on Saintes in 1706 by Jennings,[9] major raids were launched on the Provençal coast in 1707 and 1710, the second leading to the temporary capture of Cette before re-embarkation in the face of a build up of French forces.[10] In 1708 the fleet under Leake took part in the capture of Minorca and Sardinia. As in the previous war, the fleet devoted much time both in the Mediterranean and elsewhere to protecting trade from the damaging ravages of French privateers[11] and also to attacking French commerce.

This period of naval superiority was not without its problems, not least those posed by the expectations raised by allies: Austria and Savoy-Piedmont. In 1701 one of the Under Secretaries, John Ellis, wrote to George

Stepney, the envoy in Vienna, expressing interest in the possibility of using Adriatic ports, adding:

> I cannot but join with you in thinking that nothing considerable can be done in that part of the world, without a force at sea in the Mediterranean, to procure respect from the princes and inhabitants of the coast, and to set them at liberty from the apprehension and constraints they lie under from the marine power of France and Spain in conjunction.[12]

Yet, the following year, the English felt obliged to resist Austrian pressure for the dispatch of naval forces to Spanish-ruled Naples, which the Austrians were seeking to conquer. The English cited the need to retain naval superiority in the Channel and William Blathwayt, the Secretary-at-War, informed Stepney:

> You say right of our noble fleet and number of seamen but I don't conceive how you think we can venture twelve sail alone in the Mediterranean unless it be for a sacrifice,[13]

a reference to the threat posed by the French fleet in Toulon. Instead, in 1702, the English sought to intercept the Spanish treasure fleet from the New World. By thus deploying the bulk of their fleet in Channel and Atlantic waters, they were also able to keep an eye on the French fleet in Brest, the crucial strategic position of which threatened both the Irish Sea and the Channel approaches. The Spaniards were not intercepted at sea, but were, instead, attacked at Vigo by an Anglo-Dutch fleet under Rooke. The treasure fleet was protected by a boom and strong batteries, but the southern battery was captured by an amphibious force and the boom was broken by the *Torbay* under heavy fire on 12 October 1702 and the following engagement decisively won by Rooke's fleet: the French and Spaniards set fire to their ships. The previous month, Rooke had failed to capture Cadiz in an amphibious attack.

If the 1700s revealed the difficulties of combining naval strategy with the exigencies of alliance politics, it also indicated the problems facing naval forces operating outside that context, but within that of a different but often more difficult alliance, that with the English army. In 1703 Blathwayt wrote to Stepney about English attacks on the wealthy French West Indies:

> our attempt upon Guadaloupe under the command of Captain Codrington has been so far unsuccessful that after plundering and spoiling the greatest part of the island we were forced to retire to our own islands by the fresh succours the French had received from Martinique. This they say has been chiefly occasioned by the

Action off Cartagena, May 28, 1708 by Samuel Scott. HMS *Expedition* under Rear-Admiral Charles Wager attacked the far-stronger Spanish treasure fleet. The flagship, the *San Jose*, blew up after its powder magazine was hit and most of its crew were killed. Despite damage to the *Expedition*, Wager pushed on to bombard another ship into surrender. The captains of two other warships were court-martialled for failing to help Wager sufficiently. Most of the Spanish treasure went down with the *San Jose*, but Wager still gained considerable spoils. *National Maritime Museum, London.*

> disagreement of the sea commander with our land general which
> has been the bane of all expeditions from that against Hispaniola in
> Cromwell's time downwards to this last instance but the influence
> of the Admiralty will always prevail to make it so.[14]

Nevertheless, the English fleet in the West Indies was able both to threaten Spanish treasure fleets and to capture St Kitts (1702). Twenty-two warships under Vice-Admiral John Benbow were sent to the Caribbean in 1701. Spain was no longer a British ally as she had been in the Nine Years' War. Seizure of her treasure offered profit to naval commanders, bullion for Britain and the dislocation of the Bourbon financial system. French warships, however, convoyed the treasure ships and fought Benbow off Santa Marta on 19–24 August 1702. Before Benbow was fatally injured by a chain-shot, he had lost control of his captains, and most failed to give him sufficient support in the battle. As a result two were court-martialled and shot. In 1708 Rear-Admiral Charles Wager attacked the Spanish treasure ships off Cartagena, destroying the Spanish flagship and capturing one of the other ships. Two of Wager's captains were court-martialled and dismissed for failing to press home the pursuit. In 1711 Commodore James Littleton captured two more galleons off Cartagena.

Further north, Leake, then Governor and Commander-in-Chief at Newfoundland, used his warships to wreck the French fishery off the island in 1702. In 1711 an attempt was mounted on Québec, the major French base in Canada, but it failed in part due to poor navigation in the St Lawrence River. The experience in amphibious operations that was to be displayed in mid-century was not to be gained without failures.[15]

Anglo-French Alliance, 1716–31

Despite the limitations of naval warfare, first French naval weakness and then the Anglo-French alliance (1716–31) greatly helped the position of the British navy. Furthermore, Spain was the seat of war during the War of the Spanish Succession and although the Spanish navy revived subsequently, the crushing British victory over it off Cape Passaro in July 1718 demonstrated that Britain was the strongest naval power in the Mediterranean. Twenty British ships of the line and two frigates, under Admiral Sir George Byng, destroyed a poorly deployed fleet of 13 more lightly gunned ships of the line and eight frigates.[16] The victory, in which seven ships of the line were captured, led to euphoria about British naval capabilities. The *Weekly Journal*, a Whig London newspaper, in its issue of 18 October 1718 claimed, "This single action renders the King of Great Britain as much master of the Mediterranean as he has always been acknowledged to be sovereign over the British seas". An account of naval operations in this period, the third edition of which appeared significantly in 1739, the year when war with Spain next broke out, misleadingly exulted over "the war of Sicily, wherein the fleet of Great-Britain bore so illustrious a part, that the fate of the island was wholly governed by its operations, both competitors agreeing, that the one could not have conquered, nor the other subdued without it".[17]

Indeed, the extent to which Britain was the leading naval power of the period was demonstrated by her most intractable problem, the difficulty of intimidating or defeating Peter the Great of Russia when his navy refused to fight. Such problems in the Baltic were a far cry from 1690–2 when France had effectively challenged Britain for control of the Channel. Even so, in the 1720s the British were confident that their navy would prevent the Russians from dominating the Baltic and attacking Britain's allies, Denmark and Sweden, a view that was shared by other commentators, such as the Duke of Richelieu, French envoy in Vienna, later victor over Cumberland at Hastenbeck.[18]

An over optimistic view of British naval capabilities was held in political and diplomatic circles. It was assumed that through the use of naval power

Britain could solve her foreign policy difficulties. It was against this background that the resort to naval force can be best understood. Twice during the reign of George I the British ministry chose to intervene in distant quarrels by means of the navy: the dispatch of Byng to the Mediterranean in 1718 and the decision to use the navy as part of the 1719–21 diplomatic offensive to force Russia to return some of her conquests from Sweden as a part of the peace between the two powers. In both cases the government miscalculated the impact of naval intervention. In 1718 it hoped that the threat would persuade Spain not to attack Sicily, but Philip V called Britain's bluff, and, although he lost his fleet off Passaro, this did not and could not lead to the reconquest of Sicily, a point made then and again, in similar circumstances, when Spain threatened and then invaded Sicily during the War of the Polish Succession (1733–5). The British were able to do little in 1719 to aid the reconquest of Sicily by a weak Austrian military effort, and the war led to financial and political problems in Britain.

The 1718–20 crisis in the Mediterranean revealed what was to be underlined in 1733–5 and again in 1740–1, that without a permanent squadron in that sea, British intervention would tend to be too late. In 1741 the British were unable to stop the dispatch of Spanish forces to Italy across the Mediterranean. Foreign policy commitments, especially treaty obligations, in southern Europe could only be effected by naval force, but the capabilities of naval preparation and warfare did not permit as rapid a mobilization and deployment of naval forces as politicians envisaged. Whereas former army commanders held important political posts – George I, George II and Secretaries of State such as Stanhope and Harrington – this was not true of former naval officers. A successful naval strategy that matched political expectations called for Mediterranean bases where a major squadron could be based permanently, repaired completely and victualled adequately. Neither Gibraltar nor Minorca, captured in 1704 and 1708, respectively, and ceded to Britain by the Peace of Utrecht, was suitable. Gibraltar was small and some of the bay was exposed to Spanish artillery fire, Minorca was vulnerable to attacks by the Toulon squadron, and both were dependent for grain on precarious supplies from the Barbary states (Morocco, Algiers and Tunis). Britain lacked the well-positioned, well-supported naval base in the Mediterranean that its foreign policy required, but this policy also relied upon allied land forces to be effective.

The attempt to force Russia to restore her Baltic conquests in 1719–21 was similarly problematic. Naval action was seen as crucial to the fulfilment of the British diplomatic strategy, but naval opinion was contrary, to the disgust of one politician: "Sir John Norris has in a manner protested against it. He has now 17 ships of the line . . . he comes out like all your blusterers a very very little man".[19] This was unfair, for the hope that Norris could sink the Russian fleet was defeated by Peter's unwillingness to fight. Furthermore, bombarding coastal towns would have been pointless for, as with the Anglo-Russian Ochakov crisis of 1791, the principal targets would have been the warehouses of British merchants. In truth the blusterers were the members of the ministry who had negotiated themselves into a false position.

Nevertheless, in diplomatic circles there was still considerable faith in naval power. The politics of bombardment were regarded by several diplomats as perfectly possible. Just as in 1717–18 the British considered bombarding the Papal port of Civitàvecchia in order to ensure the release of the Earl of Peterborough held captive by the Papacy at Bologna, so the idea recurred in late 1727 when the Stuart Pretender, "James III", was sheltered in the Papal town of Avignon. In addition, Henry Davenant wrote in uncompromising terms concerning alleged Tuscan infringements of the religious liberties of the British factory (community of merchants) in Livorno (Leghorn): "it will be to no purpose to treat any further on this business . . . you must get the grievance redressed by force". John Hedges suggested the despatch of Wager to Genoa, during a dispute with the government: "if 10 or a dozen men of war made them a short visit it would convince them there were other people in the world, besides a family with a great lip [the Habsburgs]". James O'Hara, envoy in Lisbon, was also a strong believer in the efficacy of violence. In 1729 he proposed that the Portuguese should be brought to reason "by the roughest means", adding that, as Portugal lacked allies, nobody would intervene if George "had a mind to lay this country to ashes".[20]

Actual use of the fleet was more cautious, although it remained the most important aspect of British military preparedness and projection. In 1726, when Britain was in a state of cold war with Austria, Russia and Spain, the navy was mobilized in a truly impressive display of strength, and deployed in several areas of the world in a marked demonstration of logistical capability. In the Baltic a squadron helped to dissuade Russia from an attack upon Sweden, while in home waters the fleet threatened both Spain and the potential Austrian invasion port of Ostend with attack. A squadron under Vice-Admiral Francis Hosier blockaded the Spanish treasure fleet in Porto Bello. Viscount Townshend, the Secretary of State for the Northern Department, wrote with some satisfaction:

It is indeed a reflection which must afford His Majesty a great deal of comfort and satisfaction as it redounds highly to the glory of the British nation and the honour of our navy, that whilst one of his fleets is preserving the tranquillity of the North against the ambitious and pernicious designs of the Czarina [Catherine I], and another is keeping the Spanish treasure in the West Indies and thereby preventing the Emperor and Spain from disturbing the peace of the South, the very report of a third squadron going out has caused such alarm and confusion in the Austrian Netherlands, and has put Spain, in the low and miserable condition of their finances, to the trouble and expense of marching their troops and fortifying their seaport towns.[21]

A high level of naval activity was maintained over succeeding years. In the autumn of 1727, fearing a Spanish-supported Jacobite invasion, and angry about Spanish intransigence in peace negotiations, the British kept a strong squadron off Cadiz. Wager was ordered to destroy the Spanish fleet if it should sail towards Britain.[22] In the summer of 1729 a powerful squadron was prepared and based at Spithead, ready to sail against Spain,[23] although the fleet, which was reinforced by a Dutch squadron, did not sail, thus provoking opposition derision about its cost, lack of action and lack of effectiveness.[24]

Despite these preparations, the government deliberately avoided action, in part by keeping the navy away from stations that might have provoked confrontation, as off Cadiz in 1729. There were clearly advocates of action. In 1726 St Saphorin, George I's envoy in Vienna, suggested the movement of the fleet to Italian waters to counteract Austrian deployments in Silesia. Three years later, the Lords of the Council, anxious about the prospect of Spain duping Britain and fearing that they would have nothing definite to present to the next session of Parliament, argued that Spain should receive an ultimatum, suggested a blockade of Spain and the Spanish West Indies, and proposed an attack on Puerto Rico. Townshend noted, "As to the destroying of the Spanish fleet in Cadiz, I found before I left England, that the knowing people in those affairs thought it an enterprise very practicable, as looking upon the batteries either new or old to be of little significance to hinder our fleet going into that harbour, provided the Spaniards did not sink ships to stop up the passage".[25]

However, such schemes were not followed up. In 1729 Townshend informed the Lords of the Council that their plans were precipitate and blocked the sailing of Wager's fleet. In 1726 and 1730 there were no amphibious attacks upon Austria's Italian possessions. In 1727 British ships were withdrawn from the approaches to the Baltic, not to reappear there for many years. In place of active confrontation, the naval strategy was one of a threat of violence to be suggested by naval armaments. The *Weekly Medley* claimed on 19 July 1729 that "the British squadron without going out of our ports can incomparably hasten matters towards a conclusion much quicker than bare negotiations". Three years earlier, the Duke of Newcastle thought that the dispatch of Admiral Sir John Jennings' squadron towards Cadiz would have a great effect even though he was not to commit hostilities, "for his barely appearing in those seas, which would not fail to alarm them, might in the uncertain conditions they are in at present, produce the best consequences imaginable". In 1727 Townshend suggested that the recall of the Baltic squadron would influence Spain as it would increase the naval force that could be sent to Spanish waters.[26]

There was also scepticism about the effectiveness of naval power both on diplomatic and practical grounds. In 1726 Frederick William I of Prussia, fearful of Russian hostility, told the British envoy, "as to your fleet, it is of no manner of service to me".[27] Two years later, the Duke of Parma, who had angered Britain by his Jacobite sympathies, was reported as claiming, "he did not fear the English, for their fleet could not come to him at Parma".[28] Jacobites and Jacobite sympathizers, keen to persuade Austria and/or Spain to support an invasion of Britain in the period 1725–9, claimed that the British navy could not guarantee control of home waters.[29]

The very decision not to use the fleet for conflict kept its potential strength a mystery, and therefore enhanced its value as a diplomatic counter. It also meant that unrealistic public estimations of naval capacity could be maintained, that talk of seizing the Spanish empire without difficulty could continue. Had such a policy been attempted and failed, as it doubtless would have done given the logistical difficulties of the task, the primitive state of amphibious warfare and the strength of the Spanish West Indies, then public attitudes to naval strategy would have had to have been reconsidered. They were not, and this contrast in the domestic situation between public attitudes – continued faith in naval power and in the Blue Water strategy of self-sustaining maritime power – and ministerial scepticism and disinclination to accept the risks and cost of naval warfare, continued into the 1730s.

Conflict with the Bourbons 1739–48

The international naval situation abruptly changed with the collapse of the Anglo-French alliance in 1731, because naval capability was dependent on political circumstances. The immediate response was war panic at the prospect of a French invasion on behalf of the Jacobites.[30] The longer term consequence was a realization that naval superiority and strategic security would require war with France, if, as seemed likely, there was no reconciliation with her. The strategic problem of the years after 1731 was laid out clearly in an important pamphlet of 1742 which argued that, without a substantial army, the British position was very parlous:

> with respect to other powers, particularly France, we are now obliged to lie upon the defensive, and can only hope to protect ourselves from being invaded, without any ability to attack that kingdom . . . a considerable body of regular troops at hand, which alone can convince the people of France of our power to give them assistance. This is, perhaps, now the only method of breaking the strength of the French monarchy, which is abundantly fortified on its inland frontiers; whilst it has the whole body of its people within undisturbed, will always be able to exert a prodigious force at these extremities: but an attack by sea in the heart of its most

fruitful provinces, would interrupt its commerce, and suppress its revenues, and raise a spirit in their people, which they might never afterwards be able to break; but all this it is in vain to think of, without we support a sufficient land-force.

Admitting the utmost that can be attributed to our fleet alone; Allowing, though it is by no means true, that it can effectually guard our own coasts; is it not evident that our weakness at land must diminish its force? for we must always reserve our most potent squadron at hand, for our own defence against an invasion; and the remainder is all that we can employ at any distance; which, probably, may not exceed the French squadron in the Streights, or West Indies: so that our weakness at land actually deprives us of a superiority at sea. This at the same time is sure to create an ignorant clamour; and the wisdom of a minister in not leaving us unguarded at home, should be branded for cowardice; and the squadrons that are reserved for our own defence, shall be ridiculed, and stigmatised with being pacific . . . it is thought by some projecting persons, that we ought, in the beginning of this war, to have dispatched almost all our fleet, and our experienced regiments to the West Indies. This might have been done indeed, if our regular land force was at all numerous, and would admit of any deduction for foreign service, consistent with our own domestic security. But if we had thus ventured in our present circumstances, and left this nation exposed with only eight or ten thousand disciplined soldiers, and a weak squadron, the least motion of the troops of France towards Dunkirk, Calais, or the coasts of Normandy and Brittany, would justly have given us severe uneasiness: And the equipment of a French squadron, or an account of their collecting transports together, would have immediately thrown us into the utmost terror and confusion.[31]

This was an accurate account of the strategic situation. Sir Robert Walpole, the first minister, had himself pointed out in November 1739 that naval force alone would not force Spain to accept British terms in the War of Jenkins' Ear, the conflict over Carribbean trade that began that year and lasted until 1748. The author of the pamphlet, however, overlooked the extent of political opposition to a larger army, while the argument that amphibious operations against continental France could make a material difference was not to be proved when it was tried during the Austrian Succession and, even more, Seven Years' wars.

The central point that, without a large army, British naval options were limited so long as the French kept a fleet in being, was correct. The Spanish fleet was not a major threat, although it posed a potential challenge in Atlantic, Caribbean and Mediterranean waters. This was made far more serious by the possibility of French intervention. At a moment of tension in 1740, James, Earl Waldegrave, envoy in Paris, reported, "Their preparations in the sea-ports go on. I really think they mean nothing more by them than to keep us on the watch and oblige us to increase our armaments and consequently our expenses". Newcastle replied, "the truth is the French preparations do necessarily oblige us to keep such a fleet here as is in other respects useless and might be much more advantageously employed elsewhere".[32] As Walter Titley, envoy in Copenhagen, pointed out after the inconclusive battle of Toulon in 1744, "it is not their interest to risk their moderate sea-force against the English, which is so much superior and can soon be repaired in case of ill success".[33] By keeping a fleet in being, the French limited what the British could hope to achieve against Spain.

British naval strength did not preclude fears of invasion. William Hay, a government MP, told the House of Commons in 1738, "It may be thought, and I have often heard it said, that our fleet will protect us: but our fleet is not always sure of meeting an enemy; and if that expectation should fail what reserve have we then left but our land forces?".[34] Nine years later, Newcastle was worried about the build up of French forces in the Channel ports, including conquered Ostend.[35] This strategic situation put a premium on the destruction of the French navy, lending military point to the sense of humiliation and dissatisfaction that followed failures to achieve this end. The nature of naval operations in the age of sail was not, however, conducive to forcing an unwilling opponent to fight in a position of inferiority.

A parallel can be drawn with the land warfare of the period. This was frequently inconclusive from the point of field engagements. At the risk of pushing the analogy too far, further comparisons can be made between, on the one hand, blockades and the struggle to protect trade from privateers, and, on the other, sieges and the attempt to control areas in order to use them for logistical purposes. Generals could generally avoid unwelcome engagements by retiring behind natural or artificial defensive features, and it was not easy to force them to fight. However, a comparison between the naval and land warfare in which Britain was involved in 1688–1815 suggests that it was more common for her to fight battles on land and that most of her victories, and defeats, were on that element. In part, this reflected the comparative numerical advantage that she enjoyed at sea, and the consequent unwillingness of her opponents to fight, but it would be going too far to say that the British army had to fight for the dominance the navy already had at sea, because such naval dominance had to be fought for in each of Britain's wars with France. It is also clear that land operations were more conducive to engagements.

The continued existence of the French fleet had considerable, potentially crucial, strategic consequences at the time of the '45. This existence reflected the British failure to defeat the French in 1744. Then opportunities had presented themselves both in the Channel and in the Mediterranean. The Brest fleet under de Roquefeuil had moved down the Channel to cover a projected invasion of England, but the British attempt to defeat the French fleet had been wrecked by a storm that hit both fleets, and also sank many of the invasion transports in the Channel ports. In the Mediterranean, the battle of Toulon (11 February) had been indecisive, leading to political controversy within Britain, although it was not easy to decide how best to engage a Franco-Spanish fleet when Britain was not at war with France. The British pressed the Spaniards hard, while the French exchanged fire at a range from which they could not inflict much damage. The British rear under Vice-Admiral Richard Lestock did not engage due to Lestock's determination to keep the line. Lestock and the British commander, Admiral Thomas Mathews, had had disagreements and he was wilfully unhelpful, but Mathews had given contradictory instructions. The net effect was that the British squandered their numerical advantage. The French were able to come to the assistance of the Spaniards, the British withdrew, and when on 12 February they returned to pursue the Bourbon fleet, the latter was able to retire with the loss of only one already badly damaged ship, the Spanish *Poder*: the damage it suffered was a testimony to the impact of British broadsides. Mathews was cashiered, and the battle discredited the 80-gun ships of the fleet: lacking the firepower of 90 and 100-gun three-deckers, they appeared undergunned for their limited seaworthiness.[36] Nevertheless, the Franco-Spanish fleet in the Mediterranean did not subsequently mount a comparable challenge.

In 1745 the continued existence of a powerful French navy increased the danger of a French landing on the south coast, an event which was in fact erroneously reported. The government ordered the navy to prevent French moves in the Channel, Vice-Admiral William Martin being instructed in July, when information was received that the French had decided to invade, to prevent any ships from leaving Brest.[37] Newcastle wrote in October 1745, "Admiral Martin is cruising off the Lizard with a very considerable squadron. Admiral Vernon continues in the Downs; and we have a great number of small ships in different parts of the Channel".[38]

Confidence on this head, however, was limited. In August 1745, Newcastle's private secretary, Andrew Stone, observed:

> We hope we shall soon have a pretty strong squadron in the Channel: But I know too well, the great delays and uncertainties that service is liable to, to depend very much on it. When Ostend is gone (as it will soon be) I tremble to think of the constant alarms we shall be subject to.

That December, Stephen Weston, an Exeter cleric, complained:

I doubt should any attempt be made from Brest or St Malo at this time we should fall a too easy prey since land forces we have none but the garrison at Plymouth, that just now reduced by a draught for Bristol; part of our Western Squadron too being lately sailed to strengthen Vernon in the Downs, I think we are in a state to be pitied, and the utmost to be hoped from us is to run away with the money we are raising, leaving our estates and houses to the rage of the invaders. We must pray therefore for a North East or North West wind to shut up the western ports of France, since a South East or South West brings our enemies upon us, and at the same time denies us the assistance of our friends.[39]

These fears were to be justified in part. Cumberland's pursuit of Bonnie Prince Charlie was to be constrained by the fear of an invasion of the south coast. In December 1745, Newcastle wrote to him:

His Majesty having received an account from Admiral Vernon, that a considerable number of vessels, besides small boats, are assembled at Dunkirk, and that there is the greatest reason to believe that an attempt will be immediately made to land a body of troops from hence on some part of the southern or eastern coast . . . your Royal Highness should immediately return to London, with the rest of the cavalry and foot, that are now with you.[40]

The order was to be countermanded, but it reflected the impact of French naval power on British military planning. Nevertheless, the British were able to take for granted the use of the sea to move troops across the North Sea and up the east coast, thus avoiding many of the problems posed by an invasion when most of the army was abroad, and also enabling British forces to operate or maintain a presence in two spheres at once. British naval power also blocked French invasion schemes.[41]

No crisis comparable to the '45 was ever again to occur. During subsequent French invasion attempts in 1759, 1779 and 1805 there was no indigenous pro-French activity and, therefore, the strategic situation was different. In December 1770, when war with the Bourbons (France and Spain) over the Falkland Islands appeared imminent, there was opposition in the Council to the idea of sending a fleet to Gibraltar and Jamaica, because it was feared that it might leave the British "coasts exposed to be insulted", not because of the prospect of any co-operation with domestic rebellion. In 1745–6 the British army was torn between two competing demands: the Jacobite army and the prospect of a French invasion. By making the latter more or less likely, the balance of naval power affected operations against the Jacobites who were the more immediate military threat. In contrast, during subsequent invasion years, it was possible to match British army and naval strength and deployments to a common threat.

95

During the remainder of the War of the Austrian Succession there was an obvious divergence between growing British naval superiority and the dismal progress of the campaigns in the Low Countries. In consequence, and in marked contrast to the situation during the War of the Spanish Succession, the hope developed that naval success could compensate for continental defeats. Theophilus Leigh, Master of Balliol, observed in July 1747, "We have had better success by sea than land; I wish one might balance the other".[42] This expectation placed a new politico-strategic responsibility on the navy, for it was now required to obtain trans-oceanic advantages, an obligation that necessitated a mastery of home and European waters that would permit the trans-oceanic dispatch of major naval forces. In part, these ideas were of long standing, reflecting a traditional optimistic public assessment of naval capability, but the political need for them can be traced to 1745. It was then that the hopes of defeating France on the continent that had been so marked in 1742–3, especially after Victory at Dettingen in 1743, were replaced by the realization that it would be difficult to stop the French triumphing by land.

In 1745 the French lost Cape Breton island and its major base of Louisbourg to a force of New England colonists supported by British warships under Sir Peter Warren. The proposition of an exchange for French gains in the Austrian Netherlands as part of a peace, based on the *status quo ante bellum* (return to the situation before the war), emerged speedily. This placed an immediate strategic task on the navy, the defence of Cape Breton. That led to problems the following year, when the French sought to regain the island. There were, therefore, by then heavier strategic and political burdens on the British admirals entrusted with keeping the French fleet in its harbours or defeating it if it sailed out. In June 1746, Stephen Weston wrote to his brother from Exeter,

> We are very much troubled by the news we have had several days, of the French fleet having slipped Admiral Martin, and fear we must expect some severe blow in some sensible part or other; Cape Breton, Jamaica, Minorca, and Ireland are all guessed at.

Newcastle complained more pointedly to Cumberland:

> The only contretems we have had, was Admiral Martin's ignorance or, what is worse, letting the French fleet get clear of him. Should they go to North America, and make conquests there, we shall lose both the means of making peace or war. For when once they have either retaken Cape Breton or taken Newfoundland or Nova Scotia (which will be the equivalent for it) we have no longer in our hands the means of purchasing peace of France; or of inducing this nation to carry on the war.[43]

Anville's squadron was wrecked by bad weather and disease, fortunately for the British, for it is far from clear what the consequences of the loss of Cape Breton would have been.

From 1747 the British kept more warships to the west of the Channel approaches, and this proved crucial in affecting the course of the war at sea. On 3 May 1747 Vice-Admiral George Anson defeated La Jonquière off Cape Finisterre. Anson, with a fleet of 14 of the line, had been long cruising off the Cape, waiting for the French fleet which was instructed to escort ships sailing for both the New World and the East Indies: the French could not keep their fleet in being in Brest if they wished to maintain an imperial commercial and political system. The French were heavily outnumbered off Cape Finisterre. Rather than fight in line, Anson ordered his captains to close with the French as fast as they could, and therefore fight in a series of individual actions, in order to prevent the French from escaping under cover of darkness. Despite inflicting heavier casualties than they suffered, the French warships were captured, and Anson gained great prestige and a peerage.[44] More generally, French merchantmen were increasingly vulnerable. That August the *Duc de Chartres*, an important East Indiaman, was captured off Ushant.

On 14 October 1747, Rear-Admiral Edward Hawke won the most brilliant naval action of the war, the Second Battle of Cape Finisterre. Concerned to re-open their trade with the West Indies, eight of the line from the Brest fleet, under the Marquis de L'Etanduère, sailed to protect a large convoy. They were intercepted by Hawke with 14 more lightly gunned ships of the line. Hawke followed Anson's tactics, in order to beat the French quickly and enable pursuit of the convoy. The French fought well, but the British benefited from having taken the initiative, and from abandoning the rigid tactics of a line in order to direct heavier concentrations of gunfire on individual French ships. Six of the French ships were forced to surrender and the French also lost 4,000 sailors, a crucial limitation of their maritime strength.[45] This led Newcastle to write to Cumberland, "All difficulties that could be apprehended in Parliament will by this be removed, the pride of France a little humbled, and I hope our allies so far encouraged, that your Royal Highness will find them willing and able to exert themselves for their own safety and support". The Duke was also confident that the victory would disappoint Jacobite hopes of a possible invasion.[46] The French fleet could no longer escort major convoys bound for French colonies, and this destroyed the logic of the French imperial system.

The parliamentary consequences of naval victory were widely grasped. Lady Elizabeth Yorke, Lord Chancellor Hardwicke's daughter, who was shortly to marry Anson, wrote to her sister-in-law, Marchioness Grey, pointing out the military advantages of the victory and added:

Admiral Hawke has likewise disappointed the designs of more than the French, it having been intended by the opposition to begin their attack this session by falling upon the Admiralty; now it is thought that this scheme must be defeated, since after the late repeated successes, such an attempt cannot be very popular or successful.[47]

Seven years earlier, the situation had been very different for Sir Robert Walpole, Lady Cecilia Finch writing then

the season is so far advanced that it is almost impossible to flatter oneself anything considerable can be performed time enough to open the Parliament with a speech giving an account of the success of our arms abroad which would silence the babblers at once by leaving no room to inveigh against the conduct of the present administration which their zeal and malice will prompt them to blame without making any allowance for the bad winds.[48]

Victory transformed the invasion threats of 1744–5 and the danger of the loss of Cape Breton in 1746 into a completely different political, strategic and diplomatic situation. The angry debates over naval policy that had characterized the earlier years of the war ended, so that the Earl of Sandwich could write in November 1747, "it is plain that our fleet has honour and great support".[49] At the very close of the war, on 1 October 1748, Charles Knowles, Commander-in-Chief at Jamaica, engaged a Spanish squadron off Havana, and, although the failure of many of his ships to engage led to recriminations, court martials and a fatal duel, the Spanish warships were less effective in close action. One of the Spanish ships was captured and the flagship was driven ashore.

The navy ended the war in a rich glow of success, at the same time as the disadvantages of alliance politics and a continental military commitment were abundantly brought home by the French advance into the United Provinces. Newcastle wrote after another naval success in early 1748, "though we have our mortifications, the enemy have theirs also. Their trade is absolutely ruined for the present".[50] French wine became very scarce in Berlin in 1748, and the British envoy there was worried about the diplomatic consequences of British privateering.

The British pressure on Bourbon trade was world-wide. On 20 June 1743 Anson captured the treasure-laden Manila galleon, *Nuestra Señora de Covadonga*, off the Philippines. In 1744 Edward Peyton captured a large French merchantman in the Straits of Malacca. On 26 January 1745 Commodore Curtis Barnett captured three large French East Indiamen in the East Indies. Later that year, Warren captured several large French merchantmen at Louisbourg, by keeping the French flag flying after the base

Vice-Admiral Sir Peter Warren c.1703–52 by Louis François Roubiliac. One of the more successful naval commanders, Warren's career reflected the range of British power. Born in Ireland, he served off Africa in the Baltic, in the West Indies and in the Channel in the 1720s, off North America in the late 1730s, and in the Caribbean in the early 1740s. In 1745 he was sent with the Leeward Islands squadron to help capture Louisbourg. Second in command at the first battle off Cape Finisterre (1747), Warren made a fortune from prizes. The freedom of the city was conferred on him after the battle off Cape Finisterre and he was also elected MP for Westminster. Warren married a New Yorker and bought a 300 acre farm on Manhatten. *Courtesy of the Huntington Library, Art Collections,* and *Botanical Cardens, San Marino, California.*

99

had been seized and waiting for them to sail in. In August 1746 a squadron under Cornelius Mitchell confronted a weaker French force escorting a convoy through the Windward Passage, but Mitchell abjectly failed to press the attack, was court martialled and cashiered. In the winter of 1747–8, however, Commodore George Pocock captured 30 merchantmen in the West Indies. Warships based at English Harbour, Antigua, a naval base developed from 1728, successfully blockaded Martinique in 1746–7.

Privateering entailed a fusion of patriotism and profit: indeed more than 6,600 prizes were taken in 1702–83, nearly half by privateers.[51] The prospect of privateering profits was important in mobilizing support for imperial warfare within the British colonial mercantile community. Spanish colonial trade was hit from 1739. It was also necessary to protect British trade against Bourbon privateers: it was damaged in the 1740s, both by the Spaniards and by the French. The agricultural staple trades of the Carolinas, the Chesapeake and, especially, the Caribbean sustained serious losses, and in 1747–8 Bourbon privateers off the Delaware Capes brought Philadelphia's trade to a halt.[52] The contrast between the private enterprise that could produce so many privateers, and the state warfare that made such little difference to the disposition of Caribbean territories in the 1740s, was marked, but Britain was more successful than its rivals in using trade for warfare.

The war had shown that the navy was an effective fighting force and administrative body, and this was true not only in European, but, also, in trans-oceanic waters. In the West Indies, British failures, as at Cartagena, were not primarily due to administrative deficiencies, although victualling caused problems. The difficulties of operating in the West Indies were not new: the main change that the war introduced was in the size of the forces deployed in the Caribbean, and thus in the quantity of supplies required. The Admiralty's failure to keep the fleet in the Caribbean adequately manned was a reflection of the degree to which it had not yet solved the problem of manning in general. This manning situation was exacerbated by the effects of disease. The Sick and Hurt Board supplied all the medicines it was asked to, the Admiralty consented to the building of a new hospital, and the sick were given the best treatment that the medical knowledge of the day allowed. However, the nature of the diseases was not understood. Although convoying was poorly organized, the men on the spot were generally able to make good the administrative deficiencies that were revealed. British ships in the West Indies were able to fulfil their operational role, the decisive test of a naval administration.[53]

Naval power and British policy, 1749–55

In the years after the Peace of Aix-la-Chapelle of 1748, British foreign policy was to be dominated by an active diplomacy that placed little weight on naval power. The consequences of this policy for naval affairs are open to discussion. It could be suggested that the deterioration in Franco-Spanish relations that led to the Austro-Spanish Treaty of Aranjuez of 14 June 1752 was the single most important factor behind British naval success in the Seven Years' War (1756–63). Spain remained neutral until 1762, and thus the arithmetic of naval confrontation that had in the previous war limited British flexibility was vitally altered, a change that helps to explain France's subsequent determination to win Spanish assistance in the War of American Independence (1775–83). The British government, indeed, offered naval assistance in 1751 to the new Austro-Spanish alignment, the Earl of Holdernesse, Secretary of State for the Southern Department, writing: "The very notion of His Majesty's supporting this great alliance with his maritime force gives the greatest weight and sanction to it".[54] However, the alliance cannot be ascribed to British diplomacy.

The bulk of British diplomatic attention in 1749–53 was devoted to attempts to improve the so-called Old Alliance with Austria and the United Provinces and, in particular, to secure the imperial succession for the son of Maria Theresa, the future Joseph II. This represented a classic instance of preparing to fight the last war. Because the imperial succession had helped to undermine Austrian strength in the early 1740s, the issue was to be settled. Similarly, because, in British minds that tended to forget the '45, the defence of the Low Countries in 1745–8 had been inhibited by Austrian and Dutch weaknesses and commitments, both powers were to be strengthened. This was to be done by settling differences over the Austrian Netherlands, and by creating an alliance system that would comprise most of the German states and restrain Prussian aggression.

Naval power was essentially immaterial to this diplomatic strategy, especially because Austrian defensive and offensive interests in Italy, which had played such a major role in Anglo-Austrian relations in the 1700s and 1710s and during the periods of effective alliance between 1731 and 1733 and 1742 and 1748, and which could be assisted by a British fleet in the Mediterranean, had been settled by the reconciliation with Spain. Nevertheless, the British government believed that the strength of the fleet influenced the continental powers. In 1753 Newcastle wrote to Robert Keith, the envoy at Vienna:

> His Majesty's fleet (though at a very great expence), is in a better condition, than it ever was known to be, in time of peace: and the great effect, which the superiority of the King's navy, the last war, had towards obtaining the peace; shows how necessary and effectual, the keeping up that fleet may be for the preservation of it.

Keith dutifully replied that the Austrian Chancellor, Count Kaunitz, "was very glad to hear, that the King's Royal Navy is in such a condition, as to

promise us a superiority at sea in all events. He knows of what consequence our naval force is; how much it contributed to our obtaining the
last peace; and how necessary and essential the keeping up our fleet is for
the preservation of it".[55] In practice, the powers of central and eastern
Europe were less impressed by or interested in British naval power and,
indeed, a failure to consider the views of other powers sufficiently has
weakened discussion of British naval capability.

There is evidence of episodes in which British naval power featured as a
possible factor. In July 1748 the French foreign minister, Puysieulx, warned
the Marshal-Duke of Richelieu, who was to conquer Minorca in 1756, that
if he was to form a plan of operations for an Italian war he must anticipate
that any use of the Mediterranean would at least be contested. The following month Frederick the Great wrote to his sister, the Princess Royal of
Sweden, asking what help France could provide her Swedish ally in her
confrontation with Russia, which was allied with Austria and Britain, and,
in particular, how a French squadron could sail through the Channel in the
face of likely Anglo-Dutch opposition. The following year Sir Charles
Hanbury-Williams, the British envoy in Dresden, noted the suggestion of
an Austrian minister that Russia should ask the British to send a fleet to the
Baltic if Marshal Saxe pursued his plans to acquire Courland.[56]

Naval power was clearly important in the Baltic and this had allowed
Britain to play a major role in Baltic diplomacy, especially in the Dano-
Swedish conflict in 1700, the last stage of the Great Northern War in 1718–
20, and in 1726–7. In 1747 the Russians had pressed for naval assistance
against Sweden, Lord Hyndford reporting from St Petersburg that Czarina
Elizabeth thought

> that His Majesty seemed to expect too much of her, in that she
> should, without any assistance of money or troops begin the war
> against Sweden alone, upon bare appearance; but that, if His
> Majesty would enter into a treaty for that purpose, and send a
> squadron of ships into the Baltic, she would attack Sweden on
> the side of Finland.

In an interesting reference to the possibility of using naval action against
privateers in order to cover a political commitment, as had indeed happened in the Great Northern War against Sweden in 1715–16, Hyndford
continued,

> His Majesty had a very good pretext for sending a squadron into
> that sea, as she was positively informed, that there would be a
> number of French privateers sent thither as soon as the season was
> open, to disturb the English navigation and trade with this empire.

Hyndford later wrote, "I believe this court has so great a mind to drive the successor and all his French adherents out of Sweden, that, if the king could spare but five or six ships of war for the Baltic to sustain the Russians, the Empress would undertake the thing of herself".[57]

However, the limitations of British naval power as a diplomatic tool in the Baltic had been exposed when Peter the Great had refused to back down in the face of threats of naval attack in 1720, and were to be again in 1791, and it is difficult to believe that Russia decided not to attack Sweden in 1747 because Britain would not supply a few warships. In the case of the Holy Roman Empire (Germany), which became the focus of diplomatic activity and speculation in 1750 after the ending of the Baltic crisis, British naval power was of little value. In 1753 the Prussian envoy in Paris, the Jacobite Lord Marshal of Scotland, pointed out to Frederick the Great that he had no reason to fear a British maritime war, and he referred to the vulnerability of the Electorate of Hanover,[58] the central question mark against British diplomatic and military plans. In their German diplomacy the British relied not on offers or threats of naval power, but on financial inducements and talk of shared interests. Militarily, they referred to the support of Austria and Russia, specifically to the possibility of those powers attacking Frederick if he invaded Hanover. There was no role for naval power comparable, for example, to its importance in sustaining Anglo-Piedmontese co-operation for much of the first half of the century.[59]

There was the usual post-war military demobilization, one that was aided by the relatively more peaceful post-war atmosphere, certainly in contrast to the situation after the Nine Years' and Spanish Succession Wars. Nevertheless, ministers remained convinced of the importance of naval power. They found themselves, however, accused of failing to take adequate steps to counter Bourbon colonial and naval moves and, indeed, both France and Spain greatly increased the size of their fleet in this period. The opposition used this as evidence of an alleged failure to protect national interests, complementing criticism of an excessive concern for Continental diplomacy and serving to illustrate a supposed failure to define national interests adequately that the latter was alleged to indicate. In 1748 the *Craftsman*, a London opposition newspaper, claimed "The French see our superiority at sea, and are providing against it; therefore our countrymen should think what proper instructions to give their representatives on that account". The following spring, another such paper, the *Westminster Journal*, pressed the need to defend Britain's rights in North America firmly, "We need not fear the consequences of such strictness, while we have a fleet capable to vindicate the justice of our conduct". The *Remembrancer* claimed, "we have exhausted ourselves completely, in a cause, that of all the powers in Europe, we were the last, and least, concerned in. The balance of power at land was the bubble we fought for; whereas the commerce and navigation of the world, and the sovereignty of the ocean, ought to have been the principal objects of their attention". Another newspaper, *Old England*, stated that France "will not be forward to show that resentment further than in words, if they see us forward to vindicate our claim in the way of our natural strength, by a maritime force, without engaging in fruitless and expensive alliances on the continent".[60]

Such language was also used in opposition political circles. Admiral Vernon wrote in 1749

> I look on the fate of this country to be drawing to a speedy period whenever France shall attain to a superior maritime power to Britain, which by the present [return] of Cape Breton, we have given them an extensive foundation for . . . I may say without the spirit of prophecy, that whenever they think themselves so, the first blow they will strike, will be to strip us, of every one of our sugar colonies, which I know to be easily attainable by them, whenever they have a superior force by sea; and that the natural consequence of that will be that you will by the same blow, lose all your American colonies as to their dependence on Britain.[61]

The ministry kept a close eye on French naval developments and they were the prime target of British espionage.[62] Although French naval power revived, there was a certain amount of confidence in British ministerial circles, not least thanks to Bourbon disunity. At the same time, there was an awareness that British naval power might not be equal to all the demands that might be placed upon it. Newcastle wrote in 1753 to Joseph Yorke, envoy in The Hague, about the negotiations between the British and French East India Companies:

> You may assure the Princess Royal, that the King will not suffer anything to be done, that may tend to secure France, in case of war, against the superiority of His Majesty's fleet, in any part of the world . . . Our Directors think that a neutrality, confined to the other side of The Cape, would be found more advantageous to us than to France; as the French East India ships, in the Indies, could easily be turned into ships of force, which ours could not; and we should, by that means, be obliged to have a constant squadron there, in times of war, which would lessen our naval strength in other parts.[63]

Despite this concern about possible naval deployment, the ministry was more worried in 1753 by the defence of Hanover against possible Prussian attack. This concern dictated alliance politics, and British policy justified the response the Earl of Rochford had given in 1749 to a Sardinian minister who "had heard we were going to put our naval force upon a better foot than ever, and that we intended for the future to place our chief strength in it", to which Rochford had replied that the government thought that it could only preserve the balance of power in co-operation with allies. The same year, Newcastle suggested that France would outdo Britain in any maritime struggle unless Britain had continental allies to divert her strength.[64] Indeed, the response of the ministry to the worsening of relations with France over North America in 1754–5 was a determination to strengthen Britain's Continental alliances. Far from there being any notion that maritime strength could bring conquests that would compensate for Continental vulnerability, the ministry based its diplomacy on the defence of Hanover.

The Seven Years' War, 1756–63

Political context

In the event, Britain ended up fighting the Seven Years' War without the support of her former partners in the Old Alliance, and with only one significant ally, Prussia. This diplomatic failure helped to free naval strategy from alliance politics, although there was pressure for the commitment of naval forces to the Baltic, a point pressed hard by Frederick the Great who anticipated that it would help him with Russia and Sweden, both at war with Prussia, but not Britain. Frederick's demand was supported by Cumberland, who wrote to Holdernesse in 1757:

> I am sorry to say that, though the dispositions which you have acquainted me are made for the sea operations this year, I see but little hopes of a squadron co-operating with the King of Prussia in the Baltic this year. Had the measure been thought proper, which I can not help thinking still, might have been, as I see three great such fleets sent to sea (viz the Western squadron, that of the Mediterranean, as well as Holburne's reinforced to North America) which, according to the best account sent from France, will nowhere meet with any kind of opposition from their naval force; a very small diminution from those three great fleets, would have formed such a squadron, as might, and would in all probability, have restored His Majesty's weight in the North, where it is but too apparent, that the scale of France, at present preponderates.

Holdernesse made clear that diplomatic obligations had to take second place to naval priorities:

> The utility of sending a strong squadron to the Baltic becomes every day more apparent; but I cannot pretend to say there is any great prospect that such an additional number of men, as this service would require, are to be found; although if we credit some fresh

advice from Toulon, there are but eight ships of the line in that harbour fit for the sea, since the departure of the four, supposed to be gone to America; in which case the force destined for the Mediterranean might be diminished, and other objects in part answered by it.[65]

This was a long way from the Wars of the Spanish and Austrian Successions and the War of the Quadruple Alliance (1718–20), when the navy had had an important politico-strategic commitment, namely the control of the Western Mediterranean in order to further the plans of allies in Italy and, in the case of the War of the Spanish Succession, Spain. The absence of any such commitment during the Seven Years' War helped to release British naval power to concentrate on the challenge of France, though it would be misleading to suggest that politics played no part in the deployment of naval power; a point underlined by the policy of raids on the French coast. During the Seven Years' War discussion of naval capability and policy was conducted in terms of what Britain could achieve through the use of naval power against France. The Continental dimension was almost entirely absent. Whereas in the 1720s statesmen had discussed whether British naval power could affect actions by Austria and Russia that essentially owed nothing to maritime considerations, during the Seven Years' War the central question was one of the direct impact of naval power. Instead of contemplating whether the bombardment of Naples or Riga might influence policy, it was possible to assess the implications of seizing particular French colonies. It was not surprising that this shift encouraged a more optimistic assessment of the navy.

It was not simply that the navy and amphibious operations were more successful in the Seven Years' War than in the previous conflict, but also that their activities and triumphs could be seen clearly as designed to further what were particularly seen as British objectives. The contrast between the popularity of naval operations off Canada during the Seven Years' War, and operations in Mediterranean waters during the War of the Austrian Succession was clear, and it was not only relative success that played a role. In the Seven Years' War it was the European operations, especially when unsuccessful or only partially successful, that enjoyed limited popularity. In contrast, colonial operations were generally seen as obviously serving national interests. It was important, to this end, that in these operations Britain did not need to consult the views of allies. She had last had to do so in the colonial sphere in the Wars of the Spanish Succession and Quadruple Alliance, but, thereafter, the damaging accusations of surrender to the views of allies or the Hanoverian interests of the monarch, that so often compromised the public reputation of European operations, were absent. This was very significant in enhancing political and popular support for British naval activity.

Thus, between 1688 and 1763, there was a major shift in naval commitments that reflected diplomatic and strategic exigencies, and, in turn, affected the political context that helped to shape expectations concerning naval power. The move away from Europe helped to create a different political context for the use of naval power that altered the politico-naval capabilities and weaknesses of the Royal Navy. It became freer to undertake more in Atlantic waters and more distant oceans. The navy had always been helped in its public and political reputation by the minor degree to which it required the support of allies, a marked contrast to the army. The growing weakness of Dutch naval power furthered this process. By the Seven Years' War, this trend was complete, and naval action could be envisaged simply in an Anglo-Bourbon context, as also in the plans to support trans-oceanic pretensions after the war ended. The navy could be seen as truly British, not only in its composition, but also in its objectives. If the possible use of naval power would have been no more able to prevent the First Partition of Poland (1772) or to intimidate Russia during the Ochakov Crisis (1791), than it had been able to persuade Peter the Great to restore some of his conquests from Sweden, the navy could, nevertheless, be seen clearly as a force designed and commonly used to support what were generally seen as the national goals: the security of Britain and her colonies, and maritime hegemony.

The political context explains the willingness of the British political nation to spend substantial sums in order to gain and maintain naval superiority. It explains expenditure on new vessels, on maintenance, dockyards and equipment, a continuous pattern of support that facilitated improvements in operational practice. The political context also explains the objectives that the navy was set. Britain's global triumphs rested on naval power. By 1762 the navy had about 300 ships and 84,000 men, a size that reflected political support, the growth of the mercantile marine, population, economy and public finances, as well as a heavy shipbuilding programme during the Seven Years' War. There was also good naval leadership, although the Navy Board of the 1750s did not always welcome innovation. An experienced admiral, George, Lord Anson, was First Lord of the Admiralty in 1751–62, while admirals such as Boscawen, Hawke, Pocock, and Rodney were bold and effective commanders. Anson and the outstanding designer Sir Thomas Slade were responsible for major innovations in warship design. The old types with 80, 70 and 60 guns were abandoned, in favour of 74s and 64s; the 50-gun ship was discarded as a ship of the line, but retained in limited number as a heavy cruiser; the small two-deck cruisers of 44 guns were abandoned, in favour of the single-decked frigate; and better three-deckers were designed. These changes helped increase the operational effectiveness of the navy. The large number of single-deck frigates that were built made a notable contribution to British success in the later years of the war.

The war at sea

Once at war, Britain needed to destroy her opponents' fleets, as both France and Spain were increasing their naval strength. Together, they launched warships with a total displacement of around 250,000 tons in 1746–55, while Britain launched only 90,000, losing its previous superiority over the combined Bourbon powers. Fortunately for Britain, Spain did not join the war until 1762 and, by then, France had been defeated at sea, losing about 50,000 tons of warships to British captures. Thanks to captures and ship-building, the British navy in 1760 had a displacement tonnage of about 375,000, at that point the largest in the world. The potential strength of her opponents' united naval power, combined with the danger of invasion, made it necessary for the British to blockade the principal French bases, especially Brest. Fortunately, improvements in revictualling at sea and the development of watering facilities at Torbay made this possible.[66]

Initially, the naval war went badly for Britain. In 1755 Admiral Edward Boscawen had failed to intercept the French fleet taking reinforcements to Canada. In 1756 the French had successfully invaded Minorca. Most of the British fleet was in home waters, prepared to resist a feared French invasion of England. England thus served like a moored convoy that admirals had to seek to defend, although, unlike a convoy, the impact was strategic rather than tactical.

Due to concern about naval strength in home waters,[67] only a small squadron of ten ships of the line under Vice-Admiral John Byng was sent to the Mediterranean in 1756. Reinforced by three ships from Gibraltar, Byng attacked a French fleet of comparable size under the Marquis de La Galissonière 30 miles southeast of Minorca on 20 May. Approaching the French line, Byng heaved too in order to dress (re-organize) his own, but there was a failure to concert operations between the parts of his force. The van, under Rear-Admiral Temple West, engaged with the French at close quarters, but, approaching nearly head on, was badly pummelled by the heavy raking broadsides of their strongly-gunned opponents. The rear, under Byng, failed to come within effective gunshot and by the time it was ready to act the van was in a bad way, and Byng decided not to renew the attack on the French, who remained on the defensive. Instead, Byng withdrew to Gibraltar, the besieged British garrison at Fort St. Philip surrendered, and in the ensuing political furore the government incurred much criticism and Byng was court-martialled, sentenced to death with a recommendation of mercy, and shot,[68] leading to Voltaire's quip in *Candide* (1759): "The English shoot their admirals from time to time to encourage the others". Such punishments were believed to be an effective way to inculcate bold leadership. In 1770 George Paterson, secretary to Commodore Sir John Lindsay, Commander-in-Chief in the East Indies, complained that the officers of the Bombay Marine were not subject to military law:

Hence one would imagine arises the so frequent miscarriages in all their expeditions where their Marine have been concerned. There is a great difference between a man fighting with a conviction if he does not behave well his life is to answer for it and another who knows that the only punishment can be dismissal from the service. A man is rich and this is called a punishment.[69]

The indecisive clash off Minorca, like that off Ushant in 1778, reflected the difficulty of ensuring victory at the outset of wars. The individual ships' companies were newly recruited or pressed, their captains were still working up the sailing capacities of their ships and crews, and the admiral was still working up and determining the capacities of his captains, who were equally unsure of their commander. Line tactics required experienced crews and commanders used to working together. In both 1756 and 1778, the component parts of the British fleet displayed a serious lack of cohesion. The chances of boldness going wrong were therefore far higher than, for example, in 1759 when Boscawen and Hawke won the battles of Lagos and Quiberon Bay with well-tried and experienced ships and captains on whose capacities they could rely.

In 1757 another fleet, this time under Admiral Francis Holburne, failed to fulfil expectations when a planned attack on Louisbourg was abandoned. The expedition against Rochefort also failed. Nevertheless, French trade was under increasing pressure, both in European waters and further afield. This affected French power. For example, British ships in the Gulf of Mexico captured most ships bound for New Orleans, and weakened the colony of Louisiana, not least by increasing discontent among the Native Americans.

In 1758 the situation improved, and the ability of the navy to act both as an offensive strategic force and as a restraint on French trade was fully demonstrated. Admiral Henry Osborne pursued a section of the Toulon fleet into Cartagena on the Mediterranean coast of Spain, and then defeated the squadron sent to support it. On 4–5 April Hawke successfully attacked Basque Roads, destroying and dispersing a fleet preparing to reinforce Canada. Commodore Charles Holmes sailed up the unbuoyed channel of the River Ems, and, by cutting the supplies of the French garrison of Emden, led to the withdrawal of the French. This provided the British with a landing port in Europe. Holmes thereafter patrolled the River Ems and supported the deployment of British troops in Germany. Captain Richard Howe covered the amphibious attacks on St Malo and Cherbourg. Louisbourg fell.[70] Pocock, however, fought two indecisive battles in the Bay of Bengal; in these engagements the effect of French defensive tactics was exacerbated by the cautious nature of the British "fighting instructions". French commerce dried up by the end of 1758; the rise of captures by the British navy was indicative of its superiority in most Western waters.

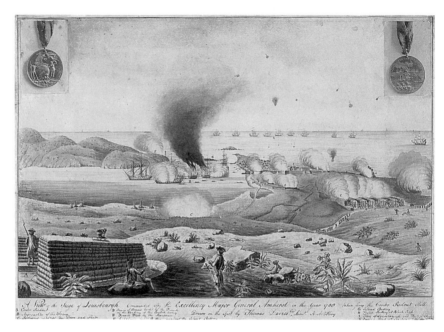

A View of the Siege of Louisbourg, 1758 by Thomas Davies, who captured one of the crucial aspects of the engagement, the destruction of the French warships in the harbour. The British force benefited from the recent development of a nearby base at Halifax. The presence of such bases – storage and safety points in the imperial system – was important to British military capability, and improved the confidence of British military planning. Louisbourg was a major fortress that had taken 1–2 per cent of the annual budget of the French Ministry of the Marine from 1716 to 1740. *Courtesy of the Royal Artillery Historical Trust, Woolwich.*

Individual French warships also proved vulnerable to the increasingly insistent British naval pressure in European water and the cumulative effect weakened the French. For example, on 29 May 1758 the *Raisonable* was captured by three British warships. On 17 July 1761 the *Achille* was captured off Cadiz. The large number of warships captured by Britain and incorporated into her navy played a major role in affecting the balance of naval strength. This incorporation aided the process by which the British changed the nature of their navy, copying the Bourbon large two-deckers. These were more manoeuvrable than the small three-decker 80- and 90-gun ships that had been so important earlier in the century. The new ships were better sailers and better fighters, both manoeuvrable and capable of holding their own in the punishing artillery duels of the line of battle engagements that the British preferred to conduct at close range, in contrast to the French preference for long-range fire.[71]

The crucial mid-century naval victories occurred in 1759, although, again, the battle in Indian waters was indecisive. That year, the French planned a knockout blow. Choiseul, the leading French minister, proposed a joint invasion, with Russian and Swedish forces transported by a Swedish fleet to Scotland. Neither power agreed, and, instead, the French planned an invasion of 100,000 troops, with landings in the Clyde and at Portsmouth, the latter subsequently being altered to Essex because of a British naval blockade of the embarkation port of Le Havre. Choiseul's plan was unrealistic, insofar as it anticipated significant Jacobite support, and it is unlikely that the invasion force could have conquered Britain. Nevertheless, had even only part of the French force landed, it would still have posed serious problems for the British.

The division of the French navy between Brest and Toulon made it difficult for them to concentrate the necessary covering force, and the blockading British squadrons sought to maintain the division, while attempts were also made to disrupt invasion preparations: Rear-Admiral George Rodney attacked Le Havre with bomb vessels on 4, 5 and 6 July and blockaded the port for the rest of the year. Although the Toulon fleet, under the Marquis de La Clue, managed to leave first the harbour and then the Mediterranean, it was defeated by the pursuing British under Boscawen near Lagos on the Portuguese coast on 18–19 August 1759. Stubborn resistance by the rearmost French warship, the *Centaure*, held off the British while La Clue sailed the rest of his fleet into neutral waters, but, on the following day, Boscawen violated Portuguese neutrality and launched a successful attack. Mortally wounded, La Clue ran his vessel ashore and burnt it to prevent British capture, and the outnumbered French lost a total of five ships, three captured and two destroyed. The rest of the fleet was then blockaded in the Tagus.

Bad weather forced Hawke, the chief exponent of close blockage, to lift his blockade of Brest in November 1759 and to take shelter in Torbay, but the French fleet, under the Marquis de Conflans, failed in its attempt to reach Scotland via the west coast of Ireland. Conflans could not sail direct for Scotland. He had first to meet transports from Bordeaux and Nantes at Morbihan, and this led to a fatal delay. Conflans was trapped by Hawke while still off the Breton coast. He took refuge in Quiberon Bay, counting on its shoaly waters and strong swell to deter Hawke's ships. The British had scant knowledge of the Bay's rocks.

Nevertheless, on 20 November, Hawke made a bold attack. With topsails set, despite the ferocity of the wind, which was blowing at nearly 40 knots, his ships sailed into the confined space of the bay, overhauled the French rear division and forced a general action. British gunnery and seamanship proved superior in this confused engagement and seven French ships of the line were captured, sunk or wrecked. French casualties were heavy. The *Superbe* sank with the loss of its entire crew of 630 after two broadsides from Hawke's *Royal George*. Like Jutland (1916), this was a battle that could have decided the fate of the war had the British lost.

111

All possibility of a French invasion of Britain was shattered by these two decisive victories of 1759. Much of the Brest fleet took refuge in the River Vilaine, further up Quiberon Bay and stayed there for the remainder of the war,[72] others took refuge in Rochefort, while political and financial[73] support for the navy ebbed in France, and the British were left to take the initiative at sea. Thus, the French navy did not disrupt the attack on Belle Isle in 1761 or the dispatch of troops to Portugal in 1762, despite the fact that both enterprises were vulnerable to naval forces based in Brittany. A squadron under Commodore Augustus Keppel covered the Belle Isle expedition, while in 1762 a fleet based at Gibraltar under Admiral Saunders discouraged a junction between Bourbon naval forces in the Atlantic and the Mediterranean. More generally, British warships were increasingly successful both in limiting French privateering and in damaging French trade. Such actions also hit French naval strength. Thus, in March 1759 two British warships captured a French frigate after attacking the frigates escorting a convoy off the Breton coast. That November, East India Company ships helped defeat an attack by Dutch frigates on the Company's positions in Bengal.

It was still necessary to be vigilant. In 1762 a French threat to the convoys sailing to the West and East Indies had to be beaten off in the Western Approaches. That June, a French squadron of five warships captured St John's in Newfoundland. The following February, French warships that the British had failed to capture off Ceylon (Sri Lanka), blockaded the Ganges.

Conclusions

Victory at sea, combined with successful amphibious operations, altered the strategic situation. It did not prevent the Bourbons from a massive programme of naval rearmament after the war was over, but British colonial conquests during the war ensured that the geopolitics and infrastructure of power were different. North America now appeared to be securely British. When, in 1770–1, there was the prospect of war with the Bourbons over the Falkland Islands, there was little need to consider the security of North America; the situation was totally different to that of 1754–6. Bengal was also secure. There were to be new strategic challenges in the two decades after 1763 – the rebuilding of the Bourbon fleets, a Russian-led League of Northern European powers in the Baltic, the combination of France and Mysore in southern India, and, most obviously, rebellion in the Thirteen Colonies – but in 1763 the situation appeared promising. Whereas in the 1690s the British had had to rely on Dutch support to achieve a naval edge over the French, and that only with difficulty, in the Seven Years' War Britain, alone on the oceans, had defeated France and Spain.

British naval success was not due to superior weaponry. Neither the ships nor their equipment were substantially different from those of the Bourbons. Instead, the crucial factors were: first, a level of continuous high commitment and expenditure that helped to ensure that a high level of both was regarded as normal and necessary and that naval strength never collapsed; secondly, the inculcation of an ethos and policy that combined the strategic offensive with tactical aggression; and, thirdly, within the constraints of naval warfare and technology, an effective use of the warships of the period.[74] British naval commanders generally took the initiative and were therefore best placed to obtain propitious circumstances. At a gut level, the British fought to win, not to survive for another day, and this was apparent in the victories that gave them the commanding position in the European world.

CHAPTER FIVE

The conquest of Empire, 1688–1763

The European world expanded considerably in the eighteenth century, and the British took a disproportionate share of that expansion. This was especially true of the period from mid-century. This larger share reflected a number of factors, some of which, such as emigration policy, had only an indirect relationship with military capability. Nevertheless, war played a major role in British expansion. Their share was won at the expense of two groups: indigenous peoples and other Europeans, and it is necessary to consider each, in turn, while appreciating that the military challenge was frequently simultaneous and that the same forces could be expected to deal with both groups.

It is also necessary to appreciate the variety both of the British forces involved and of the challenges they confronted. The first encompassed regulars, the units at the disposal of chartered companies, especially the East India Company, militia units and other forces raised in British colonies. The latter included the substantial armies of Indian rulers and the very different challenge posed by the smaller but still effective forces of the Native Americans ("Red Indians"). There was also a considerable variety in ecosystems in which the British had to operate, from the tundra near Hudson's Bay to the tropical marshes of Bengal. Despite these challenges, the British proved reasonably effective in obtaining their ends, although this was less true by 1748 and even 1756 than it was to be by 1763.

Seventeenth-century background

The English had been less active and successful in trans-oceanic expansion in the late-fifteenth and sixteenth century than both Portugal and Spain; the Scots scarcely featured. As a result, their expansion, like that of the Dutch, in the seventeenth century, was, in part, at the expense of already existing European empires. Thus, in the lucrative slave trade with West Africa the

English challenged the Portuguese, in the Caribbean the Spaniards, and in the Indian Ocean both the Portuguese and their Dutch assailants.

More important, however, from the early seventeenth century, was expansion into areas not already occupied by other Europeans. This was especially so in North America. The Virginia Company, chartered in 1606, established a colony in the Chesapeake region, while in 1620 the *Mayflower* made a landfall at Cape Cod. Virginia and New England had an English population of 26,000 by 1640. Working for the Dutch East India Company, Henry Hudson entered what became known as Hudson Bay in 1610. The English also colonized Bermuda (1613), and made an impact in the West Indies, colonizing St Kitts (1624), Barbados (1627) and Nevis (1628). These scarcely equalled the economic and strategic value of such Spanish possessions as Cuba, but they were a permanent presence. The East India Company, chartered in 1600, was the basis of commercial activity, and later political power, in the Indian Ocean, but its prime logic was commerce, not conquest, and its military strength in the late seventeenth century was very limited.

The pace of English territorial expansion increased in the second half of the seventeenth century. The Interregnum regime wrested Jamaica from Spain in 1655, while the benefits of dynasticism were illustrated under the restored Stuarts when Charles II peacefully gained Bombay as part of the dowry of his Portuguese wife. His government then turned against the Dutch and the capture *and* retention of New Amsterdam (renamed New York) anchored the English presence on the eastern seaboard of North America. New colonies were founded, including Carolina (1663) and Pennsylvania (1681). Possibly 200,000 people emigrated from the British Isles to North America during the century, far outnumbering the French settlers in Canada and Louisiana, and the settlements founded included Charleston (1670) and Philadelphia (1682), both important ports. The English also made a major impact in their West Indian islands, where they developed a sugar economy based on slave labour brought from West Africa, where English coastal bases included Accra (1672).

Prior to the Nine Years' War with France, conflict with other Europeans was largely kept separate from that with indigenous peoples. The major conflict with the latter in 1660–88 was a rising in New England in 1675–6 known as King Philip's War after the English name for Metacom, the Sachem (chief) of the Pokanokets. This war was unrelated to England's rivalry with other European powers. Furthermore, the English had few regular troops in their colonies outside Europe. Distance, cost and relative danger ensured that, whatever their value, all these colonies together had a garrison far smaller than that in Ireland. Instead, the North American colonies had to rely on their own forces, as in King Philip's war,[1] and in campaigns against the Pamunkey, Occaneechee and Susquehannock in Virginia in 1676. Sir William Berkeley, the Governor of Virginia, similarly

called out the militia to resist the 1676 rising among the European popula-
tion, Bacon's Rebellion. When many of the militia supported the rebellion,
Berkeley turned to other local Loyalists, although he was unable to hold
Jamestown and the rebellion only collapsed when Bacon died.[2]

The military and political situations were very different in India, where
in 1686, the Mughal Emperor Aurangzeb vigorously pursued a dispute
with the East India Company. A powerful force advanced against Hooghly,
the English base in the Bay of Bengal, and the English under Job Charnock,
without cavalry or field guns, were pushed back, and evacuated by sea
to Madras. Another Mughal force attacked Bombay, forcing the English
to retreat into the fort and then surrender. The English were only able to
continue trading after they apologized for their conduct and paid an indemnity.[3] The English were vastly outnumbered; unlike in North America, the
demographic balance was greatly against them.

Imperial rivalries, 1689–1697

Concern about trans-oceanic interests and possessions increased during 1689–
1713, the first imperial crisis of the period. Anxiety was particularly intense
during the negotiations over a possible future partition of the Spanish empire in 1698–1700 and in the subsequent war that began, for England, in
1702, but even in the Nine Years' War (1689–97) there was heightened concern about the colonies. This was especially so over North America and
the West Indies. Louis XIV's reign was a period of greater maritime and
colonial activity on the part of France and this was readily apparent in
North America. There both England and France competed to control the
fur trade and thus to influence native tribes at a great distance from their
bases. In 1685 the French had sent 500 regulars to the St Lawrence and in
1686 they mounted a successful overland thrust against the English bases
on James Bay, which was claimed by France. Although no more than 105
strong, the French force, commanded by Pierre de Troyes, seized Moose
Factory, Fort Rupert and Fort Albany and a rich booty in beaver skin.[4]

After war broke out between England and France, the struggle widened
in North America. "English" military activity there was almost entirely
locally generated, with little impact from England. Angered by English aid
to the Iroquois, who had proved a formidable foe during a conflict in 1682–
4, the French responded in 1690 by attacking Schenectady (northwest of
Albany) and English positions on the coast of what is now Southern Maine:
Forts Casco (Falmouth) and Loyal (Portland). These overland raids pleased
Native supporters, but were countered by an advance by New York militia
in 1691, that was ambushed, and by maritime attacks on the part of the
New England colonies. In May 1690 an expedition of eight ships and 700 men
under Sir William Phips sent by the Court of Massachusetts successfully

117

captured an unprepared and poorly defended Port Royal in Acadia. The fort was burnt down.

That July, however, an expedition of 32 New England ships and 2,200 troops, again under Phips, failed to drive the French from the St Lawrence. A diversionary attack overland against Montréal under Colonel Winthrop did not advance beyond Lake George, allowing the French to concentrate on defending Québec, which Phips unsuccessfully bombarded. He had failed to co-ordinate land and sea operations, never an easy task, and suffered from adverse winds, a shortage of ammunition, and smallpox. With Québec clearly too formidable for Phips' force, it re-embarked and returned to Boston. Phips visited England in 1691 and pressed on William III the need to continue the attack on Canada and the value of its fur and fisheries. That year, New England was largely quiet, but New England militia advanced in the Hudson–Champlain corridor and, in alliance with Mohawks and Mohicans, attacked the French south of Montréal. Phips returned to Massachusetts as Governor in 1692 and planned a second expedition against Québec, but nothing was done and he restricted himself to building Fort William Henry at Pemaquid. However, this fort was taken as French privateers and overland raids maintained pressure on New England for the remainder of the war. York was raided by the French-backed Abenaki in 1692. When Rear-Admiral Sir Francis Wheler in command of a squadron returning from the West Indies that was badly infected with yellow fever reached Boston in 1693 unannounced, he found no troops available and shelved his instructions for an attack on Québec in conjunction with New England forces.

The war flared up further west, with the French taking the initiative, successfully attacking England's Native allies and destroying the villages of the Mohawks (1693) and those of the Onondaga and Oneida (1696–7). In 1701 the Iroquois and the French negotiated peace. The Iroquois were to choose neutrality in the next Anglo-French conflict: Algonquian enemies, raiding the Iroquois after the French ceased to do so directly in 1697, were of consequence in the coming of Iroquois neutrality by 1701.[5] Further east, the French took most of the British bases in Newfoundland in 1696, including St John's which was burnt, but a British expedition in 1697 rebuilt the latter, adding barracks and defences. The Nine Years' War was not therefore a success for the English in North America. The option of the direct attack on the St Lawrence had failed. Overland pressure had not been maintained and, instead, the French had defeated England's Native allies and thus created a buffer zone to the south.

A successful attack on the St Lawrence was not beyond English capability. Indeed Québec had been captured in 1629 and held until returned in 1632. However, with time, the French presence had become stronger. A wall was constructed at Montréal in 1688. The early 1690s was certainly a moment of opportunity. Québec in 1690 was poorly fortified, but by 1694 redoubts and ramparts had been added, and this process of fresh fortification was to be maintained.[6] As a consequence, any attack on Québec would require more powerful forces, especially artillery. Such forces would likely be regulars, yet the dispatch of regular units raised the issue of priorities in England. In the 1690s Ireland and the Low Countries definitely came first. The same was true of France. Louis XIV did not send the resources sought by his governor in order to mount attacks on Boston and New York. Nevertheless, the opportunity was taken to expand French influence west from the St Lawrence. Forts were built at Michillmackinac (1700), Detroit (1701) and Niagara (1720). These interior fortifications altered the strategic situation. They narrowed the frontiers, required regular garrisons, and offered targets, for a fort taken was far worse than no fort at all. The best forts required attack by units supported by cannon, implying larger, if not regular, forces, roads and improved logistics.

Fighting in the Caribbean in 1689–97 was also a matter of local initiatives and occasional interventions by metropolitan forces. Thus, St Kitts, taken by the French in 1689, could not be retaken until English reinforcements arrived in 1690. This force, under Commodore Lawrence Wright, consisted of only eight small ships of the line, a contrast to the large fleets deployed in home waters. In 1691 Wright and Christopher Codrington, Governor of the Leeward Islands and commander of the troops there, attacked Guadeloupe. Troops were successfully landed, but the strength of the fortifications, the arrival of a French squadron, and disease among the English troops and sailors led to the abandonment of the expedition. It had been plagued by poor relations between the two commanders and was followed by bitter recriminations. Wright was acquitted at a court martial, but he never commanded a squadron again. He was succeeded by Commodore Ralph Wrenn, who, on 22 February 1692, fought off and successfully withdrew from a greatly superior French fleet off Desirade, before falling victim to disease shortly after at Barbados. In 1693 Rear-Admiral Sir Francis Wheler, who had fought at Beachy Head and Barfleur, was sent in command of a squadron to the West Indies. He landed a force on Martinique, but it failed to capture the French positions, in part due to the effects of yellow fever and of poor leadership. No expedition was sent in 1694, the year in which a large fleet was sent to the Mediterranean, but in 1695 a squadron under Commodore Robert Wilmot co-operated with the Spaniards in raiding Saint-Dominque, acquiring substantial booty. The expedition however was marred by serious differences between the army and naval commanders and by the disease that claimed Wilmot and many others. The operations in the West Indies did not determine the outcome of the war. Conflict there still bore many of the characteristics of buccaneering, as in the French capture of the Spanish base of Cartagena in 1697. English and French forces were able to launch major attacks in the West Indies, but found it much more difficult to sustain operations in the face of opposition and the logistical and ecological problems of campaigning there.[7]

War of the Spanish Succession, 1702–13

The English were more fortunate in this conflict as French naval weakness from the outset gave the English a greater freedom to mount expeditions. However, this freedom led to more operations in the Mediterranean, rather than in the Caribbean. Far less effort was devoted to seizing French-held West Indies islands. St Kitts was captured in 1702, but Guadeloupe resisted attack in 1703, although much damage was inflicted by the English troops who landed. The French did not take the initiative, except when they sacked both Nevis and St Kitts in 1706; this was just as well for the English, as the colonies took a low priority in their allocation of naval strength. Campaigning in the West Indies was seen as destructive. In 1703 Lieutenant-Colonel James Rivers wrote of his wish to leave Jamaica, "to get out of this unhealthy climate as soon as possible which diminishes the forces both sea and land very considerably every day . . . for fear of this service several of the officers quitted their commission".[8]

A major effort was made by Governor James Moore of Carolina. In 1702 he invaded Florida at the head of 500 Carolina volunteers and 300 Yamasee allies, but the fortress of St Augustine successfully resisted attack. It was too strong to storm, Moore's cannon were inadequate and warships from Cuba relieved the garrison, forcing Moore to retreat precipitately, without his cannon or eight of his fourteen ships.[9] This failure exhausted the resources of the Carolina government and indicated the importance of command of the sea. In 1704 Moore, with a largely Native army, ravaged western Florida, attacking the Spanish missions among the Apalachees near Talhahassee; having defeated a Spanish–Apalachee counterattack, he returned with over 1,000 slaves. Charleston repelled a Franco-Spanish privateering attack in 1706 and, thereafter, the British and their Native allies resumed the pressure on Florida, raiding Pensacola in 1707 and 1708, and advancing as far as Mobile in 1709. The English had very much gained the initiative, but this was dependent on Creek support.[10] Colonel John Palmer's later attempt, at the head of a force of 100 Carolinians and 100 Native allies, to take St Augustine in 1728, was thwarted by the strength of the citadel.

Further north, there was bitter fighting in Newfoundland in which, from 1706, the French largely took the initiative. Neither side, however, won lasting success or received adequate support from the regular forces. On the mainland, the French pressed on the New England settlements largely by arming the Abenakis of Vermont and launching raids from 1703, not least a destructive one against Deerfield in 1704, in which 48 militia and 200 Natives successfully marched nearly 600 miles in the depth of the winter.[11]

The previous December, Colonel Dudley, the Governor of Massachusetts, wrote to Marlborough:

> The first year by frequent visits and a free trade with the Indians I kept them at peace, but the French Jesuits amongst them have about six months past persuaded them to break all oaths and promises, and the first three days of their irruption, they destroyed one hundred and fifty poor people in the out and scattered parts of the province of Maine next them, but since I have not had any great damage, but am at a great cost of about two thousand pounds per month to maintain forces upon the frontiers, and cruising sloops upon the coast to prevent their supply of themselves and depredations upon us, which they do in small parties and avoid [sic] an hundred miles into impassable places whither it is impossible to march after them, and carry our necessary provisions being desert grounds where neither carriage nor horse can pass.[12]

In 1706 he was more optimistic:

> I have ever since [the initial raids] had so good intelligence of their marches that I have met them everywhere and disappointed them so as I have not lost one village . . . keep me in continual hurry marching of small parties all along the frontiers.[13]

The New Englanders struck at French bases, but they were happier mounting amphibious attacks than engaging in frontier warfare, a harsher course where they had to face Natives, the rigours of the terrain and their opponents' effective transport system, which was based on birchwood canoes. In 1704 a 550-strong Massachusetts force attacked Castine, but decided that Port Royal, the leading French base in Acadia, was too formidable an objective. The latter was attacked in 1707, but, although the New England army was over 1,000 strong and greatly outnumbered the defending force, the attack miscarried badly.

The failure increased pressure for the use of regulars, although that was delayed by the demands of the European theatre, which consistently received greater priority. As a result, there was no support for an advance on Lake Champlain in 1709, an advance that was wrecked by disease. The following year, 400 British marines joined with 1,500 militia to capture Port Royal: the garrison was only about 100 strong. Instead of burning down the settlement and then leaving with their loot, the captors left a garrison in Port Royal.[14]

In 1711 the government sent a major force under Rear-Admiral Sir Hovenden Walker and Brigadier-General John Hill, to attack Québec: 5,300 men in 31 transports escorted by 14 ships of the line. This expedition, the largest hitherto to North America, was designed to improve Britain's position in negotiations with France, to distract attention from Marlborough, and to vindicate the "blue water" policies advocated by the Tories. Preparations were hasty and the government relied too much upon their own overoptimistic assumptions of logistical support from New England. Difficult relations between the New Englanders and the British commanders did not prevent the assembly of a large force at Boston, including over 1,000 militia, but on 23–4 August 1711, due to a night-time error in navigation, eight transport ships and nearly 900 men were lost on rocks near Ile aux Oeufs in the St Lawrence estuary. This led to the abandonment of the expedition, an abandonment that ensured that the landward prong of the advance on Canada, a force of 2,300 under Francis Nicholson that advanced from Albany, gave up its march on Montréal at Wood Creek.[15]

Canada had not fallen. However, the Peace of Utrecht left Britain with Nova Scotia, Newfoundland and Hudson's Bay. These increased the British stake in North America and weakened the defences of New France. Given that in any future war the British would only have several years campaigning, they could only benefit from not needing to capture Port Royal again.

Britain and non-European opponents 1700–39

North America was again the major overseas field of military activity, although the British presence was by no means restricted to it. Elsewhere, however, there was only limited interest in territorial expansion, especially among ministers in London, although there was concern to maintain the security of possessions. In Jamaica this led to operations in the 1730s against the Maroons, runaway, or in some cases freed, slaves, who controlled much of the interior. They were unsuccessful, the governor, Edward Trelawny, reporting in 1738, "The service here is not like that in Flanders or any part of Europe. Here the great difficulty is not to beat, but to see the enemy . . . in short, nothing can be done in strict conformity to usual military preparations, and according to a regular manner; bushfighting as they call it being a thing peculiar by itself". The Maroons were finally granted land and autonomy by treaties in 1738 and 1739. Seven years later, Trelawny had to deal with a serious slave rising.[16] There had also been a slave rebellion in South Carolina in 1739: the Stono rising in which 100 slaves rose and killed twenty colonists before being defeated by the militia and their Native allies.[17]

British traders in West Africa relied on their fortifications. Although the minor secondary English factory [fortified base] at Sekondi fell in 1694, the leading English base at Cape Coast Castle was never taken, and was successfully defended against African attack in 1688. British cannon drove off Dahomey forces that attacked their fort at Glehue in 1728.[18]

Cape Coast Castle on the Gold Coast. The European presence in West Africa was anchored by coastal forts that served as protected bases for trade. Cape Coast Castle was the overseas headquarters of the Royal Africa Company. Powerful European-colonial fortifications were of limited use against European assailants enjoying naval superiority and not suffering from tropical diseases, but such fortifications were generally able to resist assailants who lacked the skills, resources and organization required for a lengthy siege. They were part of the process by which the European presence rested on the ability to dig and build. In 1788 Earl Cornwallis, the British commander in India, took an interest in the purchase of entrenching tools. Having ordered "4,000 good iron shovels", he wanted "2,000 iron spades to be made immediately". *National Maritime Museum, London.*

In India in 1717 the East India Company's forces behaved badly in unsuccessful attempts to relieve the besieged base at Kawar. The following year attacks were mounted against Gheria and Khanderi, coastal forts on the Konkan coast of the Maratha naval commander Kanhoji Angria, who launched piratical attacks on British trade. Neither attack succeeded. Angria's ships avoided battle and the thick walls of his forts saw off poorly-conducted attacks. In 1720 the British used against Gheria a "phram", a floating platform mounted with cannon, but it sank. The following year, another of Angria's forts, Colaba, was attacked by land and sea, but the land force was dispersed by Maratha cavalry and, despite the involvement of the Royal Navy, the bombardment from sea failed to destroy the fort. The East India Company made little impact until after Kanhoji died in 1729, his navy was divided between his sons, and a policy developed of seeking to exploit their rivalries and of gaining local allies against one of them.[19]

Whereas the frontier of British control did not advance in either Africa or in India in this period, the situation was very different in North America:

unlike in the former two areas, there was interest in territorial expansion. The war with the French in 1702–13 interacted with tension and conflict with Native Americans. Furthermore, the demographic growth of the British colonies exacerbated land hunger. There was conflict from north to south of the colonies. In the north guerrilla warfare by the western Abenaki under their chief Grey Lock in 1723–7 kept settlers out of what was to be Vermont.[20]

Further south, the Tuscaroras responded to the advance of settlers by raiding settlements in North Carolina in 1711. Colonel John Barnwell led counterattacks in 1711 and 1712, but did not win any decisive victory. In contrast, James Moore, with the support of a larger Native force, defeated the Tuscaroras in 1713: their fortified base of Neoheroka was stormed and nearly 600 were killed or enslaved.

Provoked by exploitation by Carolina merchants and landowners, the Yamasee of the Lower Savannah River attacked South Carolina in April 1715, raiding to within 12 miles of Charleston. Other tribes, including the Lower Creek, Cherokee and Catawba, provided support. The initial South Carolina military response was unsuccessful, but the Native alliance was not sustained. The Cherokee came round to help the Carolinians in 1716, and in 1717 the Creek deserted the Yamasee. The Yamasee were pushed back, but continued raiding South Carolina. This collapse of the alliance system with the Native Americans forced South Carolina to increase expenditure on defence, creating a military system that was to be employed against the Cherokees in 1760–1, although to limited effect. However, the alliance system with fellow colonists had worked: Virginia helped South Carolina in the 1710s, much to the surprise of Natives who were used to their disputes.[21]

The British were helped by the demographic and political situations, especially by the European diseases that killed Native people, particularly smallpox. Emigration ensured that the British increasingly outnumbered the Natives, close to the Atlantic, although in South Carolina the European population was probably outnumbered by the Cherokee as late as 1730, and both were outnumbered by African slaves. British colonies were disunited and had competing territorial claims west of the Appalachians. Nevertheless, they were not in conflict, and could provide mutual support. In contrast, the Native Americans were greatly harmed by their rivalries. In 1711 the Yamasee helped the North Carolinians defeat an attack by the Tuscaroras; in 1716 the Cherokee helped the Carolinians defeat the Yamasee. Defeat had a crucial demographic impact on the Native Americans. The number of Tuscaroras fell from 5,000 to 2,500. Many took refuge with the Iroquois and those that remained, were grouped by the colonists in a reservation, which by 1760 contained only about 300 people. From 1715 most of the Yamasee were killed or enslaved by the colonial militia. Such losses helped to ensure permanent moves forward in the frontier of European control.[22]

British advance was not solely a matter of conflict. Under the Treaty of Utrecht of 1713, the British claimed influence over the Iroquois (although the French did not accept this interpretation of the Treaty), and, although no control existed, relations were reasonably good: they supported each other's pretensions in order to reap mutual benefit. In 1725 the Iroquois permitted the Governor of New York to construct a stone fort at Oswego. This was the first British base on the Great Lakes and it served to extend the British trading network, for example into Southern Ontario. Rum was available and inexpensive at Oswego.

More generally, British merchants increasingly traded among Native groups west of the Appalachians. In the 1710s the French were convinced that the British were conspiring with the Fox and the Chickasaw against them. In the 1720s British merchants established temporary posts on the upper Ohio and on an eastern tributary of the Wabash. In the 1740s, the Miami were increasingly drawn to the British by trade.

Although Britain and France were at peace, the expansion of their rival trading networks in the North American interior involved the use of force. Intra-Native and intra-European rivalries were connected. They were a crucial means by which the British and French furthered their interests and influence. For example, suspicious that the Fox tribe from the Mississippi–Illinois region was plotting with the British, the French, with Native American support, launched five attacks on them in 1712–34, finally breaking Fox resistance, particularly thanks to a victory on the Illinois Grand Prairie in 1730. In 1724 Governor Shute of Massachusetts sent an expedition into modern Maine to destroy the mission of the French Jesuit Sebastian Râle at Norridgewock, and thus French influence among the eastern Abenakis; it had already been burnt during earlier punitive expeditions in 1705 and 1722.

British activity was a matter of initiatives by British-Americans. The British government took little interest in the interior of North America. In contrast, the French followed an active policy of expanding their power in the interior. This was to lead to conflict in 1754, but the two powers first fought in 1743–8 as a result of rivalry in Europe.[23]

Conflict outside Europe, 1739–48

Georgia and the Caribbean

Britain was involved in two wars in this period. The first, with Spain, known as the War of Jenkins' Ear, arose from the British response to Spain's attempts to prevent illicit trade with its New World colonies, most famously with the ear removed from the captured Captain Robert Jenkins. The war began in 1739 and was subsumed into the Anglo-French conflict that began in 1743, because Spain was an ally of France. War with Spain was largely waged in the New World. Unlike in the War of the Spanish Succession, there was no civil war in Spain for the British to intervene in, Portugal was neutral, and it appeared more profitable to strike at Spain in the New World, rather than to mount amphibious attacks on Spain itself, although the last were considered.

The war in the New World was waged in a number of areas, including the Mosquito (Caribbean) coast of Nicaragua, where the British supported native peoples against Spanish authority.[24] The most important operations on the mainland occurred in North America: the British had spread south from the Carolinas, initially with the construction of a fort on the Altamaha River in 1721 in order to forestall possible French influence over the Native Americans. However, this activity was turned in an anti-Spanish direction as a result of the foundation of the colony of Georgia in 1732. This appeared to threaten Spanish Florida and tension between the two led to hostilities at the outbreak of the war. After inconclusive skirmishes in 1739, Colonel James Oglethorpe, the Governor of Georgia, led an expedition against St Augustine in 1740. He encountered no serious resistance en route, but Oglethorpe's plan for a methodical siege was thwarted by the South Carolina Assembly's insistence on a short campaign. The Spaniards resisted bravely, mounting an effective night sortie, the naval blockade failed to prevent the arrival of supply ships, the well-fortified position resisted bombardment and, once the momentum of advance and success was lost, Oglethorpe's force was struck by desertion, especially on the part of his Native American allies and troops from South Carolina. The effects of disease exacerbated the situation and Oglethorpe retreated.[25]

Two years later, the Spaniards counter-attacked, invading Georgia with 1,900 men and capturing St Simon's Island, but Oglethorpe used the wooded terrain effectively to ambush their force near Frederica and the Spaniards were also discouraged by reports of British naval reinforcements. The Spaniards retreated. Thereafter, the situation quietened down, becoming a matter of raids, such as that mounted on the St Augustine area in March 1743. Oglethorpe returned to Britain in 1743, never to revisit Georgia. Instead, he led the cavalry pursuit of Charles Edward Stuart as he retreated to Scotland in December 1745.

The effective end of operations in the region reflected the limited local military resources of both sides, and the unwillingness of distant imperial sources of military power to provide sufficient additional resources. This was due to the greater appeal and importance of operations in the Caribbean. Florida was of slight economic importance, much of it covered by swamps, and operations there served no domestic political imperative within Britain.[26]

Instead, the British government devoted its resources to securing a spectacular victory in the Caribbean, a sea containing a series of wealthy targets. This was made more necessary because in 1739, at the outset of the war,

Vice-Admiral Edward Vernon, with six ships of the line, attacked the port of Porto Bello on the isthmus of Panama, which was defended by three well-sited fortresses. The British warships were becalmed alongside the first and, with a heavy fire, silenced the Spaniards. They then landed sailors and marines who climbed through the embrasures and took the surrender of the position. The other forts and the town then surrendered.

Vernon's success led to a wave of jingoism that encouraged political commitment of military resources to empire and created high expectations about the prospects from action in the Caribbean.[27] In the volatile political atmosphere of Britain in the closing years of the Walpole ministry, the government felt it necessary to respond to these expectations. However, the situation was far less promising than was generally believed in Britain. Vernon had destroyed the fortifications of Porto Bello, for he was in no position to retain them. Vernon, who had already served in the Caribbean in 1708–12, was wary of the benefits from large amphibious operations and preferred to rely on naval power, but in 1740 he achieved little bar an ineffective bombardment of Cartagena and the capture of Chagres. Vernon was affected by a serious shortage of sailors, a lack of naval stores, and concern about the movement of Bourbon ships. Although France was neutral, the Brest squadron had been sent to the Caribbean, and Vernon believed that his chief duty was to be ready to repel a French attack.

In 1741 the situation appeared to change with the arrival of a substantial British force under Rear-Admiral Sir Chaloner Ogle and Brigadier General Thomas Wentworth. This force was launched against Cartagena, on the coast of modern Colombia. Supporting fortresses were captured in March 1741 and the fall of the town appeared imminent, but an assault on the hill fort which dominated the city failed and, after disagreements about the best way to launch another attack in the face of heavy losses through disease, the troops re-embarked in April. Don Blas de Lezo had proved an able commander of the defence. The unexpected failure led to bitter recriminations, with Vernon blaming Wentworth for moving too slowly to attack Cartagena. The most recent study exonerates Wentworth from much of the criticism and directs attention to Vernon's volatile nature and to the problems this created for combined operations. In addition, Vernon, totally misjudging the strength of the Spanish position and the determination of the defenders, refused to land his seamen, and this ensured defeat.[28] The Cartagena expedition was carefully planned, but failed, in part due to a failure to mobilize sufficient resources. Later success during the Seven Years' War was due not to an innovative strategy, but rather to greater resources and better co-operation between army and navy commanders.

Subsequent operations in the Caribbean suffered from the impact of failure at Cartagena and the consequent loss of impetus, morale and confidence. Cuba appeared the next prize and an attack on Santiago de Cuba was planned, but it was not realized. The troops were landed, but they did not reach their goal and, instead, suffered heavily from disease before being re-embarked. Vernon's decision to land the troops at Guantanamos Bay, over 80 miles from Santiago, foolishly exposed them to a long and dangerous advance through woody terrain ideal for Spanish guerrilla action. A planned attack on Panama was similarly ineffective. Despite the agreed plan to land an outflanking force that would prevent the Porto Bello garrison from reinforcing Panama, Vernon adopted a course that allowed the garrison to retreat and reinforce Panama. The Council of War then decided not to attack Panama, a caution encouraged by losses due to disease. The army remained on Jamaica doing little until ordered back to Britain in late 1742.[29]

This was not the end of amphibious operations in the Caribbean, but, from 1743, military and naval resources were concentrated on the threat from France in Europe and in home waters. The war with Spain became a side-show and, indeed, the death of Philip V in 1746 led to hopes of reconciliation with Spain and thus of dividing Spain from France. An unsuccessful naval attack on St Augustine in September 1742 ended naval pressure on Florida.

Nevertheless, fighting continued. In early 1743 Captain Charles Knowles commanded a squadron sent to act against La Guaira and Porto Cabello, the ports on the Caracas coast, but he was beaten off.[30] In contrast, in 1748 Knowles captured Port Louis on French-ruled Saint-Domingue by sailing his ships close in to the defending fort and bombarding it into ruins. The expedition was supported by troops from Jamaica under the Governor, Edward Trelawny, but the position was not retained. Saint-Domingue was far larger than the other French possessions in the Caribbean and the capture of one port alone was not sufficient to ensure its fall. On the mainland, British-supported Natives of the Mosquito Coast of Nicaragua surprised, captured and burnt the fort of San Fernando de Matina in 1747. The same year, the Spaniards destroyed a small English settlement at the mouth of the San Juan River in Guatemala.[31]

North America

In North America, fighting with France during the War of the Austrian Succession was largely restricted to the Atlantic littoral. This owed much to the nature of the military aid sent from the metropolis – naval rather than army – and to pressure for neutrality from the Iroquois and for the maintenance of peaceful trade with New France from the Albany Dutch and major landholders in the region such as the Livingstones. These factors kept the peace south-east of the Great Lakes, while distances between the Carolinas and French positions along the Mississippi were too great for any significant operations there. The French-backed Abenaki of what was to be Vermont, New Hampshire and Maine raided British settlements in New England, drove the settlers from what was to be Vermont and ambushed militia patrols, but the French lacked regular troops to support large-scale offensive operations. However, in 1745 and 1747, the French launched inland offensives against New York and Massachusetts, capturing both Saratoga and Fort Massachusetts. This ended the *de facto* neutrality on the New York frontier and reflected the degree to which the French were able to take the initiative in the interior. Their base at Fort St Frédéric (Crown Point), at the southern end of Lake Champlain, threatened the Hudson valley. In 1746 the British planned a joint attack with the Iroquois on Canada, beginning with the capture of Fort St Frédéric, but the British forces did not arrive and most of the Iroquois remained neutral. War began between France and the Mohawks, and the latter, encouraged by William Johnson, New York's agent with the Iroquois, raided far to the north, but an Anglo-Mohawk raiding party was ambushed at the Cascades of the St Lawrence in June 1747.

Sea power, however, could both lessen distance and permit the concentrated application of force. The French acted first. Taking the initiative on the outbreak of war in 1744 warships from Louisbourg, the major French base on Ile Royale (Cape Breton Island), attacked the British positions on Acadia. The fishing port of Canso, the British position nearest Ile Royale, was captured, and Annapolis Royal (formerly Port Royal) was raided.

Louisbourg and its warships were not only a threat to Acadia. They also challenged New England interests in fishing, trade and territorial expansion. As a result, the government of Massachusetts organized a force of 3,000 militia under William Pepperell that sailed for Louisbourg in 1745. The force was transported by New England ships and supported by the small Leeward Islands squadron under Commodore Peter Warren. Louisbourg was the best-fortified position in New France, newly created on the Vauban plan. However, it was designed to resist attack from the sea, was most vulnerable by land and the morale of the garrison was low. In April 1745 Warren blockaded the harbour, and the New England militia was able to land safely in Gabarus Bay. The attackers bombarded the land defences, although inexperience led to casualties among the artillerymen, while Warren's blockade reduced the food available to the defenders. With the walls breached and Warren also able to force his way into the harbour, the governor capitulated in June. The Massachusetts forces had acted like European regulars; the siege of Louisbourg was not an exercise in wilderness warfare.[32]

Pepperell next suggested an invasion of Canada, but the British government was unable to provide support in time. Instead, in 1746, Lorient on the French coast, the base of the *Compagnie des Indes*, was attacked. The main French fleet was still undefeated, and the British feared a fresh Jacobite rising backed by the French. In these circumstances, it did not seem appropriate to devote substantial resources to operations outside Europe.

Instead, it was the French who sent a major fleet to North American waters, 15 warships including ten ships of the line, 45 transports and 3,500 troops, the largest force they sent in the mid-century wars. However, d'Anville's attempt to regain Louisbourg fell victim to bad weather, disease and inadequate supplies. The fleet anchored at Chibouctou on the site of modern Halifax, but was affected by typhus and typhoid fever. The inexperienced Duke of Anville, a kinsman of the naval minister, was among the casualties. His successor, La Jonquière, wanted to press on to attack Annapolis Royal, but losses among his force and the arrival of British reinforcements had altered the situation and the plan was abandoned. The fleet returned to France with the loss of 8,000 men.[33] In some respects, this was a French parallel to the Cartagena expedition. It illustrated the difficulties of amphibious operations, and showed that disease was not only a problem in tropical environments. The French faced very serious organizational and operational problems in mounting trans-Atlantic expeditions and had less experience in such operations than the British; this gap was to become more important in the next war.

The capture of Louisbourg deprived d'Anville of a base and enabled the British, again dominant at sea, to blockade the St Lawrence. This cut supplies to New France and destroyed the basis of the French fur trade. Amerindian alliances were sustained by presents and trade goods. British fur traders were now able to undersell the French dramatically, and this encouraged both the Miami and the Huron to break with the French. Louisbourg was returned in the Peace of Aix-la-Chapelle (1748), much to the fury of the New Englanders. Nevertheless, its fall had shown that it could be captured, while the economic benefits to Britain of French weakness had been fully demonstrated. As a result of the war, British colonial interest in the Ohio country greatly increased. The Ohio Company, a group of Virginian landowners and London merchants, was granted half a million acres in the Ohio Valley by the British Crown.

The British government was also interested in circumnavigating North America by discovering a navigable Northwest Passage to the Pacific. In 1741 the Admiralty sent the *Discovery* and *Furnace* to Hudson Bay under Christopher Middleton. The following year, he sailed further north along the west coast of the Bay than any previous European explorer, but he could not find the entrance to a passage.[34]

War in India, 1746–8

Louisbourg was not the only gain restored in the peace. The British regained Madras, their principal base in the Carnatic, the south-eastern coastal region of India. Madras had been lost in 1746 to the Governor-General of the French positions in India, Joseph François, Marquis de Dupleix, supported by a squadron under La Bourdonnais, Governor of Mauritius, and 1,200 French regulars. Mauritius was a base from which the French could threaten British positions in India. British forces, in contrast, were inadequate: in 1740 the British East India Company controlled only 2,000 troops throughout India and their fortresses were in poor condition. The first companies of their artillery were not formed until 1748. In 1746, the British fleet in the area, six warships under Commodore Edward Peyton, refused to attack La Bourdonnais' larger force. Peyton was sent home under arrest. His successor, Thomas Griffin, was tried for failing to engage a French squadron. Fort St George at Madras itself fell after only a two-day siege; the garrison suffered six dead.

Dupleix successfully defended Madras against the Indian allies of the British: at the battle of Adyar a force of about 1,000 French and French-trained and -equipped Indians drawn up in advancing ranks of musketeers drove a larger force from the field. Dupleix, however, was unable to capture Cuddalore and Fort St David, adjacent to the French headquarters at Pondicherry. The fort was finally relieved by Boscawen who arrived with six of the line and troop reinforcements in July 1748, having decided the previous month that Mauritius would be too difficult to take. Boscawen, appointed Commander-in-Chief by sea and land of British forces in the East Indies, had been ordered to capture Pondicherry, but surprise had been lost and the position was well defended. As at Cartagena in 1741, it proved easier to plan than execute a bold step. Instead of a rapid attack, operations were delayed by preparations and by the capture of an outlying position, and the siege was abandoned after an ineffective bombardment and heavy losses to disease.[35]

War in India, 1749–65

The Peace of Aix-la-Chapelle ended formal hostilities between Britain and France. Boscawen lost his flagship, *Namur* in 1749, but it fell victim to a hurricane, not the French, and that year he set sail for Britain. However, the growing European presence in India ensured not only that conflict arising from war between Britain and France in Europe had to be considered, but also that events on their periphery, in India, would now draw the Europeans in. The two powers were soon indirectly involved in war through their participation in the internecine disputes of the local rulers, particularly a succession struggle over the Carnatic.

Dupleix's ally, Chanda Sahib, became Nawab of the Carnatic in 1749, and Dupleix established an effective system of allied rulers across southern India. The British East India Company resisted the French and supported Muhammad Ali, the rival claimant to the Carnatic, sending forces to assist him at the walled city of Trichinopoly, about 200 miles to the south of the capital Arcot and about 200 miles from Madras. In 1751, Chanda Sahib besieged Trichinopoly. The young Robert Clive led a diversionary force of

500, which captured Arcot in a surprise attack and then held the fort against a 50-day siege by a force of about 10,000. After the siege was raised, Clive pursued the retreating besiegers and defeated them at Arní. He followed this up by defeating Chanda's son, Rájá Sahib, a second time at Cáveripák.

These defeats wrecked the momentum and appearance of success on which Dupleix depended and his alliance system collapsed. In 1752 both Chanda and a French force surrendered, the latter to Stringer Lawrence, the able and energetic commander of the forces of the Madras Presidency of the East India Company, and a former major in the regular army. Lawrence created a Company field army in the Carnatic, ensuring that the Company was not restricted militarily to a few coastal positions, and enabling it to take a more proactive role in politics. Lawrence, who had already captured Devikotai in 1749, established garrisons in Trevadi and Trichinopoly in 1752. Another French force was defeated by Lawrence at Bahur outside Pondicherry on 26 August 1752: British-trained Indian sepoys dispersed their French counterparts, before British troops, firing as they advanced, drove their French opponents from the battlefield with a bayonet charge.

Although Chanda, then a prisoner, died in 1752, the war continued. That year, Lawrence's army amounted to 1,200 European troops and 2,000 sepoys. In 1753 the French again besieged Trichinopoly, but Captain John Dalton defended the position until it was relieved by Lawrence that autumn. Lawrence then campaigned actively around Trichinopoly until an armistice was arranged in October 1754. The battles Lawrence fought in 1753, such as Golden Rock and Sugarloaf Rock, are now forgotten, but, with Bahur, they marked Britain's first successful attempts to use Indian troops on the battlefield, and secured the British position in a strategic area, greatly expanding the area of British power south-west from Madras. Because both sides put so much effort into gaining Trichinopoly, British success was a major blow to the French. In 1754 Dupleix was recalled to France.[36]

Britain was left as the dominant power in South India, but the French remained influential in Hyderabad in the Deccan, much to the concern of the East India Company which wanted them driven thence. When Clive returned from Britain he found no shortage of military duties. In February 1756 he co-operated with Rear-Admiral Charles Watson in capturing Gheria, the stronghold on the west coast of India of Tulajee Angria, and destroying his fleet. Tulajee had rejected the suzerainty of the Peshwa and this ensured that Maratha troops helped the British to capture Suvarnadurg in 1755 and Gheria in 1756.[37]

The British position was soon after challenged in Bengal in east India. In June 1756 the newly acceded Nawab of Bengal, Siraj-ud-daula, stormed poorly defended and fortified Fort William at Calcutta after a brief siege. He confined his captives in the "Black Hole". Clive, then Lieutenant-Governor of Fort St David, and Watson were instructed to retake Calcutta.

Clive was in command of 850 British soldiers and 2,100 Indian sepoys, an important deployment of British strength. This force reached Bengal in late December and regained Fort William, largely thanks to the guns of Watson's squadron. The Nawab then advanced on Calcutta, but was checked by Clive in a confused action fought in a heavy morning fog. The adaptability of naval power was demonstrated by the 500 seamen Watson added to Clive's force.

Siraj-ud-daula then agreed terms of peace, and on 9 February 1757 he recognized Calcutta as British. Concerned about the French presence in Bengal, Clive next attacked their fort at Chandernagore, with crucial support from the navy, made possible by excellent navigation in the waters of the Hooghly River. Skill in such operations was again to be crucial when the British attacked Québec in 1759. However, unlike Québec, Chandernagore was not supported by an army. Close-range fire from Watson's warships was instrumental in its fall on 23 March.

Clive was suspicious of intrigues between the French and Siraj-ud-daula, who was indeed seeking Maratha support against the British. Clive determined to replace the Nawab and reached an agreement with one of his generals, Mir Jaffir. Clive then marched towards the Nawab's capital at Murshidabad, taking the fort at Cutwa en route. The Nawab stationed his army to block Clive's advance near the village of Plassey, and it was there that the two forces met on 23 June 1757. Clive deployed his men, about 850 British troops and 2,100 sepoys, in front of a mango grove with an acute angle of the river behind him, the sepoys on the flanks and his ten field guns and howitzers in front; 50 sailors acted as artillerymen. An artillery duel began and Clive withdrew his men into the grove, where they sheltered behind the mudbanks and among the trees. The Indians, about 50,000 strong, made no real effort to attack the British position (Mir Jaffir's men were totally inactive), with the exception of a cavalry advance that was driven back by grapeshot. A torrential midday downpour put most of the Nawab's guns out of action, but the British gunners kept their powder dry. As the Indian artillery (manned by Frenchmen) retreated, Clive advanced to man the embankment surrounding the large village pond to the front of his position. An Indian infantry attack was repelled by Clive's artillery and infantry fire and, as the Indians retreated, Clive's men advanced rapidly, storming the Indian encampment. The Nawab had already fled.

Clive's force suffered about 60 casualties, his opponent's only about 500 dead; but the political consequences were important. The battle was followed by the defection of Mir Jaffir whose son had the Nawab killed. Mir Jaffir was installed as his successor and Clive received over £250,000 from him. This enabled Clive to establish himself as a politician, able to influence a number of parliamentary seats when he returned to Britain.[38] Clive's fame and fortune was deserved. Clive's bold generalship was both crucial in itself and an inspiration to others. John Carnac, a major in the Bengal army, wrote to his patron Clive after winning a victory in January 1761, "If I have any merit in our late affair it is entirely owing to the lesson I have learned from you, always to push forward". A willingness to advance against vastly greater forces was to be crucial to British military success in India, and to link Clive to Wellesley. This was not only a matter of the commanders. Carnac noted how his infantry bravely advanced into the face of cannon, as Wellesley's men were to do at Assaye in 1803, adding "I was so happy as to have under my command a set of people who were as ready to advance as I could be to lead them".[39] The troops, themselves, were often discontented with their conditions, Eyre Coote noting in July 1757, "the soldiers during the whole of the march uttering expressions full of discontent; complaining of the fatigues they suffered . . . their want of shoes and arrack; and that their prize money had not been paid them".[40]

The path from Plassey to British control of Bengal was not smooth: the British had to face both attempts to reimpose a Muslim ascendancy and the problems of establishing a stable regime there. In 1760, the Company's sepoy force in Bengal rose to 5,000 and, under Major John Caillaud, it repelled an invasion of Bihar by Shah Zodah, the eldest son of the Mughal Emperor. The British were short of men and uniforms and were delayed by the need to have the road made passable for their artillery.[41] Nevertheless, Caillaud was victorious on 22 February. Gilbert Ironside reported that, although the British cannon inflicted casualties, the Mughal forces continued to advance bravely and pressed hard the forces of Britain's ally, the young Nawab of Bengal:

> It was then the Major advanced at the head of his sepoys. They drew up quite close to the flank of the enemy while they engaged the Nawab, threw in their fire, then rushed in with their bayonets.

The Nawab's cavalry then attacked and the Mughal forces collapsed.[42] British tactics, based on firing once or twice and then charging, greatly impressed Indian opponents. Chittagong on the east side of the Bay of Bengal was seized by the British the same year.

With the encouragement of Caillaud and the Company's officials, the increasingly distrusted Mir Jaffir was removed by his son-in-law, Mir Qasim, but he fell foul of the excessive financial demands of the Company and the private interests of its avaricious officials. War broke out in 1763, the British helped by the absence of another rival able to divert their forces.[43] Indeed, troops that had taken part in the successful siege of Pondicherry were transferred to Bengal. Mir Qasim's substantial force included infantry trained to fight like sepoys and effective artillery. His opponent, Major Thomas Adams, commander of the far less numerous forces of both Crown and Company in Bengal, engaged Mir Qasim at Gheriah and Andwanala. The former was a particularly close-fought battle in which Mir Qasim's men broke through part of the British line and captured two of its guns, but they were at last beaten back. By the end of October Mir Qasim had been heavily defeated.

Fighting resumed the following year, but, again, the British were victorious. The Company's Bengal army was increased to 16,000 men. At Patna (3 May 1764) British grapeshot halted the advance of hostile infantry, and, when a cavalry attack was launched by the Indians, they were driven back by heavy artillery fire.[44] At Buxar (23 October 1764), Sir Hector Munro and 7,000 men of the East India Company army, including 1,500 British soldiers, defeated Mir Qasim and his allies, Shah Alam II, the Mughal Emperor, and Shuja-ud-dowla, the Nawab-Wazir of Oudh, who together fielded a force of 50,000 men. The Indian army had more cannon, but British grapeshot, musket fire and bayonets blocked the Indian cavalry and the Indians were driven from the field. The British troops were provided with 24 rounds each. Nevertheless, the hard-fought battle lasted three hours.[45]

Buxar was followed by the Treaty of Allahabad (1765), which recognized the British position in Bengal and Bihar, and thus stabilized the situation from the Indian as much as the British perspective. The Mughal Emperor conferred the right to collect revenue and conduct civil justice, the *diwan*, on the Company. Shuja-ud-dowla accepted the settlement as a result of the Company's invasion of Oudh, while Mir Qasim was left as an inconsequential exile. Bengal and Bihar were to provide a solid source of revenue and manpower, and to be the basis of British imperial power in Asia; the Madras and, to a greater extent, Bombay presidencies of the East India Company lacked the resources of the Bengal presidency, and were frequently poorly governed. Neither for a while made great headway against local rivals, but Bengal enabled the East India Company to act as an effective territorial power, not only in the Ganges valley, but also elsewhere in India.

Conflict in North America, 1749–63

The Peace of Aix-la-Chapelle was followed by a determined French effort to reimpose control in the hinterland of New France. Fort St Jean was rebuilt in 1748, in order to strengthen the French position near Lake Champlain: a new wagon road linked the fort to Montréal. Niagara was also rebuilt and in 1750 the French erected Fort Rouillé (Toronto).

In 1749 a small expedition under Céleron de Blainville was sent into the Ohio Valley, but it had little effect, bar burying lead plates asserting French sovereignty. The previous year, the British government had given the Ohio Company title to half a million acres in the region and the French found the Native Americans trading with British merchants. In 1752 the French tried again, attacking the Miami who were openly supporting the British. The Miami chief, Memeskia, was killed and eaten by pro-French Natives in a raid on the village of Pickawillany where the British post was destroyed.

The expulsion of British traders was maintained as French troops moved into the area and in 1753–4 the French built four forts between Lake Erie and the junction of the Ohio and the Monongahela Rivers, although this alienated many of the Native population and led some of the Ohio Natives to seek British support.[46] Further north the French competed actively with the Hudson's Bay Company: by 1753 a line of French posts lay across the canoe routes to the bay.[47]

The recovery of French activity after 1748 threatened to exclude the British not only from the Ohio Valley, but also from the entire interior of the continent. This threat exacerbated and was exacerbated by the failure of commissioners to settle the North American boundaries of Britain and France in negotiations.

There was also tension on the Atlantic seaboard. The French strengthened Louisbourg once it was returned to them. The British in turn developed a major base on the east coast of Nova Scotia at Halifax. Begun in 1749, a set of fortifications was completed the following year. Halifax enhanced the British military and political presence in the sensitive region near the mouth of the St Lawrence, and this presence was strengthened by the settlement nearby of German and Dutch Protestants.[48]

The British government had no wish for war, but could not accept French claims in the Ohio Valley. British complaints, however, were rejected and on 17 April 1754 a 500-strong French force forced the small colonial garrison of 40 men in Fort Prince George (near modern Pittsburg) to surrender. This indicated the duality of great power confrontation, when conflict on the periphery could be entered into, despite the huge implications in Europe and even when there was no intention on the part of the metropolitan governments to wage war.

In May 1754 George Washington advanced at the head of a small force of Virginia militia into the contested area, defeating a smaller French detachment on 28 May. The French, however, in turn advanced in greater numbers and on 3 July Washington was obliged to surrender at Fort Necessity: he was outnumbered 400 to 700. That summer, Native Americans from Canada and Abenakis raided settlements in Massachusetts, near New Hampshire and New York, advancing to within 15 miles of Albany.[49] At that point, the British had fewer than 900 troops in North America. Charles Townshend MP, a Lord of the Admiralty, sent the Duke of Newcastle an account of the situation:

> The military force, maintained by the Crown on the continent of North America, consists of seven independent companies, usually stationed in South Carolina, Virginia and New York, and each company, when complete, consists of one hundred men, but, as neither the officers or private men have ever seen any service and the companies are generally at a great distance upon separate duty,

they can not be thought as they are now employed to be of any general service.

The memorandum proposed that the troops be gathered together and placed under a commander who had "served in America, where there are so many peculiar circumstances attending the manner of carrying on war". Locally raised troops were seen as best: "If a regiment should be sent from hence, the transportation will be extremely expensive, and the men both new to the service and strangers to the climate. But if a regiment should be raised there, the expense will be much less, and the men not only accustomed to the climate, but in a degree to the service". Rather than resting on the defensive, and offering inadequate protection, the memorandum proposed an advance to cut the forward French positions and their Native supporters off from Montréal. It was claimed that only offensive operations would deter the French from future attacks.[50]

Domestic political pressures obliged the British government to adopt a firm attitude in 1755 and regulars were dispatched in order to mount attacks. However, having decided not to attack the major French bases of Louisbourg and in the St Lawrence, the British dissipated their strength with three separate attacks, although that also reflected the varied priorities of the northern colonies that produced appreciable numbers of troops. The most successful was that in which naval power could be used, an attack on the French forts that threatened Nova Scotia. Fort Beauséjour fell on 16 June 1755, to a force of 250 regulars and 2,000 New England militia under Lieutenant-Colonel Robert Monckton, and two days later Fort Gaspereau surrendered.[51]

The British marked their presence by renaming the forts Cumberland and Moncton, but, more harshly, by deporting the Acadians. Ruled by Britain since 1713, they were suspected of disloyalty. In 1755 more than half the 13,000 Acadians were deported, others following in 1758. Their treatment was less harsh than that of the Native Americans, but it served as a clear indication that the victims of British power were not only non-Europeans. The deportation was ordered by British officials in Nova Scotia, not London. It was an indication of the extent to which policy was set at the imperial periphery.[52]

Another force, largely of regulars under the inexperienced Major-General Edward Braddock, had already been defeated on 9 July near Fort Duquesne by the out-numbered French and their Indian allies, who made excellent use of tree cover. Braddock's army, fresh from Britain, lacked experience of North American operations and Braddock had deprived himself of the possibility of effective Native support by refusing support from Shingas, the Delaware chief, who had sought a promise that the Ohio region should remain in Native hands. From a Native viewpoint, one crucial issue was whether the British or French posed the greater threat to the Ohio hinterland

and river systems. Braddock had very few Native auxiliaries, and none of the expected Cherokee and Catawba, and lacked British light infantry, an arm which the British had as yet failed adequately to develop. The Virginia militia in his force had very little experience of frontier warfare.

Braddock left Fort Cumberland on 30 May, cutting a road through the trees in order to move his cannon and supplies. By 9 July, he was within eight miles of his target. Fort Duquesne would have been vulnerable to cannon – indeed in 1758 the French were to abandon it before such an attack could be mounted – but in 1755 they took the tactical advantage from the British strategic offensive by advancing to attack. The army's response to the ambush was inadequate, unsurprisingly so, as they were not prepared for such an engagement. Instead of attacking the ambushing forces, they held their ground, thus offering excellent targets. Lieutenant-Colonel Thomas Gage reported

> a visible terror and confusion appeared amongst the men . . . The same infatuation attended the whole; none would form a line of battle, and the whole army was very soon mixed together, twelve or fourteen deep, firing away at nothing but trees, and killing many of our own men and officers. The cannon were soon deserted by those that covered them. The artillery did their duty perfectly well, but, from the nature of the country, could do little execution . . . the enemy always giving way, whenever they advanced even on the most faint attack . . . I can't ascribe their behaviour to any other cause than the talk of the country people, ever since our arrival in America – the woodsmen and Indian traders, who were continually telling the soldiers, that if they attempted to fight Indians in a regular manner, they would certainly be defeated . . . the only excuse I can get from them is that they were quite dispirited from the great fatigue they had undergone and not receiving a sufficient quantity of food; and further that they did not expect the enemy would come down so suddenly.

Braddock was killed and his force fled after two and a half hours. Of the 1,459 British troops, 977 were killed or wounded; the French lost only 40 from their force of about 250 regulars and militia and 640 Natives.

Braddock's defeat posed the challenge of how best to operate in North America. Sackville had expressed the confidence of a regular that the conflict would be a conventional matter of sieges:

> If Braddock gets his cannon over the mountains and through the marshes I do not doubt of his success, but I apprehend great difficulties in Crown Point, because that is the strongest fort, and is the nearest at hand to be reinforced from Montreal and Quebec. If they force that, Canada is open to us.

James De Lancey, Lieutenant Governor of New York, responded to the defeat by emphasizing the need for central direction and the value of artillery: "the expediency of having, at all times, in this city, as being nearly the center of the British colonies, a number of cannon and arms, and a large quantity of ammunition ready, on all occasions, to be disposed of for such services as the general His Majesty shall think fit to appoint for North America, shall judge proper". In contrast, Horatio Sharp, the Governor of Maryland, took note of frontier conditions and suggested that "in case of another campaign against Fort Duquesne . . . there ought to be two, or at least one, thousand of our woodsmen or hunters, who are marksmen and used to rifles, to precede the army and engage the Indians in their own way".[53]

Not only regulars were defeated. A militia force under William Johnson advancing from Albany towards Fort St Frédéric was ambushed near Lake George on 8 September 1755. The advancing force fled back to Johnson's camp, pursued by the French. The latter then attacked the camp, but were unsuccessful and took heavy casualties from cannon and musket fire: they no longer enjoyed surprise and were now fighting on ground of Johnson's choosing. Fortified positions gave a marked edge to defenders, but only if the battle came to them. The advance was abandoned.

War was formally declared in 1756. Greater French interest in Canada had led to a growth in the size of the Louisbourg garrison to 2,500 regulars with a supporting naval squadron. Six battalions, totalling 3,000 men, had been sent to Canada in 1755, although 330 were captured when two ships were seized by Boscawen. Louisbourg and Québec were well fortified. The French were outnumbered, however, both in regulars and in local militia, the latter a reflection of greater British settlement in North America. Nevertheless, their new commander, Louis Joseph, Marquis de Montcalm, a Major-General with no experience in North American warfare, decided that it was best to take the initiative and thus counter the British numerical advantage by achieving a local superiority in strength. In August 1756 he captured Forts Ontario, George and Oswego, taking 1,620 prisoners for the loss of only 30 men. The British were therefore driven from Lake Ontario. The French also established Fort Carillon as an advanced base at the southern end of Lake Champlain.

That year the British did not mount an effective response. The government was weak and demoralized, and concerned about the defence of Britain from possible invasion. The new commander in North America, John, 4th Earl of Loudoun, a veteran of the '45, was unwilling to search for a compromise on the reimbursement and control of colonial troops and, as a result, there was scant co-operation. In 1757, however, a large fleet was sent to Halifax. This was designed for an expedition against first Louisbourg and then Québec,[54] but poor weather and then the presence of a French squadron deterred the British commanders from attacking. Instead, it was Montcalm who advanced, besieging Fort William Henry at the head of

Lake George with a far larger force. The fort was bombarded with 30 cannon Montcalm had had hauled overland, and it fell rapidly.

Thus, as a result of three years of operations, British forces had secured Acadia, but made no impact on Louisbourg, while in the interior the Ohio River valley remained in French hands and Montcalm had driven the British from Lake Ontario and back towards the Hudson. He had successfully taken the initiative. British failure led to criticism in London and attacks on poor leadership. The *Herald* claimed in its issue of 20 October 1757,

> With a vast land and sea force in North America, nothing has been done. And with the odds of twenty inhabitants to one against the French on that continent, our forts are taken, the out-settlements of our colonies continually ravaged, and the whole body of every one of them kept in perpetual terror and alarm!

An unimpressed William Pitt the Elder was determined to do better.[55] He had Loudoun, whom he blamed for failure removed, promised to provide funds from Britain and restricted the authority of Loudoun's successor over the colonial authorities. In 1758 Pitt took a leading role in planning a massive three-pronged offensive on New France, that took the initiative from the French. Separate expeditions were to attack Louisbourg, Carillon (Ticonderoga) and Fort Duquesne. The largest force was sent under General James Abercromby against Carillon,[56] but it was the smaller Louisbourg force, under Generals Jeffrey Amherst and James Wolfe, and Admiral Boscawen, that was successful. It contained first rate units and the intention was for it to proceed that same summer to Québec.

Troops were landed on Cape Breton on 8 June. As in 1745, they concentrated on the landward defences of Louisbourg. British cannon breached the walls and Louisbourg surrendered on 26 July. The British force of 13,000 suffered 560 killed or wounded, but 3,000 French were taken prisoner. In addition, the French naval squadron of five warships was lost – three to bombardment by the British artillery and two when British warships penetrated the harbour on the night of 25–6 July – and thus there was no challenge to British naval operations in the St Lawrence.[57]

In contrast, the advance against Carillon was a costly failure. A frontal assault, an "unlucky ill conducted attack",[58] on 8 July 1758, led to heavy casualties. The British abandoned the operation, having lost 1,900 killed or wounded out of a force of 6,400 regulars and 9,000 American provincials. In contrast, Montcalm's 3,500 strong force suffered only 400 casualties.

The third offensive was successful. An army of 7,000, mostly American provincials under Brigadier-General John Forbes, advanced on Fort Duquesne, building a road as they moved forward, and the 300 poorly supplied defenders withdrew on 30 November. The advance indicated the value of experience and the ability to learn from mistakes. Forbes was

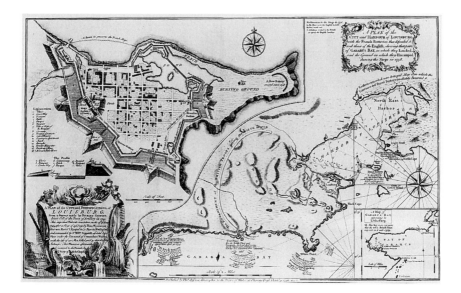

A Plan of Louisbourg to show the siege of 1758. Devoting attention to the landing sites, the plan captured the importance of army–navy co-operation in the amphibious deployment of British striking power. The publication of the plan testified to public interest. *National Maritime Museum, London.*

determined to learn from Braddock. He took a shorter route and cautiously advanced from one fortified position to another. As a result, an attack on his vanguard failed: Forbes' men fell back behind breastworks where they could be supported by cannon. The French position was weakened when in October Pennsylvania authorities promised the Native Americans that they would not claim land west of the Appalachians. The consequent shift of Native support obliged the French to give up the Ohio region. Forbes' success strengthened Native advocates of conciliation. Viewed from Europe, this was still a two-sided conflict, whereas on the ground the shifting support and fears of Native groups could be decisive. The captured and rebuilt Fort Duquesne was named Fort Pitt.

In August, another British force, composed largely of American provincials under Lieutenant-Colonel John Bradstreet, sailed across Lake Ontario and destroyed crucial French supplies and the French lake squadron at Fort Frontenac. It was so far from the major British bases that the French had failed to defend it adequately. Due both to greater experience of conflict in North America and to the growing importance of irregular warfare in Europe, British forces were becoming more used to "wilderness warfare", a valuable enhancement of the capability of part of the army.[59] Further east, also in August, a British amphibious force from Louisbourg captured Port La Joie on Ile Saint-Jean. Fort Amherst was built at the port, the island

141

became Prince Edward Island and its population was largely deported to France. British raiding parties from Louisbourg also successfully raided the French fishing stations on the Gaspé Peninsula that September.

Despite these successes, British strategy and its execution were weak in 1758. The British offensives had failed to provide mutual support and Montcalm had been able to concentrate his efforts against Abercromby. The loss of Louisbourg, however, increased the danger of a British amphibious attack up the St Lawrence, while the fall of Fort Frontenac and Fort Duquesne increased the vulnerability of the French on and near Lakes Erie and Ontario and cut French supply links, rendering the positions to the west of the Appalachians indefensible. This undermined Montcalm's defensive success at Carillon. Yet had the war ended in the winter of 1758–9 the British would have had relatively little to show for their campaigning.

In 1758 the British had made the Hudson–Lake Champlain axis a major priority. In 1759 they concentrated on the St Lawrence, where their naval power could be used most effectively.[60] American provincial troops garrisoned Louisbourg, freeing regulars for the advance on Québec. Benefiting from reliable pilots and nearby harbour facilities at Halifax, both of which had been lacking in 1690 and 1711, the navy convoyed a force of 8,600 men under Wolfe to near Québec. Although young, Wolfe (1727–59) was very experienced. He had served at Dettingen, Falkirk, Culloden and Lawfeldt, taken part in the Rochefort expediton of 1757, and had a well-deserved reputation for energy and determination.[61]

Wolfe arrived near Québec on 26 June, but the natural strength of the position, French fortifications and the skilful character of Montcalm's dispositions thwarted him for over two months. Wolfe's initial operations along the Beauport shore were unsuccessful. On 31 July an attack on French positions was repelled by Montcalm's larger army, with the British suffering 440 casualties to the French 60. As winter approached, it seemed increasingly likely that the British would fail. Wolfe risked a bold move. James Cook, later famous as the explorer of the Pacific, had thoroughly surveyed the St Lawrence and British warships had passed beyond Québec from 18 July onwards and made upriver raids on 8 August. The army was to follow. On 1–3 September, British troops left the Montmorency camp and moved along the southern bank of the river opposite Québec. On 10 September, Wolfe, having reconnoitred the river, decided to land at Anse au Foulon to the west of the city. After delays due to the weather, the British landed in the early hours of 13 September. Some 200 light infantry scaled the cliffs and successfully attacked a French camp of 100 men. The remainder of the British force, fewer than 4,500 men, then landed and advanced to the Plains of Abraham to the south-west of the city.

Montcalm, with a total of 13,000 men in the area, was in a strong position, with fresh troops approaching Wolfe's rear, but, instead of waiting on the defensive and uniting his forces, he chose to attack with the men immediately available. The French advanced in columns, but their centre veered to the right and their formations became disorganized. The British waited until the French were about 100 feet away, then opened regular volley fire. This close-range onslaught caused the French columns to disintegrate and retreat before the British began their bayonet charge. A British participant recorded:

> About 9 o'clock the French army had drawn up under the walls of the town, and advanced towards us briskly and in good order. We stood to receive them; they began their fire at a distance, we reserved ours, and as they came nearer fired on them by divisions, this did execution and seemed to check them a little, however they still advanced pretty quick, we increased our fire without altering our position, and, when they were within less than a hundred yards, gave them a full fire, fixed our bayonets, and, under cover of the smoke the whole line, charged.

Wolfe had already been fatally wounded before the French advance, and Montcalm was mortally wounded as his troops retreated. French and British casualties were comparable, about 650 each, but French morale was shattered. Although Québec had not been captured and more French troops arrived immediately after the battle, the French officers decided at a council of war not to risk battle again, but to retreat upriver. The decision to retreat was reversed a few days later, but, even as a French relief force approached Québec, it surrendered on 18 September.

The capture of Québec dominated attention, but there were other important successes in 1759. From Albany, the British advanced to Lake Ontario. The French, short of Native American support, abandoned some of the forts there and near Lake Erie. The French did contest the Niagara positions, but their advancing force was defeated by defensive fire at La Belle-Famille (24 July) by a force of regulars, provincials and Native Americans under Colonel William Massey. The well-fortified Fort Niagara surrendered to a large British force two days later. The original British commander of the besieging force, Brigadier-General John Prideaux, had been killed when a shell from a British mortar exploded prematurely. As at Québec, although on a far smaller scale, the defeat of the local French field force had been followed by the surrender of their principal position; hope of relief had been lost.

Further east, the British under Amherst were also successful on the Hudson–Lake Champlain axis. Their attack on the St Lawrence obliged Montcalm to pull back. In the face of Amherst's advance, Carillon was abandoned on the night of 26–27 July, occupied by the British and renamed Ticonderoga. Crown Point followed four days later: the French were short of men, and supplies. Amherst introduced a number of tactical changes to increase the effectiveness of his men in the forest environment. The customary three rank formation was replaced by one two deep, and Amherst tried to develop a light infantry capability. One-tenth of his regulars were chosen to form a light infantry unit, and they were armed with fusils.

The death of Wolfe and the capture of Québec are generally seen as marking the end of New France. This is mistaken. The caveat, had the war ended then, is especially appropriate in 1759, given that that was the year of the planned French invasion and, indeed, had French forces landed in Britain, then the British troops in North America would have been sorely missed.

Indeed, the French forces left in Canada, although cut off from supplies and reinforcements from France, were no passive victims, no more than Lally was in India. Six months after the fall of Québec, the substantial French army still in Canada under Lévis advanced to recapture it. Brigadier James Murray had been left in command of a garrison of 4,000 troops, but his position was weakened by the closure of the St Lawrence by ice, which deprived him of both naval support and supplies. The latter contributed to the scurvy that weakened the garrison; other diseases also caused serious inroads. When Lévis' much larger army advanced to threaten British outposts, Murray repeated Montcalm's mistake, engaging on the Plains of Abraham when it would have been wiser to remain on the defensive in the city. In the battle of Sainte-Foy (28 April 1760), one of the numerous engagements forgotten in the teleological account of Britain's imperial rise, the French carried the day with a bayonet charge that benefited from a lack of order in the British force and the British retreated with heavier casualties into Québec: 1,088 dead and wounded out of 3,866 troops, compared to 833 French casualties.

The city was then besieged, but the French batteries did not begin firing until 11 May. They had little time to do damage: a British fleet destroyed the French ships in the St Lawrence and arrived with reinforcements on 16 May. Lévis raised the siege and fell back to Montréal. In the summer of 1760, the three-pronged British advance finally triumphed. Troops advanced from Québec, Crown Point and, in largest numbers, Lake Ontario, under Murray, Colonel William Haviland and Amherst, respectively. The outnumbered French abandoned most of their positions, although there was fighting around Fort Lévis in August. The surrender of Chambly on 1 September opened the way for Haviland. By 6 September, Amherst's force lay above the city on the St Lawrence, Murray's below it and Haviland was approaching, like Amherst using water transport as much as possible. On 8 September, the Marquis de Vaudreuil, the Governor-General of New France, and the 3,520 French in Montréal surrendered to Amherst's force of 17,000. Trois Rivières surrendered three days later. Canada had fallen.[62]

The 1760 campaign was an impressive triumph of resources and planning.[63] It is, however, appropriate that the fall of Québec should receive most attention. At that stage, the fate of war was more in the balance. Moreover, Wolfe in his death provided a powerful icon of self-sacrifice and success, an image of imperial warfare that was to possess great potency.[64]

The Cherokee War, 1760–1

The surrender at Montréal did not bring conflict to an end in North America. In 1760 war broke out with the Cherokee, a generally pro-British tribe whose hunting lands in modern east Tennessee and west North Carolina were under pressure from the advancing frontier of European-American activity, control, and settlement. Cherokee pressure on the frontiers led Governor William Lyttleton of South Carolina to plead with Amherst for military assistance. The force of 1,300 regulars, including 400 Scottish Highlanders under Colonel Archibald Montgomery, that was sent in the Spring of 1760 to suppress the Cherokee faced logistical problems and also met guerrilla resistance organized by Oconostota, and fell back; Montgomery had been instructed to return for the campaign in Canada while the Cherokee's rifles were more effective than Montgomery's muskets. In turn, the Cherokee laid siege to Fort Loudoun and captured the starving garrison on 9 August as it retreated. The garrison had surrendered the fort two days earlier, on the promise of a safe pass to Fort Prince George, but many of the Cherokee wanted revenge for the earlier murder of some of their kinsmen held as hostages in the fort. British commentators linked the conflict to the war with France, John Leland fearing "if the war should continue that the French will molest our southern colonies, as South Carolina is already attacked by Indians instigated by them".[65]

After a truce, the British invaded Cherokee territory again in 1761. Their mixed force – of regular troops, Carolina Rangers and allied Native Americans – under Major James Grant indicated the variety of forces that officers had to learn to command and combine. A scorched-earth policy in which settlements and crops were burnt was countered by Cherokee resistance based on highland hideouts but food shortages and despair engendered by failure led the Cherokee to agree terms, return Fort Loudoun, and yield territory in 1761.[66]

This was a very different struggle to that against the French regulars, one that indicated the variety of tasks that the army and auxiliary forces was expected to discharge. Already, in 1759, Amherst had sent 200 American rangers under Major Robert Rogers to surprise and destroy the main Abenaki village of St François, a task they successfully accomplished, although a collapse of supply arrangements on their retreat forced the men to eat the corpses of colleagues. The raid on their hitherto invulnerable base greatly wrecked Abenaki confidence.[67]

145

Fighting the French: Africa, the West Indies and India, 1756–63

Africa

Although Canada offered the most spectacular and lasting successes, British forces were victorious elsewhere against France during the Seven Years' War. Forts St Louis and Gorée, the French bases in West Africa, were easily taken in May and December 1758, respectively. They were poorly fortified and inadequately garrisoned, lacked hinterlands that could provide support, and were particularly exposed to naval attack.[68] Their fall lent support to earlier mercantile claims that the British position in West Africa was supported better by "men of war properly stationed and timely relieved", rather than by forts.[69] The British were in part motivated by a desire to gain control of the trade in gum arabic, which was important to the textile industry.

However, the expeditions had an improvized quality. In April–May 1758 the troops lacked fresh water, tents and a plan. Their success was fortuitous, largely a matter of being in the right place. A chance crossing of the bar at the mouth of the river and the beating off of a French attack, led the French to surrender. The British squadron, carrying 200 marines and "a detachment of Artillery People", had left Plymouth on 9 March and arrived off the Senegal River on 24 April, crossing the bar five days later. That day

> the enemy with seven vessels three of which were armed with ten guns each, made a show of attacking our small craft, and kept a kind of running fire, but were soon repulsed and obliged to retire up the river. The marines and seamen, to the number of seven hundred landed, and got the artillery on shore.

On 30 April, before this force could attack Fort Louis, the French offered terms; on 1 May these were accepted and on the 2nd the British took possession of the fort; 232 French troops surrendered.

The British were less successful with the local population. A dispute over the right to pillage goods from ships that ran aground on the bar led to a clash two months later with the Wolof state of Kajor. A surprise night attack on an encamped British force led to 53 casualties among the latter.[70]

West Indies

The major French possessions in the West Indies were tougher targets, not least because they were more strongly fortified and garrisoned. Nevertheless, Guadeloupe was captured in 1759 and Martinique in 1762, with naval firepower playing a major role. Such a bland summary, however, omits Major-General Peregrine Hopson's failure at Martinique in 1759. Hopson's troops landed successfully, but encountered strong resistance from the largely mulatto militia that fought in a dispersed fashion and took advantage of the natural cover, denying the British easy targets. Hopson felt he had inadequate forces to both besiege the citadel at Fort Royale and maintain his lines of communication to the landing base. Guadeloupe was a second best in 1759. The French position at Basseterre was heavily bombarded by Commodore John Moore's warships and, after the defending batteries had been silenced, troops were able to land and occupy the town. Driven into the mountains, the French soon surrendered.[71]

In 1761 a large force under Andrew, 5th Lord Rollo, freed by the fall of Canada, was sent from New York to the West Indies. In co-operation with a squadron under Sir James Douglas, that provided covering fire, Rollo conquered Dominica in two days: it surrendered on 8 July, the day after Rollo landed. In a domino process, Rollo then joined the force assembling on Barbados for the attack on Martinique.

This force, under Major-General Robert Monckton, twice as large as that commanded by Hopson, landed on Martinique on 16 January 1762. Supported by sailors and marines from the fleet, Monckton was able to clear the fortified hills behind Fort Royale, to build a battery on Mount Garne from which the fort could be bombarded, to cut it off from its hinterland and to maintain his own communications. With no hope of relief, the French surrendered less than three weeks after the landing. The fall of Fort Royale was followed by the surrender of the island on 4 February, and by the collapse of the French position in the Windward Islands. Grenada, St Lucia and St Vincent all fell to the British in 1762. St Lucia surrendered as soon as a small British squadron under Captain Augustus Hervey approached the principal settlement. The French were left with only Saint-Domingue, a far larger island, and one that was not attacked.

India

The war in Africa and the West Indies was one of amphibious operations and sieges. The French lacked field armies in both areas, sent few reinforcements, and remained on the defensive. In contrast, in the Carnatic in India the French took the offensive, seeking to regain the position they had only recently lost. Their commander, Thomas, Count de Lally, the son of an Irish Jacobite and a veteran of Dettingen, Fontenoy and Lawfeldt, went with his troops aboard d'Aché's squadron and reached Pondicherry in the spring of 1758. Fort St David, which had successfully resisted the French in the War of Austrian Succession, was rapidly besieged and it fell on 2 June 1758. Lally moved on to nearby Madras, beginning the siege on 13 December 1758. However, d'Aché provided insufficient support, the British under Stringer Lawrence were superior in artillery, Fort St George had been strengthened since the siege of 1746, a force commanded by Caillaud harassed French communications with Pondicherry, and the French were also affected by the victory of the British under Francis Forde in the Northern Circars. As a result, Lally, who was continually rowing with the French Company's authorities in Pondicherry, raised the siege of Madras on 17 February 1759. The dynamism of the French recovery had been lost.

Forde had been a major in the regular army before transferring as colonel to act as second-in-command to his friend Clive in Bengal. Clive believed that the British would only be secure if the French were driven from the Circars: the coastal region between Orissa and the Carnatic. From there pressure could be brought to bear on Hyderabad, while control of the Circars allowed the British to transfer troops overland between Bengal and the Carnatic. The Circars thus served to add a useful axis to British power and also to emphasize the possibilities of co-operation between Calcutta and Madras.

At the start of 1759 Forde was sent to the Circars at the head of a force of 2,500 men and 12 cannon. He landed at Vishakhapatnam, defeated a French force under Conflans at Condore, captured Rajahmundry, and, on the night of 25–6 April, stormed Masulipatam at the head of 900. Forde's force suffered 284 casualties, but the poorly led French force of 2,600 surrendered and, with Masulipatam lost, the British were established at a crucial point on the east coast of India. The Circars were ceded to Britain in 1766.

The British had regained the initiative and they exploited it to effect. Returning to Bengal, Forde in November 1759 ambushed and defeated a Dutch East India Company force that was trying to capture the British positions in Bengal, at Bedara near Chandernagore while the Dutch ships were seized by East India Company ships at Kalpi. On 22 January 1760 in the Carnatic the French commander Lally was defeated at the battle of Wandewash, the decisive engagement of the war in India and one in which British artillery played a crucial role. Relying on British troops, rather than sepoys, Eyre Coote, whose forces outnumbered Lally by 5,400 to 2,800, captured the French camp and artillery. Coote had served under Clive at Plassey. He had captured Wandewash on 30 November 1759, been besieged there by Lally, and the battle arose when his army sortied out against the French.

Wandewash was followed by the rapid fall of hostile positions such as Cuddalore. Arcot was besieged at the beginning of February. John Call, the Chief-Engineer on the Coromandel Coast, recorded that on the 5th "we had three batteries playing on Arcot. The garrison being strong made a great fire, dismounted two of our guns the first day, and killed or wounded 40 of our men in carrying on the works, but on the 10th when our approaches were on the glacis", the French surrendered.[72] Karikal was also captured. The French abandoned many of their posts as they fell back on

Pondicherry. The remaining French possessions in India were captured by early 1761; Pondicherry, the major French base, was besieged on 7 April 1760 and Lally surrendered on 15 January after he had abandoned hope of relief. Call deployed a large number of cannon,[73] Rear-Admiral Charles Stevens' powerful blockading fleet dissuaded the French squadron under Raymond at Pulicat from attempting a relief and the garrison was desperately short of food. Lally was taken to London, returned to France, imprisoned for surrendering Pondicherry, tried and beheaded, treatment that fired Voltaire to rage.[74]

War with Spain, 1762–3

The effectiveness of British amphibious operations was demonstrated most dramatically against Spain. British successes in 1762 also offered an obvious contrast to earlier failures and disappointments during the War of the Austrian Succession: there was to be no repetition of the failure at Cartagena in 1741.

The major British effort was directed against Havana, the principal Spanish base in the West Indies and their leading naval facility in the New World. A British force of 12,000 under George, 3rd Earl of Albemarle, a protégé of Cumberland, covered by Admiral Sir George Pocock and 22 ships of the line, landed to the east of Havana on 7 June 1762. Operations were concentrated against Fort Moro which commanded the channel from the sea to the harbour and was protected by a very deep landward ditch. On 1 July the British batteries opened fire, supported by three warships, but damage from Spanish fire forced the latter to abandon the bombardment. The summer passed in siegeworks, which were hindered by the bare rock in front of the fortress, and in artillery duels. A third of the British force was lost to malaria and yellow fever, but the Spanish batteries were silenced by heavier British fire.[75] On 30 July, the British exploded two mines on either side of the ditch, creating an earth ramp across it and a breach that was stormed successfully, enabling them to capture the fort. From there, British artillery could dominate the city and it surrendered on 13 August. The fleet in the harbour, which included 12 ships of the line, also surrendered. By attacking Havana, the British had wrecked Spanish naval power in the West Indies.[76] Albemarle and Pocock each received £122,697 10s 6d as their share of the prize.

The expedition against Manila, the capital of the Philippines, was on a smaller scale and more daring, but Manila lacked the defences of Havana: the fortifications were weak, the garrison small, and attack was not anticipated. The project was mounted from Madras where its commander, Colonel William Draper, complained that the small numbers he had been allocated "will sufficiently evince the impossibility of my acting against the place with the formalities of a siege. My hopes are placed in the effects of a bombardment or *coup de main*". Draper could only dispose of a single battalion of regulars, which, with additional sepoys, pioneers and French deserters, provided a force of only 1,700 men. Fortunately co-operation with the naval force, of eight ships of the line and two East Indiamen under Rear-Admiral Samuel Cornish, was very good. The admiral landed about 1,000 sailors and marines to help the attack. Arriving in Manila Bay on 23 September and landing on the 25th, Draper captured Manila on 6 October after a vigorous advance that contrasted with the purposeful, but slower operations against Havana. He had to move fast because of the breaking of the monsoon. This was a serious problem, as was the opposition from Filipino irregulars. Fortunately, Captain Richard Kempenfelt's capture of the well-equipped naval dockyard of Cavite enabled repairs to the British warships, while Manila fell rapidly. Colonel George Monson recorded:

> An eight gun battery was finished about three hundred yards from the wall the 2nd of October at night, and opened the 3rd in the morning on the south west bastion, which immediately silenced the enemy's guns and made a breach in the salient angle of the bastion, the fourth at night batteries were begun to take off the defences of the south east bastion and of the small bastions on the west side of the town; which were opened the fifth by ten o'clock in the morning and had so good an effect, that the general gave out orders for storming the place next day; which was done about seven in the morning, with very little loss, on our side.[77]

However, the fall of Manila did not end Spanish resistance. British plans had dangerously exaggerated the co-operation to be expected from the Filipinos. Pasig was taken, but, after initial success, the British were unable to maintain their position in Bulacan. Nevertheless, the capture of Manila encouraged British interest in the Pacific that did not cease when the city was returned to Spain in 1764.[78]

Conclusions

Although successful, the operations against Havana and Manila indicated the parameters within which the British had to operate. The very ability to mount such expeditions safely presupposed naval superiority. Once landed, the troops had to overcome fortified positions before disease could attenuate their numbers and energy.

Yet the expeditions also displayed the strength of the British position at the close of the Seven Years' War. Naval superiority gave them the ability to choose where to direct efforts and enabled the application of strength to achieve a local superiority at a time of choosing at crucial points. The danger of losing naval control was demonstrated in 1762 when a French squadron of five warships under Louis, Count of Haussonville reached Newfoundland. On 27 June an 800 strong force attacked St John's, defeating the 80 defenders. The British mounted a counter-expedition from Halifax and on 18 September the town was regained in an assault by 1,560 regulars and American provincials. Augustus Hervey had already captured a French frigate carrying supplies for the force in St John's. Earlier, in November 1758, the French had sent a squadron to the West Indies to try to counter British operations, but it was greatly outnumbered by Commodore Moore's fleet and was unable to prevent the fall of Guadeloupe.

If Britain's opponent was another European imperial power, the seizure of major bases was sufficient to cause the collapse of their position. It was not necessary to conquer New France, Cuba or the Philippines, only the principal positions. Similarly, had the British captured New Orleans they would have gained effective control of Louisiana. The British did not defeat France's Native American allies, but won a largely conventional war against French Canada. The situation in mainland Spanish America with its relatively high European and creole population might have been different, but French colonies lacked such population, were more dependent on trade, and were much more vulnerable to the fall of their principal base and, indeed, to blockade. The latter was difficult to maintain, but trade with the St Lawrence could be effectively cut, and Canada was thus particularly vulnerable. Demographic factors were also important; indeed in 1750 François-Marie Durand, the French chargé d'affaires in London, had urged his government to pay attention to the large number of emigrants to British America.[79]

The French empire depended on the maintenance of its major bases, but, unless the French could threaten the British at sea, these bases could be isolated and attacked with overwhelming force. Fortifications could prolong the defence and force the British to resort to siege, but fortifications were only designed to last so long against an effective siege; indeed they were principally designed to force attackers to resort to a siege. The effectiveness of British sieges could be lessened by poor leadership, inadequate resources, especially manpower, and disease. Proposing an attack on Havana in the event of war with Spain in 1727, Lieutenant-Colonel Alexander Spotswood, a veteran of Blenheim and former Lieutenant-Governor of Virginia, warned of the need to have troops inured to the climate and to tropical illness. Disease and the effects of rum caused heavy losses among the troops that arrived in Jamaica in 1731.

Poor leadership and inadequate resources, nevertheless, were increasingly overcome as the British developed considerable and unmatched experience in amphibious operations. The creation of naval bases, providing refitting and repair facilities overseas, English Bay, Antigua from the 1730s and Halifax from 1749, helped considerably. British military successes depended on the detailed co-operation of army and navy, for example Wolfe and

Saunders at Québec or Coote and Stevens at Pondicherry. Hodgson wrote from Belle Isle in 1761, "The two services have acted as one corps ever since we left England. The Commodore [Keppel] has left himself so bare of ammunition by the supplies he has, from time to time, given me, that he has hardly a sufficiency to give the enemy's fleet a proper reception". Thus the navy which also received its supplies from the Ordnance Board made up for the deficiencies of the supply to the army.[80]

By 1762 much of the army and navy had had experience of amphibious operations. Hodgson had earlier commanded a brigade in the Rochefort expedition of 1757. Experience was distilled in Thomas More Molyneux's *Conjunct expeditions, or expeditions that have been carried on jointly by the fleet and army* (London, 1759). Success depended also on a more general systemic co-ordination: the ability to mount amphibious operations stemmed from a degree of naval superiority in home waters that both made invasion improbable and could permit the dispatch of fleets to distant waters. These fleets had to ensure superiority there, sufficient both to cover expeditions and to provide supporting firepower. In 1755 the Duke of Newcastle emphasized the need for naval superiority off Nova Scotia.[81]

Such an account may make the task seem both obvious and easy. It was neither. It was necessary to make calculations about relative strengths in a context in which reliable information was scanty. Strategy was also challenged by operational uncertainties, most obviously disease and the weather. Thus, the expeditionary force destined for Gorée in 1758 was damaged and delayed by bad weather. The siege of Pondicherry was hampered by rain, while the blockading fleet was driven away for four days by a strong storm. More generally, both in Europe and further afield, the British faced the problems of being a maritime power using amphibious forces against Continental states. In 1707 Major-General John Richards wrote from Alicante that "with a very little help upon the arrival of the fleet, we might do anything upon this neighbouring coast or within 4 or 5 leagues of it". Yet this confidence was dependant upon the Franco-Spanish troops having pulled back.[82] British options were far less in the face of powerful opponents whose coastal strength was supported by an extensive hinterland. This was the problem facing amphibious attacks on France during the Seven Years' War, and on other occasions. In that war, the British were fortunate in that attacks on metropolitan France were subordinated to those on the more vulnerable French empire. Similarly, in 1762 it was Havana not Seville that was besieged.

Nevertheless, despite British success in lessening the deleterious impact of distance and the challenge of the oceans, the French empire was not conquered rapidly. Pondicherry did not fall until 1761. Looking at the total of British conquests it is easy to forget that many took years to acquire: Louisbourg, Ticonderoga and Martinique only fell at the second attempt. An ability and willingness to sustain the war was part of the reason for

British success. Again, however, politics and the factor of timing were crucial. By 1761 war weariness was growing, and the new king, George III (ruled 1760–1820), and his favourite, John, 3rd Earl of Bute, both sought peace. War with Spain broke out despite them. In 1762, however, they were able to insist on the settlement with France and Spain that was signed on 10 February 1763 as the Peace of Paris. In hindsight, as with the War of Spanish Succession, it is clear that the political parameters made the military task more difficult by adding a crucial dimension of timing. Resources alone were not the issue. It was necessary to win before the political basis on which their availability rested, and, more generally, the continuance of the war depended, disappeared.

CHAPTER SIX

Rebellion successful: the American War of Independence

The American War of Independence (1775–83) was a great defeat for the British political and military systems. The intervention of France (1778), Spain (1779) and the Dutch (1780) on the American side also ensured that the war became a global conflict in which Britain was sorely pressed around the world, from India to the Western Mediterranean, home waters to the West Indies. It is instructive to consider the conflict on its own, but it is also useful to examine it against the background of the military challenges Britain had faced since the end of the Seven Years' War in early 1763.

A variety of challenges, 1763–74

Aside from the continuing conflict in Bengal already referred to in Chapter 5, the British faced a number of military challenges in this period. They were very varied. Non-Europeans were fought in North America, the West Indies and India. A serious confrontation with Spain in 1770–1 over the Falkland Isles nearly led to war. Rising problems with discontent in the Thirteen Colonies tested military resources and methods. All these challenges had to be confronted against the background of post-war demobilization. Furthermore, the return of many of the conquered territories to the Bourbons as part of the peace settlement helped to restore their military potential and this was exacerbated by a major programme of Bourbon naval re-armament.[1]

Pontiac's War, 1763–4

The Seven Years' War was followed by renewed British–Native American tension. The Peace of Paris had not taken note of Native American views. Tension rose as the British failed to provide the Native Americans with customary presents, which were seen by the Natives as compensation for the right to trade and travel, while British American merchants acted in an arbitrary fashion and settlers moved into Native lands, breaking agreements. The British were very fortunate that the crisis followed the Seven Years' War. They would have found war with the French very difficult had they had to face a major Native rising, while French support would have made such a rising far more serious.

Mounting tension led to Pontiac's War (1763–4), which involved a number of tribes, especially the Ottawa under Pontiac, but also the Saulteaux, Sauk, Miami, Mississauga, Wyandot, Delaware and Shawnee; however, the "northern nations" were generally quiescent, and there was no unified effort among the Natives who rose, unsurprisingly so given the vast area at stake. Pontiac's influence was limited. Attempts at securing Native unity centred less around him than around nativist religious revival leaders, such as Neolin, the Delaware prophet. This began a movement for unified resistance to Anglo-American expansion which continued until the War of 1812.

A series of attacks was launched by the Natives in May 1763. The British American settlers fled back over the Appalachians, although about 2,000 traders and settlers were killed or captured in the uprising. The army was left to hold the forts to the south of the Great Lakes. Most of the forts were small and not designed for large garrisons, and most of the garrisons were small and unable to hold their positions. The 16 defenders of Fort Sandusky were killed by the Wyandot on 16 May and the fort was burned. Fort Miami fell to the Miami on 27 May: one of the defenders was killed, the other 11 captured. The Miami pressed on to capture Fort Ouiatenon on 31 May. All 21 defenders were taken prisoner. More forts fell the following month, largely as a result of ruses. The Sauk and Saulteaux captured Fort Michilimackinac on 2 June after gaining entry to follow a lacrosse ball: 18 of the defenders were killed, the other ten taken prisoner. The defenders of Fort Venango were killed on 13 June when the Delaware Senaca captured it. Other forts were abandoned – Edward Augusta (15 June), Le Boeuf (18 June) and Littleton (20 June) – the forts failing as a system of control and forward defence.

The Native Americans were helped by the small size of the British army in North America and the vast area it had to cover. A series of Native victories in battle also prevented the British from relieving besieged forts, hit their communications and lessened their confidence in their ability to move troops safely. Unaware that fighting had begun, 96 troops from Fort Niagara, sailing in 18 small boats along Lake Erie towards Detroit, were ambushed at Point Pelée on 28 May 1763 and 63 were killed or captured. On 5–6 August 350 regulars and 110 American militia, advancing to relieve Fort Pitt, were attacked at Bushy Run. 118 were killed or wounded; their opponents only suffered 60 casualties.

However, Fort Pitt was relieved. The British force was more effective in forest warfare than Braddock's had been. Instead of milling around as confused targets, Lieutenant-Colonel Henry Bouquet's men retained operational effectiveness, mounting a bayonet attack, and a feigned retreat; the latter was effective in causing Native casualties on the second day of the battle because the Natives abandoned their distant fighting tactics and came within reach of the British bayonets. Nevertheless, Bouquet's force had been hard hit and was unable to mount further operations that year. In addition, on 14 September, in the "Devil's Hole Massacre", 139 British regulars were ambushed near Fort Niagara and 127 were killed. Bushy Run was not typical. The British were less effective at fighting in the woodlands of the frontier zone than their opponents, especially in acting offensively, and British dependence on supply routes made them vulnerable to attack.

Despite these successes, the major forts, with their sizeable garrisons and artillery, resisted siege; the Native Americans were least effective at siegecraft. They lacked cannon and their ethos and method of warfare were not well suited to the lengthy, methodical, arduous and unheroic nature of siegecraft. Detroit held out from 9 May 1763 until the unsuccessful siege was lifted on 31 October, Fort Pitt from 26 June until the siege ended on 7 August. Despite hit and run attacks in June, Forts Ligonier and Bedford did not fall, while the forts on Lake Ontario – Niagara and Oswego – remained in British hands.

Their opponents were affected by shortages of supplies. Owing to the British conquest of Canada, the Natives had no access to firearms other than those they captured. The Anglo-French rivalry that had given a measure of opportunity, providing for example arms and ammunition to the Abenakis, had been ended. Native Americans opposed to the British had lost their French supporters. By 1764 the Native Americans were probably short of gunpowder: the British received reports to this effect. This had also been a problem for the Cherokee.

They anyway found it difficult to sustain long conflicts, an instance of the advantage that professional permanent forces had over societies in which conflict involved the bulk of the adult male population. Furthermore, the British planned to distribute blankets infected with smallpox – an early example of biological warfare, and whether this was carried out or not, the tribes were ravaged by a smallpox epidemic. The Native Americans did not launch attacks in 1764, possibly because they were satisfied by the 1763 Royal Proclamation establishing a line beyond which colonial settlement was prohibited. A threat to Native towns in the Muskingum Valley also encouraged the Natives to negotiate. As, more generally, with French Canada, a threat to opponents' bases was more effective than successes in encounter warfare. The conflict was settled in a series of treaties, for example that of 6 August 1764 with the Seneca and another in November with the Delaware and Shawnee. The Royal Proclamation – and the resumption of presents to the Natives – indicated that the settlement was a

Sir Jeffrey Amherst by Reynolds. A protégé of Ligonier, Cumberland and Pitt, who had served at Dettingen, Fontenoy, Roucoux and Lawfeldt, Amherst rose to prominence as Commander-in-Chief of the forces conquering Canada from 1758. After the surrender of Montréal, Amherst became Governor-General, but he proved less than adept in his response to Pontiac's War in 1763. Amherst did not understand how best to use the colonial militia. In effect Commander-in-Chief of the British army during the War of American Independence, Amherst lacked flexibility. He was replaced by the Duke of York in 1795, but created Field-Marshal in 1796. *National Gallery of Canada, Ottawa.*

compromise,[2] just as had been the treaties with the Maroons of Jamaica in 1738 and 1739. The Natives returned all prisoners, but ceded no land.

The crisis had revealed deficiencies in the British military system. Amherst, Commander-in-Chief in North America from September 1758 and Governor-General of British North America from September 1760, lacked flexibility in his treatment of the Native Americans and failed to appreciate the potential of the colonial American militia. Yet, the ability to retain hold of key fortresses at the beginning of the rising and also to prevent the Native Americans from rolling up the supply route to Fort Pitt ensured that, once the initial energy of the rising had been spent, the British were well placed to mount a response. Raids on Forts Ligonier and Bedford were not sufficient to dislodge their garrisons and, further east, Fort London, Carlisle and Lancaster remained under British control, and could serve as bases for countermoves. Attacks on settlements in rural Pennsylvania and neighbouring colonies did not translate into an assault on the region of cultivation and settlement serious and systematic enough to force the British to adopt a reactive strategy in which they concentrated their troops on holding defensive positions to the east and south of the areas of Native settlement. Indeed, the very weakness of the Native position in areas that had been colonized was a vital resource for the British.

In the American War of Independence the situation was to be very different: the British did not enjoy a safe base area for recruitment, supply, communications and manoeuvre similar to that they had benefited from during Pontiac's War. Indeed, the rising highlights, by contrast, the nature of the military challenge in the War of Independence. The latter was at the centre of Britain's North American empire, not at its margins.

St Vincent, 1772–3

Another conflict at the margins of empire in the New World occurred in the West Indies in 1772–3. Again, the British benefited from the safety of their crucial bases. The native Caribs were not able to attack other islands and the war was largely a matter of the buildup of the British ability to deploy resources on the island. Unlike in the case of the initial stages of Pontiac's War, the British possessed the initiative.

It was not easy for European troops to operate in St. Vincent and there was no equivalent to the large sepoy forces employed by the East India Company: the British did not have a slave army in the West Indies (not that sepoys were slaves). Instead, they had to rely upon regulars. The British commander, Lieutenant-Colonel William Dalrymple, a veteran of the 1762 campaign in Portugal, who was made a local Major-General for the duration of the conflict, wrote to the Secretary at War at its start:

> Your Lordship is doubtless too well acquainted with the natural and uncommon strength of this island to doubt that a vigorous

opposition may be expected. The fatality attending the climate at this season particularly joined with the numbers of the savages, present difficulties only to be overcome by our utmost diligence and perseverance.

By the end of the year, Dalrymple had reached the end of the existing road: "no white man has ever been in their concealed places of retirement . . . neither guides nor intelligence can be procured . . . this fatal climate". Yet, despite losses through ambushes and by "the neglect of a villainous set of surgeons", Dalrymple obtained a satisfactory treaty. The British had 636 casualties, 394 of them "sick", but what was striking was their ability to deploy a force of over 2,000 effectives. Troops had been moved from elsewhere in the West Indies and from North America: Dalrymple had been serving in Boston. The returns indicated that the troops had been armed with good, new flintlocks. The global potential of British power was amply displayed.[3]

Lord Dunmore's War, 1774

A brief and localized war with the Native Americans preceded the outbreak of the War of American Independence. John, 4th Earl of Dunmore, the Governor of Virginia, had allowed settlement in Shawnee territory west of the Appalachians, but the Shawnees attacked the settlers. In response, Dunmore sent a force of volunteers, only for this to be ambushed and routed along the Kentucky River. Thereupon, Dunmore assembled a force of 1,500 militia, which advanced in two columns. Weakened by the refusal of the Iroquois to provide help, the Shawnees attacked one of the columns under Andrew Lewis at Point Pleasant on 6 October 1774. The Virginians lost 50 dead, but the Shawnees had heavier casualties and hastened to make peace. The short conflict indicated the greater force that the colonists could employ against their Native neighbours, but also the importance of divisions among the latter.

India

Elsewhere in the world, the British were also acting as a major power. In India, Caillaud successfully besieged Vellore in 1762, and Madurai fell in 1764 as the result of another successful siege. It had been under the control of Yusuf Khan, an outstanding sepoy officer in the Madras army in the 1750s and 1760s. He had been given a gold medal in 1755 and appointed commandant of sepoys. Yusuf Khan had then become ambitious and become a renter for the Nawab in Madurai, before quarrelling with the Nawab's son and breaking away. As the sponsor of the Nawab, the East India Company had to suppress Yusuf Khan. Indicating one of the disadvantages of mobility and interdependence, Call blamed his defiance on the dispatch of much of the Madras army on the Manila expedition. In 1763 Call described the difficulties of campaigning against Madurai:

> We should not be the least uneasy about the certainty of defeating him were it not for the difficulty of penetrating through the woods to get at him . . . The narrow roads are at all times difficult to an army, but retrenched and secured as they are at present we are well assured it is impracticable to penetrate by any route but that of marching by the sea side . . . Another grand obstacle is the want of water . . . as well as rice . . . in spite of all we should have marched against him and could have drawn together a body of 600 Europeans . . . but such was our weakened state that we could not send half that number into the field.[4]

The campaign demonstrated the increased military commitments that stemmed from the spread of British political interests. Yusuf Khan was betrayed to the British by one of his French officers and hanged. In 1766 the East India Company gained the Northern Circars as the price of their alliance with the Nizam of Hyderabad. Caillaud, now a Brigadier-General, occupied the area with little resistance. Benares, acquired from Oudh, followed in 1775.

In 1767–9, however, the British fought a rising ruler, Haidar Ali of Mysore, an effective general whose forces were particularly strong in light cavalry and who was seen as a threat by the Madras Council. A British officer recorded in 1768 "a large body of the enemy's horse constantly hovering about us, and often carrying away numbers of our bullocks, baggage etc". Short of cavalry, the Company's forces could not respond effectively.

Despite this, Mysore was invaded and the British were able to use their artillery to reduce opposing forts in 1768.[5] Nevertheless, the resources and determination to sustain an invasion were absent, and Haidar's cavalry, described in 1791 as "the most diligent and enterprising light troops in the world", hit the Company's ability to raise taxes. In 1769 this cavalry ravaged the Carnatic, advanced as far as Madras and dictated peace to the Council, whose army was far smaller.[6] Haidar Ali respected and feared Major-General Joseph Smith, the commander of the Madras army, but Smith had insufficient means and it was difficult to respond successfully to the Mysore cavalry. The failure to defeat Haidar Ali, like the earlier blows in the initial stages of Pontiac's War, indicate the danger of reading too much from Britain's success in the latter stages of the Seven Years' War. War on land against non-European opponents, who not only fought in a different fashion but were also products of contrasting socio-political systems, was more difficult than conflict with other European powers.

In the 1770s the British were not as powerful in southern India as in the lower Ganges valley, although Vellore was stormed in 1771 and Tanjore successfully besieged in 1775. Further north, Bengal forces under Lieutenant-Colonel Thomas Goddard moved into Oudh in 1772–3 in order to retain influence there. In 1774 the British helped Shuja-ud-dowla of Oudh conquer Rohilkhand. The following year, the Company's troops helped suppress a mutiny amongst those of Oudh against its new ruler, although this entailed heavy casualties.

British power was increasingly apparent at their coastal centres. The consolidation of the British position was noted by George Paterson when he visited Bombay in 1770. He thought the original square fort which the British had sheltered in against Mughal attack in 1686 "by no means fit to sustain a modern attack", but noted more modern fortifications including those on a hill overlooking the town. The speed of the work greatly impressed Paterson:

> it must be fortified. Well this being agreed to, the fortifications were well planned and immediately carried into execution, and all the time they were employed about this, there were several thousands also constantly at work to take away the hill and blowing it up like fire and smoke. They both come on apace and very soon there will be no hill; but there will be fine fortifications . . . All these works put together may be very well defended by 10,000 men, an army sufficient to meet any power in the field that can attack this place; but one may as well fight under cover as not.[7]

The dockyards at Calcutta were improved in the late 1760s and the construction of ships to British design using naval shipwrights began. The East India Company's yard at Bombay contained docks that could be used for proper ship maintenance, avoiding the need to send warships home with all the attendant consequences for naval strength. Further east, however, the Company's settlement of Balambangan off Borneo was wiped out in a local rising in 1775.

The Pacific

Over distant horizons, the British navy played a major role in exploration, especially in the South Seas. In 1767 a naval officer, Samuel Wallis, "discovered" many islands in the Pacific, including King George the Third's Island, better known as Tahiti. The collaborative international observation of Venus' transit across the sun in 1769 took another naval officer, James Cook (1728–79), to Tahiti in HMS *Endeavour*. From there, he conducted the first ciruit and charting of New Zealand and the charting of the east coast of Australia. Here in 1770 Cook landed in Botany Bay and claimed the territory for George III. In 1772–5 Cook's repeated efforts to find a great southern continent, including the first passage of the Antarctic circle, failed. Cook, however, "discovered" New Caledonia and Hawaii. He used one of the chronometers invented by John Harrison to measure latitude; Harrison's chronometers made organized maritime exploration like that by Cook possible.

Exploration helped to fire a view of Britain as a global maritime power. Accounts of exploration, for example of the voyages of Cook or Dalrymple's *Collection of voyages to the South Seas* (1770–1), were very popular.[8] The projection of British power in the southern hemisphere in the 1780s, including the establishment of a settlement in Australia in 1788, was to be easier as a result of the information gathered in the previous decade.

The Falklands

Britain's maritime strength and preparedness was put to the test in 1770. Port Egmont, the British base on the Falkland Islands, was seized by Spain, which claimed the islands. The government responded with a substantial armament that demonstrated the effectiveness of the navy. A fleet of 55 ships was prepared and by May 1771 it was three-quarters manned. Spain and its French ally could not match these preparations and this accentuated political tensions within the Bourbon camp. The more bellicose French foreign minister, Choiseul, was dismissed on 24 December 1770, and Louis XV pressed Charles III of Spain to make concessions. The matter was settled by compromise on 22 January 1771. Spain promised to restore Port Egmont while declaring that this concession did not affect its claim to sovereignty, and the British gave a secret, verbal assurance that they would evacuate Port Egmont. The British, however, did not withdraw their troops until 1775, and then only on the grounds of economy.[9] The crisis ended for a while French planning for an invasion of England.

This was not the sole example of British naval mobilization and sabre-rattling in this period. In 1771 four ships of the line were sent to the Indian Ocean to deter a possible French threat to British interests in India. The French indeed sent military advisors to Haidar Ali that year.[10] In 1772 the threat of action led the Danes to release into exile Caroline Matilda, George III's sister and their adulterous Queen.

The world power challenged

Yet, these were also years in which Britain lost the edge in naval strength to the Bourbons. Due, especially, to French and Spanish launchings in the late 1760s, that were each greater than those of Britain, and also to greater Spanish launchings in the early 1770s, the Bourbons had a quantitative superiority in tonnage of about 20 per cent by 1775.[11] This loss of naval superiority was to cost Britain dear during the War of American Independence, but the situation was more complex than one of peacetime failure leading to wartime problems. The British navy in 1765 was in terms of tonnage the largest of any navy hitherto. Given the problems of manning the fleet and maintaining ships, the advisability of further construction was limited. The Seven Years' War and the Falkland Islands crisis both indicated the weakness of Bourbon co-operation. A full-scale rebellion in the American colonies, especially in co-operation with France, seemed unlikely.

Such a rebellion was to break out in 1775. The crisis in imperial relations was part of a more general collapse in European control in the New World in the century from 1775. Yet, rather than suggesting any inevitable clash, it is necessary to explain why the process of reaching and endlessly redefining a consensus that underlay and often constituted government in this period broke down. In northern India, for example, the British initially successfully adapted themselves to the social system as they found it, conciliating the local elites of Muslim service gentry and Hindu merchants and benefiting from their power.

In the American colonies, however, especially those of Britain, constitutional ideas and political practices derived from Europe led to increasing disagreements over the nature of the colonial bond. These directly touched on the nature of the British empire, helping to create a steadily more volatile atmosphere as British ministries responded with wavering acts of firmness. The policing of North America was a difficult task for the British army and navy. Between 1763 and 1775 nearly 4 per cent of the entire British national budget was spent on maintaining the army in North America.[12] The landing of troops in Boston in 1768 helped to increase tension. Policing involved the use of military force. The "Boston Massacre" of 5 March 1770, in which five Bostonians were killed, was seen by many Americans as demonstrating the militarization of British authority. Disorder, indeed, encouraged governmental reliance on the army. The Boston Tea Party of December 1773 led to tough action against Massachusetts, including the dispatch of more troops. General Thomas Gage, the Commander-in-Chief in America, was appointed Governor of the colony. Gage was ordered to use force to restore royal authority and this led to the outbreak of war.[13]

The American War of Independence

War began with an attempt to seize a cache of arms reported to be at Concord, a town 16 miles from Boston, past the village of Lexington. The British found about 70 militia drawn up in two lines at the village. Heavily outnumbered, the militia began to disperse, but a shot was fired and the British fired two volleys in response, thereby scattering the militia. The shedding of blood outraged New England, and a substantial force, largely dependent on their personal arms, soon encircled the British in Boston. Elsewhere in the Thirteen Colonies, British authority collapsed: governors were provided with no military assistance due to a concentration of troops in Massachusetts.

The first battle of the war was that of Bunker Hill on 17 June 1775. The previous night, the Revolutionaries marched to Breed's Hill on the Charlestown peninsula and began to fortify the position which commanded the heights above the city of Boston; the battle is named after the more prominent hill behind Breed's Hill. Gage, who had command of the harbour, decided on a landing at high tide that afternoon, followed by an attack on the American entrenchments. He moved ponderously, spending about two hours deploying his men and advancing in a traditional open-field formation. The British artillery failed to damage the American positions significantly. The Americans waited until the advancing British were almost upon them before shattering their first two attacks with heavy musket fire. An attempt to turn the American flank was repelled. The Americans, however, were running short of ammunition and a third British attack took the American redoubt. The exhausted British, harassed by sharpshooters, were unable to stop the Americans from retreating.

British casualties were heavy. Thereafter, the army in Boston was singularly cautious in mounting operations. As a consequence, the British lost the strategic offensive; their troops did no more than control the ground they stood on.

Canada held, 1775–6

The rebellion of the Thirteen Colonies in 1775 and the declaration of independence the following year was a seminal event in world history in part made possible by British military failure. Nevertheless, the British military system was also, in part, responsible for another major event: the sundering of the British North American world thanks to the British retention of Canada.

Initially, it looked as though the British would also be thrown out from there, although by invasion rather than rebellion. The main American invasion force, 2,000 strong under Richard Montgomery, advanced via Lake Champlain. Fort St Jean fell after a six-week siege (2 November), and Chambly (17 October) and Montréal (13 November) surrendered. The Governor of Canada, Guy Carleton, fled from Montréal to Québec. Meanwhile, another American force of about 1,200 men under Benedict Arnold crossed Maine to arrive, after much hardship, opposite Québec on 14 November. Montgomery advanced on Québec down the St Lawrence and the combined American force besieged the city.

The Americans attacked the Lower Town on the night of 30–31 December 1775, but were checked with heavy losses: 60 killed (including

Montgomery) and wounded (including Arnold), and 426 taken prisoner, compared to 18 British casualties. The siege continued until the ice on the St Lawrence melted and the arrival of the British relief fleet on 6 May 1776 led the Americans to retreat. They attacked the pursuing British at Trois Rivières on 8 June, but were defeated, losing 623 casualties, compared with ten on the part of the more numerous British.[14]

The Americans suffered in their invasion from a lack of sufficient local support, from long and difficult lines of communication, and from the peripheral nature of the conflict to most Americans, especially while the British remained in Boston until March 1776. However, the war in Canada was more than a matter of American weakness; it also revealed British strengths. The length of time it took the Americans to capture Fort St Jean indicated the role of British defensive positions as, more obviously, did the retention of Québec. Carleton emerges as a capable general.[15] In the end, however, Canada had to be reconquered; the campaign of 1776 there indicates the importance of the British state being able and willing to send a large force. The importance of control of the sea was shown by the relief of Québec.

Campaign of 1776

The role of sea power was also displayed in the 1776 campaign in the Thirteen Colonies. In March the British withdrew from Boston to refit at Halifax. Under General William Howe, they then landed on Staten Island, at the entrance to New York harbour, on 3 July. This began a second stage in the war that was more widespread, bitter and sustained than had at first seemed likely, the stage of the British counter-attack.

A battle that could have been decisive was that of Long Island on 27 August. Based on Staten Island, the British made an unopposed landing on Long Island on 22 August to find the Americans divided between entrenchments at Brooklyn and a force strung out along the Heights of Guan, a ridge in advance of this position. A failure to guard Jamaica Pass on the left of the American line was exploited by the British, who outflanked the outnumbered Americans, while the left of the British army engaged the American front. The Maryland and Delaware troops on the American right under "Lord" Stirling mounted a rearguard action, but were captured or dispersed as the Americans fell back to their positions on Brooklyn Heights. The terrain caused some problems for the British. Captain William Congreve, later Colonel Commandant of the Royal Artillery, found his artillery unit vulnerable to American riflemen: "the riflemen being covered by trees and large stones had very much the advantage of us, who were upon the open ground", but he was relieved by British light infantry.

Once the battlefield had been cleared, Howe failed to order the storming of the Brooklyn positions, and, instead, decided on "regular approaches".

166

With hindsight, it is argued that Howe should have pushed his men, who were ready and willing to keep advancing, at the American lines. But, mindful of heavy casualties at Bunker Hill, he was unwilling to lose troops when, as soon as the winds abated, his brother, Admiral Howe, could bring his fleet up the East River and cut the Americans off. In fact, when the wind abated, a fog rolled in and, even as the British fleet was lifting anchor preparatory to sailing, Washington used the cover of the fog to row his men across the river to Manhattan.[16]

The British, however, retained the initiative and used the navy to mount out-flanking amphibious operations on Manhattan Island, thanks to which the outnumbered Americans were driven from New York. The British also seized Newport, Rhode Island, and overran New Jersey, reaching the Delaware at Trenton on 8 December. Nevertheless, George Washington's successful surprise counter-attack across the Delaware at Trenton against the Hessian soldiers in British service on 25–6 December stemmed the tide of British success and led them to abandon much of New Jersey with disastrous consequences for the Loyalists and for future chances of winning Loyalist support.[17]

1777: Philadelphia and Saratoga

In 1777 Howe decided to attack Philadelphia, the American capital. Instead of marching across New Jersey, he proposed to use the flexibility provided by British naval power. However, this led to serious delay, not least because Howe chose the longer approach, via the Chesapeake, rather than that via the Delaware. Once the British had landed, Washington sought to block Howe at Brandywine Creek (11 September), but was outflanked and defeated. Howe pressed on to capture Philadelphia (26 September) and to beat off a surprise American counter-attack at Germantown (4 October).

Success in Pennsylvania did not bring victory, because the British strategy of cutting the Thirteen Colonies in half along the Hudson corridor failed. The British had followed up their success in clearing Canada by advancing south to Lake Champlain in late 1776. Their advance revealed another facet of British military capability, for on 11–13 October, on the lake near Ile Valcour, the British fought an inland naval engagement defeating an American flotilla under Arnold and destroying 11 American ships. The British flotilla had been built from scratch. Nevertheless, the British failed to consolidate their position on the lake that winter.

In 1777 a bolder strategy prevailed. The British, under General John Burgoyne, captured Ticonderoga (6 July) and then advanced to the Hudson through difficult wooded terrain. Not to have pressed on, having taken Ticonderoga so easily, would have been to make no contribution to what appeared likely to be a decisive campaign.

However, a detached part of the British force was defeated near Bennington (16 August), while, having crossed the Hudson, Burgoyne foolishly pressed on towards an American army that was growing in numbers. Burgoyne attacked at Bemis Heights (19 September), but suffered heavy casualties from American riflemen and was unable to dislodge the Americans from their positions blocking his advance south. Burgoyne's force was now dangerously exposed. Another British attack was repelled on 7 October. An attempt was made to relieve Burgoyne from New York by advancing north, but it was too late. On 17 October 4,812 troops under Burgoyne surrendered to 21,000 Americans at Saratoga.[18] The Americans broke the surrender convention and refused to allow the British troops to return to Britain.

The loss of the troops was serious, but so also was the defeat. Thereafter, the British did not attack south from Canada. As a result, they adopted a maritime strategy that centred on control of ports and coastal areas without the additional dimension of overland capability provided by an offensive force based in Canada. This reduced the strategic options open to the British. Saratoga marked the end of any serious prospect of cutting off New England from the rest of America. The campaign was also a warning of the folly of thinking that the Americans had really only one important field army and, consequently, that its defeat would signal the end of the war. When Burgoyne's advance had first been considered, it had been assumed that the sole significant risk would be if Washington moved against him. Instead, Burgoyne had been defeated while Washington's army had been deployed against Howe.

The war moves south, 1778–80

Victory at Saratoga and Washington's ability at Germantown to mount a riposte to the fall of Philadelphia helped lead France to enter the war on the American side in 1778: France no longer seemed to be risking supporting the losing side.[19] French intervention changed the nature of the conflict in America, especially by increasing the number of Britain's commitments elsewhere, and thus lessening the availability of fresh troops for operations in America. British interest was increasingly focused on the South where it was hoped to benefit from Loyalist support. The war in the middle colonies largely became a low-level struggle in which partisan operations by American militia and raids by British troops inflicted much damage, but did not alter the strategic situation.[20]

Meanwhile, in the South, Savannah fell to a British amphibious force in December 1778; as did Charleston in May 1780, one of the most serious American defeats of the war thanks to the size of the force that surrendered and the consequent collapse of the American position in coastal South Carolina. The British, however, found it difficult to consolidate their position in South Carolina. Thanks to the poor quality of the Virginia and North Carolina militia, Cornwallis defeated the American southern army under Horatio Gates at Camden (16 August) and left it in ruins, but it proved impossible to control the back country, and Major Patrick Ferguson and Colonel Banastre Tarleton were defeated at King's Mountain (7 October 1780) and Cowpens (17 January 1781), respectively.[21] American partisans also undermined the attempt to create stability under British rule nearer the coast. By Yorktown, the British controlled an area extending only about five miles beyond Charleston.

1781: year of decision in America

By 1780, the Americans faced growing exhaustion and war-weariness[22] while, despite the financial strain, the British continued to fight on. In light of the limited experience of Revolutionary leaders in logistical questions, the lack of an adequate central executive authority or centralized governmental machinery, the rivalries between the colonies and the active defence of local interests, logistical support for the army was, when vigorously managed, adequate; but, at other times, as a consequence of incompetence, inefficiency and selfishness, unsatisfactory. The resources that existed were mismanaged and the rebels lacked an effective political organization and system of taxation. The limited creditworthiness of Congress and the reluctance of the states to subordinate their priorities and resources to Congress meant that the army had to live from hand to mouth. Much of the supplying of the Continental Army relied on the issue of largely worthless certificates. In January 1781, short of pay, food, and clothes, and seeking discharge, both the Pennsylvania line and three New Jersey regiments mutinied. The Pennsylvania mutiny was ended only by concessions, including the discharge of five-sixths of the men. The episode was a salutary warning to the Revolutionary cause and can only give rise to speculation as to what would have happened if the American army had been forced to endure another harsh winter without (as in that of 1781–2) the prospect of success.[23]

Early in 1781 Cornwallis invaded North Carolina. On 15 March he defeated the larger army of Gates' replacement, Nathanael Greene, at Guilford Court House, although the Americans fought well and the battle was no rout. Cornwallis then invaded Virginia, eventually establishing a base at Yorktown on the Chesapeake. This was a poor defensive position, but it had an anchorage suitable for ships of the line. At this crucial juncture, however, the movement from the West Indies of the French fleet under de Grasse and the failure of Rodney to send a matching number of ships denied the British command of the sea: the approach to the Chesapeake was barred by the French. Furthermore, without interference from Clinton's army in New York, Washington and a French expeditionary force under

The Surrender at Yorktown, 19 October 1781 by Louis Nicolas von Blarenberghe. Two days earlier, Johann Conrad Döhla, a member of the Ansbach-Bayreuth forces in Cornwallis' army recorded, "At daybreak the enemy bombardment resumed, more terribly strong than ever before. They fired from all positions without let-up. Our command, which was in the Hornwork, could hardly tolerate the enemy bombs, howitzer, and cannonballs any longer. There was nothing to be seen but bombs and cannonballs raining down on our entire line". *Lauros-Giraudon/Bridgeman Art Library.*

Rochambeau were able to achieve a concentration of strength outside Yorktown which placed Cornwallis in an untenable position. Blockaded, under heavy bombardment, and without relief, Cornwallis surrendered on 19 October 1781.[24]

Although the British still held Charleston, New York and Savannah, Yorktown was effectively the end of British efforts in North America. The defeat led to the replacement of Lord North's ministry by a British government more ready to accept American independence. Thereafter, the British concentrated on their conflict with the Bourbons.[25]

Could the British have won?

American victory was not inevitable and the war was a series of highly contingent events. Even the American folklore of the conflict, to the extent that it immortalizes Washington's crossing of the Delaware at Trenton as a turning point in the struggle for independence, affirms contingency. The British had a serious chance of winning in 1776 and 1780. The notion of victory depends on an understanding of the goal of the war. Both Lord

North and the Howe brothers assumed that the war would end with the restoration of government by consent under the Crown, a very different objective from those pursued against the Jacobites, and one that presumed a measure of compromise. Had the navy moved into the East River earlier in 1776, it would have cut off Washington's men in Brooklyn. To have captured most of Washington's army on Long Island in 1776 would have meant more than 10,000 prisoners and probably a long series of treason trails, which would have left much bitterness behind. An America subdued by 40,000 soldiers who would then have to remain as an army of occupation was not a viable plan for an area as huge as the Thirteen Colonies. The Howes had a better idea; they understood the voluntaristic character of American military service (willingness to serve for a single campaign of six to nine months, and then it would be someone else's turn), and they very nearly succeeded in turning it against the settlers. As the British scored one local victory after another between August and December 1776, Washington's army did indeed all but disintegrate. Men were laying down their arms and returning home, which is exactly where the Howes wanted them to go. Washington's Trenton campaign was, at bottom, a desperate recruiting device, an effort to persuade veterans to re-enlist. Though largely a failure at this overt level, it and the subsequent victory at Princeton on 3 January 1777 did revitalize resistance and permit Congress to raise a new army in 1777, including many who agreed to serve for three years, a luxury Washington had never enjoyed before.

An emphasis on these social dynamics which were crucial to recruitment leads to an interesting counterfactual: what if Cornwallis had responded to defeat at Princeton in the way he reacted to opposition in the Carolinas four years later? Having identified Washington's most loyal supporters, what if he had decided to hound them to death, as he later tried to do with Nathanael Greene? If he had been able to crush Washington in January 1777, perhaps somewhere near Morristown, and if the British had continued to garrison New Jersey, would the Revolution have collapsed? In addition, Trenton was a gamble for the Americans, a dangerous operation that was dependent on surprise and that, anyway, partly miscarried. What if Washington had failed to achieve surprise? What if the Hessians had driven them back to Pennsylvania, would anything have changed? Would Congress have been able to raise a new army for 1777?

By 1780 hyperinflation had wrecked the American economy. The war reduced median household wealth by more than 45 per cent. General Sir Henry Clinton, who succeeded Howe as Commander in Chief, did see in all this misery an opportunity to win the war, and in the South everything went well for the British until King's Mountain and Cowpens. But the real key to victory in 1780 was New Jersey. Clinton did have a plan for crushing Washington. It involved landing two armies on the Jersey shore, each larger than Washington's, and sending them through the two passes of the

Watchung Mountains. If Washington waited (and he did not have enough horses to move all of his artillery), he would have been overwhelmed at Morristown. If he attacked either invading force, he would have been out-numbered and on the offensive, conditions under which Americans always lost during the Revolution. Had Clinton achieved that objective, he would have moved against the French when they landed that year in Rhode Island. The French would not have been able to withdraw into the interior. With Washington's army gone, he probably would have captured West Point thanks to the treachery of Arnold and thus gained naval access to the entire Hudson Valley.

But he told nobody in New York about this grand plan, and before he returned from Carolina the Loyalists, who were convinced that Clinton was incapable of decisive action, persuaded the Hessian commander General Wilhelm von Knyphausen to land in New Jersey with a smaller force than Clinton had envisioned. By the time Clinton returned, there was no chance for surprise, and he pulled back to New York after the indecisive engagement at Springfield. This was the last major engagement north of Virginia and it was a major morale-boosting encounter for the Revolution-aries: a fighting withdrawal by the Americans in the face of larger British forces, was followed by the establishment of a stronger defensive position, and a British retreat that led to the abandonment of New Jersey.

After Springfield, King's Mountain and Cowpens, British victory was unlikely. Neither Cornwallis nor Clinton still had any clear vision of what a victory might look like by 1781. Cornwallis brought devastation to the Chesapeake, not a coherent plan of conquest; and, after a while, he dis-played a dangerous level of inactivity. It took the French navy to produce Yorktown, and without Yorktown the war would have dragged on. But no one was voluntarily returning to British rule, and the British lacked the manpower for another large offensive. It is difficult to see what combina-tion of British initiatives could still have been construed as a victory.

Earlier in the war, the Americans suffered severe, but not fatal, blows. In 1776 they were defeated in Canada and at Long Island and lost New York; and in 1777 they were defeated at Brandywine and lost Philadelphia. Yet in neither case did this lead to the collapse of the revolution. First, the defeated forces were able to retreat; there was no total loss, as the British suffered when they surrendered at Saratoga and Yorktown. The import-ance of this factor is indicated by the seriousness of the consequences when American forces were forced to surrender. Fort Washington at the north-ern end of Manhattan Island, with its 2,818 strong garrison, surrendered, after a successful attack on 16 November 1776, and this helped to lead to a collapse in the American position near New York. The surrender of about 5,500 men in Charleston on 12 May 1780 led to the speedy spread of British control over most of South Carolina, especially the Tidewater. There was no comparable disaster from 1777 in the Middle Colonies.

Secondly, even if the British had achieved a more decisive victory in the field they would still have had to face an undefeated New England. Each colony or state had military and economic resources of its own, so that a British victory in one part of America had only a limited effect elsewhere. Compared to the Jacobites, the Americans benefited from having more space and resources, a diffuse leadership and more military and political autonomy.[26]

The war at sea

The limitations of naval power in the American crisis, given the then size of the British navy, had been revealed prior to Bourbon entry. The concentration of naval vessels in Boston harbour and along the New England coast, as occurred in 1774–5, was only achieved by leaving the rest of the American coast largely unsupervised, and thus permitting trade to continue essentially without imperial regulation and restrictions.[27] Once war had broken out, the navy proved unable to protect trade from American privateers, in American, Caribbean, Nova Scotian and European waters.[28] It also failed to block the crucial supply of European munitions to the American revolutionaries.[29]

Such tasks were arguably beyond the capability of any eighteenth-century navy. The task of blockading fleets of ships of the line was difficult enough and they could only operate from a restricted number of ports. Dealing with individual merchantmen and privateers was far more difficult. There was a parallel with the problem the British army encountered in protecting Loyalists from their Revolutionary opponents. In great part, the Loyalists had to be left to their own devices, while the army garrisoned major posts and prepared for field engagements. The British navy, however, did not have a comparable task prior to France's entry into the war, because the Continental Navy of the Revolutionaries was not a formidable force. Not large enough for fleet actions, it made less of a contribution to the Revolutionary war effort than the privateers.[30]

On the other hand, British naval options were limited dramatically by the need to support the operations of the army. This was, of course, in keeping with the general pattern of amphibious operations at the expense of France and Spain earlier in the century. There were, however, important differences. During the Seven Years' War, the British were essentially obliged in their colonial warfare to defeat small armies composed of regular European units supported by native irregulars. Campaigns centred on the capture of major fortresses and centres of government that could be reached by sea. There was no need to overrun large areas.

Such a strategy clearly subordinated naval power to the exigencies of amphibious operations. Seeking to mount a permanent blockade of Bourbon or American ports in order to prevent privateering or other maritime activities was an alternative use of naval strength. However, it was not one that offered anything in terms of the economy of territorial gains and losses that would determine the terms of the eventual peace unless it served as a basis for amphibious expeditions by land forces.

In the pre-Bourbon stage of the American war the British navy readily fulfilled its task of supporting the army. Substantial reinforcements were moved to Boston in 1775, and in 1776 the army was evacuated to Halifax and then transported to New York, while Québec was relieved.[31] In 1777 Howe was transported to the Chesapeake. British control of the sea was not only crucial to their own logistics, it also threw an excessive burden on the land transportation available to the Revolutionaries.[32]

Each of the tasks placed major burdens on British naval resources, and yet it can be argued that the British did not achieve enough. This was not so much in terms of the failure to prevent American privateering or to block their supplies from Europe which were very difficult tasks, but rather that British naval power was not used more extensively for offensive operations along the Atlantic seaboard.

Two counter-arguments can be advanced. First, one such major expedition was attempted. It was planned that it should sail from Cork for Cape Fear in early December 1775, restore royal authority in North Carolina, where there were many Loyalists, and then join the major force under Howe as early in the spring as possible. The plan was not without value. Rather than pitting British troops against the hostile population of New England, it made sense to try to intervene in the more volatile and favourable situation in North Carolina. Had the arrival of the force been co-ordinated with the rising by the Loyalists there, it might have divided the South and crucially encouraged Loyalists in South Carolina and Georgia. The plan was unduly optimistic about timing, but the British enjoyed the naval superiority that enabled them to plan how best to employ the troops they were transporting to America. As it was, bad weather and administrative deficiencies fatally delayed the expedition which arrived after the Loyalists had been defeated. A subsequent attempt to attack Charleston's defences was unsuccessful.[33]

The second counter-argument is that attacking the American coastline would have had a detrimental effect on American opinion. On 18 October 1775 naval bombardment, supported by marines, destroyed most of Falmouth (now Portland, Maine). This inspired bitterness on the American side and contributed to their growing literature about British atrocities. Later raids on the Connecticut coast, for example the burning of Fairfield and Norwalk in 1779, had the same effect. Thus, the argument about how British troops should conduct themselves, in particular concerning how best to preserve and encourage Loyalist sentiment, can be seen to have had a naval echo.

Despite these considerations, it can still be argued that naval power could have been used more effectively and in a more *politically* acute fashion prior to the entry of the French and the consequent need to consider the vulnerability of dispersed units and the possibility of fleet actions. War is an option of difficulties, and it can be argued that ministers, generals and admirals failed to grasp opportunities. However, British generals and admirals did not like to disperse their strength, and amphibious operations were difficult to execute successfully. Units that landed might have found it difficult to obtain supplies and might have risked defeat at the hands of larger American forces, the retreat from Concord being repeated up and down the eastern seaboard. In addition, the naval strength in American waters before the late spring of 1776, and usually even after that, was possibly insufficient for the task of supporting Loyalists sufficiently to give them much confidence.

Nevertheless, the specific character of the war at this stage, as an armed struggle in which it was crucial to seize the local initiative in order to inspire Loyalism and while Britain's opponents were poorly organized and trained, was not properly grasped by British leaders who were unduly cautious in the aftermath of Bunker Hill. A pamphlet of 1776 complained that the Americans had been given "the advantage of gaining time to form a union of counsels, to adjust plans of action, to turn their resources into the most convenient channels, to train their men in regular discipline, and to draw to their camp ammunition and stores, and all the necessary implements of war".[34]

Arguably the same problems that were to face the British in the South in 1780–1 would have affected earlier operations there: to make a sufficiently widespread impact it would have been necessary to disperse forces and thus the army could have been defeated in detail. On the other hand, aside from the success of dispersed units in fortified positions repelling attack, as at Québec in 1775 and Savannah, Stono Ferry and Castine in 1779, the Revolutionary position in 1775–6 was far less consolidated than it was to become, while British control of the sea was not seriously challenged until 1778.

Prior to that, the British failed to make adequate use of their naval power. The easy capture of Newport in December 1776 and of Savannah in December 1778 suggests what might have been achieved earlier. It should have been possible to capture ports in the Middle and Southern colonies, even if a major force had not been sent to operate in the interior. A "Southern strategy" offered both these alternatives, and the eventual failure of the attempt to control the interior does not invalidate the alternative of garrisoning crucial ports, a policy that was dependent on naval power.

If it is argued, however, that the linchpin of American resistance was Washington's army then an advocacy of dispersal may be inappropriate. The greatest failure of the navy can then be seen as the failure to cut off

175

The Destruction of the American Fleet at Penobscot Bay, 14 August 1779, by Dominic Serres. The British base at Castine was besieged by the Massachusetts militia supported by a squadron under Dudley Saltonstall. The arrival of a smaller British squadron under Commodore Sir George Collier led to panic. Most of the American ships fled up the Penobscot River where they were beached and set alight. The other ships were captured by Collier. The American soldiers and sailors fled into the woods. Castine was held by the British for the remainder of the war. The debacle indicated both that the Americans were not as successful at amphibious operations as the more experienced British could be and that in offensive operations their militia were not necessarily an impressive force. Saltonstall was court-martialled and dismissed from the service. *National Maritime Museum, London.*

Washington's retreat from Brooklyn after the battle of Long Island in 1776. America, even during the Revolutionary War, was a continental power and the issue could not be decided except by an army. Any policy that did not concentrate on destroying Washington's army arguably would not have worked, although a series of amphibious diversionary attacks might have made it difficult for Washington to prevent men from returning to protect their homes.

French entry into the war altered the parameters of amphibious operations. Instead of simply considering the American military and political response, it was necessary to face the prospect of a loss of maritime superiority. Naval resources were redeployed as Britain responded to the integration of the American conflict into a wider struggle in which the naval balance in American waters was interrelated with that in European and, more obviously, Caribbean waters.

After French entry into the war, the threat of French naval action was a major factor in operations in North America. The entry of Spain (1779) and the Dutch (1780) further complicated the situation for the British. By 1780 France and Spain had a combined quantitative superiority in naval tonnage over Britain of about 25 per cent. As a result, the British were unable to repeat their success of the Seven Years' War. The Dutch, who had not taken part in the Seven Years' War, prepared 14 ships of the line in 1781 and 19 in 1782, and opened the North Sea as a new theatre of war. Bourbon numbers and the late mobilization of British naval strength meant that for most of the war the British navy was fighting on the defensive against heavy odds, and the only real possibilities of taking the initiative was before Spain entered the war in 1779, and in 1782, by which time Britain was winning the naval race.

The British military effort was also complicated by ministerial rivalry. In his quest to establish himself as the dominant war minister, Lord George Germain, the Colonial Secretary, sought to undermine the Earl of Sandwich, the First Lord of the Admiralty. Germain was temperamentally unsuited to creating the necessary co-operation of army and navy. After the entry of France into the war, America "became a strategic backwater" as British interests were threatened elsewhere, including, crucially, in European waters, but Germain was unwilling to accept the political and strategic consequences as it threatened his position.

The British navy gained control of neither European nor American waters. The arrival of the French in American waters, where d'Estaing was first spotted by the British on 5 July 1778, reflected the failure to keep the French fleet in European waters. The desirability of blockading French ports, for which there was arguably too few ships, clashed with Sandwich's prudent argument that British naval strength should be concentrated in home waters, not only to deter invasion but also to permit a serious challenge to the main French fleet which was based at Brest, and thus to gain a position of naval dominance. This could be better obtained by concentrating naval strength, rather than dissipating it on distant stations. In the latter, squadrons could support amphibious operations and protect trade, but they could not materially affect the struggle for naval dominance and were too distant to control effectively; in short a strategy that lacked strategic possibilities. Parcelling out much of the fleet among distant stations, the commanders of which jealously guarded their autonomy and resources, produced an inflexibility that was ill suited to the need to react to French initiatives.

Keeping a close eye on Brest and failing to blockade Toulon or block the Straits of Gibraltar left the Toulon fleet free to sail to North America. Given the troops deployed on land, it was dangerous to risk the loss of naval control in American waters. If the French made such an attempt, a matching squadron could theoretically be sent in pursuit, although it was possible that the French fleet might inflict serious damage before the British arrived. Alternatively, the opportunity could be taken of defeating the Brest fleet, if it sailed forth.[35]

A fierce government dispute over strategy[36] was matched by public concern over the level of naval preparedness, and there were no victories to ease political tension. Proposing in 1779 a motion of censure on the government for not sending sufficient ships to Admiral Lord Howe at New York the previous year, Charles James Fox, the leader of the opposition in the Commons and a former Lord of the Admiralty, claimed that

> if Lord Howe had been reinforced or the Streights of Gibraltar watched, in either event the effect would be similar; that of securing to Lord Howe the full advantage of the force under his command, or giving him a superiority in case the Toulon squadron was permitted to cross the ocean.[37]

The failure to blockade Toulon looked back to Byng's failure off Minorca in 1756 and to the refusal to act over the French acquisition of Corsica in 1768. It contrasted with the more assertive use of naval power in the Mediterranean between 1694 and 1748, in 1793–6 and from 1798.

In 1778 the navy failed to defeat the French before Spain entered the war. Had it done so, the British position would have been far stronger; indeed Charles III of Spain, who had already experienced the consequences of British naval strength in 1762, and also as King of Naples in 1742, might have been deterred from acting. Lacking the naval superiority that would have been provided by the addition of Vice-Admiral John Byron's squadron, detached to pursue d'Estaing to North America, Admiral Augustus Keppel failed to destroy the evasive Brest fleet under Admiral Louis-Guillouet, Comte d'Orvilliers in the battle off Ushant on 27 July 1778. John Blankett, then 4th Lieutenant on Keppel's flagship HMS *Victory* and a critic of British naval preparedness, reported,

> We fell in with the French fleet on Thursday the 23rd about 1 o'clock in the afternoon, they were then 42 sail amongst which we counted 32 ships of the line. Both fleets were then a good deal scattered and distant from each other about three leagues. Our fleet stood towards them, and they from us, till the evening when the French fleet being all collected, they tacked and stood towards us in regular order. As we had no doubt but they meant to give us battle, we tacked and lay too, for that night, blowing hard, expecting to begin the action in the morning but the French availing themselves of a change of wind in their favour, made sail and in the morning were to windward of us, in good order except two ships, who being to leeward bore away, and never after joined the

fleet. The French fleet kept the advantage of the wind by the most steady attention and good management, until Monday the 27th having worked to windward in regular order, in a manner we did not expect. About 11 o'clock on Monday morning Sir Robert Harland who led our van, stood near to the French line they being on the other tack. The French van fired on our ships who were the farthest to windward, which was soon returned and the engagement began to be general in the van of both fleets about 11. Admiral Keppel thus situated was obliged to make the signal to engage, on which the French ships bore away and run down to windward of our fleet, who were chasing to windward and of course not in order and the firing continued till a little after one.

The French fired first and very effectually destroyed our rigging and sails, and very much damaged our masts and yards; however, the Admiral made the signal to wear and stand towards the enemy; but finding our ships to be so much shattered, he wore again in order to give them an opportunity to repair their damage. The French wore about 3, and stood towards us, in good order, only one of their ships appearing to be disabled; on this the Admiral made the signal to form the line but as our disabled ships formed very slowly it was evening before our fleet were in any order. The French advanced in a most regular line and in a masterly manner, until the close of the evening, when their van was to leeward in a line with our center – In the night they bore away and to our surprise were out of sight by day light.

Your Lordship will recollect that the forcing a fleet to action, equal in force, and with the advantage of the wind must always be done with great risk, and our fleet was not equal to that manoeuvre, but chance, which determines many events, put it out of the Admiral's power to choose his disposition, the eagerness of our van when fired on, putting all regularity out of the question. The French behaved more like seamen, and more officerlike than was imagined they would do, their ships were in very high order, well managed, well rigged and . . . much more attentive to order than our own. In short, they are truly formidable, nor will I admit the general received opinion of their inferiority in any one point . . . their fire was brisk and well directed, nor was there the least appearance of fear, many of their ships passing us as close as we could wish . . . As our fire was directed low and was well kept up, I have reason to think killed a great number of their men and did them great damage in their hulls. But the truth is, unless two fleets of equal force are equally determined for battle, whoever attacks must do it with infinite risk, but a fleet to leeward attacking one to windward is a dangerous manoeuvre indeed.[38]

In 1779, France and Spain sent a fleet of 66 ships of the line under Orvilliers into the Channel, in response to the Spanish demand for a short war. The attempt to invade Britain was thwarted by disease and poor organization, rather than British naval action, for the out-numbered Western Squadron under Admiral Charles Hardy failed to mount an effective response.[39] The loss of Grenada (1779), West Florida (1779–81) and Minorca (1782),[40] and the build up of a powerful Franco-American force around Yorktown (1781), revealed that the Bourbons could mount successful amphibious expeditions. The French navy also destroyed the British factories at Churchill and York in Hudson's Bay in 1782.

The French were also more successful at sea than in the Seven Years' War, in part thanks to determined and effective leadership. When Byron attacked d'Estaing off Grenada on 6 July 1779 he was outnumbered and roughly handled. In three engagements in the West Indies in 1780 Rodney was unable to defeat the Comte de Guichen. The failure of Admiral Thomas Graves to defeat the French off the Virginia Capes (5 September 1781) was an indecisive battle in terms of the damage inflicted, but, as it prevented British relief of Cornwallis' encircled army at Yorktown, it was an important success for the French. Graves was out-numbered, 24 to 19 in ships of the line, and instead of taking the risky course of ordering a general chase on the French van as it sailed in disordered haste from the Chesapeake, manoeuvred so as to bring all his ships opposite to the French line of battle, which was given time to form. The engagement lasted for just over two hours, neither side having any ships sunk, but both suffering considerable damage.

The temporary and localized French superiority that the battle reflected and sustained was not, however, the consequence or cause of a climatic battle in which one fleet destroyed the other and, as a result, it did not lead to a decisive shift in naval superiority.[41] Nevertheless, in the summer of 1781 another Franco-Spanish fleet was able to cruise in the Channel approaches without the out-numbered British risking battle. In the same month as the battle of the Virginia Capes, the British were concerned about a possible invasion of England or Ireland from Brest and also about the danger that the French fleet there would be employed against Gibraltar. There was no sense that Britain controlled the war at sea.[42]

It was not until the Battle of the Saints that there was a decisive British naval victory to rank with Quiberon Bay or Lagos: the French were threatening to invade Jamaica, but, on 12 April 1782, off the Iles des Saintes south of Guadeloupe, the out-numbered French commander, de Grasse, was soundly defeated by Rodney. He broke through the French line, capturing five ships of the line, including the flagship, the *Ville de Paris*, with de Grasse himself, after a long fight. Thanks in part to innovations introduced by Captain Charles Douglas of the *Formidable* that increased the ease of serving cannon, of firing them instantaneously, and the possible angles of training them, including improvements in flintlocks, tin tubes, flannel cartridges, wedges to absorb recoil and steel compression springs, British cannon fire was particularly effective. The French strategy was wrecked and, thereafter, the Bourbon fleets remained on the defensive in the Caribbean. Regarded as the saviour of Jamaica, Rodney became a hero. In Bristol,

> his Lordship made his triumphal entry into this City to dine by invitation with the Society of Merchants at their hall in King Street . . . several hundred of the citizens met and formed a magnificent cavalcade consisting of equestrians and carriages forming a long line interspersed with bands of music embossomed in laurels in boats placed upon wheeled carriages. Also three persons in the characters and costumes of Mars, Britannia and Minerva seated upon thrones likewise upon wheeled carriages with their attendants at their feet. In the cavalcade was a vessel about 40 tons burthen drawn also upon a wheeled carriage by horses (having swivels on board which were fired occasionally) . . . every insignia and trophy that could add splendour to the scene were resorted to. The cavalcade passed through the principal streets of the city amidst the acclamations of the spectators, the music playing, bells ringing, flags flying and guns firing, [word obscure] by the smiles and the waving handkerchiefs of the fair lasses of Bristol.[43]

Elsewhere, the navy was also able to relieve Gibraltar on three occasions, permitting the fortress to resist the long siege of 1779–83, and on the first a Spanish squadron was defeated off Cape St Vincent on 16 January 1780: Rodney and 21 of the line chased 11 Spanish of the line in a battle conducted on a stormy night. One Spanish warship was destroyed, and six, including the flagship, captured. A naval engagement nearby off Cape Spartel on 20 October 1781 was indecisive. Further north, Vice-Admiral Sir Hyde Parker fought a costly, close-range but indecisive battle with the Dutch on Dogger Bank on 5 August 1781. The Dutch succeeded in keeping a British squadron busy watching them.

The navy also responded to the conflict both by arranging a major programme of construction and by technological advances. Copper sheathing reduced the difficulties caused by barnacles, weeds and the teredo worm, and the consequent loss of speed, and made refits easier. It was pressed forward from February 1779 by Sir Charles Middleton, Comptroller of the Navy 1778–90. In 1780, 42 ships of the line were given copper sheathing. In 1781 the Marquess of Rockingham claimed:

> The copper bottoms occasioning our ships to sail so much better enables us either to go and attack if we should see an inferior fleet or to decline the attempt if we should see a superior fleet.

The value of copper sheathing in the conduct of naval operations has recently been queried, but the administrative achievement was considerable.[44] The demand for copper also brought great wealth to Wales. Another development was the introduction of the carronade, a new, light short-barrelled gun that was very effective at close quarters and was adopted in 1779. It was used with effect at the Saintes.[45]

World war

French naval efforts on entering the war were chiefly aimed at securing the profitable sugar islands of the West Indies. They captured Dominica (1778), Grenada (1779), St Vincent (1779) and Tobago (1781), but lost St Lucia in December 1778. D'Estaing's attempt to regain St Lucia was unsuccessful. After the Dutch came into the war, Rodney captured St Eustatius in the West Indies in February 1781, but it was subsequently recaptured by the French. Naval superiority enabled the French to capture Nevis in January 1782 and St Christopher (St Kitts) and Montserrat the following month, but the arrival of naval reinforcements under Rodney from Britain in February ended the crisis. In early 1783 the French seized Turks Island. Nelson and a relief force unsuccessfully counter-attacked the garrison at Grand Turk in March.

The Spaniards conquered West Florida: Baton Rouge fell in September 1779, Mobile in March 1780, and Pensacola in May 1781. An attempt to regain Mobile failed in January 1781. In Pensacola, the major base in West Florida, a 2,000 strong garrison successfully resisted a siege by 7,800 troops under Galvez until a Spanish shell hit one of the magazines and blew up part of the fort.[46] In Central America the Spaniards captured St. Georges Cay, the principal port of the British loggers at Belize, in September 1779. A British expedition in 1780 against Fort San Juan in modern Nicaragua intended to push through to the Pacific port town of Realejo, fell victim to yellow fever. Fort San Juan fell in April 1780 after a three-week siege, but the British force was then greatly weakened by yellow fever and in February 1781 the British withdrew to Jamaica. They had lost 77 per cent of the men that had been sent. In May 1782 a Spanish force escorted by an American frigate and privateers captured Nassau, the capital of New Providence, the major island in the Bahamas. The poorly defended position put up no resistance; but when a counter-invasion was mounted in April 1783 a strong Spanish garrison resisted before surrendering at the close of the war.[47]

In Europe, however, the Spaniards failed, despite major efforts, to take Gibraltar, which was well fortified and ably defended by Lieutenant-General George Eliott. Their blockade began in 1779, and a formal siege began in the summer of 1781. On 13 September 1781, a major attack was made with floating batteries, but most were sunk by British fire and thereafter the siege became a less intense blockade and bombardment. The British ability to relieve the position by sea was crucial, although it depleted naval strength elsewhere.

Minorca, however, surrendered in February 1782 to a vastly greater Franco-Spanish force after a long siege without relief had let scurvy ravage the garrison. In West Africa the French took Gorée in January 1779, but it was recaptured later in the year. In India, Pondicherry surrendered on 17 October 1778 after a month's siege, and, as after its fall in 1761, the fortifications were demolished. The success of the British siege owed much to the retreat to Mauritius of the covering French squadron after an indecisive action on 10 August. Captain George Vandeput and HMS *Asia* captured the French base of Mahé in 1779.

In the latter stages of the war, the Indian Ocean also became an important sphere of hostilities. The British attempt to capture Cape Town from the Dutch in 1781 was prevented by a French fleet under Admiral Pierre André Suffren that brought reinforcements, although four Dutch East Indiamen anchored nearby in Saldanha Bay were seized on 21 July. Dutch bases in India and Sri Lanka (Ceylon) were rapidly captured: Sadras and Pulicat were seized by troops from Madras. Negapatam was captured in November 1781 by troops supported by ships under Vice-Admiral Sir Edward Hughes, Commander-in-Chief in the East Indies. Hughes then embarked about 500 soldiers and sailed to Trincomalee on Sri Lanka, the only all-weather harbour in the Bay of Bengal. The commanding fort was successfully stormed on 11 February 1782. The Dutch bases on the west coast of Sumatra fell in 1781 to attack from the East India Company's base of Benkulen.

In 1782 the able and energetic Suffren arrived in Indian waters to provide support for Haider Ali, the Sultan of Mysore. This led to a series of battles with Hughes in the Bay of Bengal and off Sri Lanka from February 1782 until June 1783: the battle of Sadras (17 February 1782), Providien (12 April 1782), Negapatam (6 July 1782), Trincomalee (3 September 1782), and Cuddalore (20 June 1783). Suffren proved a redoubtable opponent who sought to scatter Hughes' fleet and defeat it piece-meal by concentrating strength against vulnerable sections. However, Hughes avoided defeat and was thus able to prevent Suffren from determining the course of the war on land. Suffren suffered from the lack of a well-equipped local base and had poor relations with some of his captains whom he thought timid and incompetent. Nevertheless, he forced the British garrison in Trincomalee to capitulate in August 1782, a major blow, relieved Cuddalore in June 1783, and, in the last battle, attacked the more numerous British at close range and inflicted greater damage than he suffered.[48]

War in India, 1778–84

The arrival of Suffren's fleet was made more serious by the challenges to British power in India. Indeed, although less lasting in their impact than the War of American Independence, the conflicts in India from 1778 can be seen as an aspect of a wider crisis for the emerging British empire. The British were involved in war with two major opponents. In western India a conflict with the Marathas in 1774–6 had left a peace that was unsatisfactory to both sides. Seeking to emulate the gains made in Bengal, Bombay, the weakest of the East India Company Presidencies, was drawn into struggles between the Maratha leaders, but its intervention proved ineffective. In late 1778 a slow-moving army of 3,200 infantry, with 12,000 bullocks pulling guns and supplies, advanced from Bombay into the difficult terrain of the Ghats.[49] The army was not up to the task and failed to master the crucial equations of mobility, logistics and terrain. As it advanced, it moved less than a mile a day. The Marathas made a stand on 9 January, but retreated when the British formed up and advanced. Two days later, however, John Carnac, now a member of the Council at Bombay and one of the civilian committee with the army, told its commander, Lieutenant-Colonel William Cockburn, that it was necessary to retreat. Carnac argued that difficulties in obtaining supplies made it essential to fall back in order to open communication links with Bombay, and he also pointed out that Ragunath Rao, their Maratha ally, seemed to be winning no support.

In what was an administrative shambles, the powers of the committee were ambiguously phrased. Cockburn thought it important to press on towards Pune (Poona), the Maratha capital and the objective of the expedition, and said that it would be dangerous to retreat in open country in face of the Maratha forces, especially as their cavalry moved very rapidly. The committee, nevertheless, ordered a retreat, but Cockburn's force, now 2,800 strong, was rapidly surrounded by a far larger force. Cockburn wrote of the 12th, "we remained under a severe cannonade, having the whole flower of the Maratha horse ready to charge whenever an opportunity offered, but our well served artillery and the steadiness of the infantry prevented them". However, the following night the army was badly affected by falling morale. Desertions sapped its strength and, with ammunition falling, it signed a convention at Wadgaon that provided for the withdrawal of the army to Bombay. Subsequently, everybody blamed everybody else and the Directors sacked the lot of them.[50]

This convention rarely features in the annals of British military history, but it is instructive for a number of reasons. The parallel with Burgoyne's advance on the Hudson in 1777 is interesting. A well-trained force could only achieve so much, especially if on difficult terrain, in the face of considerably more numerous opponents and if reconnaissance was inadequate. In India, unlike America, the British suffered from the greater mobility enjoyed by their opponents thanks to the role of their light cavalry.[51]

On 15 January 1761 Carnac, then a major in the East India Company's Bengal army, had defeated a Mughal force supported by a French contingent. On that occasion he had argued that it was foolish to have European (i.e. non-native) cavalry in the British forces, "nor will our establishment of Europeans admit of their being otherwise employed than as infantry, in which alone our immense superiority over the country [Indian] powers will always consist".[52] Carnac was correct. The British could not have competed with the Indians, but this led to a potential disadvantage that was very serious. In 1770 a member of the Bombay Council opposed hostilities with the Marathas on the grounds that the British could do nothing to prevent their cavalry from invading the Carnatic.[53]

Much of the blame for the British failure can be put on logistics and the command structure. Goddard, later, did quite well in this theatre. Compared with the other two Presidencies, Bombay was inexperienced in mounting expeditionary forces. One of the reasons for the committee going along was a feeling that Cockburn was not up to the task, but this only created command problems. The supply train was too long and this delayed progress up the Ghats. Such a long train was not uncommon in India: the British emulated Mughal luxury in the field.

Another British force, however, successfully marched 785 miles from Bengal to Surat in 1778–9, much of it across unfriendly territory. Covered by artillery, the British crossed the Jumna in the face of Maratha forces on 19 May 1778. The following month, the expedition was delayed by bad roads, a lack of water and of bullocks, and by the "scorching heat". On 3 June, "the scorching hot winds with the intense heat of the sun on a dry extensive plain . . . exposed us to sufferings of the superlative degree. About twenty sepoys dropped down quite exhausted for want of water". Nevertheless, the march continued, helped by the Maratha failure to block wells. The breaking of the monsoon delayed the expedition in Bundelkhand, but detachments continued to operate. The infantry volleys that had played a major role in the crossing of the Jumna, also helped drive off an attack on 1 September. There was much criticism of Colonel Leslie's slow progress at Calcutta. Patronage and seniority had got him the command. Lieutenant-Colonel Thomas Goddard, not Leslie, was the preferred choice of Warren Hastings, the Governor General. Leslie took his wife with him, and it was alleged that his delay was really due to his diamond dealing in Bundelkhand. Leslie died on 3 October and was replaced by Goddard. He resumed the march, despite frequent desertions and an absence of reliable news about the fate of the Bombay army. When Goddard heard of its failure, he marched on Surat, which he reached in February 1779.[54]

Although he arrived too late to prevent the defeat of the Bombay army, Goddard subsequently pressed the Marathas hard. The ruler of Baroda was intimidated into alliance and into ceding territory near Surat, and the Maratha garrison of Dabhoi fled when the British erected batteries. The rapid breaching of the walls of Ahmadabad demonstrated the effectiveness of British artillery and led to its fall on 15 February 1780. The British had arrived on 10 February, and on the 12th established a battery for three 18 pounders and two howitzers within 350 yards of the wall. The defenders "attempted to disturb the workmen with some small pieces of artillery from towers on the walls, but these were soon silenced by 2 long six-pounders sent down with the covering party". By the evening of the 13th the cannon had battered a breach 100 yards wide "besides the defences taken off for a considerable distance to the right and left"; by the evening of the 14th a level breach 150 yards wide had been made. The fortress was stormed at dawn on the 15th, the defenders being taken by surprise. Many "behaved nobly, drawing their swords and dealing blows around them even after the bayonets were plunged in their bodies".[55] Goddard then pressed on to defeat the Maratha leader Sindia on 3 April and to attack Bassein, which fell on 11 December. Another force under Captain William Popham, sent to help the Rana of Ghodi against the Marathas, defeated them and then stormed by escalade the fortress of Gwalior, which was generally reckoned impregnable (3 August 1780). Popham, a mere captain, upset a lot of higher Bengal officers by his enterprise which they called reckless. He was superceded.

Goddard was less successful the following year. The heavy cost of the war led to pressure for its end. Hastings became keen for a negotiated solution because of the problems that Haidar Ali of Mysore was causing in the Carnatic. Goddard decided to strike at the Maratha centre of Pune (Poona). He advanced from Bassein in January 1781, overrunning the Bhore Ghaut, but failed to defeat the Marathas, suffered from their attacks on his supplies and was forced to retreat with serious losses. The indecisive nature of the war in 1781 was due to the greater effectiveness of the Marathas, who increasingly emulated the infantry artillery combinations of European armies, while maintaining their superiority in cavalry, to the problems of terrain and logistics confronting the British, and to their need to fight Mysore at the same time. Nevertheless, Goddard was able to recruit cavalry. His allied forces included Mughal and Pathan mounted units.

The Treaty of Salbai (May 1782) ended the war, with most British gains restored to the Marathas, and committed both powers to unite against Mysore, a necessary result for the hard-pressed British. The suppression of the rebellion of Raja Chayt Singh in Benares in 1781 also helped, by reducing the pressure on the forces in Bengal. The war in Benares had been brief, but the heavy casualties suffered when one unit advanced into the narrow streets of a town indicated the potential hazards of that kind of fighting.[56]

The expansionism of Haidar Ali, and his co-operation with the French threatened the East India Company's position in southern India, while the British capture of the French base of Mahé, which Haidar saw as under his protection, and their refusal to provide help against the Marathas as they were obliged to do under the treaty of 1769 angered Haidar. Anglo-Maratha hostilities gave Haidar an opportunity to attack. In July 1780 he invaded the Carnatic, advancing through the Changama Pass. The British response was inadequate. A force in the Circars under Colonel William Baillie was instructed to join near Madras with the main Madras army under Sir Hector Munro, the victor of Buxar, in order to block the Mysore advance, but Baillie moved slowly, while Munro failed to advance to his relief. The initial error was not to order Baillie down earlier when Haidar was clearly threatening. In addition, the route he took was ill-advised. Munro was past his prime.

On 10 September 1780 Baillie was attacked by the entire Mysore army at Perumbakam. He drew up his men in a defensive position, only to find that badly disrupted when his numerous camp followers fled. Baillie was heavily out-numbered and, in the end, the square of his troops, under fire from cannon, was fought down by repeated attacks by Mysore cavalry and infantry. The wounded Baillie died in captivity, as did many of the other prisoners. The British situation deteriorated as Haidar pressed on to make gains in the Carnatic. Furthermore, his capture of magazines of supplies in the Nawab's hands and the devastation spread by his cavalry created serious supply problems for the Company's army, problems exacerbated by the size of the army. Thus, the maintenance and protection of its supplies became the major operational objective of the army.

Both sides generally took positions by storm. It was often remarked by British officers who had seen service in Europe how much weaker and more irregular were the numerous mud forts which peppered India. Some, such as Gwalior, were only strong because they were situated on precipitous rocks. The flavour of storming operations was captured by Lieutenant-Colonel Henry Cosby, who described one such attempt in 1780. Delays in raising the ladders proved fatal to the British:

> by this time the enemy's whole force were collected to oppose us, numbers of blue lights hoisted all along the face attacked and rows of pikes presented through every embrasure so that it now became impossible to enter, as a man no sooner got to the top of the ladder, than he was knocked down by a shot or a pike.[57]

The situation deteriorated when the French landed 3,000 men to help Haidar Ali. In response, Hastings sent Eyre Coote, now a Lieutenant-General and Commander-in-Chief in India, from Calcutta by sea to Madras, while five regiments from the Bengal sepoy corps under Colonel Thomas Pearse marched overland via Orissa and the Northern Circars, arriving in the summer of 1781.

Coote reported a lack of cannon, ammunition, tents and provisions in Madras. He requested money from Bengal, which Hastings sent. The interdependence of the different parts of the British system was amply demonstrated. Bengal was placed under great pressure in meeting the financial demands from Madras, but, as it was peaceful, revenues rose, while money provided by Oudh was crucial.[58]

Coote raised the siege of Wandewash, only to be cut off at Cuddalore from his base at Madras. Coote, however, was re-supplied by sea. In June 1781 he advanced from Cuddalore, but was repulsed by Haidar Ali at Chelambakam. Coote fell back to Porto Novo pursued by Haidar Ali. The latter deployed his more numerous troops in a good position with the sea on the flank, but on 1 July Coote's men turned that flank by advancing along the sandhills under covering naval fire, and the British front line then advanced.

Haidar Ali's army was heavily defeated, and Coote followed up his victory, helped by the addition of Pearse's force. Perumbakam was stormed on 27 August. Coote went on to win more victories in 1781. Madras was saved. Coote's health, however, was wrecked and he returned to Bengal. His successors were less effective. Major-General James Stuart fell out with the Governor of Madras, George, Lord Macartney. Macartney believed it crucial to subordinate military commanders to the civil power and felt that Stuart was less than energetic and competent. Stuart was too slow, but there was also a major difference over strategy. Coote and Stuart both felt the French enemy should have priority over Haidar and Tipu. Macartney had contrary views, and also wanted to divide the army into three divisions so that it could fight in different theatres. Coote and Stuart, perhaps with Baillie in mind, wanted to keep it concentrated. Macartney particularly wanted to detach part of Stuart's army to help Colonel Fullarton, a royal officer, who dynamically invaded Coimbatore (Southern Mysore) west of Trichinopoly in 1782. Stuart countermanded Macartney's orders to make the detachment. This was the cause of the conflict. Stuart was suspended from his command, and sent back to Britain.

The hazards of operating in India were amply demonstrated at the start of 1782. On 18 February a British force under Colonel Braithwaite was defeated just south of the Coleroon river by Haidar Ali's son, Tipu Sultan, who had been trained by his father's French military advisers. Failing to take adequate precautions, Braithwaite had been surprised. The British attempt to retreat was unsuccessful. In a repetition of Perumbakam, Braithwaite held off the Mysore cavalry for a day, until his ammunition ran out. Braithwaite's force consisted of 1,400 infantry, 200 cavalry, 80 artillerymen, six six-pounders, two three-pounders and a howitzer. Including a French force, Tipu's army, according to a British source that may have exaggerated, contained 12,000 infantry, 6,000 cavalry and 20 cannon.[59]

Tipu succeeded his father in December 1782 and pressed the British hard, but he suffered from the cessation of French support after they made peace with Britain in 1783. The French had been handicapped by the limited military forces they could deploy in India and by the mutual antipathy of their potential allies, Mysore and the Marathas. However, they had assisted Mysore, by providing advisers, co-operating in specific operations, as against Cuddalore, and by diverting British efforts.

Tipu Sultan continued to press the British hard, although he was affected by British forces operating from three separate directions: Coote and Stuart's concentration on the Carnatic was replaced by a more multifaceted approach, including operations on the Malabar coast and an attack on Mysore from the south. Nevertheless, the cost of the war to the Company led to pressure for its end and in January 1784 the British garrison at Mangalore surrendered after a ten-month siege. The subsequent Treaty of Mangalore of 11 March 1784 was based on the *status quo ante bellum* (a return to the situation prior to the war); but it was severely criticized by Warren Hastings for failing to protect the position of Britain's ally, the Nawab of the Carnatic.

War reviewed

The British had at least preserved their position in India. They were helped greatly by the divided nature of their opponents: the Marathas made peace before Mysore and by the Treaty of Salbai agreed to act against Haidar Ali. The British were also helped by the absence of any serious military challenge to Bengal and by their ability to move troops from Bengal to the Carnatic. The greater British commitment to India was indicated by the decision to retain regular Crown troops there once peace was restored.

Elsewhere, the British had been less successful, and this was reflected in the terms of the peace signed at Versailles on 3 September 1783. France won minor gains, including Tobago and Senegal and consent to the fortification of Dunkirk. Spain obtained Florida, East and West, and Minorca. The most important loss was the Thirteen Colonies, and contemporaries suspected that this loss would mark a fundamental weakening of the British empire and be followed by French challenges to British power elsewhere.

The seriousness of the failure of the British military system should not be exaggerated. The British had held on to Canada, Jamaica, Gibraltar and Madras. Britain had not been invaded and there had been no rebellion in Ireland. The French fleet had been defeated in 1782. Indeed, an appreciation of British resilience and successes, in the teeth of a powerful European–American coalition, is a necessary part of any assessment of the war. In terms of resources, the war had revealed the problems posed by the absence of a large enough army. There was indeed a major expansion in the size of British land forces. The army establishment at the beginning of 1775 was about 36,000 strong, while the envisaged strength of land forces for 1776 was 96,314, although that included German auxiliaries and North American Loyalists. A force of over 60,000 in North America might seem substantial, but they were spread out from Canada to Florida, many units were committed to garrison duties, and others were deployed in hostile country. The British forces operating in the field were often quite small and thus especially vulnerable to casualties. The limited forces at their disposal affected the strategic plans and tactical moves of British generals, but their American opponents were also short of troops.

In India, in contrast, the size of the East India Company's force expanded greatly, rising to 113,000 by 1783, enabling the Company, albeit with difficulties, to wage offensive war against Mysore and the Marathas simultaneously. The Indians that the British recruited and trained were good soldiers. In 1780 Captain Samuel Kirkpatrick marched from Patna to Midnapore – "a route no body of troops ever went before, and a most disagreeable trip from the badness of the roads, woods and jungle" – at the "head of so good a corps as the 31st Legion of Sepoys".[60]

The initial stages of the war with France had also revealed a crisis in naval preparedness, but, by the end of the conflict, the British were outbuilding Bourbon rivals. Resources played a major role in the conflict, but the war was about far more. The need to confront a number of challenges around the world placed considerable burdens on the ability to control and allocate resources and also raises issues of strategic understanding and of the accurate assessment of threats. The nature of communications prevented the exercise of close control and made it difficult to respond to developments adequately.

Furthermore, there were serious problems in co-operation between army and navy, as well as problems in co-ordination in both land and sea operations, problems that raise questions about both the calibre of British military leadership and the ability of the military system to execute plans. Blame has been widely distributed: some generals, such as Burgoyne and Cornwallis, accused of rashness, others, such as Clinton, of excessive caution.[61]

Poor operational decisions were indeed responsible for specific failures on land and sea. However, poor leadership in this war was not restricted to the British, the British did enjoy important successes, there had been many failures of command in conflicts that had been successful for the British, including the Seven Years' War, and the tasks facing British commanders on both land and sea were formidable.

Britain's opponents were able to take the initiative in North America, the West Indies and the Indian Ocean, and on many occasions the British were unable to fight more than defensively. Some operations, such as Carleton at Québec, the defence of Gibraltar, and Coote's campaign in 1781, were successful, others, such as the Carnatic campaign in 1780, Cornwallis at Yorktown and the defence of Minorca and Trincomalee in 1782 were unsuccessful. The British found themselves in the same position as the Bourbons in the Seven Years' War: once their opponent had gained the initiative they might be able to fight them off, but it was difficult to do so, and even harder to regain the initiative. In resisting, the British were fortunate that their opponents lacked their degree of land–sea co-operation. The Americans and the Indian rulers lacked sufficient state-directed naval strength to support their land operations. Thus Québec was not also attacked by sea, while in 1778, when Clinton retreated from Philadelphia, he was able to sail from New Jersey to New York. Haidar Ali and Tipu Sultan had no Indian squadron to support operations against ports such as Cuddalore, Madras, Mangalore and Porto Novo.

The French had the necessary naval strength both in American and Indian waters to attempt such goals, but it was hard to arrange consistent co-operation, especially if circumstances were difficult. Furthermore, the French themselves faced serious problems in balancing their naval commitments and sustaining their squadrons, and these affected the operations of particular fleets.

British strategic options were different before and after French intervention, for that transformed both offensive and defensive options. The campaigns of 1775 and 1777 were seriously mishandled; that of 1776 less so. Yet, the net effect was the same. The Thirteen Colonies had not been reconquered by the time Britain found herself in a world war and, moreover, one in which the Bourbons did not have distracting European commitments. The British lacked any technological leading edge over their European opponents and did not display any special tactical aptitude until Rodney's victory at the Saintes. The Indian forces that the British fought differed in tactics, weaponry and balance between the various arms. The British did not necessarily enjoy an advantage in weaponry and tactics in India, and it is anyway inappropriate to think of their forces as simply depending on firepower, or of military success as a product of the advantage of firepower. Furthermore, the limitations of Britain's military power in India and the growing strength of her opponents was apparent. The Secret Committee at Fort St. George noted of the 1781 campaign,

> large body of French troops was daily expected to come to the assistance of Haidar, without which he had been able to maintain his ground in the Carnatic notwithstanding every exertion made against him . . . that those [forts] we held did not impede his progress or prevent his possession of the greatest part of his country.

Haidar was also able to avoid defeat:

> though he had engaged three times in the late campaign he discontinued the combat on each occasion before any durable impression could be made on his army, that Sir Eyre Coote always possessing the field of battle had a fair title to the laurels due to victory but that Haidar suffered few of the disadvantages of a defeat, that his numerous bodies so far from dispersing as had in general been the case with Indian armies in contest with our troops were for the most part as well kept together as before, and did not seem to feel

the humiliation or adopt the fears of the vanquished that they were driven to no permanent distress nor did they abandon the territory they had invaded, that the decided superiority of the British arms in Indostan had been maintained but the solid purpose of the war to expel the enemy remained to be effected.[62]

War with the Bourbons and, especially, the Dutch, provided the opportunity of making territorial gains to offset losses elsewhere, but the situation was less favourable than in the Seven Years' War. This was demonstrated most clearly when Suffen intervened to block the British at Cape Town and Trincomalee: individual conflicts were no longer shaped by an overarching British naval dominance. Local dominance was still crucial. Hector Munro's successful siege of Pondicherry in 1778 owed much to support from Sir Edward Vernon's squadron: the town was cut off on 21 August; delayed by heavy rain, the British batteries – 28 heavy cannon and 27 mortars – opened fire on 18 September; and Pondicherry surrendered on 17 October. Vernon both blockaded it and landed marines and sailors to help Munro. However, such dominance was no longer certain. The situation was to be different by the latter stage of the Napoleonic Wars, but, only, at the cost of a protracted struggle first.

CHAPTER SEVEN

Conflict in Europe, 1793–1815

With the exception of its garrison in Gibraltar, the British army had been absent from the European continent since the Seven Years' War. When it returned in 1793, it was to face a new and more formidable opponent, Revolutionary France. The British army was not ready for such a conflict; its small peace time establishment was far smaller than the armies already deployed in Western Europe. In 1793 the peacetime establishment in Britain was only 17,013 men although, when troops in Ireland, Canada, the West Indies, Gibraltar and royal units in India were added, the total was just over 50,000. In 1793, due to recruitment efforts during the Nootka Sound crisis of 1790, this establishment was virtually complete. The French Revolutionary Wars had broken out in 1792, and in 1793 Britain joined the conflict in order to thwart a French threat to the Dutch.

Thus began a period of conflict that involved British troops campaigning across much of the world. St Lucia, Martinique and Guadeloupe were not novel spheres of operation, but the Plate estuary in South America, Egypt, Denmark and Calabria in southern Italy were. Operations outside Europe are considered in Chapter 9 but, even within Europe, the diversity of tasks that the army was ordered to perform is impressive. Initially, the prime commitment was to operations in the Low Countries, but the French success in overrunning them in 1794–5 forced the British army to range more widely. The scope for amphibious attacks in Europe was enlarged. Whereas for most of the Seven Years' War the potential targets were restricted to those on the French coast, the extension of French power and influence across most of Western Europe led the British to attack targets such as Ferrol in Spain (1800), Copenhagen (1807), and Walcheren in the Scheldt estuary (1809). Troops were sent to the Baltic in 1807 and 1808.

In addition, efforts were made to send large forces to the Continent, not only to attack specific targets, but also in order to begin more extensive operations. Thus, in 1799 over 36,000 troops were sent to Den Helder in

Holland, in 1805 a large force was ordered to Hanover, and in 1813 another was sent to Holland. These operations were intended to put long-lasting pressure on France and also to offer support to Britain's allies; in short, a return to the policy followed when troops were sent to Germany in 1758. The dispatch of troops to the Continent was a feature of an alliance strategy that rested more securely on Britain's subsidies to her allies. Such operations depended on co-operation with other powers. Russian troops were also sent to Holland in 1799, while in Germany the British sought to assist Prussia. However, they faced both the difficulties of securing and sustaining such co-operation, and the problems of confronting stronger French forces that were more mobile once the British had landed. Just as the French lost the advantage of a fleet "in being" when they left port, so the British compromised their amphibious capability by mounting expeditions and, still more, landing and keeping a large force on land. Once they had done so, logistics also became a more serious problem.

The Peninsular War in the Iberian peninsula (Spain and Portugal) was the most important British military contribution to the Continental war, prior to the Waterloo campaign of 1815, but it did not begin until 1808. Before that, the British army had a less than distinguished record.

The 1790s

When the British troops arrived in the Low Countries in 1793, the war had already begun a year earlier, and the French were hard pressed, attacked by a coalition that included Austria, Prussia, Spain and the Dutch. Including German auxiliaries, 17,000 of whom were hired in 1793, the British army in the Low Countries rose to 37,500 by late 1794. As in previous wars in the Low Countries, the British army, under George III's son, Frederick, Duke of York, found itself confronting the problems of co-operating with allied forces operating to a different agenda. The campaign faced problems from its inception, although an Anglo-Austrian force defeated the French at the Camp de Famars on 23 May, Valenciennes surrendered on 28 July, after a successful siege, and on 18 August, at Linselles, the Guards under Major-General Gerard Lake drove back a larger French force under Jourdan and Béru at bayonet point. However, the British army, assisted by Hanoverian and Dutch forces, was ordered to besiege Dunkirk, a potent symbol of Anglo-French hostility and one whose fortification had only been permitted by the Treaty of Versailles of 1783. It was mistaken to attack Dunkirk, for it was not a crucial target and, by failing to remain with the Austrians, the British became a more tempting target for French attack. Once York reached Dunkirk, he found himself without the necessary siege artillery. Delays in its dispatch enabled the French to regain the initiative, first by flooding the marshes near the town and then by moving up a relieving army that pushed back the less numerous British and Hano-verians at Hondschoote (6 September). Dispersed French units wore down the defenders, and the French were then victorious, with a final attack. York abandoned the siege and withdrew to winter with the Austrians at Tournai.

In 1794 the Austrians and British had some initial advantages in the Austrian Netherlands, winning engagements at Villers-en-Couches (24 April) and Beaumont (26 April). In the latter cavalry attacks on the French flanks defeated advancing columns with heavy casualties. The British cavalry proved stronger than its French counterpart, which had been greatly dis-rupted by the Revolution, not least because the bloodstock was hit when many horses were eaten. British success culminated in the battle of Willems (10 May): the French cavalry was swept aside and their infantry broken. Repeated cavalry attacks supported by infantry and cannon broke a French square.

However, on 17–18 May 1794, in the battle of Tourcoing near Tournai, the French under Pichegru used their local numerical superiority to defeat British and Austrian units: in the battle, York's army was given inadequate support by the Austrians, and it was forced to stage a fighting withdrawal. Thereafter, York retreated, pushed back by stronger French forces, aban-doning the Austrian Netherlands and falling back through the United Prov-inces during a hard winter. The British fought well when they engaged, but they were outnumbered and had lost the initiative, and the river lines could not be held, not least when the rivers froze. Nijmegen, which the French had attacked, was evacuated on 7 November, and, although the more numerous French were driven across the Waal in the battle of Tüyl on 30 December 1794 and defeated by a British attack at the battle of Buren on 8 January 1795, the outnumbered British, now under Lieutenant-General William Harcourt, retreated through inhospitable terrain. Their medical, transport and supply systems proved inadequate and the army suffered greatly from sickness, reducing its effectiveness. There was a terrible short-age of shoes, bread and uniforms. In April 1795 the British were evacuated from Bremen, although a small cavalry force remained in Germany until that December.[1]

They were not to return to the Low Countries until 1799, but, by then, British forces had been involved in a number of other expeditions. Troops were sent to Toulon in 1793. Royalists had seized control of the city and the British, under Admiral Lord Hood, came to their aid, but they were poorly supplied and out-numbered by the Revolutionary French, while co-operation with a Spanish force also there proved difficult. Alliance strategy and warfare both failed. Toulon was the sole engagement prior to Moore's retreat to Corunna, and later Waterloo, in which Napoleon, then an artil-lery officer, encountered British troops. He used his artillery to drive back the British and established a battery that made the harbour untenable by the

195

British fleet. The British also seized island positions: on Corsica in 1794, off Brittany in 1795, Minorca in 1798. The conquest of Corsica involved some hard fighting, including the successful sieges of Bastia and Calvi.[2]

A raid on Ostend was mounted in 1798 in order to destroy the lock gates of the Bruges canal and make it harder for the French to use the canal system for invasion preparations. Major-General Eyre Coote, nephew of the victor of Wandewash, led 1,300 troops who disembarked and cut the sluices at Ostend on 18 May. However, a strong wind prevented the ships from coming in to allow the troops to re-embark, French reinforcements arrived, and Coote was attacked and forced to surrender. None of these expeditions made any material difference to the war. Instead, the First Coalition against France collapsed as its members were defeated by her armies. Austria, crucially, made peace in 1797.

The British decided to make a more direct contribution to the war on the Continent as part of the War of the Second Coalition. In 1799, in co-operation with a Russian force, they planned an attack on the Low Countries. The options chosen were the islands at the mouth of the Meuse, the estuary of the Ems or the northern coast of Holland, and the expedition was finally launched at the last. It was designed to seize the Dutch fleet and to encourage an uprising in favour of the exiled Orangists and against the pro-French Batavian Republic. The expedition, however, was mismanaged and, more to the point, for many expeditions were mismanaged, unsuccessful. Its goal was unclear and the necessary planning had not been carried out: too little was known about the terrain, the opposing forces and the attitude of the population, and much of the available information was inaccurate. The French were expecting an attack.

The expedition at first went well. The British force under Sir Ralph Abercromby landed safely south of Den Helder on 27 August and a French counter-attack was driven back, in part thanks to covering fire from the British fleet. The capture of Den Helder, and 13 disabled warships, opened the Texel passage to the British fleet and on 30 August Vice-Admiral Andrew Mitchell led a squadron into the Zuider Zee. The best ships in the Dutch fleet had withdrawn from Den Helder into the Zuider Zee in order to defend the channel leading to Amsterdam, but a mutiny among the sailors led to the surrender of the entire fleet, including eight ships of the line.

However, Abercromby rested inactive for three weeks and the expedition lost the dynamic of success. It was not until 13 September that the Duke of York and the Russians arrived. Six days later, the Anglo-Russian forces attacked those of the French south of the Zype, but were checked. They were more successful on 2 October, but were then defeated at Castricum (6 October), a formless and confused battle fought in driving rain. The French commander, Guillaume Brune, proved an able general, making the most of a difficult position, despite being only slowly reinforced. Trapped in an impasse, and affected by poor weather and sick troops, York signed the Convention of Alkmaar (17 October) under which the British were able to evacuate in return for handing over their French prisoners. Mitchell had led his squadron into the Zuider Zee again on 18 September, and had captured three towns on its shores, but he lacked troops to support extensive amphibious operations. The army failed to take up the option for a joint operation against Amsterdam or the eastern shore of the Zuider Zee.[3] York received severe criticism at home as a result of the failure of the expedition and was never again permitted to command outside Britain, despite calls for him to be given the Peninsula army.

In 1800 attempted landings at Belle Isle, Ferrol and Cadiz, all failed. Cornwallis described the army as "the laughing stock of Europe"; although others were more understanding of the problems faced by British commanders. Henry Dundas, the Secretary of State for War, replied to Brigadier-General Maitland's explanation of why he had decided not to attack Belle Isle:

> it was certainly judicious in you under all circumstances not to expose the troops under your command, by attempting a landing in the face of a superior force, possessing in addition to the natural strength of their position, a strong fortress to support their operations.[4]

Nevertheless, unlike the navy, the army was apparently playing little role in the war with France. Vice-Admiral William Young wrote to his wife from Vigo Bay on 30 August:

> We arrived here yesterday from Ferrol Bay, where the troops landed, and made a kind of attempt on Ferrol, where several sail of Spanish men of war lay; but the General did not think it adviseable to make a formidable attack on it – therefore after being on shore about 24 hours the troops embarked again, with a trifling loss – I confess myself, as well as the navy gentlemen in general, are at a loss to account for landing the troops at all, unless a more formidable attack was made – and I cannot conceive the reason of our laying here . . . I am heartily tired of such ridiculous expeditions.

The following month, he commented on the problems of amphibious operations, writing from Tetuan Bay:

> We may truly be considered as a wandering army, at the mercy of the winds and waves – for we left Gibraltar meerly on account of the anchorage there being unsafe, for a large fleet, in case of a westerly gale, and if we should meet with a *Levant*, or *Easterly* wind here, we must then weigh from this, and push out of the Streights.[5]

The campaigns of the 1790s revealed serious deficiencies in the British army. Commanding the 33rd regiment, Lieutenant-Colonel Arthur Wellesley, the future Duke of Wellington, learned in the Low Countries, "what one ought not to do". General John Moore noted of his troops in the West Indies in 1796, "great want of discipline and confidence in their officers . . . The men of our regiments are mere recruits – the officers young and without either zeal or experience".[6]

However, the British were not alone in falling victim to the tactics, numbers and enthusiasm of the Revolutionary French. The armies of Britain's allies were also defeated, so that, for example, the strategy of the entire Second Coalition against France collapsed in 1799, and, to a certain extent, the French Revolutionary War revealed and was the high point of a crisis of a general politico-military system. The tactical system adopted by the British in 1792 drew on that of Prussia. It was based on Colonel David Dundas' *Principles of military movements chiefly applied to infantry, illustrated by manoeuvres of the Prussian troops, and by an outline of the British campaigns in Germany* (1788), in short on the experience of Continental warfare. This represented a deliberate rejection of the more flexible tactics of the American War of Independence, and, indeed, Dundas, who was to succeed York as Commander-in-Chief in 1809–11, belonged to what was termed the "German" rather than the "American" school of officership. Dundas placed the organized firepower of the close-order line at the centre of military practice, claiming that such a line could resist cavalry in open country. He was much less concerned with light infantry, believing that interest in it had led to a decline in the close-order line. The British neglect of such troops served them ill in Holland in 1799.

The French successfully combined columns and covering skirmishers, and also had large numbers produced by the *levée en masse*. Traditional close-order linear formations were vulnerable to French soldiers in open order, and also to the impressive French artillery. This was shown near Tournai in May 1793:

> The [Coldstream] Guards marched in excellent order through the wood keeping as good a line as their situation would permit . . . the masked battery of the French (of which the Guards were completely ignorant) commenced the heaviest firing of grape shot . . . within 30 yards . . . The second discharge of the French knocked down whole ranks . . . as the Prussians observed what business had the Guards in the wood when it was only the duty of light infantry and riflemen.[7]

Yet it would be mistaken to see the period simply in terms of a clash between an anachronistic *ancien régime* that was bound to fail and the future represented by the armies of Revolutionary France. Such an approach ignores the defeats France suffered and also the degree of dynamism that *ancien régime* forces possessed. The British army had light infantry and riflemen and had responded to the failures of the War of American Independence with a period of limited reform. This was part of a more general period of reform in British government under Pitt the Younger. However, the concern about public finances ensured that the rapid increase in army size during the recent war was swiftly reversed and that the pattern of a small peacetime army was retained, although it was bigger than that in the early 1720s. The Pay Office Act of 1783 put the army in the mainstream of public finance for the first time.

It was not only public finance that was the issue. Disbandment in 1783 had been poorly handled, in part due to rapid changes in government and, by the end of the year, the army was under strength and poorly deployed, while its morale had suffered badly from the recent defeat. Sensitivity to the idea of a powerful military led to political hostility to aspects of military preparedness, shown most clearly in successful parliamentary opposition in 1786 to plans to re-fortify Portsmouth and Plymouth, although there were also objections on the grounds of cost and practicality. Charles O'Hara, a Major-General on the staff at Gibraltar, complained of "defenceless works, unserviceable artillery, exhausted stores, weak garrison etc. etc. all of which is most true, to a scandalous degree". When in 1797 a French expedition approached Fishguard Harbour, the garrison in the fort there had only three rounds of ammunition.[8]

The low level of peacetime capability was further manifested in an absence of large-scale manoeuvres and of adequate training. This caused problems when Britain went to war in 1793 as, more generally, did the need to increase greatly and rapidly the size of the army and to introduce an effective command and planning structure. The peacetime military administration was not up to the challenge of war and the army was to be found wanting in 1794.

Nevertheless, there were improvements, not least in response to a near-war with France in 1787, the Dutch crisis. The size of the army was increased, and the organization of recruitment was improved. In addition the Corps of Engineers was transformed into the Royal Engineers in 1787 and a corps of Royal Military Artificers was created. Army pay appreciably increased in 1792. The following January, the Royal Horse Artillery was formed, an important enhancement of the army's mobility. A mobile mortar-brigade followed. Tactical conventions were standardised in 1792 with the publication of *Rules and regulations for the formations, field exercise and movements of His Majesty's Forces*, which was based on Dundas' book and Prussian drill.

The pace of reform accelerated during the period of war with France. Deficiencies were highlighted by failure. John Hill, an officer in the 23rd Foot (Royal Welsh Fusiliers), recorded "we had the regiment fire ball some time ago, about 4 in an hundred hit the target . . . some of them do not know how to load their piece. The badness of the musket, the ball not firing . . .". An atmosphere of urgency encouraged reform and reformers. Again, this was part of a period of national reform, one that included the introduction of income tax (1799), parliamentary union with Ireland (1800–1) and the first national census (1801). Compared both to them and to changes in the French army, those in that of Britain were modest, but they increased the capability of British forces.

Much was due to the efforts of the Duke of York, who succeeded Amherst as Commander-in-Chief in 1795, and was a more effective administrator than he was a field commander. He faced a formidable challenge. Britain was up against a strong opponent, and it was necessary both to manage the major expansion in army strength that had begun in 1793 and to cope with the consequences of the defeat and retreat suffered by the army in 1793–5. The army needed to be revived. York took particular care to raise the quality of British officers. He could not abolish the practice of purchasing commissions, but he made it less deleterious both by raising the number of free commissions and by establishing minimum periods of military service for promotion. However, he was unsuccessful in ending absenteeism among officers. The appointment of a Military Secretary to the Commander-in-Chief was designed to encourage bureaucratic procedures, especially with regard to appointment and promotions.

York also encouraged schemes for military education, especially the plans of Lieutenant-Colonel John Le Marchant for a military college that would both train cadets and also staff officers. The former was opened in 1802 at Marlow, and developed into the Royal Military College at Sandhurst; the latter in 1799 at High Wycombe: it was the basis of what in 1856 was to be the Army Staff College. Le Marchant had already produced two important cavalry manuals.

York also addressed the conditions of the ordinary soldiers, including food, accommodation, medical care and punishment regimes. The soldiers were provided with greatcoats. He was a supporter of the standardisation of drill, and in 1796 the Adjutant-General, Sir William Fawcett, published *Instructions and regulations for the formations and movements of the cavalry*; a third edition appeared in 1799. Consistency was a standard theme in York's policies, and this helped to turn a collection of regiments into an army. It aided the transfer of troops and equipment, and improved operational flexibility. However, there was little improvement in some areas of training, such as bayonet training, where a system for the entire army was not introduced until 1857.

York was also a supporter of the cause of light infantry, a cause associated in particular with Sir John Moore who in 1803 was appointed Commander of a new brigade at Shorncliffe Camp in Kent which was designed to serve as the basis of a permanent light infantry force. Particular emphasis was placed upon marksmanship. Moore had been much impressed by the system of training and manoeuvring light infantry developed by Major Kenneth Mackenzie the previous decade. Moore's force was to become the Light Brigade and, subsequently, the Light Division.[9] York was forced to resign in 1809 when a former mistress, Mary Anne Clarke, falsely accused him of selling promotions, but he was reappointed Commander-in-Chief in 1811, holding the post until he died in 1827.

War with Napoleon

The collapse of the Second Coalition led to negotiations between Britain and France, but the Peace of Amiens of 1802 solved little and by 1803 the two powers were at war again: disagreements over particular issues were less serious than mutual distrust. In particular, the British government felt suspicious of the French leader, Napoleon, who had seized power in the "Brumaire" coup of 9–10 November 1799; he crowned himself Emperor in 1804.

The British were again faced with the problem of deciding how best to employ their smaller army against France. Initially, this issue was over-shadowed by that of preparing to cope with a possible French invasion. The British deployed part of the army to respond to threats of an invasion of south-east England, and also sought to improve the defences of the region with both the digging of the Royal Military Canal and the building of numerous Martello towers, modelled on a tower attacked in Corsica; although much of the fortification work took place after 1805. Militia and Volunteer units staged elaborate manoeuvres and both were familiarized with military conditions. A mock landing at Swansea on 23 April 1804 was driven back by infantry fire and cavalry. On 9 January 1804, in Devon,

> the Exeter Volunteer regiment, with the First Somerset Militia, the Royal Miners, a detachment of the 10th regiment of reserve, a squadron of the Royal Dragoon Guards, the Exeter Artillery, and the Artificer's Corps, attended by their field pieces, were brigaded on Haldon, where they were met by Lord Clifford's squadron of yeomanry cavalry, Lord Courtnay's regiment of volunteer infan-try, the Chudleigh volunteers, and the light company of the Sec-ond Somerset. The business commenced by an attack on a strong position, at the entrance of Haldon, on the Newton road, which was difficult of access, and strengthened by artillery; the light troops having, however, driven in the advanced posts, and the sharp-shooters sent out to annoy them, the artillery, etc. retreated towards the race stands, where they were vigorously pursued by the attacking army. The firing was kept up on each side with great vivacity, and different positions were taken to show the manner of

forming, in case of actual service; after which the whole body were marched into line, several feus de joi were fired from the centre to flanks, after which the cavalry, drawn up on the right wing, advanced and charged, when the business concluded.[10]

Expecting militia, and to some extent Volunteers, to operate alongside regular troops raised their level of military skill.

In 1803 Britain lacked any powerful allies, and was therefore not in a position to plan combined operations against France. Instead, the resumption of war brought opportunities to attack the overseas bases of France and her allies: an expedition against Dutch Surinam was dispatched in 1804. The situation changed in 1805 as the War of the Third Coalition began. Napoleon moved the Grande Armée, originally deployed at Boulogne in preparation for the invasion of England, into Germany in order to attack Austria. The defeat of the Franco-Spanish fleet at Trafalgar also lessened invasion fears, although they lingered until 1813. These developments encouraged plans for the movement of a British army to north Germany. 25,000 men were deployed by late January 1806 and Bremen was occupied. Napoleon's rapid victories over first Austria and then Prussia, the slower pace of British preparations and the delays caused by storms in the North Sea ensured that the strategic situation collapsed before the British could contribute. They speedily evacuated northern Germany in February.

In southern Italy the British landed a force in the Bay of Naples on 21 November 1805 that was designed, in co-operation with a Russian expeditionary force, to protect the Kingdom of Naples against French attack. However, after Austerlitz the French advanced in force and in January 1806 the Anglo-Russian forces withdrew, the British to Sicily and the Russians to the Ionian Islands. The French in southern Italy concentrated on besieging Neapolitan forces in Gaeta and Major-General John Stuart decided to strike at the French force under General Reynier in Calabria. Landing on 1 July, he found Reynier near Maida. On 4 July the French, about 6,500 strong, advanced, but were stopped by the heavy and accurate fire of the well-drilled lines of British infantry.

The battle served as the cornerstone of Sir Charles Oman's influential but dated theory of the struggle between column and line as the tactical characteristic and key to that between French and British forces. However, recent work on the French sources has suggested that French tacticians were more flexible than Oman thought and that the French probably deployed in line. Reynier needed a quick victory to prevent the strategic situation from deteriorating, and his troops were ordered to attack with the bayonet and without firing. An attempt to use cavalry and skirmishers to turn the British left was repelled by the advance of a British regiment. Due to poor timing and co-ordination, the French lacked artillery support at the point of contact. Ordering a bayonet assault on an intact infantry line was foolish, and the French suffered from overconfidence and from the lack of battle experience of their commanders who were essentially staff commanders.

The checking of the French assault was followed by a firefight after which the French unsuccessfully sought to renew the advance.[11] Stuart had no cavalry and was unable to follow up his victory. He did not display the attacking spirit that Wellington was to show in the Peninsula: there the British line advanced after the French had been checked. After a brief and successful siege of a local castle, Stuart returned to Sicily, and he was criticized for failing to exploit the victory sufficiently.[12] Nevertheless, the victory was an important morale boost, not least because it showed that the British could defeat the French in open battle. Sicily was to be held by a British garrison for the remainder of the war serving as a base for operations elsewhere in the Mediterranean, for example in Egypt and east Spain.[13]

The following year, another expeditionary force, this time of 18,000 troops sent against Denmark, was successful. The British landed on Zealand on 16 August, eight miles north of Copenhagen, and besieged the city the following day. On 29 August 1807 Sir Arthur Wellesley and 5,000 men rapidly routed an attempt by 14,000 Danish militia under Castenskjold to relieve the city at Kjöge: the combination of a quick charge and a single volley brought victory. A destructive artillery bombardment of a weakly defended Copenhagen that began on 2 September caused heavy casualties and led the Danes on 5 September to seek terms. The Danes were forced to hand over their fleet, the major purpose of the expedition. The government's hopes of retaining control of Zealand ended when Wellesley and other generals advised that it would be difficult to do so.[14] Some of the troops available for the expedition reflected an earlier disappointment: most of the King's German Legion had been sent to Swedish Pomerania in July 1807, only to withdraw in the face of the Franco-Russian Tilsit agreement.

In 1808 a 12,000 strong force under Moore sent to help Sweden resist Russia and conquer Norway found itself unwelcome: the troops never disembarked, while in the Mediterranean Capri fell to French attack that October: the commander, Hudson Lowe, surrendered after the defences had been breached in a 13-day siege. The withdrawal of Moore and 8,000 men from Sicily and their dispatch to the Baltic, had greatly weakened the British in the Mediterranean, but Lowe blamed the loss of Capri in large part on a lack of adequate naval assistance. Thus, Britain's Mediterranean positions were as dependent on the navy as those in the Caribbean had been.

A worse fate awaited the 44,000 strong force sent in 1809 to destroy the dockyards at Antwerp, and, it was hoped, help the Austrians by mounting a powerful diversion. The planning was inadequate and the weather hostile. Landing on the island of Walcheren, the British force was poorly led and decimated by disease, particularly malaria, while the French responded rapidly, blocking the British advance.[15] Besieged on 1 August, Flushing, the main port on Walcheren, fell on the 16th, but, by then, the French had greatly reinforced Antwerp. On 27th August a council of war decided to abandon the expedition, but the withdrawal was very slow, permitting sickness to spread. The last troops did not embark until 9 December; the French did not need to drive them away. This operation, like that against Copenhagen, reflected the importance of naval considerations in British military operations. It was crucial to disrupt Napoleon's attempts to assemble and develop his naval power.

Stuart was more successful, capturing Ischia and Procida in the Bay of Naples in June 1809: this was an effective use of the British land and naval forces designed to protect Sicily, but it did not contribute materially to the defeat of Napoleon, and Stuart re-embarked when Admiral Collingwood warned of the danger of French naval attack. Stuart was successful, however, in thwarting a French attempt to invade Sicily in September 1810. A rapidly moving British force attacked the French when they were only in part disembarked; those who had done so, nearly 1,000 men, were forced to surrender and the others were driven off. Another British expedition overran Cephalonia, Ithaca and Santa Maura in the Ionian Isles.

Napoleon's defeat at Leipzig in 1813, in which a British battery of William Congreve's rockets had participated, encouraged the British to resume operations in northern Europe. A force under Sir Thomas Graham was sent to the Netherlands to co-operate with the Prussians against Antwerp, but only 8,000 troops could be spared for what was to be one of the forgotten campaigns of the war. The French had reduced their forces in the region in order to concentrate on the defence of eastern France against Austria and Prussia. The British landed at Willemstad on 18 December 1813. After establishing a bridgehead, they advanced towards Antwerp. On 11 January 1814 they helped the Prussians drive the French from Hoogstraaten. The French were defeated at Merksem, north of Antwerp, but in February 1814 two attacks on Antwerp failed. The siege was raised on 6 February and the British troops then went into cantonments. An attempt to storm the nearby strong fortress of Bergen-op-Zoom on the night of 8 March also failed: the British fought their way into the town, but the fighting then turned against them, the columns that were in the town received insufficient support and were, instead, ordered to retreat, and they were driven out with 3,000 casualties. Under pressure from invading Austrian and Prussian forces and faced by a collapse in domestic support, Napoleon abdicated before operations could resume in the Low Countries. The British then occupied the fortresses in the area, moving their headquarters to Antwerp and, later, Brussels.

The net effect of such expeditions was limited. The French had to keep troops around their empire and in dependent territories anyway in order to prevent uprisings. None of the British expeditions elsewhere had the success obtained by the army sent to Iberia.

The Peninsular War

Success against Austria, Prussia and Russia in 1805–7 encouraged Napoleon to turn further afield. In November 1807, the French successfully invaded Portugal, a major British trading partner. Her conquest would help to cement the Berlin and Milan Decrees that sought to establish commercial quarantine of Britain and her goods, and thus weaken her economy. However, Napoleon's attempt to place his brother Joseph on the throne of Spain, a move that would have increased French control over Spanish resources, led to a popular uprising in the spring and summer of 1808. The British exploited the situation with an expedition of 11,000 troops under Lieutenant-General Sir Arthur Wellesley, later Duke of Wellington, that landed in Portugal at Mondego Bay on 1–5 August.

The 39-year-old Wellesley had won fame as a result of his victories over the Marathas. The fourth son of the Anglo-Irish Earl of Mornington, Wellesley (1769–1852) had entered the army in 1787, purchased a Majority and been promoted to Lieutenant-Colonel, both in 1793, and first seen action in 1794, in the defence of the United Provinces against the French advance. He took part in the subsequent winter retreat. Wellesley's rapid rise to positions of command made him accustomed to taking responsibility and making decisions. In October 1795 Wellesley's regiment embarked for the West Indies, only to be driven back by storms. His regiment, instead, went to India, arriving in Calcutta in February 1797. Wellesley took part in the Mysore campaign of 1799, fought the Marathas in 1803–4 and returned to Britain in 1805. Having taken part in the Danish expedition of 1807, he was promoted Lieutenant-General in 1808. An MP from 1806, the well-connected Wellesley was appointed Chief Secretary in Ireland in 1807. The following June he expressed his confidence about taking on the French, "first, because I am not afraid of them, as everyone else seems to be; and secondly, because (if all I hear about their system is true) I think it a false one against steady troops. I suspect all the continental armies are half-beaten before the battle begins. I at least will not be frightened beforehand".[16]

The superior firepower of Wellesley's army and his flexibile generalship defeated attacking French forces under Marshal Junot at Vimeiro (21 August 1808). Wellesley had sheltered his lines of infantry from the French cannon by deploying them behind the crest of the ridge. He placed his riflemen in open order down the slope and used them to prevent the French skirmishers who advanced before the columns from disrupting the British lines. The advancing columns were halted by British infantry and cannon fire, and driven back by downhill charges. The French attacks were poorly co-ordinated and, having beaten them, Wellesley was on the point of ordering a general attack when he was overruled by the more senior Sir Harry Burrard. The British lost 720 men, the French about 2,000. Burrard superseded Wellesley and was in turn superseded by Sir Hew Dalrymple. Neither wanted to push on against the French who were able to negotiate the Convention of Cintra (30 August). By this, the French evacuated Portugal, but were returned to France in British ships and were then free to resume hostilities. The British also agreed to ship the French baggage and booty. This agreement caused a stir in Britain and Wellesley, Burrard and Dalrymple were recalled to face a court of enquiry in London.[17] Moore, who did not join the army until after Cintra, was left in command.

Napoleon responded to the crisis by invading Spain, defeating poorly trained and commanded and outnumbered Spanish troops and entering Madrid on 4 December 1808. Instructed to provide support to the Spanish government in northern Spain, Moore advanced from Lisbon, entering Spain on 11 November and reaching Salamanca on 13 November. An absence of promised Spanish support led Moore to order a retreat, but an urgent request for help from the government in Madrid, led him rashly to decide to press on, in order to strike at French lines of communication, and a French cavalry force was defeated at Sahaguan (21 December). News of French strength led Moore to decide to retreat. The French threat to his communications with Portugal led him to fall back towards the port of Corunna in north-west Spain. Moore withdrew from 24 December 1808, in difficult wintry conditions, in the face of overwhelming French strength. Discipline collapsed in the leading divisions as the army retreated, but the well-trained rear maintained order and held off the pursuing French.

Napoleon abandoned the chase on 1 January 1809 and entrusted the pursuit to Marshal Nicolas Soult who caught up with the British at the embarkation port of Corunna. The British fought the French off on 16 January. Soult's army was little larger and the nature of the terrain limited his use of his cavalry. Moore stood on the defensive, anticipated Soult's moves and handled his reserves ably in order to block them. The army was successfully evacuated the following day, but Moore had been killed in the battle, his death making him a hero. About 7,000 men had been lost in Moore's brief expedition and it had revealed the difficulty of co-ordinating operations with Spanish forces. However, Napoleon's plan for the conquest of Iberia, a rapid advance to Madrid and then Lisbon, had been thrown into disarray.[18]

Soult next moved south to destroy the British forces in Portugal, then garrisoning Lisbon under Lieutenant-General Sir John Francis Cradock, a cautious commander who felt that evacuation might be necessary. Soult stormed Oporto on 27 March, but fresh British troops under Wellesley were sent to Portugal. Wellesley assumed command of the British army there on 22 April. On 12 May he made a surprise crossing of the Douro, fought off counterattacks, and captured Oporto, in a well-executed offensive action that was helped by poor dispositions and slow responses on the part of Soult who had wrongly thought he had seized all the boats that could be used for a crossing. Another British force had been deployed to block a French advance on Lisbon from the east along the Tagus, but the French, under Marshal Victor, halted their advance, before they could reach the British force, after the news of Wellesley's victory at Oporto.

Wellesley then turned against Victor's army in Spain. On 27 June he crossed the frontier. On 22 July Wellesley joined with Spanish forces, with which he had been instructed to co-operate, at Talavera, but the French were rapidly assembling a powerful response. Wellesley's boldness had left him exposed. On 27 and 28 July the French attacked the Anglo-Spanish army at Talavera, concentrating their attack on the outnumbered British. Wellesley employed his infantry firepower to repulse the French columns, but the pursuit of the retreating French threw the British into confusion and fresh French units drove them back. The final French attack on the centre of the allied line was only just held with Wellesley committing his reserve, but held it was, although the British suffered 5,400 casualties; more than a quarter of the force. However, Wellesley subsequently had to retreat in the face of fresh, larger French forces under Soult who advanced on his lines of communication, placing the British in a dangerous position. Wellesley learned the problems of campaigning with the Spaniards: their failure to provide promised supplies had been a serious blow forcing Wellesley to drop his men to one-third rations, and the victory at Talavera had led to no gains. A victory, however, it was, and Wellesley was raised to the peerage, becoming Viscount Wellington in September 1809. In addition, he had been given supreme command of the Portuguese army.

From September 1809 until the following summer the French concentrated on their Spanish opponents, while Wellington adopted a more cautious generalship after Talavera. After Soult's victory at Ocaña (19 November 1809), the French were able to move south, which they did in January, capturing Seville. The fall of Andalusia left Wellington's army more exposed, as France's major opponent in Iberia, but it also tied up a large French force in maintaining control of the region. However, more troops were freed for operations in Spain by the negotiation of the Austro-French Peace of Schönbrunn on 14 October 1809. Nearly 140,000 reinforcements were ordered to Iberia. Marshal André Masséna was given command of the Army of Portugal and ordered to conquer Portugal. Masséna was an excellent commander, but he was ill in 1810 and tried to resign before he was sent. The Army of Portugal proved a terrible command. The allocated complement of troops was cut, and Masséna responded to the lack of promised resources by complaining that this greatly hindered his operational possibilities. Masséna also had serious disputes with his subordinates, Junot and Ney.

The threat of French attack led Wellington to fall back, avoiding battle with the far larger French army: his strategy was one of defence in depth and he was given added time when Napoleon ordered Masséna first to capture Ciudad Rodrigo and Almeida. Both fell, the second after the powder magazine was blown up on 27 August, but the sieges delayed Masséna. Wellington was convinced that Portugal could be held, and developed a strong fall-back fortified position – a line of forts and natural obstacles, the Lines of Torres Vedras – to cover nearby Lisbon. Wellington chose to resist Masséna's advancing force further forward in a good defensive position at Bussaco (27 September 1810). The French found the British drawn up on a ridge, and their poorly planned attacks were repulsed with nearly 5,000 casualties.[19] However, the position was then out-flanked, and Wellington fell back on the Lines, the most successful defensive move of his career. The French reached the Lines on 12 October. They were too strong for Masséna's weakened force to breach and the French suffered heavily in the devastated countryside.[20] Masséna lacked a siege train, while Wellington had followed a scorched-earth policy. Captain John Hill recorded "The country is dreadfully ravaged. I saw nothing except a few pigeons left about the villages; the floors and rafters taken out either to burn or make huts. All the inhabitants had retired before our army, so that what a few months before had been a fine country is literally now a desert".[21]

Wellington devoted himself to strengthening his position. Masséna was denied the opportunity to display his ability as a battlefield commander and his army suffered serious malnutrition. Napoleon thought that the British navy did not have the capacity to supply the million people within the lines, but he was wrong, as were the British officers, such as Wellington's second-in-command, Major-General Sir Brent Spencer, who doubted the viability of Wellington's plan of defence. Napoleon also mistakenly thought that the Prince Regent, the future George IV, would abandon the war. Masséna appealed for aid and Napoleon ordered Soult to provide it, but he was not insistent and Soult did not send help. However, leaving Masséna outside the Lines kept the British hemmed in at Lisbon and thus unable to affect the Napoleonic position in Spain, let alone Central Europe, the strategic region on which Napoleon focused.[22]

The winter did its damage, not least by greatly exacerbating French supply difficulties, and on 5 March 1811 Masséna began to retreat. He was followed by Wellington who launched harassing attacks, that were held off by Ney's rearguard actions. On 5 April the French evacuated Portugal after a well-conducted retreat. Masséna was relieved of his command, and 1811 was the end of his career as a field commander. The centre of hostilities moved to the Spanish border fortresses. Almeida was besieged and Masséna's attempt to relieve it successfully blocked at Fuentes de Oñoro on 3 and 5 May. Almeida fell and the British under William Beresford besieged Badajoz on 8 May, only to raise the siege on 12 May when the French armies under Marmont (who had succeeded Masséna) and Soult advanced to relieve it. This led to the battle of Albuera on 16 May. Wellington then besieged Badajoz, only to withdraw on 19 June in the face of larger French forces under Marmont. The increase in Wellington's forces had not translated into success in Spain.

In early 1812 Wellington stormed by night the two key Spanish border fortresses of Ciudad Rodrigo (19 January) and Badajoz (6 April), the well-defended positions falling when costly attacks on breaches created by artillery fire were supported by subsidiary attacks at other points. This opened the key invasion routes into Spain. Wellington invaded northern Spain in June, abandoning the often excessive caution that had characterized his generalship after Talavera, a caution that was justified by the fact that he was commanding Britain's only field army. The French were weakened by Napoleon's concentration of resources on his forthcoming invasion of Russia. On 22 July the French were defeated at Salamanca: Marmont's strung-out disposition allowed Wellington to defeat the French divisions in detail in a battle that had some similarities to naval tactics. Noting that the French were overextended, Wellington rapidly and effectively switched from defence to attack and ably combined his infantry and cavalry in the destruction of three French divisions. One division was ridden down by the cavalry under Le Marchant, now a Major-General, although he was mortally wounded in the charge. The French had 14,000 casualties including 7,000 prisoners, the allies 5,200, one-third of whom were Portuguese. Private William Wheeler of the 51st Regiment left a record of the difficulty of the conditions on the battlefield:

> Our support being required on the right of the line we now moved on in double quick time. This raised such a dust that together with the heat of the day we were almost suffocated. The want of water now began to be severely felt, those who had some in their canteens were as bad off as those that had none, for what with the heat of the sun and the shaking it got it was completely spoiled. Those who drank of it immediately threw it up. As we proceeded the fire increased. We were wet with sweat . . . and so great was the quantity of dust that settled on our faces and clothes that we scarce knew each other. In fact we more resembled an army of sweeps or dustmen than any one thing I can conceive. Almost fagged to death we arrived at our position on the right of our line; in our front was a hill on which was posted the enemy's left. They welcomed us opening about 16 guns and several howitzers.[23]

Wellington pressed on to occupy Madrid on 12 August, only to be forced to retire in the autumn in the face of larger French forces after his attempts to storm the fortress of Burgos had failed, not least because he had insufficient artillery. This failure, which arose from Wellington's risky strategy and tactics and in which the British lost 2,000 men to no purpose, led to criticism of Wellington's generalship and disputes with his subordinates. The

French had recovered the strategic initiative by abandoning Andalusia and thus concentrating an overwhelming field force. The British suffered many casualties in the retreat, in part thanks to a breakdown of the supply system.

Having spent the winter building up his army's strength, in May 1813 Wellington invaded Spain again. He was encouraged by news of Napoleon's failure in Russia and advanced rapidly, outflanking the French and forcing them to retreat. Joseph Bonaparte, the French-appointed King of Spain, abandoned Madrid in order to block any British advance on France. Burgos fell on 12 June. Joseph's army was weakened by the detachment of substantial forces to deal with guerrillas in Navarre and the Basque country. Wellington's skill at wideranging flanking movements, combined with inadequate French generalship and poor French battlefield dispositions, led to a crushing French defeat at Vitoria (21 June 1813): Wellington took both the strategic and the tactical offensive, and his ability to plan a battle was particularly necessary on a battlefield that extended for over eight miles. The outnumbered French suffered 8,000 casualties, the victors 5,000 including 3,300 British. The French lost about 400 cannon. Wellington was rewarded by being made a Field-Marshal.

Their morale shattered, the French retreated towards the Pyrenees, although further east they retained their positions in Catalonia on the Mediterranean coast. Wellington pursued them towards the Pyrenees, attacking their fortified bases. Pasajres fell on 31 August, San Sebastian on 9 September after a difficult siege in which the attackers lost heavily in two assaults, Pamplona on 25 October. French forces that attempted counter-attacks to relieve the besieged positions initially pushed back advanced British covering forces, but were defeated at Sorauren in the battles of the Pyrenees (28 and 30 July) and at San Marcial (31 August). The British made plentiful use of bayonet attacks, and Wellington described the battle of Sorauren as "fair bludgeon work". His victory ensured that San Sebastian and Pamplona would not be relieved, and indeed that a full siege could be reimposed on San Sebastian. Success in northern Spain enabled the British to use the harbours there and thus to shorten the lines of communication that had hitherto been via Lisbon, although there were problems in developing an effective supply system. Operations in the Pyrenees led to the formation of the first Royal Artillery mountain battery which was equipped with three-pounder cannon.

Wellington was able to invade southern France, but because he had first tackled San Sebastian and Pamplona, the French under Marshal Soult had been able to regroup and prepare their defences. Soult held the line of the River Bidassoa. At low tide early on 7 October 1813, the British used fords to cross the estuary, before defeating the defenders. France had been invaded. Soult fell back to the River Nivelle, only for his defences there to be outflanked and stormed on 10 November 1813. The French retreated to the River Nive which Wellington crossed against slight opposition on

9 December. The following morning, Soult attacked the spread out Allied forces, pushing them hard, yet failing to do more than gain the line where the piquets had been. On the 13th, Soult attacked again, at the other end of the British line, but he was held off. In these engagements, the battle of St Pierre d'Irube, the French had lost about 4,900 men, the Allies 3,400. Bad weather then forced both armies into winter quarters. Wellington's numerical advantage gave him a decided advantage, and this was accentuated as Napoleon transferred units from Soult in order to build up his own army in east France in the face of Austrian and Prussian advances.

The following year, Wellington crossed the Adour River on 23 February. Bayonne was besieged, although without success, and Bordeaux fell to a detached British force on 12 March, while Wellington pursued and defeated Soult's field army, after hard-fought attacks at Orthez (27 February) and at Toulouse (10 April). Wellington was wounded at Orthez, but the French lost heavily in their retreat. At Toulouse Wellington's Anglo-Spanish army outnumbered Soult 50,000 to 42,000, but the strong French defensive position and the exposure of the attacking forces to heavy defensive fire, ensured that the victory was won at the cost of heavier Anglo-Spanish casualties: 4,500 to 3,200. The French mounted a successful sortie from Bayonne on 14 April and did not surrender the city until 27 April, after Napoleon's abdication. Under the pressure of overwhelming Allied, principally Austrian and Prussian, forces advancing on Paris from the east, the Napoleonic regime had collapsed.

Other British forces in the Peninsular War operated away from Wellington's direct control, often to his frustration. It was not until 1813 that Wellington was given permission to send back generals that he found unsatisfactory. Lieutenant-General Thomas Graham, who had been Moore's aide-de-camp at Corunna, was in 1810 appointed commander of the British forces aiding the defence of Cadiz. On 5 March 1811 he defeated the blockading army at Barossa. On 16 May 1811 another detached force, an Anglo-Portuguese-Spanish army under William Beresford, was attacked by a smaller army under Soult at Albuera. The British infantry fought well, but they were drawn into a static firefight. Beresford mishandled the engagement, the French cavalry attacked to effect, the Polish lancers inflicting heavy losses on three British battalions and 40 per cent of the British troops were casualties. Hill recorded ". . . it was nothing but the steady determined attack of the infantry on the right that saved the day . . . the carnage was without exception far more terrible than any I ever before have seen".[24]

An Anglo-Sicilian amphibious force sent from Sicily to the east coast of Spain achieved little in 1812, but on 13 April 1813, under its new commander, Lieutenant-General Sir John Murray, it defeated the French under Suchet at Castalla: attacking columns were brought down by the firepower of British lines. Murray then sailed from Alicante to Tarragona and began a siege of the latter, but on Suchet's advance he hastily re-embarked his men, abandoning his cannon. This led Wellington, who had recommended in 1804 that Murray be relieved of his command in India, to urge that he now be court martialled. Although British operations in eastern Spain were less successful than those in the south, they also played a role in tying down French forces. However, the subsidiary operations did not lead to the expulsion of the French from the Peninsula.[25]

French forces in Iberia outnumbered those under Wellington's effective command and yet the French were checked and defeated at a time when Napoleon was dominant elsewhere. Their defeat can be attributed to the problems of campaigning in Spain, especially Spanish guerrilla resistance, to British fighting qualities, generalship and naval and financial resources, and to the poor quality of French command. The Spaniards were generally unsuccessful in formal conflict, and British generals could be critical of their organization, but their regular and guerrilla operations denied the French control over the countryside and, in particular, greatly harmed their communications and logistics. The French were unable to concentrate their superior forces against Wellington, but they would have been able to do so once they had knocked out the Spaniards, which would have been a distinct possibility but for the invasion of Russia. Spanish guerrillas also provided Wellington with useful intelligence. Thanks in large part to Spanish and Portuguese assistance, it was more sensible for the British to attack France in Iberia than to use Malta and Sicily as a base for large-scale operations in Italy.

The disciplined firepower of the British infantry played a major part in Wellington's victories, although this firepower was not necessarily immobile, but, rather, often used as a prelude to a bayonet charge. Wellington ably executed fire and movement tactics. The British succeeded in balancing the well-drilled line that represented the legacy of Frederick the Great and the extensive use of light infantry in battle, the conservatism of an emphasis on linear firepower formations with a greater role for manoeuvrability. Wellington never had more than 60,000 British troops under his personal command; he commanded 70,000 men at Vitoria, but only 35,500 were British. The army in Spain had a high sick rate, which rose after 1810 as "Walcheren fever", probably malaria, spread to the army with units moved there after the failed expedition. Wellington was always heavily outnumbered in both cavalry and artillery and his siegecraft suffered from the absence of an effective engineering branch, but his troops were among the best in the British army, a contrast to the situation among his opponents. He was also a fine judge of terrain and adept at controlling a battle as it developed. At Vimeiro the well-positioned British lines succeeded in blunting the attacking French columns, while at Salamanca he used his lines in attack with great effect.

The French, conversely, suffered from a number of poor commanders, especially, in 1810, the tired Masséna, who was well past his prime and

Joseph Bonaparte in the Vitoria campaign and in the battle itself. Most of the commanders had been very successful generals, but the problems facing them in the Peninsula were just too much. The French were also affected by the frequent unwillingness of their generals to co-operate, and, as seriously, by Napoleon's continued interference from a distance. Napoleon did not understand the Peninsular war, its topography and ramifications; he went to Spain in overwhelming force, and then forgot about the nature of campaigning there. Napoleon was consumed with his own projects and jealous of his subordinates. His misguided attempt to direct plans through written instructions was compounded by the absence of a clear command structure within Spain itself. In 1810 Napoleon tried to micro-manage Masséna's campaign, ordering him to take the border fortresses first. Wellington, in contrast, had far more control over military operations and benefited from this unity of command. He was appointed Commander-in-Chief of all allied forces in November 1812. His logistical arrangements were also far superior to those of the French, and Wellington was better able to rely on them than his opponents were.

The French also had inadequate battlefield tactics. In place of *l'ordre mixte*, the interplay of lines, columns and skirmishers that had proved so effective in the 1790s, especially in weakening lines of opposing infantry, the French relied on crude attacks in dense columns. Thus the firepower of the British lines was not compromised, and the French themselves provided an easy target for the British.

Despite the deficiencies of the Brown Bess, the British flintlock musket, with its stiff trigger, powerful recoil, poor performance in wet weather if the powder became damp, and the large bore that ensured a loose fit for the musket ball and thus increased the problem of accurate fire, British firepower was more effective than that of the French. Tests carried out by the Prussian General Gerhard von Scharnhorst in 1813 suggested that, whereas French and Prussian flintlocks were more effective at 100 yards, their British counterparts were better at a greater distance and, therefore, better for engaging French columns at a distance. Furthermore, the large bore of the Brown Bess meant that it could take all calibres of musket ammunition, while the loose fit of the ball helped ramming and thus contributed to the rate of fire. However, the loose ball would have meant that accuracy was lost with distance. In addition, despite textbook suggestions of a rate of fire of up to five times a minute in the hands of a trained soldier, modern tests suggest that the real rate of fire was closer to two times a minute.

Superior firearms should not be stressed too much. The French acquired 30,000 British muskets when they captured Ferrol in 1809 and thousands more were issued to Britain's continental allies over the years, many falling into Napoleon's hands in the wake of his victories. Although some muskets were slightly better than others, this can only be a minor factor in explaining the outcome of battlefield clashes.

Most British infantry continued to be armed with smooth-bore weapons, if only because of the financial and other costs attached to rifled ones; they were expensive and difficult to produce, required special ammunition, and, though more accurate, were much slower to load and fire than muskets. This last drawback could prove very disadvantageous against an enemy who closed in during a firefight, offsetting his poorer accuracy with sheer volume of fire. The British neglected the use of rifled weapons in the period between the American War of Independence and the creation, in 1800, of the Experimental Rifle Corps, which eventually developed into the 95th Regiment.

The decline in the quality of the French army, due to near-continual campaigning, affected its tactical sophistication, not to mention its morale. Success in battle had greatly turned on the exploitation of the synergy between cavalry, close-order infantry, artillery and skirmishers. A combination of attacks by different arms reduced both the enemy's physical means to resist – by silencing his guns with counter-battery or skirmisher fire, by neutralizing his command and control by picking off officers, or by using cavalry, especially to force infantry from lines into defensive squares, thereby cutting their frontage and, thus, firepower – and chipped away at his will to resist. The French experienced great difficulty in Spain in trying to achieve this. Terrain factors frequently precluded the efficacious use of their often superior cavalry and artillery. Attacks were often executed sequentially, rather than simultaneously, and by one arm, usually the infantry. Much of the same happened at Waterloo, although with fewer excuses.

Any French failure to weaken the British lines, by the use of artillery or skirmishers, before the column attack, was especially serious. Wellington's reverse-slope ploy, his policy of locating his troops behind the crest of hills in order to protect them from artillery, was important, as at Bussaco on 27 September 1810. Because of the breakdown of their "system" in engagements with British troops, French infantry columns were too often left exposed to fire from intact, unshaken lines with neither the time nor the space to redeploy. They therefore either had to run for it, or try to bludgeon their way through. The latter, however, was often more than flesh and blood could achieve. A bayonet charge against an adversary who stayed ordered and calm, pulling the trigger and throwing up a hail of lead, was generally ineffective.

Wellington was also very active in counter-attacks and the well-timed bayonet charge, launched when the French were disorganized by their approach march and by British fire, was as effective a tactic as the volley.[26] Medical records on casualties and other sources suggest that the bayonet was essentially a psychological weapon in most Napoleonic engagements. Firepower caused more casualties and was therefore crucial to the decision of the battle. However, the bayonet charge permitted exploitation of the advantage. Such a charge, preceded by a volley, had become a standard

British tactic from the late 1750s, used with effect in the War of American Independence, and, with his fine grasp of timing and eye for terrain, Wellington brought the system to a high pitch of effectiveness.

Waterloo, 18 June 1815

The British also played a crucial role in the defeat of Napoleon in 1815. Having escaped from Elba and regaining power in Paris, Napoleon was threatened by the forces of a powerful coalition. Wellington argued that the coalition should begin "when we shall have 450,000 men", including Prussians and Russians, and he was confident that Napoleon could bring no more than 150,000 men to strike at any one point.[27] However, Napoleon took the initiative and struck first at his nearest opponents: a British–Dutch–German army under Wellington at Brussels and the Prussians under Blücher at Liège. Wellington's army included inexperienced units and, more generally, was not accustomed to fighting as a united force.[28]

On 15 June 1815 Napoleon invaded the Netherlands and gained the strategic advantage. Wellington's initial assessment that the French advance was a bluff was mistaken. The following day Napoleon's forces engaged Blücher at Ligny and Wellington at Quatre Bras. Blücher was defeated by Napoleon with heavy casualties, but Marshal Ney had less success against Wellington: there was no French victory. Instead, British lines brought down French columns, and formed squares to repel their cavalry, although these squares formed tempting targets for the French artillery. A counterattack regained most of the original allied position. The *Times* reported on the 22nd that "many of the British officers present in the affair of the 16th declared that they never witnessed more severe fighting in the Peninsula than that which took place on the plains of Fleurus and its vicinity. The duke of Wellington exposed himself as usual to imminent danger". However, threatened by Blücher's defeat, Wellington fell back towards Brussels, to a ridge at Mont Saint-Jean: Ney had failed to pin him down and a somewhat listless and possibly ill Napoleon was unable to overtake him as he withdrew on the 17th. Late that day, the British cavalry charged the pursuing French lancers at Genappe in order to hold them off.

The subsequent battle of Waterloo found Wellington with 68,000 men, 31,000 of them British, holding his position against attacks by Napoleon's 72,000. This was not, however, the army with which Wellington had won the Peninsular War. Many of those units were involved in the war with America. Instead, many of Wellington's British units were untried in battle. Nevertheless, although uncertain of Prussian moves, Wellington decided to stand and fight.

As in the Peninsular battles, the British line was not weakened by prior engagement, although the French attempted to do so with an artillery bombardment. Its impact was weakened by Wellington's use of the reverse slopes, while, as in the Peninsula, he deployed light infantry to keep the French skirmishers at bay. The British line was anchored by the farms at Hougoumont and La Haye Sainte. Wellington had to fight the battle as a defensive engagement, and the offensive tactics that had characterized his generalship at Salamanca and Vitoria were absent, although that did not preclude small-scale advances during the battle. British firepower decisively defeated a number of separate and poorly co-ordinated French assaults, including that of General Drouet's corps in the early afternoon, Ney's cavalry attacks in the late afternoon, and the Guard infantry at the end of the day. The defensive nature of Wellington's tactics was captured by Edmund Wheatley, an ensign in the King's German Legion, who wrote of the squares which Wellington's troops formed to resist the French cavalry, "we dashed them back as coolly as the sturdy rock repels the ocean's foam . . . we presented our bristly points like the peevish porcupines assailed by clamorous dogs". There were also British counter-attacks. The French infantry that advanced in the early afternoon to the east of La Haye Sainte was stopped by the British lines and then charged down by the British heavy cavalry. However, in the heat of the battle, the charge was misman-aged as the cavalry failed to stop and regroup and, instead, advanced too far and were driven back with heavy casualties by the French.

With more men and time Napoleon might have won. The British centre was in a dreadful state by late afternoon: Napoleon's costly frontal attacks, greater in scale than any Wellington had hitherto encountered, did have an effect. Wellington regarded it as his hardest battle, and he suffered over 15,000 casualties. It has recently been suggested that he came close to losing the battle by under-garrisoning Hougoumont.[29] La Haye Sainte fell at 6 pm when the remains of the garrison, their ammunition exhausted, withdrew. Wellington's centre was badly exposed, and the attack by the Imperial Guard was a crisis, not the last fling of a defeated opponent. However, the Guard was stopped by British firepower and then successfully charged by cavalry. As the Guard fell back, Wellington ordered a general advance. Victory, numerical advantage and the availability of fresh Prussian forces, especially numerous cavalry, permitted the launching of a pursuit that was more destructive than those after Wellington's Peninsular victories.

With more men and time Napoleon could also have threatened Welling-ton's flanks. He had no more of either. The Prussians had regrouped after Ligny within striking distance of Waterloo and from mid-afternoon their advance units began attacking the French right: Napoleon was forced to send most of his reserves to block them. Marshal Grouchy, whom Napo-leon had sent in pursuit of the Prussians after Ligny, failed both to prevent Prussian intervention at Waterloo and to join Napoleon himself in the battle. The Emperor thus lost the numerical strength he worked best with.

Yet Napoleon did not fight well with the troops he had. Having moved slowly on the morning of 17 June, he had simply followed Wellington north and had made little attempt to take strategic control of the situation; nor were the heavy rain and mud of 17 June conducive to boldness. Napoleon's subsequent tactical lack of imagination on 18 June was in keeping with his earlier failure to obtain a decisive success while his opponents were divided. He was less brave and decisive on the battlefield than Wellington; more a distant commander who lost touch with the progress of the battle and failed to manoeuvre.

Furthermore, due to the steady decline in the quality of the French army, ruined by incessant warfare and only a shadow of its former self, there was little to choose between the quality of the Allied and French armies at Waterloo. At best, Napoleon might have secured a Pyrrhic victory. Wellington had constructed a strong defence in depth which, even under better weather and other conditions, would have proved difficult to crack. Napoleon had only a slight numerical advantage, while Wellington had another 18,000 men guarding his immediate right flank, which he saw as his Achilles' Heel, and some 70,000 to 80,000 Prussians closing in on his left. Indeed, as the day wore on, Wellington was able to abandon his position on the left entirely to the Prussians, who also got round Napoleon's right flank and rear.

Yet for all Napoleon's failings and the maladroit conduct of several of his generals, the French at Waterloo were a formidable army and their defeat a major achievement for Wellington and his force.[30] It is unclear that Napoleon's grand strategy was sustainable anyway. He had triumphed in battles enough without winning the war. Large Allied forces, especially Austrians, were approaching France from the east. Yet Waterloo was not a strategic irrelevance. Napoleon was crushed, the war ended beyond any hopes that events or Allied divisions would provide him with opportunities.

After the battle, Wellington and the Prussians advanced into France, although the British army had been much weakened by its victory. Resistance was minimal: Napoleon's army was broken. Cambrai and Peronne were stormed. Paris surrendered on 3 July, while the advancing British forces were building a bridge across the Seine nearby at Argenteuil, and Anglo-Prussian forces occupied the city on 7 July. Forces at Genoa under the command of Hudson Lowe, now a Major-General, co-operated with a squadron under Lord Exmouth to occupy Marseilles in July. In conjunction with local royalists, they then advanced on Toulon and restored it to Bourbon control. Napoleon, who had taken refuge in Rochefort, surrendered on 15 July to Captain Frederick Maitland of HMS *Bellerophon*. The British naval blockade made it impossible for him to leave France by sea. The British were concerned to prevent Napoleon taking refuge in America, and Admiral Hotham had been ordered to "keep the most vigilant lookout for the purpose of intercepting him".[31] Napoleon was taken to St Helena, where he died, his imprisonment a consequence and sign of British power.

Napoleon's gaoler at St Helena was Hudson Lowe, appointed Governor of the island in 1815. His career was a testimony to the range of British power. Lowe's father was an army surgeon, and the young Hudson accompanied his father's regiment to the West Indies and America. He himself served in Gibraltar, Toulon, Corsica, Elba, Portugal, Minorca, Egypt, Malta, Italy, the Ionian Islands, France, and, after St Helena, in Antigua and Ceylon (Sri Lanka). Other Britons found their careers cut short. Napoleon's Irish Legion was stood down after the restoration of the Bourbons.

Conclusions

Waterloo was greeted with joy in Britain, an anonymous correspondent reporting from Devon,

> At length our day of tumultuous exultation is ended, the bells have ceased their clattering peals, the ringers have reeled to their heated beds and our rustic politicians wearied with their own huzzas dream of peace and plenty for years to come, or plan, for years of deprivation that are past, schemes of punishment and revenge is to be inflicted on that reptile now fangless, who lately "made a world turn pale". Our towns and villages have been walking groves of laurel, and our atmosphere is still glowing with the embers of many a bonfire.[32]

The British contributed greatly to this achievement. Their role at Waterloo was far greater than that in 1812–14 when it was Russian, Prussian and Austrian forces that had defeated Napoleon. Furthermore, had Napoleon remained on the defensive in 1815, the British would probably have borne a smaller share of the renewed war on land, because Austrian and Russian forces would have played a major role.

Britain had fought France for longer than any combatant, keeping the resistance to Napoleon alive in 1810–12, but her achievements on land in Europe had been limited. British forces had been driven from their traditional sphere of operations in the Low Countries and many of their subsequent amphibious expeditions had been unsuccessful. The seriousness of the challenge posed by the Peninsular War may be gauged from the fact that Napoleon only campaigned there once. The army was criticized by informed British commentators in the 1790s and 1800s; for lack of success and operational inadequacies, including poor planning and officers.

Yet these deficiencies should not be exaggerated. The fighting quality of the British infantry was evident from the campaigns of 1793–4 on and was to be demonstrated anew in the Egyptian campaign of 1801. The victory at Maida was not a bolt from the blue. Soldiers and commanders learned from successive campaigns and indeed were forced to do so. For example,

Brigadier-General Robert Anstruther, who died in Corunna on 14 January 1809 shortly after commanding the rear-most units in the retreat there, had already served in the Low Countries, the West Indies and the Dutch expedition in the 1790s, and in the Egyptian and Portuguese campaigns in the 1800s.

Furthermore, the British did make an important contribution in the Peninsula, and thus found a way to make an impact in Europe. The Walcheren expedition did not save Austria in 1809; it was an unimpressive diversion. In contrast, thanks to the Peninsular War, Napoleon had fewer troops available to campaign against Russia in 1812 and to defend France against Russia, Prussia and Austria in 1813–14. Wellington could not have fought his way to Paris in 1814; he lacked the troops to do so, but Soult's men were not available to protect the city from Britain's allies. The British had found a way to use their limited military power to maximum effect, something that was not possible in the Low Countries.

The army did not have to face the ultimate challenge: the defence of Britain against a major French invasion. In 1795, after the harrowing retreat through the icy United Provinces, it was in a poor state to do so, rather as was the army in 1940 after the retreat from Dunkirk. In 1797 Napoleon's Army of England was encamped on the Channel coast. By 1805 the British army, supported by the militia and the Volunteers, was much more prepared to resist invasion than had been the case in 1795–7. Thanks to the naval campaign by 1805, Trafalgar and Napoleon's other commitments, it was not necessary, but the army's subsequent move into a major offensive role in Iberia was appropriate: despite continued fears of invasion, the defensive function had been fulfilled. Although an appreciable portion of the army remained in the British Isles for home defence, its task was as much prompted by fears of domestic troubles as by the prospect of invasion. The chance of a French fleet driving away British blockading squadrons was far more remote than hitherto.

Nevertheless, the scale of Britain's global commitments, the proportion of the army tied up holding outposts around the globe, exerted such a huge drain on manpower that comparatively few troops could be spared for offensive operations on the European mainland or elsewhere. This was essentially a defensive mission which deprived Britain of the forces necessary for important offensive operations such as that in Holland in 1813–14.

Despite this, thanks to the army, the British were able to take the war to French Europe, not least by playing the major role in preventing Napoleon from successfully integrating Iberia into his system. This was no mean achievement. The same is true of the army's role in the conquest of much of the extra-European Napoleonic world, which is discussed in Chapter 9.

Wellington links the extra-European world, Iberia and Waterloo. Although he was unsuccessful in several campaigns, was repulsed in his first attempt to take Burgos and some of his other successes were heavily qualified, nevertheless, he never lost a battle or an army. His victories in Iberia were not the prelude to an evacuation by sea, as had been Moore's at Corunna. Wellington's understanding of, and ability in, strategy, tactics, intelligence work, and organization[33] made him the best general the British had; seeing more service than any other senior commander, he had more opportunities to develop his command abilities. Combined with self-confidence, bravery, diligence and stamina, they ensured that Wellington's command, although not always successful, was generally at least highly competent and frequently brilliantly impressive. Both in India in 1803 and against the French in Spain in 1813, Wellington was able to launch and sustain campaigns of manoeuvre deep into enemy territory, an achievement that owed much to the creation of an effective supply system.[34] Like Napoleon, much of his skill lay in adapting quickly to fresh intelligence and changing circumstances.

The Duke's achievements appear more striking against the background of repeated British failures, especially Holland in 1799, Argentina in 1806 and 1807, Egypt in 1807, Walcheren in 1809, and New Orleans in 1815. The contrast was unfair as Wellington had the advantage of commanding sustained campaigns, while the failures cited were expeditions, but it helped to enhance Wellington's reputation. These defeats indicate that there was no necessary superiority for British troops and tactics, nothing inevitable about British victory. It is dangerous to generalize from Wellington's experience, but, equally, this throws light on his achievement.

Without the troops, Wellington's qualities would have been of scant value. Napoleon knew that Wellington was a good general and the British good soldiers, and he said so. In the Peninsular War, the British, especially the infantry for there were few cavalry, stood up well in very difficult circumstances, firing on when the situation appeared in collapse, as at Talavera and Albuera. Their skill with the bayonet was such that the British victories were not solely triumphs for defensive firepower, and Wellington demonstrated, not least at Assaye, Argaum, Salamanca and Vitoria, his success in attack, but it is appropriate that the dominant image of this war on land is of Waterloo, of lines and squares of infantry bravely fighting off larger numbers of attacking French.

CHAPTER EIGHT

Naval success, 1793–1815

Thanks to her naval strength, Britain could be a world power, France only a European one. In 1798 Geoffrey Mowbray observed "our navy keeps every one of our enemies bound in chains upon their own coasts".[1] This lessened the ability of Britain's opponents to threaten invasion, send reinforcements to their colonies and take part in maritime trade. Much British activity was defensive: the prevention of enemy attack, both by action, such as convoying merchantmen, and keeping squadrons at sea to discourage invasion attempts, and by a continuous high level of preparation. However, the effect of such defensive activity was an offensive situation that gave Britain more maritime control than her rivals.

It was impossible, because of the difficult naval situation in 1796–8 and the policy of open blockade, to prevent the French from landing some troops in Wales (1797) and, more seriously, Ireland (1798), but they were relatively small forces unable to deliver a knockout invasion. The navy played a crucial role in 1805 when Napoleon assembled a large invasion force near Boulogne, only to find the British thwarting his plan for the French navy to gain control of the Channel for long enough to permit a crossing.

British trade was also protected, and, with it, empire. The value of colonies and trading stations was largely a function of their ability to trade. Naval power was crucial to this, because of the maritime nature of western European colonialization and long-distance commerce. The value of this trade, as a source of imports and re-exports, employment, processing and profit, and as a market for exports, could be huge. British naval power ensured that Britain gained this wealth and her opponents lost it, and this was vital to the ability to the British state to finance its actions in peace and war.

When Spain joined France in 1796, the British navy cut her links with her colonies. On 16–17 October 1799 four frigates captured the Spanish frigates *Thetis* and *Santa-Brígida*, each bearing treasure from the New World, off Cape Finisterre. The following April the British blockading squadron off Cadiz captured nearly all of a large Spanish convoy. In October 1804 the squadron off Cadiz took three Spanish frigates carrying a valuable cargo of bullion. British trade also had to be protected, an arduous task that led to the tedium and problems of convoy duty and to many sharp actions. When in February 1799 the French frigate *Forte* entered the Bay of Bengal the British frigate *Sibylle* sought it out and battered it into surrender.

By 1815 the French, Spanish, Dutch and Danish fleets had been defeated by Britain, although at the time of his fall in 1814 Napoleon was building a substantial fleet and had 40 large warships under construction. By 1815, the French and Dutch empires had been emasculated as military and strategic threats, and the route to India had been secured. Naval supremacy not only allowed Britain to capture the bases of other colonial powers, but also to develop colonies in areas with low population density, such as Australia, and to wage war with native rulers in India with only limited interference from other European powers. Naval strength and colonial power were to be the basis of Britain's ability to act as a world power in the nineteenth century. The consequences were to be crucial both for Britain and for many areas in the world.

The 1790s

Despite the well-prepared nature of the navy when war broke out in 1793, there was nothing inevitable about British victory in the naval and transoceanic struggles. The French navy was gravely weakened by the Revolution, losing 13 of the line in 1793 as a result of the British supported counter-revolutionary rising in Toulon. The combination of revolutionary zeal and mobilization was less beneficial to the French navy than to the army, and was indeed counter-productive given the effects of the Revolution on the officer corps. Nevertheless, victory on land brought France the support of other naval powers. Thus the situation during the American War of Independence was repeated: Britain was opposed by the other leading European naval powers.

As in 1759 and 1782, the British navy had again to win naval supremacy. British naval victories in the 1790s were crucial to the maintenance of national independence. There were no fleet engagements in 1793, in part because the policy of open blockade limited British opportunities and in part because the French fleet was unprepared. The following year, however, the British were to get their opportunity. At the Glorious First of June (1 June 1794), Richard, Earl Howe with 25 ships of the line attacked a French fleet of 26 of the line under Louis Thomas Villaret-Joyeuse sent to escort a grain convoy from America into Brest. Howe, who had gained the weather gauge as a result of skilful seamanship, was unable fully to execute his plan for all his ships to cut the French line so that each passed under the stern of a French ship and engaged it from leeward, but sufficient ships succeeded and British gunnery was superior enough and at close range for long enough to cost the French seven warships (six captured and one sunk) and 5,000 casualties, crucial given the difficulties of obtaining skilled manpower; the vital convoy reached France, however.[2]

This victory was followed by further, though lesser, defeats for the French off the Ile de Groix (23 June 1795) and the Ile de Hyères (13 July 1795), although the caution of Vice-Admiral William Hotham led to a failure to push home the British advantage in engagements in the Mediterranean. On 13 July Hotham outnumbered the French by 23 to 17 warships, but the French only lost one warship in an engagement that infuriated Nelson. Hotham's caution was in part justified by the limited support facilities Britain then had in the Mediterranean. Further afield, the capture of French overseas bases owed much to British naval support. HMS *Minerva* and three of the East India Company's ships blockaded Pondicherry in 1793. Two years later three of the Company's ships were fitted out at Bombay and assisted in the capture of the Cape of Good Hope, while 14 of the Company's ships were sold to the government and equipped as ships of the line. The Bombay Marine was reconstituted as a regular naval service in 1798.

Nevertheless, the situation deteriorated as France overran the United Provinces (1795) and forced Spain into alliance (1796). There was now a threat that Britain's opponents would combine their naval power in order to cover an invasion: combined, they enjoyed a numerical superiority over the British. Napoleon's occupation of Livorno closed it to the British. The British withdrew their navy from the Mediterranean in 1796; instead using Lisbon and the Tagus as their base. In 1797 the British could not mount a response when the French invaded Venice, seizing its navy and its bases in the Ionian Isles, such as Corfu. The British garrison on Elba was evacuated by Nelson in 1797. It was scarcely surprising that Britain sought peace, although talks at Lille collapsed as a result of the British refusal to return all its colonial conquests and of the intransigence of the French government.

The dangerous situation was eased by the difficulties in achieving co-operation and co-ordination between the French, Dutch and Spanish fleets, by the mismanaged French expedition against Ireland in the winter of 1796–7, and by two British victories in 1797. On 14 February 1797 off Cape St. Vincent, Rear-Admiral Sir John Jervis and 15 of the line attacked a superior and far more heavily gunned Spanish fleet of 27 of the line under Don José de Cordova successfully, using tactics similar to those of Napoleon on land, to operate on interior lines and concentrate his strength on attacking one part of the Spanish fleet. Nelson on his own initiative, and followed by others, kept the two parts separated. British captains took successful advantage of the melee Nelson created to win a number of individual ship encounters: their greatly superior rate of fire had a deadly effect. The Spaniards lost four ships of the line captured, including two 112-gunners, and had ten more ships badly damaged. Their fleet was driven back into Cadiz, thus ending the plan for them to join the French at Brest.[3]

On 11 October 1797, in the North Sea, two advancing British lines of warships under Admiral Adam Duncan broke the Dutch line under De Winter into three segments at the battle of Camperdown: each fleet had 16 warships. In the individual ship-to-ship engagements that the battle developed into, British victory owed much to superior gun power, but Dutch gunnery skill was such that British killed and wounded were proportionately closer to that of their opponent than in any other fleet action of the war. Nevertheless, the Dutch lost seven ships of the line.[4] This victory was followed during the 1799 expedition against Holland with the capture of Dutch warships at Den Helder and in the Zuider Zee.

Less well-known victories were also important. The landing of French troops in Ireland in 1798 dramatized the importance of control of Irish waters. On 11 October 1798 a British squadron under Sir John Borlase Warren attacked a French counterpart off the coast of Ireland. The smaller French force was heavily defeated; but if the victory owed much to the superior strength of the British, it was the defeat of the French that was important. Warren captured most of the French expeditionary force: 2,500 troops and Wolfe Tone. In 1800 the British under Jervis, now Lord St. Vincent, introduced a close blockade of Brest, further ensuring control of Irish waters. On the night of 12–13 July 1801 Rear-Admiral Sir James Saumarez with only four ships of the line defeated a Franco-Spanish fleet of eight of the line near Cadiz, capturing or destroying three ships of the line.

In the meantime, in a series of small engagements, the British had destroyed or captured numbers of French warships and privateers and attacked French trade, especially, but not only, in the Channel. For example, on 19 June 1793 the *Nymphe* frigate under Edward Pellew captured the *Cléopâtre* frigate in the Channel and on 20 October 1793 the *Crescent* frigate under Saumarez captured the *Réunion* frigate, which had been using Cherbourg as a base to attack British trade. Aside from individual engagements, the British also fought a number of squadron engagements that played a major role in affirming their dominance in the Channel and the Western Approaches. Frigate squadrons were ordered to cruise off Brittany and to destroy French forces preying on British trade. In 1794 a squadron under Warren twice destroyed French frigate squadrons. A squadron under Pellew captured the French frigate *Révolutionnaire* off Ushant on 21 October, and it was added to the British fleet. In 1795 a frigate squadron under Richard Strachan greatly harrassed coastal trade on the Norman and Breton coasts. The following year, Pellew, again in command of a frigate squadron, captured two French frigates. In June 1799 a squadron of frigates was captured in the Gulf of Genoa by Keith. The number of French and Dutch frigates fell dramatically between 1795 and 1800. Ships of the line also helped in the struggle against French privateers: four en route to the Mediterranean under Rear-Admiral John Gell, captured the *Général Dumouriez* off the Portuguese coast in 1793.

Five years later, the *Hercule*, a newly launched 74-gun warship en route from Lorient was attacked by the *Mars*, a 74-gun ship that was part of the fleet blockading Brest. The two ships came alongside, the bow anchors hooked and the ships exchanged fire while touching, with many of the guns fired from in-board. The British clearly won the hour-long gunnery exchange and the *Hercule* surrendered. The heavy casualties of such engagements, which included both captains, indicate how misleading it is to think of naval war in this period as limited.

Such successes helped to reduce the losses of British trade and also maintained the sense of British naval power, although French privateering revived when part of the British navy mutinied in 1797. The protection of British trade took the navy far afield. In 1795 Samuel Hood took a squadron into the Aegean to protect trade against French frigates based in Smyrna. The pursuit of commerce raiders was not restricted to European waters. In October 1799, Edward Hamilton, who had already, in command of the *Surprise* frigate, a captured French ship, taken numerous French and Spanish privateers in the West Indies in 1798–9, stormed and cut out the *Hermione*, a Spanish warship moored between shore defences at Puerto Cabello.

Nelson victorious, 1798–1805

The next three major victories were won by Rear-Admiral Sir Horatio Nelson (1758–1805).[5] The eldest son of a Norfolk clergyman, Nelson entered the navy, under the auspices of his maternal uncle. After serving in the Caribbean, the North Sea and North American waters during the War of American Independence, in 1793 he was sent to the Mediterranean. He took part in the conquest of Corsica the following year, being largely responsible for the capture of two ships of the line off Cape Poli on 13–14 March, and losing the sight of his right eye during the siege of Calvi. In 1796 Nelson commanded a frigate squadron that harassed French coastal positions and movements in the Gulf of Genoa. At the battle of Cape St. Vincent, Nelson, then captain of the *Captain*, took a prominent role, boarding and capturing two Spanish warships. As a result, he was knighted and promoted to Rear-Admiral. In 1797 Nelson lost his right arm in a mismanaged amphibious attack on a well-defended Santa Cruz at Tenerife in the Canary Islands.

In 1798, thanks to Cape St. Vincent and Camperdown, the government felt able to send a fleet back into the Mediterranean, a policy deemed necessary in order to persuade Austria to rejoin the war. Nelson was instructed to find out what the Toulon fleet was preparing to do. However, the fleet left Toulon for Egypt on 19 May while Nelson was driven away by a

Capture of French *Ça Ira* by HMS *Agamemnon* under Captain Horatio Nelson, 1795. Nelson had sailed for the Mediterranean with Hood's fleet in May 1793. Nelson took an active part in a number of engagements until his brilliant role in the defeat of the Spanish fleet at the battle of Cape St. Vincent in 1797. Aside from fleet and smaller actions, he was active in the capture of Bastia in 1794 and played a major role in attacking French coastal trade. Nelson sought to use naval power in order to hinder the French on land, but in 1796 Napoleon's successes in Italy led the British to evacuate the Mediterranean. *National Maritime Museum, London.*

strong northerly gale. A long and unsuccessful search was finally ended when Nelson found the French fleet under Brueys anchored in Aboukir Bay. Napoleon and his army had already begun the conquest of Egypt. At dusk, in the battle of the Nile (1 August 1798), Nelson unexpectedly attacked the French on both sides: on the shallow inshore side of their line, where the French were not prepared to resist, as well as simultaneously on the other side, a manoeuvre that was not without risks: *Culloden* ran aground and was unable to take part in the battle. In a battle fought at night in which the British fired at very close range, the French lost 11 of their 13 ships of the line present: the other two fled, as did the French frigates. The nature of the French position was such that Nelson was able to achieve a battle of annihilation, first defeating the ships in the French van and then pressing on to attack those moored behind; the latter had been unable to provide assistance. French gunnery proved inadequate, and the French were not only poorly deployed, but also failed to respond adequately to the British attack. The British navy worked as a well-integrated force. Nelson had ably prepared his captains to act vigorously and in co-operation in all

226

The Battle of the Nile, 1 August 1798 – Beginning of the Action, by Thomas Whitcombe. A spectacular victory that indicated the possibility of total victory at sea. As with La Hougue in 1692 and the Russian victory over the Turks at Cesmé in 1770, an attacked fleet in an inshore position was particularly vulnerable. As with Louisbourg in 1758, the loss of a distant French squadron helped to isolate the French army in the region. *National Maritime Museum, London.*

possible eventualities, and had fully explained his tactics to them, as some other energetic admirals, such as Suffren, failed to do. British seamanship was superior and the well-drilled gun crews outshot the French.

The strategic situation changed. The dangerous commitment made by the dispatch of a fleet to the Mediterranean, not least the weakening of the fleet in home waters, had been justified by victory; although that did not lessen the nature of the risk that had been taken. The French army in Egypt was now cut off. The British exploited their naval position in the Mediterranean by blockading Egypt and Malta, capturing Livorno and Minorca (1798) and by providing naval support to the Turks in their resistance to Napoleon's siege of Acre (1799). Napoleon's siege artillery, sent by sea from Egypt, was captured on 18 March by British warships under Captain William Sidney Smith. Captain Thomas Troubridge used naval power to make an important contribution to the struggle with the French in southern Italy. In 1799 he captured Ischia, Procida and Capri, blockaded the Bay of Naples and played a major role in the successful sieges of St. Elmo, Capua, Gaeta and Civitàvecchia. In 1800, the *Guillaume Tell*, the last surviving French warship that had escaped the battle of the Nile, was captured: an 80-gun ship, she was engaged at night off Malta by the 36-gun

Penelope and delayed until two British ships of the line could come up. Lord Keith successfully blockaded Genoa, materially helping the Austrian siege of the French garrison. The British fleet also bombarded French forces near Savona that year. By 1800 the British navy had a clear numerical advantage over its opponents. This was not the case in ships of the line, but in frigates the British had an overwhelming advantage, and they were crucial for trade protection.

In 1801 the British took action against the threatening Northern Confederacy of Baltic powers. Denmark rejected an ultimatum to leave the confederacy. At the battle of Copenhagen, on 2 April 1801, Nelson, who, after sounding and buoying the channels by night, had sailed his division down the dangerous Hollaender Deep in order to be able to attack from an unexpected direction, was again successful at the expense of an anchored line, this time that of the Danish fleet. Heavy Danish fire led Nelson's commander Sir Hyde Parker to order him to "discontinue the action" if he felt it appropriate, but Nelson continued the heavy bombardment and the Danish fleet was battered into accepting a truce. The 17 Danish ships of the line that were present were captured or destroyed. Neutral trade with France was thus no longer an option. Nelson's reputation rose greatly, one newspaper reporting, "The zeal, spirit, and enterprize of Lord Nelson were never more completely developed than upon this great and memorable occasion, and they happily diffused their influence through the whole of the squadron under his immediate command".[6] The British were also helped by the assassination the previous month of the hostile Czar, Paul I, by aristocratic opponents. After leaving the Baltic, Nelson was appointed to command the squadron assembled to repel the invasion force believed to be assembling at Boulogne. On 1 August, and again on the night of 15–16 August 1801, he attacked the boats in Boulogne harbour, but heavy fire from the shore thwarted the attack.

The naval situation was instrumental in the resumption of hostilities in 1803, because the British government refused to surrender Malta as it was obliged to do by the 1802 Peace of Amiens. Captured in 1800, Malta offered a naval base[7] in a sea where the British had already lost Toulon, Corsica and Elba and in 1802 given up Minorca under the peace. Nelson returned to the Mediterranean in 1803 and resumed the blockade of Toulon. However, the situation remained threatening, with France still in control of the Dutch fleet, and continuing an active programme of naval construction. Nelson hoped that Napoleon's government would be "upset by French men", which indeed appeared to be the only means to remove his power. In the meanwhile, he had to resume the long hours of blockade and cast around the Mediterranean from that perspective, finding, for example, Sardinia "an invaluable possession in every respect. It is the Ceylon of the Mediterranean", an interesting example of the degree to which the European world was increasingly refracted through the lens of Empire.[8] The blockade of other French ports was resumed and efforts were made to prevent the concentration of French invasion craft near Boulogne.

In 1805 the naval situation approached a fresh crisis, with Britain again on the defensive. Napoleon prepared an invasion for which he required naval superiority in the Channel and this seemed a prospect when Spain joined France. French squadrons successfully escaped from Toulon and Rochefort, threatening a concentration of strength to cover an invasion. Napoleon planned for his squadrons to join at Martinique and then to return as a united force able to defeat the British. He required superiority in the Channel for four days in order for his troops to cross, planned to land in or near Pegwell Bay in Kent, and intended to overrun London within a week before dictating peace.

The failure of the naval plan ensured that the detailed preparations for the landing proved fruitless. The Rochefort squadron arrived first in the Caribbean and captured Dominica, but it returned to Europe when no other squadron arrived within the prescribed time. Villeneuve and the Toulon squadron was able to join a Spanish squadron at Cadiz in April, the outnumbered blockading squadron under Vice-Admiral Sir John Orde offering no hindrance, and to reach Martinique on 14 May, but he was pursued by Nelson, who reached Barbados on 4 June.

Evading the pursuit, Villeneuve sailed back for Europe, but he was unable to join the Brest fleet, which, thanks to the British close blockade under Admiral Cornwallis, had not had the opportunity to sail to Martinique. Villeneuve fought a British fleet under Vice-Admiral Sir Robert Calder west of Cape Finisterre on 22 July. Although outnumbered, Calder engaged Villeneuve in the fog and captured two Spanish warships. Villeneuve failed to renew the battle the next day and put in first to Vigo, then to Ferrol and then to Corunna. The outnumbered Calder fell back to join the British fleet off Brest, although he was to be reprimanded by a court martial for failing to renew the battle. The increasingly hesitant Villeneuve sailed again on 15 August, but, instead of trying to fight his way into the Channel, made for Cadiz, taking advantage of discretionary orders from Napoleon, who responded with fury to the news of his admiral's caution.[9] Nelson took command of the fleet assembled to blockade the port. Napoleon cancelled his invasion plans, and marched against Austria. When the Franco-Spanish fleet set sail on 19–20 October it was for Italian waters. It was intercepted off Cape Trafalgar.

At Trafalgar (21 October 1805), Nelson's objective was to engage the larger Franco-Spanish line (33 of the line to the British 27) as rapidly as possible, attacking in two divisions in order to split his opponents into smaller groups that could be attacked in strength. By using his windward position to attack the Franco-Spanish rear and centre, Nelson achieved numerical superiority as his opponent's foremost ships could not intervene effectively. The line was penetrated as planned, making it difficult for

Double-headed shot for cutting through rigging fired at HMS *Victory* from the *Santísima Trinidad* at Trafalgar. The commander of the French marines recorded: "Four of our ships, *Héros*, *Santísima Trinidad*, *Bucentaure* and *Redoutable*, presented him [Nelson] with a very brisk and solid wall of fire as he approached". The four-deck 136-gun flagship of Admiral Cisneros lost her three masts to accurate British fire, particularly that from HMS *Neptune*. Having suffered 300 casualties and no longer able to fire a shot, the ship surrendered and was scuttled in the storm that followed the battle. *National Maritime Museum, London.*

Villeneuve to retreat or regroup, the Franco-Spanish ships were raked from the stern, and the battle became a series of small struggles between individual ships or groups of ships in which British gunnery and seamanship prevailed, albeit at the cost of heavy casualties in the close combat that such engagements entailed. Nelson was mortally wounded by a French sharpshooter firing from the rigging of the *Redoutable*. One French ship blew up and 18 French and Spanish ships of the line were captured, including the *Santísima Trinidad*, the largest eighteenth-century warship, a four-decker carrying 136 guns, although she, like many of the prizes, sank in a strong storm that followed the battle. Villeneuve was captured. The losses of sailors, including prisoners, in the combined fleet was serious, amounting to about 14,000, of whom 7,000 were dead or wounded. British dead and wounded totaled 1,690.[10] Four of the French ships of the line that escaped Trafalgar were attacked off Cape Finisterre on 4 November by a squadron under Strachan. After inflicting much damage, Strachan captured them all.

After Trafalgar

After Trafalgar, the British enjoyed a clear superiority in ships of the line. Napoleon subsequently sought, with some success, to rebuild his fleet. By 1809 the Toulon fleet was nearly as large as the British blockaders. However, his naval strength had been badly battered by losses of sailors in successive defeats, while his attempt to translate his far-flung territorial control into naval strength was unsuccessful. Due to the Peninsular War, Napoleon lost the Spanish navy, and the six French ships of the line sheltering in Cadiz and Vigo surrendered to the Spaniards in 1808. The Portuguese and Danish fleets were kept out of French hands, the former by persuasion, the latter by force, while Russia's Black Sea fleet, then in the Tagus, was blockaded until the British were able to seize it. By 1810 Britain had 50 per cent of the ships of the line in the world; up from 29 per cent in 1790. Britain's proportion of world mercantile shipping also increased: effective convoying ensured that ships could be constructed with reference to the goods to be carried, rather than their military effectiveness. Re-established in 1793, convoys were made compulsory in 1798. The profits from trade enabled Britain to make loans and grants to European allies.

The navy had numerous tasks in European waters after Trafalgar. Some were defensive. Aside from convoying trade and offering protection against French privateers,[11] it was necessary to retain control of home waters. This also entailed covering attacks on the Continent, especially the Walcheren expedition of 1809, which was intended to lead to the fall of the French naval base of Antwerp. Enemy trade was attacked wherever it could be found.

In the Mediterranean, the British sought to blockade Toulon as the first line of defence for British and allied interests, such as the protection of Sicily. The blockade was also intended to complement more offensive steps, including intervention in Iberia and moves to limit French influence in the eastern Mediterranean. These moves included Vice-Admiral Sir John Duckworth's attempt to obtain the surrender of the Turkish fleet in 1807. This was unsuccessful. Duckworth sailed through the Dardanelles on 19 February 1807, destroying a squadron of Turkish frigates, but the Turks refused to yield to his intimidation and when, on 3 March, Duckworth returned through the straits he ran the gauntlet of Turkish cannon, firing stone shots of up to 800 pounds: one took away the wheel of the *Canopus*. Turkish resistance had been stiffened with French assistance and the British operation suffered from unfavourable winds and Duckworth's indecision.[12] Captain John Spanger was more successful against the French in the Ionian Islands in 1809.

The British also had defensive and offensive objectives in the Baltic. Concern about the Danish fleet led to a successful joint attack on Copenhagen in 1807: the British fleet under Admiral James Gambier helped

231

Sir John Duckworth's Passage of the Dardanelles, February 1807, by Thomas Whitcombe. Duckworth's first passage was successful. He silenced the forts and destroyed a squadron of Turkish frigates. The return under heavy bombardment in March was less happy. George Monro had reported in 1793 "the Dardanelles are at present in no respect able to oppose a fleet . . . where they have forts, they are so situated as to be nearly useless, either from the construction or from neglect of what is well constructed". French advice helped the Turks show that such assessments were overdrawn. *National Maritime Museum, London.*

bombard Copenhagen on 2–5 September and the city and the Danish fleet surrendered on 7 September.[13] A vivid account by a young observer was provided by John Oldershaw Hewes (1789–1811), whose ship anchored in the Sound on 16 August:

> on the 17th . . . Saw the Danes burn one of our merchantmen and carry one into Copenhagen. Our boats returned with two Danish vessels. Saw our bombs, brigs and frigates engaging the enemys mortar boats on the 18th. The enemys mortar boats commenced a heavy firing. The Comus frigate took the Danish frigate Fredrickswern 23rd. Sent our boats to tow our small shipping into action. At 12 o'clock one of our boats returned with three men wounded in it. One of the men had all the thick part of his thigh shot off but is now well. On the 24th at 6 o'clock at night saw the red hot shot and shells flying which looked beautiful flying in the air. At 30 minutes past 6 saw a fire break out in Copenhagen. At 8

o'clock it thundered and lightn'd most tremendous. 25th our troops on shore and the enemys forts were firing away one at another also on the 26th 27th and 28th. On the 31st the enemy hove a shell in the Charles tender and she blew up and wounded nineteen men belonging to us besides took of one of our Lieutenant's legs broke his collar bone, cut him very bad on the head and almost knocked one of his eyes out, but he is now quite well and at Portsmouth. It killed a young man about my own age, my most particular acquaintance a masters mate, and killed two sailors besides what belonged to the vessel. On the 1st of September I went on shore with 15 sailors to make a battery close under the enemys walls. We were obliged to go when it was dark as they should not see us or else they would have certainly have shot us. We could hear them talking and playing a fiddle. It rained excessively all night and I was almost perished with wet and cold. We left it as soon as it began to get light in the morning. On the 2nd our batteries began bombarding the town. Saw the town on fire in two places . . . was on fire from the 2nd to the 7th on which day it surrendered . . . the greatest part is burnt down.

Hewes went on to serve as a clerk in the *Valiant* and purser of the sloop *Thais*, and drowned off Cape Castle, West Africa in 1811.[14]

In 1808, the British sent warships into the Baltic in order to assist Sweden against attack by Denmark and Russia. On 25 August two British ships of the line helped 11 Swedish counterparts defeat nine Russian ships of the line off south-west Finland. The following year Vice-Admiral Sir James Saumerez led a powerful fleet to the Gulf of Finland, thus preventing the Russians from taking naval action against Sweden. However, the Russians had already conquered Finland, and were able to force the Swedes to accept a dictated peace. Thereafter, as Sweden was forced into the French camp, Saumarez took steps to protect British trade and, crucially, naval stores: much of the timber, tallow, pitch, tar, iron and hemp required for the navy came from the Baltic.[15]

The general situation was more favourable than in 1795–1805, particularly after the Spanish navy and naval bases were denied France in 1808, although there were fewer opportunities than earlier to increase the size of the navy by adding French prizes. The blockaded French navy was no longer a force that was combat-ready. The longer it remained in harbour the more its efficiency declined: officers and crews had less operational experience. It remained difficult to predict French moves when at sea, but the French were less able to gain the initiative than hitherto. The French and allied squadrons that did sail out were generally defeated. These frequently overlooked engagements were important because a run of French success would have challenged British naval control.

On 25 September 1805 Samuel Hood and the blockading squadron off Rochefort attacked a French frigate squadron bound for the West Indies with reinforcements: four of the five frigates were captured, although Hood had to have his arm amputated after his elbow was smashed by a musket shot. On 6 February 1806 Duckworth and seven of the line engaged a French squadron of five of the line that had escaped from Rochefort off Saint Domingue in the West Indies. The superior British gunnery brought Duckworth a complete victory: three of the French ships were captured and two driven ashore and burnt. During the battle a portrait of Nelson was displayed abroad the *Superb*. On 13 March 1806 Warren captured two warships sailing back from the East Indies as they neared France. Further afield, the Dutch squadron in the Indian Ocean was destroyed at Gressie on 11 December 1807. On 4 April 1808 an escorted Spanish convoy was intercepted off Rota near Cadiz, the escorts dispersed and much of the convoy seized. On the night of 11–12 April 1809 a French squadron in Basque Roads was attacked by fireships. Although they did no damage to the French warships, many ran aground in escaping the threat. They were attacked by British warships on 12 April and four were destroyed. However, a failure to press home the attack led to recriminations between the admirals and a court martial. Two years later, on 13 March 1811, a squadron of four frigates under Captain William Hoste, one of Nelson's protégés, engaged a French squadron of six frigates under Dubourdieu off Lissa in the Adriatic: Lissa was a British base that the French were trying to seize. As the French approached, Hoste hoisted the signal "remember Nelson" to the cheers of his crew. Thanks to superior British seamanship and gunnery, the French were defeated with the loss of three frigates.[16] Hoste kept the Adriatic in awe. Frequently, foreign warships had to be attacked while inshore or protected by coastal positions, a situation that enhanced the value of Britain's clear superiority in vessels other than ships of the line. In August 1806 the Spanish frigate *Pomona* anchored off Havana close to a shore battery was captured by two British frigates.

These engagements were the highpoints of a prolonged and often arduous process of blockade in which British squadrons policed the seas of Europe and, to a far lesser extent, the rest of the world. The history of these squadrons was often that of storms and of disappointed hopes of engaging the French. Blockade was not easy. This was especially true off Toulon due to the prevailing winds. The exposure of warships to the constant battering of wind and wave placed a major strain on an increasingly ageing fleet. The Channel Fleet for example was dispersed by a strong gale on 3 January 1804 and the blockade of Le Havre lifted, although that of Brest was swiftly resumed. The weather claimed and damaged more ships than the French: out of the 317 naval ships lost in 1803–15, 223 were wrecked or foundered. Tropical stations could be particularly dangerous. In 1807 Troubridge and the *Blenheim* disappeared in a storm off Madagascar.

Blockading squadrons could be driven off station by wind and weather: this was the case with the small watching squadron off Toulon when the French sailed in May 1798.

Fog could cover French movements, as when the Brest fleet sailed in April 1799. Once it had sailed, the British were unsure whether the French would head for Ireland or the Mediterranean. Concern about the safety of Minorca handicapped the subsequent British pursuit in the Mediterranean, and the French were able to sail to Toulon, and eventually back to Brest, without being intercepted.[17] In January 1808 the French Rochefort squadron evaded the British blockaders in bad weather and poor visibility and sailed to Toulon. Fog was also a hazard to British warships. The 74-gun *Venerable*, part of the squadron covering Brest, sank on the Devon coast in 1804 after running ashore in a thick fog.

The poorly charted nature of inshore waters was also a problem and ships ran aground. Nearly 400 men drowned in March 1801 when the *Invincible* ran aground near Great Yarmouth. It was particularly easy to do so when enforcing blockades. Thus the frigate *Jason* was wrecked on a rock when pursuing a French convoy near Brest in 1796. Chasing a frigate off La Rochelle, the frigate *Artois* ran aground in 1797 and was lost. Shoals were also a problem when attacking enemy warships sheltering in coastal waters. The *Hannibal* ran aground and was forced to surrender in Saumarez's attack on French warships moored off Algeciras on 6 July 1801. The *Amazon* was wrecked in Audierne Bay in January 1797 when the British attacked and drove inshore the *Droits de l'Homme*. The *Amazon*'s captain, Robert Reynolds, was lost with all bar 12 of the crew of 850 when the 98-gun *St. George* was driven onto the Danish coast in a storm in December 1811; the 74-gun *Defence* was also lost on the same occasion. Fire at sea was another hazard: one such, caused by a drunken steward, put paid to *Ajax* off the Dardanelles in 1807. The *Queen Charlotte*, flagship of the Mediterranean fleet, was destroyed by fire off Livorno in 1800 with the loss of nearly 700 men.

The condition of the fleet forced the government to launch an expensive programme of repair, refitting and construction. Aside from the expense, this programme faced serious deficiencies in the dockyards and in supplies, especially of timber. A rapid rise in the demand for timber led to the use of inferior, including unseasoned, stock and thus to warships rotting rapidly. Part of the strain was met by adding captured warships to the fleet.[18] Aside from the wear on the ships, the shortage of sailors also ensured that blockade posed a major burden. Nevertheless, the very presence of blockading squadrons was crucial. Blockade was designed to prevent French squadrons from sailing out in order to mount attacks. It also served both to prevent the squadrons from uniting and becoming a more serious threat, and to limit the supplies that they could receive. The threat posed by the united Franco-Spanish fleet in Cadiz in 1805 was a salutary reminder of the need to keep French squadrons separated: Villeneuve would have had even more ships in his force had he been able to join with the Brest fleet.

After Trafalgar, the British presence off Spain and in the Mediterranean was maintained by Vice Admiral Cuthbert Collingwood, who had received a peerage for his role as second in command at Trafalgar. In 1805–7 he blockaded Cadiz, but he then moved into the Mediterranean where his main concern was the French fleet in Toulon. Threatening Sicily, this fleet forced the British to adopt a defensive strategy. At least after Trafalgar this strategy was based on clear maritime dominance. In 1808 Collingwood failed to intercept Ganteaume when he relieved the French garrison on Corfu, largely because he only received belated news of French moves and responded in an overly cautious fashion. The blockade of Toulon was more successful the following year, and on 26 October two ships of the line attempting to carry supplies to Barcelona were driven on shore and destroyed. Nevertheless, concern about the Toulon fleet continued strong, and at times the British fleet seemed stretched. In 1810 Collingwood was replaced as commander in the Mediterranean by Admiral Sir Charles Cotton, and that year, as the French continued to increase their fleet, concern about the situation in the Mediterranean reached a post-Trafalgar peak. The British command stretched over 2,000 miles and Cotton was critically short of frigates. One British squadron blockaded Corfu. In January 1811 the British feared that the Toulon squadron would be able to escape and to attack Wellington's position at Lisbon.

From 1811 command in the Mediterranean was held by Edward Pellew, then a Vice-Admiral. A sortie from Toulon was turned back in 1812. Despite the problems of British naval[19] power in the Mediterranean, there was no retreat from the sea as in 1796. In 1810 George, 4th Earl of Aberdeen, who had spent much time in Greece and the Aegean, argued that there was much interest in independence there and that Britain should encourage it. Aberdeen added that a "French connection, from the absence of naval intercourse and protection, is much less desired than the friendship of this country".[20]

It was not only in the Mediterranean that British naval resources were stretched. Elsewhere, despite the size of the navy, there were too few ships and sailors for the myriad tasks expected of the navy, and the situation could become hazardous if the French acted in strength. In December 1809 the *Junon* sailing from Halifax to the West Indies was attacked, heavily battered and successfully boarded by four French frigates near Guadeloupe. However, the successive capture of French overseas bases lessened their ability to challenge the British.

Collingwood, Cotton and Pellew had the responsibilities of fleet command in the Mediterranean and had primarily to respond to the possibility of French sorties. A more aggressive note was struck by Thomas Cochrane. As captain of the frigate *Pallas* in the Bay of Biscay, he harried French trade and destroyed corvettes. In 1808, as captain of the frigate *Impérieuse*, Cochrane attacked positions on the coasts of southern France and Catalonia. Semaphore stations, fortifications, lighthouses, batteries and bridges were destroyed. In 1809 Cochrane organized the fireship attack on Basque Roads, but fell out with Gambier when the latter failed to press home the attack. In 1810 Murray Maxwell and the frigate *Alceste* stormed a battery near Fréjus on the French Mediterranean coast.

William Hoste also had the active time that being detached on independent cruises permitted. As commander of the frigate *Amphion* and later the *Bacchante*, in 1806 he operated against French bases on the coast of Calabria and in 1808–14 ravaged French trade in the Adriatic and attacked coastal positions. Both Cochrane and Hoste showed their flexibility and all-round military skills by also operating successfully on land. In 1808 Cochrane delayed the fall of the Catalan castle of Rosas for a fortnight when he took over its defence and in 1814 Hoste established batteries on difficult positions, commanding Cattaro and Ragusa, leading their garrisons to surrender. The successes of naval forces in such circumstances were frequently obtained with allied support, for example that of the Austrians at Cattaro. Furthermore, only so much could be achieved against superior French forces: Rosas fell, and the French dominated Italy.

Nevertheless, British naval activities harassed the French and forced them to deploy considerable forces to garrison their coasts. It was a counterpart to the commercial challenge posed by British contraband. Attacks on coastal shipping and positions required less military effort and resources than amphibious operations, and were possible both when the war was going badly and when it was more successful. A squadron under Nelson harassed the French on the Ligurian coast in 1795–6; another, under Vice-Admiral Thomas Freemantle, in 1812–14 drove the French from much of the Dalmatian coast, playing a major role in the capture of Fiume (1813) and Trieste (1814). In a host of small actions, British warships put the French on the defensive. The *Sirius* frigate captured the corvette *Bergère* off Civitàvecchia in April 1806.

French ports on the Atlantic, Channel and North Sea also had to be blockaded after Trafalgar. The service was similarly arduous, although there were fewer opportunities for operations against coastal positions than in the Mediterranean. In the Channel after Trafalgar there was felt to be less need for winter blockade by ships of the line. As in the Mediterranean, there were many small-ship actions, as the British sought to stop French commerce raiding: frigate, sloop, ketch, cutter operations against French warships, privateers and merchantmen. Captain John Loring of the *Niobe* was a particularly active frigate commander, acting both on his own, for example in the capture of the brig *Néarque* in 1806 and of the privateer *Loup Marin* off Le Havre in 1811, and in co-operation with other warships, as in the destruction of two frigates off the Cherbourg peninsula in the winter of

1810–11. As commander of first the *Loire* frigate and the *Emerald*, Captain Frederick Maitland attacked French privateers and coastal batteries around the Bay of Biscay. Such actions also took place across the oceans. In the West Indies James Gordon in the sloop *Racoon* captured one brig in July 1803 and drove another ashore on Cuba the following year, continuing his attacks on privateers in 1805.

Aside from blockade and inshore attacks, the navy also played a major role in supporting operations in the Peninsular War. This involved the transport of men and supplies for the British forces and also of supplies for their Portuguese and Spanish allies. Rear-Admiral Sir Home Popham played a particularly important and active role, with amphibious operations on the north coast of Spain in 1812. British participation in the war would not have been possible without the navy.[21]

War of 1812

British naval power was also crucial in the war of 1812–15 with the United States. Naval blockades greatly harmed the American economy, amphibious forces were able to approach Baltimore and burn Washington, and it was possible to send reinforcements to Canada in order to resist successfully poorly led and unco-ordinated American attacks. In August 1814 a fleet under Vice-Admiral Sir Alexander Cochrane entered the Chesapeake. A squadron under James Gordon forced its way up the Potomac, silenced Fort Washington, captured Alexandria, Virginia and returned with a rich haul of merchantmen. Troops were convoyed up the Patuscent whence they marched on Washington. An unsuccessful attack was mounted on New Orleans in January 1815, but the British were able to send a force there, and when hostilities ceased an expedition was being planned against first Savannah and then Charleston, both of which were blockaded. The Treaty of Ghent had been signed in December 1814, but fighting continued until early 1815.

Although the Americans had the most powerful frigates of the age, they had no ships of the line and their total navy at the outset comprised only 17 ships. The Americans were to capture three British frigates in 1812, but the other British naval losses were all of smaller vessels. Nevertheless, the British suffered initially from overconfidence, inaccurate gunnery and ships that were simply less powerful and less well prepared than those of their opponents. However, British gunnery improved during the war, as, more generally, did their naval effectiveness. They developed a fleet on the Great Lakes. In 1814 the British were able to construct a 112-gun ship at the naval base at Kingston on Lake Ontario which had been founded in 1784.[22]

Naval strength

British naval hegemony rested on a sophisticated and well-financed administrative structure, a large fleet drawing on the manpower resources of a substantial mercantile marine, although there was never enough sailors, and an ability to win engagements that reflected widely diffused qualities of seamanship and gunnery, a skilled and determined corps of captains, and able leadership. This was true not only of command at sea, as with Nelson's innovative tactics and ability to inspire his captains, his "band of brothers", but also of effective leadership of the navy as an institution. Thus Jervis, created Earl St. Vincent after his great victory, was an energetic First Lord of the Admiralty in 1801–4, although his hostility to naval contractors and his campaign for economy in the naval dockyards limited the rate of construction and repair, placing the navy in a difficult position in 1804. The reversal of this policy when St. Vincent resigned in 1804 ensured that by the end of 1808 the commissioned fleet totalled 113 of the line and 596 other ships. Admiral Charles Middleton, created Lord Barham in 1805, was an effective First Lord in 1805–6. He played an important role both in developing organizational efficiency and in providing able and effective leadership during the Trafalgar campaign. Able administrators such as Samuel Bentham and John Payne did much to develop the organizational infrastructure of the navy.[23] Resources permitted and administrative systems supported the maintenance both of the largest battlefleet in the world and of a crucially large number of smaller warships

Better leadership helped in avoiding a repetition of the serious naval mutinies of 1797. That year, dissatisfaction over conditions, especially pay, provided a fertile basis for political discontent. The Spithead fleet refused to sail, there was trouble in St. Vincent's fleet off Cadiz, and, more seriously, that at the Nore began to blockade the Thames until quelled by firm action.[24] Later mutinies were on a smaller scale and more specific in their grievances. Thus in December 1801 the crew of some of the ships ordered to sail for the Caribbean mutinied. The mutiny was crushed and the ringleaders executed.

The infrastructure improved and became more farflung.[25] New naval facilities were developed, both in Britain and abroad, for example at Malta, where Nelson established a ropeworks.[26] Cape Town, Madras, Bermuda, Barbardos, Trincomalee and Bombay were developed as naval bases. Two new deep docks were created at Portsmouth in 1796–1800 and the basin was deepened in order to enable the docking of ships without unloading guns and equipment, although the facility was only occasionally used and then only for frigates requiring rapid attention.[27] Signalling at sea, crucial to operational effectiveness, communications and co-ordinated action, improved from the 1780s, and a quick and flexible numerical system of signals was developed. The Admiralty Hydrographic Office was founded in 1795, with Alexander Dalrymple, since 1779 hydrographer to the East India Company, as first hydrographer of the Navy. Before then there had been no Royal Navy facilities specially for marine surveying or chart production.

The Battle of Trafalgar by Thomas Luny. A marine painter who served in the Royal Navy. The victorious subjects he painted included *The Burning of the Spanish Batteries before Gibraltar, Admiral Rodney's Action off Cape St. Vincent, The Battle of the Nile* and *The Siege of Algiers*. His painting of Trafalgar captures the confusion of the engagement once the British had pierced their opponents' formation. The latter lost nearly 7,000 men (compared to 1,690 British), but the semi-official *Journal de Paris* of 7 December 1805 reported a serious British defeat off Trafalgar with 19 British ships wrecked and over 10,000 casualties. *By kind permission of the Trustees of the Royal Naval Museum, Portsmouth.*

Thanks to her naval resources, Britain was able to turn tactical triumphs to strategic advantage. As on land, mobility, firepower and determination were crucial in battle, although at sea these were always most readily applied in the offensive. Successive victories, particularly Trafalgar, conditioned British and foreign expectations, and the latter was crucial, because it affected French naval strategy, or rather the absence of it, for most of the rest of the war. Confidence is a vital military resource, and victory both brought it to Britain and denied it to France.

CHAPTER NINE

Britain the world power, 1783–1815

A s in earlier periods, conflict with France and other opponents within
Europe also entailed hostilities outside Europe, while, in addition,
Britain was engaged in crucial wars with non-European peoples. This was
very much the case in the years 1783–1815 and, indeed, the ability of Britain to master this combination of challenges was crucial to its success as a
power. For the sake of clarity, these challenges will be dealt with themati-
cally: first the trans-oceanic struggle with other European powers and then
that with non-European peoples. The War of 1812 with the USA will be
dealt with separately as a special case. Such an organization risks neglecting
the special problems created by the coincidence of crises, but a chrono-
logical account would be more confusing.

The global struggle with Revolutionary France, 1793–1801

The West Indies

As in the last two wars with France, trans-oceanic operations were planned
from the outset, and, as in all the wars with her since the 1690s, the forces
available and their operations were affected by the threat of French invasion
of the British Isles. Attacks on her colonies seemed the most profitable and
appropriate way to strike at France in the 1790s. Such operations would
make effective use of the striking power of the navy, and, by taking French
colonial bases, would lessen the likelihood of successful French attacks on
the British colonies.

These operations appeared more necessary after British forces were driven
from the Continent in 1795. Thereafter, it was necessary to demonstrate
that Britain was striking at the French colonies, and those of France's allies,
in order to convince actual and potential allies that she was weakening

France, and to demonstrate to domestic opinion that the war was not without point and profit.

The most important French colonies were in the West Indies. The region was crucial to French overseas trade. The British devoted much of their military effort in the decade to war there with the French. The British moved rapidly. In April 1793 Tobago, which they had lost in the War of American Independence, was regained by troops from the local British garrisons. Later in the year, an unsuccessful attack was mounted on Martinique, but a position was established on Saint Domingue. In 1794, 6,000 troops under Lieutenant-General Sir Charles Grey arrived from Britain. Grey made good use of the winter campaigning season. Martinique fell in March 1794, followed by St Lucia and Guadeloupe in April. The next target was the largest French possession in the region – Saint Domingue, modern Haiti. However, Grey's force was hit by disease and, with the British impetus lost, the French mounted a counter-attack, landing a force on Guadeloupe. Grey attempted to expel them, but his attack on Point-à-Pitre on 1 July 1794 failed: the cohesion of the British units was destroyed in street fighting and they suffered heavy casualties.

The French used revolutionary ideology to build up their military strength. Slavery was abolished and the freed slaves conscripted. This provided the troops to drive the British, whose garrison was weakened by disease, from Guadeloupe (December 1794), recapture St Lucia the following May, and stir up rebellion in Grenada, St Vincent and Dominica. It had already required considerable effort to quell the Maroons on Dominica in 1783–4. Although the rising in Dominica in 1795 was rapidly crushed, control over Grenada and St Vincent was lost. The British were driven back in Saint Domingue. In Jamaica the Maroon population rebelled in August 1795.

This was a crisis that was more serious for the British imperial system than the expulsion of the British forces from the Low Countries. The West Indies was important to British trade, and also to her public finances. The credit-worthiness of the government was threatened by these successive blows. In consequence, the British government made a massive effort to regain the West Indies, one that was more impressive than the army sent to North America in 1776, because in 1795 Britain was already at war with France. Thirty-three thousand troops under Major-General Sir Ralph Abercromby, over half the line regiments in the army, were sent in late 1795, although the expedition was delayed, first by a shortage of shipping and then by storms.

Other than Granby, Abercromby has the best claim to be the greatest British general between Marlborough and Wellington. He acted with great energy in the Caribbean. Demerara was captured in April 1796 and St Lucia in May. The rebellions in Grenada and St Vincent were crushed the following month; that in Jamaica had already ended in January.

The following year, Abercromby attacked the Spanish colonies. Trini-dad was captured in February, after four Spanish ships of the line and a frigate had been surprised at Port of Spain by Rear Admiral Henry Harvey on 17 February. The Spaniards abandoned and set fire to their ships. The destruction of Spanish naval power in the eastern Caribbean helped Abercromby to press on. However, two months later, he was unsuccessful when he attacked San Juan in Puerto Rico. Poor health then led Abercromby to resign his command.

This was not the end of British operations in the West Indies, although heavy losses to disease reduced the troops available and few could be spared from Britain: 1798 was the year of the Irish rising and the supporting French invasion. Instead, 12 regiments were raised from the negroes in the West Indies, and the pace of offensive operations was reduced. There were to be no attacks on Cuba, Puerto Rico or Guadeloupe. Brigadier-General Thomas Maitland, who had served in India against Haidar Ali and the French, ended the British invasion of Saint Domingue by negotiating a settlement with the local leader, Toussaint l'Ouverture, in 1798.

Nevertheless, the British continued to make local gains. The Dutch colon-ies – weakly held – were captured: Surinam in 1799, Curaçao in 1800 and St Martin in 1801. The Danish West Indian islands were also captured in 1801, as was the Swedish possession of St Barthélemy.[1]

The war had revealed serious deficiencies in the British army, especially in Abercromby's force.[2] The units rapidly raised after the outbreak of war were often short of combat experience and poorly trained. They were less disciplined and experienced than Grey's army and much of the command at company level was inadequate. Nevertheless, both Grey and Abercromby's armies were effective. Grey used his men in shock tactics that took advan-tage of their experience with the bayonet. Such tactics were also an appro-priate response to the debilitating nature of siege warfare: as in India, British commanders wished to avoid sieges, both in order to retain the initiative and because they feared the impact of disease if troops remained at one place in the field for long. Abercromby placed a greater emphasis on the firepower of his men, but he also adopted the shock tactics appropriate to Britain's aggressive strategy.

Success on land followed skilful amphibious operations which were the highpoint of good co-ordination between army and navy. Grey and Jervis co-operated well, as did Abercromby with Rear-Admiral Sir Hugh Chris-tian and Harvey. Naval operations were greatly affected by the prevailing winds, and also by an absence of sufficient frigates and sloops.

Operations on land were hampered by the climate, especially the heat, and by disease, particularly malaria and yellow fever. The British lost 45,000 troops in the West Indies in 1793–1801, over 95 per cent to disease. These high casualty rates affected morale, leading to desertion and mutiny. William

Pym, who took medical charge, subsequently, used his knowledge to publish *Observations upon Bulam Fever* (1815), an early account of yellow fever.

Despite these losses, the campaigns produced solid gains, and those at a time when the war was generally going badly. Both Grey and Abercromby achieved more than York and the British amphibious operations in Europe. Had the British not followed a policy of conquest in the West Indies they would still have had to deploy sizeable forces there in order to protect colonies from French attack and local revolt. Furthermore, the best way to prevent such attack was to seize the French colonies themselves.

As in 1758–9 and 1779, there was a risk that trans-oceanic operations would so denude the British Isles of troops that they would be vulnerable to French invasion. Had Napoleon struck at Britain rather than Egypt in 1798 the situation would have been very serious. By then, the British government had ceased sending armies to the West Indies, but the loss of numerous troops to disease had weakened the British militarily.

Elsewhere

Although the bulk of British trans-oceanic military effort was devoted to the West Indies, other attacks were mounted on the colonial bases of France and her allies. In the Indian Ocean, the Seychelles were captured in 1794. In India Chandernagore was captured by Commodore William Cornwallis in 1793 and Pondicherry by William Cornwallis and Colonel Braithwaite the same year. After the United Provinces was seized by France, the Dutch bases in India and Ceylon (Sri Lanka) were occupied: Cochin, Trincomalee, Jaffna and Galle in 1795. Colombo and the rest of Dutch Ceylon (Sri Lanka) surrendered on 15 February 1796. In the Malay Peninsula, Malacca and Perak were taken from the Dutch in 1795, in Sumatra, Padang in 1795, and in the East Indies, Amboina and the Moluccas in 1796, and Tidore and the base of Menado on Sulawesi in 1797. Ternate followed in 1801. Commodore Peter Rainier, who was Commander-in-Chief in the East Indies in 1794–1804, had served in Indian waters in the Seven Years' War and the War of American Independence, and proved a capable defender of British interests. He made a large sum in prize money from the conquests of the spice islands in 1796. In West Africa, Gorée was captured from the French in 1800.

In South Africa, the Dutch base of Cape Town fell in 1795. The British had hoped it would be possible to gain control without fighting, as William V of Orange had taken refuge in Britain when the United Provinces was overrun. The British expedition, under Rear-Admiral George Elphinstone, arrived off Cape Town on 10 June. The troops were landed at Simon's Bay, but negotiations were unsuccessful and the Dutch began hostilities. Naval gunfire forced the Dutch to abandon their initial position at Muizenberg on 7 August, but it was not until reinforcements arrived from India that the British were able to advance decisively. On 14 September the Dutch were defeated at Wynberg and on the 17th Cape Town surrendered. The following year, the Dutch sent a fleet to regain Cape Town, but it was caught at anchor in Saldanha Bay by Elphinstone and surrendered without fighting to his greatly stronger fleet on 17 September. Elphinstone was rewarded with an Irish peerage. The new British garrison fought the local African population on the Sundays river in 1800.

These repeated successes still left much of the French, Spanish and Dutch empires unconquered, but, thanks to them, the British acquired a general position of maritime and colonial dominance. This was important to the protection of British commerce and the harrying of that of their opponents. Furthermore, the British came to possess a good network of naval bases, and were able to mount operations with little fear of interruption. The range of British naval activity expanded. Thus, Rear-Admiral John Blankett operated in the Red Sea, in order to deter any possible French threat from Egypt to India. He did not enjoy his posting. In August 1799 he wrote from HMS *Leopard* anchored off Mocha, "I most heartily wish to be clear of this service . . . The height of our thermometer is in general about 90°, sometimes falling to 2° at night. This with exercrable water which is both salt and bitter". Blankett was to die on a second "show of force in that sea".[3]

The Egyptian expedition

Blankett's cruises in the Red Sea were part of the concerted British operations provoked by the presence of a French army in Egypt. After Nelson's victory in the Battle of the Nile and the unsuccessful French siege of Acre, Napoleon had returned to France in 1799, evading the British navy. He had, however, left his army in Egypt. It appeared both a threat to the overland route to India and a vulnerable target against which the British could use the advantages of amphibious power.

The resulting campaign of 1801 was the most successful British land operation in the Revolutionary War. Abercromby was appointed Commander-in-Chief in the Mediterranean, and in 1800–1 he carefully trained his troops so that they should be able to face the French veterans. Abercromby stressed the need for professionalism on the part of officers, trained the troops in light infantry exercises, and adapted the close-order drill to make it more appropriate to battlefield conditions. He also focused on a crucial aspect of British operations, the assault landing, and held landing exercises on the Anatolian coast, developing effective co-operation with the navy. Abercromby had learned from the confusion of the 1799 landing on the Dutch coast.

The results were seen on 8 March 1801 when the British successfully landed in Aboukir Bay in the face of French opposition. A contested landing was never an easy operation, but Abercromby's well-trained men were up to the challenge: training and tactics were applied in battlefield conditions, and with success. Hudson Lowe, Major Commandant of the Corsican Rangers, a force of Corsican émigrés that took part in the landing, wrote to his father:

> The fleet arrived in Aboukir Bay on the 1st but contrary winds prevented our disembarkation until the 8th. The French availed themselves of this interval to strengthen their position on the coast, collected about 3000 men to oppose our landing and lined the whole coast with their artillery. About 2 o clock in the morning the first division of the army were in the boats and after rowing five hours came within gun shot of the coast when the enemy opened the hottest fire upon us, at first of shell and round shot and as we approached nearer of grape and musketry. Several boats were sunk, many persons killed and in one boat alone 22 persons killed and wounded by musketry before the boat took ground, but nothing could withstand the ardent spirit and impetuousity of our troops who forced their landing in spite of every opposition immediately attacked the enemy whom they completely repulsed after an action of about half an hour. The number of our wounded and killed in this short but sharp contest was 640, that of the enemy about half the number. Their cavalry attempted to make some charges but its effects were felt alone by the Corsicans who stood the attack and had 19 men sabred but not without killing or dismounting as many of the enemy.

Abercromby then advanced towards Alexandria. On 13 March a French covering force was driven back at the battle of Mandara. Two French cavalry charges were beaten off by the steady fire of British lines, and the infantry attacks that followed were similarly defeated. Light infantry was used to hold off French skirmishers. Lowe recorded that the French had 'a numerous and well served artillery' and

> offered a powerful resistance at every step we approached but our troops continued to advance, returned their fire with the most decisive effect . . . Nothing could be more admirable than the steadiness and discipline of our troops on this occasion. Every movement was performed with more regularity and precision than I have ever seen practised at any review or field day, though the men were dropping in the ranks under the hottest fire of the enemy's grape and musquetry.

Eight days later, a French counter-attack was defeated at the battle of Alexandria, the decisive engagement in the campaign. In a somewhat confused engagement, in which Abercromby was fatally wounded, the British infantry defeated successive French attacks. Moore noted, "we have beaten them without cavalry and inferior in artillery".

The victory was important in its own right: although still numerous, the French in Egypt lost confidence and the British took the initiative. The French withdrew from Rosetta on the approach of an Anglo-Turkish force in April, and the British maintained pressure on the French in Alexandria. After the French capitulation on 30 August, the British entered Alexandria on 2 September. The victorious army was then free for other duties: units were ordered to Britain, the West Indies and Sicily, although the signature of Preliminary Articles for peace with France brought hostilities to a close. Victory also greatly raised the morale of the British army, giving it a sense of superiority over the French. This increased self-esteem was an important bridge between the failures of the 1790s and the successes of the Peninsular War. Unlike the successes in the West Indies, victory had been won at the expense of a veteran force. Furthermore, in the West Indies the fighting had been small in scale, and the British had not had to stand up to assaults by large numbers of cavalry and infantry as in Egypt. Discipline, training and courage had combined to bring success. Brigadier General Hildebrand Oakes commented on the "order and discipline" of the troops and their "utmost precision of movement" under fire.[4]

The Egyptian campaign also indicated the farflung nature of British military power. Aside from Abercromby's force which reached Egypt via the Mediterranean, another, under Sir David Baird, sailed from India, and a third under Samuel Auchmuty from the Cape of Good Hope. The two last joined, marched across the desert from the Red Sea in the summer of 1801 and then sailed down the Nile, in time to take part in the capture of Alexandria.

The global struggle with Napoleonic France

The Peace of Amiens of 1802 reflected Britain's isolation and the desire of the Addington government for peace. All Britain's gains from France, Spain and the Dutch were to be restored except Trinidad and the Dutch bases in Ceylon. These terms were bitterly criticized in Parliament, but were also viewed by the government as little more than a truce. Napoleon's aggressive policies on the Continent, especially his refusal to withdraw his forces from the Dutch Republic and his prohibition on British commerce, aroused concern. In 1803 the British demanded the withdrawal of the French troops from the Dutch Republic and an agreement that the British troops could remain on Malta, already seen as a crucial Mediterranean base. French refusal led the British to declare war on 18 May.

The European colonial world had to be conquered anew. The task was somewhat easier, because the British army and navy were both prepared, and their opponents' fleets had not recovered from recent maulings. Nevertheless, in 1803–4 there was no window of opportunity equivalent to that of 1793: France did not face a hostile coalition or attack on her landward frontiers, and, instead, the British had to consider the danger of invasion. No major force could be sent to the West Indies equivalent to those commanded by Grey and Abercromby.

However, the forces available on overseas stations were greater than those in 1793, and the British took the initiative by declaring war before their opponents were ready. In and around the Caribbean, St Lucia, Tobago, Demarara and Essequibo (now Guyana), and Surinam were all seized in 1803–4. The French army in Saint Domingue surrendered. The French islands of St Pierre and Miquelon were occupied, denying the French a possible privateering base near the mouth of the St Lawrence. The impact of disease and other problems of campaigning in the tropics ensured that the British preferred to avoid sieges. Thus Forts Leyden and Frederica in Surinam were taken on 30 April 1804 by bayonet attacks in the face of grape shot and musket fire: there was no preliminary bombardment.

Elsewhere, it took time before the British were able to make significant gains. The British army in India was more concerned about the Marathas. In the East Indies the Moluccas, Sulawesi and the Dutch trading base at Aceh on Sumatra were not occupied until 1810, Timor until 1811, Bandjarmasin (on Borneo), Bangka and Billiton (between Borneo and Sumatra), and Makassar until 1812, and Bali until 1814. Batavia, the leading Dutch position in the East Indies, fell in 1811.

Cape Town was captured again after a brisk campaign in 1806. Five thousand troops under Major-General Sir David Baird landed on 5 January, and on 8 January he won a conclusive victory at Blouberg. Cape Town surrendered on 10 January, to be followed by the Dutch forces on the 18th. Fort Louis on the Senegal River, the last French base in Africa, fell in July 1809 to a small expedition from Gorée.

In the West Indies the British had to defend a far-flung position with only 15,000 troops, but naval superiority permitted offensive operations. The Dutch islands of St Croix, St Thomas and St Johns were captured again in December 1807, the Danish islands were also captured that year, and Martinique fell in February 1809 to Lieutenant-General Sir George Beckwith and 10,000 troops after the French attempt to reinforce it had been ended at the battle in the Basque Roads. The principal French position, the well-fortified and naturally strong Fort Desaix, or Fort Bourbon, fell after an extremely heavy artillery bombardment. One of the shells detonated the principal magazine on 24 February, leading to the surrender of the fortress later that day. Thomas Henry Browne recorded:

> February 20th. Our batteries began their fire, which was truly tremendous, they threw 500 shells, besides quantities of round

shot, in the course of the evening . . . 25th . . . The inside of the work presented a shocking spectacle of ruins, and blood, and half buried bodies, and was literally ploughed up, by the shells we had thrown into it.[5]

The French in Santo Domingo surrendered on 11 July 1809 to an Anglo-Spanish besieging force under Major-General Alexander Lyle Carmichael. Naval support was important, Captain William Cumby writing of

the unremitting perseverance with which the vessels maintained the stations assigned to them, through all the variety of weather incident to the season, on a steep and dangerous shore, where no anchorage was to be obtained, as well as to the vigilance and alacrity of those officers and men who were employed in the night guard-boats, by whose united exertions the enemy's accustomed supply by sea was entirely cut off, and the surrender of the city greatly accelerated.[6]

The navy also provided crucial cannon.

The British then turned against Guadeloupe, first instituting a close blockade in order to encourage the garrison to surrender. Concern about disease led to Beckwith being instructed to avoid a lengthy campaign. The development of smallpox vaccine also reduced casualties due to disease. Beckwith landed on Guadeloupe on 28 January 1810 and by 5 February the island had fallen. St Eustatius and St Martins were also taken that month. Captain James Yeo and the *Confiance* assisted by a small Portuguese force captured Cayenne in February 1809.

Some of the conquests were not simply the recapture of earlier gains ceded at Amiens. The fall of Batavia totally altered the situation in the East Indies. The French naval presence in the Indian Ocean was destroyed with the fall of Réunion and Mauritius in 1810. Mauritius had been an important base for French warships and privateers in successive wars, and a threat to the British naval position in Indian waters. The initial British attempt ended in failure in the battle of Grand Port of 23–7 August 1810: a British force of frigates under Samuel Pym was badly battered by heavier French ships, and, then, had to surrender when a French squadron appeared. The battle indicated the danger of overconfident dispersed British forces being defeated by French squadrons enjoying a local superiority.

The situation off Mauritius was remedied by Commodore Joshua Rowley who had already silenced the batteries at St Paul's on Réunion on 21 September 1809 and covered the invasion of the island on 7–8 July 1810. Réunion lacked a strong garrison, and surrendered on 9 July. Once reinforced, Rowley was able to begin a close blockade of Port Louis on Mauritius. On 29 November a force under Vice-Admiral Sir Albemarle Bertie and Major-General John Abercromby landed on the island and the

Battle of Grand Port, 23–7 August 1810. A defeat off Mauritius of a frigate squadron under Captain Samuel Pym. Two frigates ran aground and were set on fire and abandoned and two others were captured by the French. The fighting quality of the stronger French force underlined the rash character of Pym's bold leadership. Pym was acquitted of all blame by a court martial after he had been released when Mauritius was captured that December. *National Maritime Museum, London.*

weak position of the French led them to surrender on 3 December. The navy provided 2,000 sailors for the operations on land.

The British were less successful in South America. Buenos Aires was captured by about 1,200 troops under Brigadier-General William Carr Beresford and by Commodore Sir Hugh Popham in 1806. This was an unauthorized expedition that took advantage of the presence of sizeable forces in newly captured Cape Town. The troops landed near the city on 25 June and, after a weak resistance, Buenos Aires surrendered on 2 July. Hopes of opening South America to British trade and of spreading British power by means of expeditions to Chile and Mexico took fire in Britain. However, in the meantime, the small garrison was forced to surrender on 12 August in the face of a major popular rising. The garrison was taken prisoner and the navy left to blockade the river.

The British government sent a force to recapture the city and free Beresford's troops. The first British force to arrive, 4,800 men under Brigadier-General Sir Samuel Auchmuty, successfully stormed Montevideo in February 1807, although it suffered 350 casualties. Auchmuty, who felt he had insufficient forces to attack Buenos Aires, was superseded by Lieutenant-General John Whitelocke, who brought fresh reinforcements.

A garrison was left in Montevideo and on 28–9 June 1807 about 8,000 men landed 30 miles from Buenos Aires.

Although delayed by swampy terrain, Whitelocke attacked the town on the morning of 5 July. The town was strongly defended, and, although some of the attacking columns attained their objectives, others met strong resistance in the barricaded streets from the numerous garrison, actively supported by the population. Whitelocke had been inaccurately informed that the inhabitants would be friendly. The columns failed to provide mutual support in what was a poorly co-ordinated attack, and the sluggish Whitelocke lost control of the operation. Some of the British units were cut off and then surrendered. Having suffered 3,000 casualties, Whitelocke on 6 July accepted Spanish proposals for an exchange of prisoners and the British evacuation of the Plate estuary including Montevideo.

The failure led to much criticism in Britain and Whitelocke was court-martialled and cashiered.[7] This was one of the more serious failures of a British expeditionary force in the period. It has generally received little attention because there was nothing heroic about the defeat or the general, and because it did not lead to the loss of a longheld possession. Whitelocke's failure was, however, an important indicator of the limitations of amphibious power. Although in command of a substantial force, enjoying good naval support, and not facing an eco-system as hostile as that in the West Indies, Whitelocke was confronted by a hostile population that did not want to exchange Spanish control for that of another group of foreigners, and one as well that was Protestant. This was crucial to the battle on 5 July 1807, but, even had Whitelocke won that engagement, he would have faced a sullen population and been obliged to use large numbers of troops to extend and maintain control. This was very different to the situation in the French empire where there was no large, hostile population and where the defenders were gravely weakened by the consequences of British naval power.

The British were also to experience the consequences of overseas conflict with forces supported by an active and hostile population in North America in the War of 1812. In 1807 they also discovered in Egypt the dangers of pressing on with inadequate knowledge in the face of hostile local forces. In order to prevent the French from establishing a presence there when Britain began hostilities with the Turks, a force of 6,000 men under Major-General Alexander Fraser was sent from Sicily to Alexandria, which was seen as an important naval base. Alexandria fell rapidly in March 1807. The garrison was small, the British cut its links to the south and the position was vulnerable to British warships: the commander capitulated on 20 March.

Pressure from Major Ernest Misset, the confident Consul-General in Alexandria, and misleading information about the need to expand British control in order to ensure supplies, led Fraser to send out a force under

Major-General Peter Wauchope to gain control of Rosetta, a crucial point for trade in the Nile. The over-confident British sent only a brigade, and, due to the need to advance across sand, provided no powerful cannon. Their assault on Rosetta on 31 March was a disaster. One column was ambushed and then overrun by cavalry, a second was unable to cross the outer wall, and the centre column, attacked from all sides by snipers taking advantage of the narrow streets and tall houses, took heavy casualties. In all 189 men, including Wauchope, were killed and 282 severely wounded; all four cannon were lost.

The remains of the British force retreated to Alexandria, while Mehmet Ali used the opportunity to move reinforcements down the Nile from Upper Egypt. Fraser believed it important to make a second attempt on Rosetta, both because he was convinced that the town was crucial to the food situation and because he thought it important to regain British prestige. The second force, 2,500 troops under General William Stewart, left Alexandria on 3 April, only to suffer from the effects of a hot southerly wind. Progress was delayed by the inclusion of heavy artillery.

Stewart reached Rosetta on 7 April and began to bombard it on the following day. However, the arrival on 21 April of fresh Egyptian troops, which brought their total strength to over 6,500 troops, with an additional superiority in artillery, forced the British to stage a fighting withdrawal. The main British square successfully resisted the attacks of Egyptian cavalry, although sniping infantry took a toll. Yet, the garrison retreating from Al-Hamed, four miles south of Rosetta, was destroyed on its retreat: its squares provided easy targets for Egyptian fire. By the time Stewart reached Alexandria on 23 April, his force had suffered 916 casualties and lost ten cannon. The Egyptians then blockaded Alexandria by land.

British reinforcements arrived in May but the intractable nature of the conflict and concern about southern Italy led the British to decide to abandon their presence. Under a convention signed on 10 September, the British evacuated Alexandria.[8]

The British failure underlined what was also apparent in India, that non-Western forces armed with firearms could mount formidable opposition. The British suffered from numerical inferiority and an absence of reliable information about their opponents. In such circumstances, offensive operations were hazardous, as the British were also to discover, during the War of 1812, at New Orleans in 1815. However, this was more than simply a matter of numbers. The problems of staging attacks in towns was amply demonstrated at both Buenos Aires and Rosetta. Street-fighting rewarded detailed knowledge of the terrain rather than general firepower, and also placed a premium on small-unit effectiveness for which the training of the parade ground and the linear tactics of the battleground were little preparation.

War of 1812

Disputes over trade led Britain and the USA to war in 1812. The British were determined to prevent the neutral Americans from trading with France and thus circumventing the British blockade. Yet it was the American Congress that voted for war in 1812, in part, because of bellicose overconfidence and, in part, thanks to patriotic anger with British policies.

The USA was poorly prepared for war. The armed forces were weak and British blockade hit trade and thus removed the fiscal basis for war. However, Britain had few regulars in Canada, and was fully engaged in war with Napoleon, a far more menacing threat than Louis XVI had been.

Although handicapped by opposition within New England, the Americans mounted an attack thence on Montréal in November 1812, but it collapsed due to inadequate logistics and poor command. There was far more fighting further west, where the best American troops were deployed against the Native Americans. Initially, Brigadier-General William Hull invaded Canada on 12 July 1812 with 2,500 men at the western end of Lake Erie. However, a collapse of nerve led to a retreat to Detroit and Hull then surrendered on 16 August to a smaller force under Major-General Isaac Brock.

In October 1812 the Americans advanced near Niagara. They crossed the river on the night of 12–13 October and developed a position at Queenston. A counter-attack failed when Brock was killed, but the Americans received inadequate support, in part because of the unwillingness of the militia to cross the river, and, by the evening of 13 October, in the face of British reinforcements, the Americans had been driven back or surrendered to Brock's replacement, Major-General Roger Sheaffe.

Fresh American attacks were mounted in 1813. The first under General Winchester was defeated on 23 January, at Raisin River, near Detroit. Neither side subsequently made significant advances at the western end of Lake Erie. Further east, the Americans advanced on the Niagara front in May, but were stopped in June, at Stoney Creek (6 June) and Beaver Dams (24 June). York, the capital of Upper Canada, now named Toronto, was captured by General Dearborne on 27 April, although the Americans lost more men than the number of defenders, and the British squadron on Lake Erie was defeated and surrendered on 10 September 1813. As in November 1812, the Americans prepared a bold step, designed to cut the St. Lawrence artery of British power, However, the advance on Montréal again was hit by poor leadership and logistics and the onset of bad weather. American forces were defeated at Chateauguay (25–6 October) and Chrysler's Farm (11 November). The Americans were also driven back on the Niagara front in December, losing Fort Niagara on 19 December.

Napoleon's abdication in 1814 allowed the British to send far more troops to North America than in 1812 or 1813: about 6,000 troops were sent in

1813, but close on 20,000, including many of Wellington's veterans, in 1814. The Americans attacked first, near Niagara, winning the battle of Chippawa (5 July), only to be held by the British counter-attack that led to the battle of Lundy's Lane (25 July). Far from returning to the offensive, the Americans fell back to the frontier, although they retained Fort Erie until they evacuated it in November. A British advance on Plattsburg along the western shore of Lake Champlain was abandoned when the British naval squadron on the lake was defeated by the Americans on 11 September.

A simultaneous campaign was launched in Chesapeake Bay. A force of 4,500, mostly Peninsular veterans under Major-General Robert Ross, but also including a marine battalion, landed at Benedict on the Patuxent on 19 August. Ross advanced on Washington, but at Bladensburg on 24 August he found 6,500 Americans, mostly militia, drawn up behind a branch of the Potomac. Despite being outnumbered and heavily outgunned, the British advanced across the river, and attacked the Americans in front and flanks, defeating them after three hours' combat. After the battle, Ross entered Washington that night without resistance. The public buildings were destroyed in retaliation for American destructiveness at Kingston. Ross's force then returned to the fleet, re-embarking on 30 August.

Ross then struck at Baltimore, landing at North Point on 12 September. A larger force of American militia resisted in wooded terrain and Ross was killed. Although the Americans were driven back with heavy losses, the strength of Baltimore's defences led to the abandonment of the expedition. The force successfully re-embarked on 15 September. The supporting warships under Cochrane had moved up the Patapsco and bombarded Fort McHenry on 13 September, but were unable to destroy it. The fort's resistance was the inspiration of the poem *The Star Spangled Banner* by Francis Scott Key. The operations in the Chesapeake led to no permanent gains, although they influenced the peace negotiations at Ghent. The British had sent too few troops to do more than raid and there was criticism that more troops had been sent to Canada.

Another British force, under Major-General Sir Edward Pakenham, was sent to attack New Orleans, only to be heavily defeated on 8 January 1815. The delay in mounting the attack ensured that the Americans under Andrew Jackson had time to prepare their defences. American artillery and musket fire blunted a British attack on prepared positions, with 2,000 casualties, compared to 71 among the Americans. The British attacked in a tightly packed formation on a narrow front, providing a good target for defensive fire. The assault was led by inexperienced regiments that had not fought under Wellington. Instead of pressing home the attack, they halted, losing impetus and the initiative, and increasing their vulnerability to American fire. Vice-Admiral Sir Alexander Cochrane captured Mobile the following month, but Pakenham's defeat had ensured that the war ended with a powerful impression of British military failure. In the meanwhile, negotiations had led to the Peace of Ghent of 24 December 1814 that essentially confirmed the pre-war *status quo*.

Limited goals greatly helped the British. This was no war of reconquest. There was no attempt to regain the USA. The British would have pressed for frontier changes had their advance along Lake Champlain been more successful in 1814, but the government was ready to abandon such schemes. Although the outbreak of a new war in Europe was not considered likely, the British had no wish to direct their well-honed forces against a new target. Wellington emphasized the cost of any war of conquest in North America.

Prior to 1814, the war for Britain was essentially defensive on land, but with a crucial addition provided by naval blockade. The British were greatly helped by Canadian resolve. This extended to the French Canadians, many of whom fought in the Voltigeurs Canadiens, helping to secure Lower Canada against American invasion. The British also benefited from the support of Native Americans.

American advances were poorly co-ordinated, although it was difficult to be otherwise, given the distances involved and the logistical and transport problems that any attacking force faced. The very assembly of a larger force ensured greater difficulties in moving and supplying it. The British were also assisted by the American hostility to a large standing army and by the degree to which their naval power did not match their commercial maritime strength. Resources were less important than the ability to utilize and direct them. As a consequence, despite her military efforts against Napoleon, the British were able to hold off the Americans in 1812–13 and then to carry the war to them.[9]

India

The utilization of resources was also crucial in India. As earlier, during the Seven Years' War and the War of American Independence, a military challenge to Britain within the "European" world was accompanied by a serious crisis in India. However, despite British anxieties that powerfully contributed to intervention in Egypt, the French were not able to intervene in India to the same extent as in previous conflicts and, therefore, the two spheres of challenge were essentially distinct. This was a serious failure on the part of the French. Both in the case of India, and also of Ireland in 1796–8, the French were unable to contribute greatly to what were major crises for British power; the situation had been different in North America and India during the previous war.

Tipu Sultan had been the most serious Indian opponent of the British in the early 1780s. Hostilities revived after Tipu attacked a British ally, the Rajah of Travancore, late in 1789. Seeking to isolate Tipu, the British allied with both the Nizam of Hyderabad and the Marathas. They provided cavalry and supplies, although the Marathas proved unreliable because they did not wish to see Mysore crushed. In the 1790 campaign, General Sir William Medows invaded Mysore in June and captured a number of positions, but, once Tipu began to counterattack, he was able to concentrate strength against isolated British posts, while avoiding battle with Medows' main force. Tipu then advanced into the Carnatic, forcing Medows to retreat to its defence.

At the end of the year Cornwallis, now Governor-General and Commander-in-Chief in India, took personal charge. He had already acted to reform the forces in India,[10] and in doing so reflected his openness to new ideas. Thus in 1790 he presciently wrote of the sepoy units:

> it is highly expedient and indeed absolutely necessary for the public good that the officers who are destined to serve in those corps should come out at an early period of life, and devote themselves entirely to the Indian service; a perfect knowledge of the language, and a minute attention to the customs and religious prejudices of the sepoys being qualifications for that line which cannot be dispensed with . . . how dangerous a disaffection in our native troops would be to our existence in this country.[11]

Indeed in 1806 new turbans in the army and an order against caste marks was to lead to trouble in the Carnatic forces.[12]

Arthur Wellesley was also convinced that the effective use of sepoy units depended on good British officers: "It is well known that the exertions of a native corps depend almost entirely upon their officers, and yet some of them have lately gone out with a commanding officer, and one or at most two young men just landed in the country".[13]

Cornwallis was convinced that the destructive raids on the Carnatic by Tipu's light cavalry, which threatened British logistics and communications, could only be stopped if Mysore was invaded, a policy also pressed on him by John Shore of the Bengal government.[14] Cornwallis believed in methodical planning, and had disciplined and relatively orderly military and administrative structures that could give shape to such planning. In January 1791 he wrote to Medows:

> I conceive that we can only be said to be as nearly independent of contingencies, as can be expected in war, when we are possessed of a complete battering train, and can move it with the army; and whilst we carry a large stock of provisions with us, that ample magazines shall be lodged in strong places in our rear and at no great distance from the scene of our intended operations . . . I hope that by a systematic activity and vigour, we shall be able to obtain decided advantage over our enemy before the commencement of the ensuing rains.[15]

The systematic application of power, particularly when the climate was propitious, was to characterize British military activity in the subcontinent. Theirs was not an army that dispersed in order to forage and ravage, or a force that had to be held together by booty and that thus dedicated itself to the strategy of pillage.

Cornwallis stressed the importance both of cavalry and of bullocks to move the artillery, themes voiced earlier in the Second Mysore War by Coote. Like Coote, Cornwallis was well aware of logistical problems, not least the unnecessary size of the "tail" in the field which had been criticized by Macartney. Cornwallis (and later Wellesley) were helped by the appearance of brinjaries, free-ranging Indian entrepreneurs who wandered round with bullocks and rice looking for armies to supply. Under Cornwallis' command, the British succeeded in combining the firepower, that was so effective against Mysore's fortresses, with a reasonable degree of mobility.

Cornwallis proposed seizing Bangalore in order to secure communications with the Carnatic,[16] and thus the creation of a reliable supply system for an advance on the Mysore capital of Seringapatam. The citadel of Bangalore was stormed on 21 March, and on 3 May Cornwallis set off thence for Seringapatam. Poor weather, an epidemic that hit the bullocks pulling the wagons, and a scorched earth policy by Tipu Sultan greatly hampered the advance. Nevertheless, by 13 May the British were within nine miles of Seringapatam, facing the Mysore army, "their infantry in regular files, with guns in the intervals, drawn by long teams of large bullocks as white as milk". Heavy rain thwarted Cornwallis' attempt to cut Tipu's army off from Seringapatam. Instead, he advanced to attack them. Major Skelly of the 52nd Regiment recorded:

> while our army was forming, which took up more than an hour for it was necessary to use many precautions against the horse (which were constantly threatening our flanks) the enemy brought a numerous and well served artillery to bear upon us, and we suffered very considerably from their shot.

The artillery position was stormed successfully and the British then began a general advance. One participant recorded that the Mysore army fell back:

> they soon recovered firmness, particularly the cavalry who attacked in their turn, supported by a large body of infantry, with sabre, spear, and pistol. Here was a glorious spectacle! The glittering of the swords in a bright sun shine, and the flashes of the fire arms, on both sides, was grand, and awful. Our cavalry soon found their overmatch and were obliged to give way in a masterly manner wheeling outwards to the right and left into the rear, by a signal from Colonel Floyd, at a moment when the Bengal battalions came

up between the two divisions and gave their fire, and perhaps saved the whole corps.

Skelly noted that, on the British right:

> the enemy for some time stood firm and their fire was heavy, but on our troops charging, they abandoned their guns, and fled, in confusion, towards the island of Seringapatam, which everywhere presented batteries of heavy cannon to cover their retreat . . . on the left . . . when we arrived within reach of their musquetry they gave us their fire, which, though heavy, was ill directed, and did little execution, few of our corps even returned the fire, but moved on in such perfect order, and with such fine resolution as might have commanded victory from better mettled troops than Tipu can bring into the field.[17]

Cornwallis then advanced on Seringapatam, but it was well defended and the British were very short of supplies. Thanks, in addition, to heavy rains, there was no prospect of a successful siege. Cornwallis decided to retreat to Bangalore but, short of draught animals, he had to destroy his cannon. Many sepoys deserted on the retreat, but Bangalore was reached on 11 July.[18] Major-General Robert Abercromby, the Commander-in-Chief at Bombay, who had advanced towards Seringapatam from the west, also had to fall back, his troops suffering greatly from disease and heavy rainfall.

Late in 1791 when campaigning resumed in the dry season, Cornwallis captured a series of hill forts hitherto thought impregnable. Nundadroog was successfully stormed on the night of 18–19 October after the artillery had eventually opened a breach. Sevendroog was likewise stormed after the artillery had opened a breach.[19]

In 1792 Cornwallis advanced rapidly from Sevendroog on Seringapatam. On the night of 6–7 February his army attacked that of Tipu drawn up about seven miles from the capital. Tipu's centre was routed by a bayonet charge and Tipu himself fled into Seringapatam and shut the gates. However, Medows' failure to defeat or hold Tipu's left enabled it to attack Cornwallis and his reserve, then in the Mysore camp. The attack was a serious one and Skelly noted that Cornwallis "finding that our fire was trifling in comparison to that of the enemy ordered a charge to be made this was immediately executed by the 74th Regiment . . . with a spirit which totally disconcerted the enemy – they gave way and retreated in some confusion".[20]

The following day, the Mysore forces launched repeated attacks, but they were driven back by British infantry fire, and, on the night of 7–8 February, Tipu withdrew from the north side of the river. Cornwallis then began the siege of Seringapatam. On 10 February he was joined there by

Abercromby, who had already occupied the Malabar coast. The rapid progress of the siege accompanied by much desertion among his troops, and the failure of a Mysore attack on 22 February led Tipu on the 24th to surrender and to cede much of his territory. Medows unsuccessfully attempted suicide.

French weakness at the time of the Revolution greatly helped Cornwallis in his war with Tipu, and so did the avoidance of conflict with the Marathas. The Third Mysore War was followed in 1793–4 by the Second Rohilla War, in which the British were defeated at Dalmau in 1793. The following year, Abercromby with a small force won the battle of Battina against a far larger army under Gholam Mahommed, although the victory was not easily gained. The initial Indian cavalry charge threw the British defence into disorder, but the failure to follow this up with another charge, and the preoccupation of the Indian vanguard with looting the British tents enabled the British to recover and to defeat their opponents. In 1798 the French-trained part of the Nizam's army was disbanded under British military pressure and the subsequent mutiny quelled.

In the Fourth Mysore War (1799) the British were both totally victorious and successful far more rapidly than in the Third War. Fearful of links between Tipu and the French, the British had abandoned an expedition planned against Manila, and had, instead, concentrated their energies into reducing Mysore to subordination. In 1799 they successfully coordinated forces from Bombay and Madras, and maintained the pace of their strategic offensive. Tipu failed to display the mobility he had shown in the previous war and, more particularly, that his father had displayed. He concentrated on position warfare, and this was to prove a mistaken strategy. The British, supported by Hyderabad forces, fought off an attack by Tipu at the battle of Malavelly (27 March), inflicting heavy losses. Tipu then retreated into Seringapatam. The Bombay army united there with the 50,000 strong Madras army under Major-General George Harris, who had served against Tipu in 1790–2.

The siege of the fortress began on 5 April 1799. It was a formidable position on an island in the River Cauvery, and Harris had to succeed before the monsoon swelled the river. The artillery on the opposite bank blew a breach in the ramparts. This was then stormed under heavy fire on 4 May. Part of the British force was held in savage fighting until the defenders were outflanked by British troops who had gained the inner rampart and then moved along. The defenders were then thrown into disorder and slaughtered with heavy losses, including Tipu. The victorious forces pressed on to capture the forts of Gooty, Gurrumcondah and Cuptal, and the rest of Mysore rapidly surrendered. The British then restored the dynasty displaced by Haider Ali, although important territories were annexed by the East India Company, Mysore was left land-locked, and the new ruler was forbidden to maintain an army.

The next major challenge came from the Marathas. In response to the weapons and tactics introduced into India by the Europeans in the mid-eighteenth century, Maratha armies became more professional, so that a strategy based on living off the land was less feasible. Warren Hastings in his day had been content for Indian states to try to emulate the superior European infantry formations because he was confident they would never succeed and it would take resources away from their cavalry and slow them up in the field. The new infantry and artillery units proved expensive, leading to developments in revenue administration, banking and credit. These trends created political problems. In addition, the Marathas were greatly weakened by periods of civil war that in general reflected disputed successions.[21] There was a considerable shift in power from the centre to the peripheral Maratha states, and this made the British task easier because it hindered co-operation between their opponents. The Marathas lacked the degree of co-ordination enjoyed by the Americans in 1775–83 and 1812–15.

When the Second Maratha War broke out in 1803, the British fielded 60,000 men on a number of fronts. The commander in the Deccan was General Arthur Wellesley, later Duke of Wellington, a master of methodical yet rapid warfare. He had been put in command of Mysore in 1800 and had shown himself adept at pacification operations that were fast paced, but not rash. This had led to victories at Manoli (1800) and Arrakerry (1800).

In 1803 Wellesley began operations against the Marathas by occupying Pune (Poona) on 20 April. On 7 August the British declared war on the two leading Maratha rulers, Dowlut Rao Sindia, Maharaja of Gwalior, and Raguji Bhonsle II, Maharaja of Berar. Wellesley pursued Sindia. Having taken the strong fortress of Ahmadnagar on 11 August after a two-day siege, Wellesley blocked an advance by Sindia on Hyderabad and then advanced against his army, thus encouraging Britain's allies.

At the battle of Assaye (23 September), Wellesley with 4,500 men, 17 guns and 5,000 unreliable Indian cavalry successfully confronted the combined army of Sindia and Bhonsle, a force of 30,000 cavalry, 10,000 infantry trained by French officers, and over 100 cannon. The Marathas were drawn up behind the River Kaistna and their position was too strong for a frontal attack. Wellesley, however, crossed the Kaistna to the east of the Maratha position and rapidly deployed his army in the V of land between the river and its tributary the Juah. The Marathas responded by moving their artillery and infantry and it was against them that Wellesley's men advanced in the afternoon sun. The Maratha cannon that had been organized by Pohlmann, a German mercenary, moved fast, were well served and laid, disabled the British guns, and inflicted heavy casualties.[22]

It was through a deadly fire that the 78th Highlanders on the British left moved to bayonet the Marathas gunners to death, while the infantry fled. On the right, however, the 74th Highlanders suffered far more heavily from canister and grapeshot when they attacked the numerous cannon round the village of Assaye. They were then charged by Maratha cavalry only to be relieved by the British cavalry who drove their assailants back. The Maratha centre repelled an attack by sepoys, but was driven back by the 78th. In subsequent bitter and confused fighting the Marathas drove back the British cavalry only to retreat before the infantry.

At Assaye Wellesley demonstrated what he and other "sepoy generals" believed essential for campaigning in India: speedy attack.[23] This compensated for his numerical inferiority and for poor intelligence about the location of the Maratha forces. Wellesley's success in the battle owed much to bayonet charges, scarcely conforming to the standard image of Western armies gunning down masses of non-European troops relying on cold steel.[24] Casualties accounted for over a quarter of the British force. Crucially, the fearsome Maratha cannon were captured.

British losses were less in their victory over Bhonsle at Argaon (Argaum) on 29 November, but, again, although it opened fire at too great a range, the Maratha artillery was effective. It checked the first British attack. Wellesley eventually succeeded with a second attack supported by light artillery. This victory, the subsequent storming of Bhonsle's hill fort of Gawilgarh (15 December), and Wellesley's continued ability to take the initiative, and to sustain the range and mobility of his force, were instrumental in leading to a successful peace with Sindia on 30 December: the treaty of Surji-Anjangaon. The weak command structure and lack of money of the Marathas disrupted operations; the absence of regular pay destroyed discipline and control.[25] Richard Wellesley basked in "our most glorious war and most honourable peace in India".[26]

Operations in northern India were directed by the Commander-in-Chief, General Gerard Lake (1744–1808). His career indicated the variety of tasks that the British military confronted. He served first in Germany in 1760–2, and next fought in the War of American Independence, being captured at Yorktown. Lake, by now a Major-General and an MP, served with distinction in the Low Countries in 1793–4, and in December 1796 he was appointed commander in Ulster, responsible for disarming potential rebels. He became Commander-in-Chief in Ireland in 1798 and was victorious over the rebels at Vinegar Hill. In 1800 Lake was appointed Commander-in-Chief in India and devoted much effort to creating an effective force of Bengal cavalry supported by light artillery. This increased the mobility of the East India Company's Bengal army. Cavalry assisted by horse artillery gave the British a means for quick victory. In 1793–1808 the Bengal cavalry establishment increased by a factor of 12, although the British were hindered by the difficulty of finding suitable breeding stock. This led William Moorcroft, from 1808 superintendent of the Bengal stud at Pusa, into missions to Nepal, north-west India and Tibet.[27] Lake also created a force of light infantry: a company of skirmishers in each regiment of sepoy infantry. There was a degree of hybridization of military practice between the

British and their opponents, a valuable and necessary indication of their flexibility.

In August 1803 Lake invaded the northern Maratha dominions, and on 29 August led a cavalry charge near Alegarh that drove off the Maratha cavalry. On 4 September Alegarh itself was stormed. A week later, Lake defeated a Maratha army outside Delhi. This led the Mughal Emperor, Shah Alam II, to seek British protection on 16 September. Agra fell after a brief siege on 18 October, and at Laswari on 1 November Lake heavily defeated a French-officered Maratha army.

The following year, Lake was sent against Jeswunt Rao Holkar, Maharaja of Indore, another leading Maratha leader. After initial problems, Holkar was decisively defeated at Farruckhabad on 17 November. Lake was a firm believer in mobility, and led his troops accordingly. Only through strategic mobility could the British hope to counter the Maratha cavalry,[28] and impose themselves on such a large area. Under pressure, British troops could march at least 60 miles in 24 hours, thus achieving surprise at Farruckhabad. Holkar's infantry had already been defeated at Dig on 13 November and Lake went on to capture Deeg on 23 December 1804.

Lake benefited from the Experimental Brigade of Horse Artillery, created by the Bengal Army in 1800, a step that reflected the influence of the formation of the Royal Horse Artillery in 1793. This brigade was so effective, that in 1809 the East India Company decided to form a permanent Corps of Horse Artillery. In 1816 the Bengal Horse Artillery was strengthened by a Rocket Troop.

Despite their increasing flexibility, the British had a number of serious setbacks. Colonel William Monson lost his cavalry and guns when forced to retreat in the face of Holkar's vastly larger cavalry force from Mukundra Pass to Agra in July–August 1804. The following year, Lake lost 2,312 killed and wounded in four unsuccessful attempts to storm Bharatpur: he had only four 18-pounders and insufficient ammunition and was unable both to neutralize the defensive fire and to blow the gates in, as he had done at Alyhgur. Lake also misjudged the depth of the ditch and the height of the walls, and his operations were affected by Maratha counter-mining. Nevertheless, defeated at Farruckhabad and eventually driven to take refuge in the Punjab, Holkar sought peace and a treaty was signed on 7 January 1806.[29]

The composition of Monson's force, most of which was native, indicated that the fusion of European training and Indian manpower was an opportunity as well as a threat. Indeed, such a fusion was to be a basis of British military power in the nineteenth century, helping in the creation of an imperial state of hitherto unprecedented range. The first Indian troops raised by the East India Company appear to have been two companies of Rajputs enlisted at Bombay in 1684. The mostly native East India Company army was 18,200 strong in 1763, 115,400 in 1782 and 154,000 in 1805.

Carnac had regarded this as crucial in 1761: "If we are to keep our new countries, it will be absolutely necessary to have in pay a large body of sepoys; in such case, in order to model them properly, and to render them useful, it will be expedient that an experienced officer should have the charge of the whole".[30]

Supported by the resources of the fertile areas of India under British control, Bengal and the Carnatic, including their banking networks, the army was capable by the 1800s of defeating the most powerful of Indian forces. During the Napoleonic wars, expeditions were also sent from India to Egypt, Ceylon (Sri Lanka), Mauritius and the East Indies, and an expedition to the Persian Gulf to put pressure on Persia was planned in 1808. In the Kandyan War of 1803, the British were thwarted in Ceylon (Sri Lanka) by guerrilla attacks, logistical problems, inhospitable terrain and disease. The garrison in Kandy was obliged to surrender in June and was then massacred on its retreat to the coast. In 1815, however, 900 British and 1,800 Indian troops under Sir Robert Brownrigg conquered the kingdom of Kandy as a result of concerted operations by independently moving columns. About 3,000 sepoys served in the successful attack on Mauritius in 1810.

There were 5,770 Indian as well as 5,344 British troops in the expedition under Sir Samuel Auchmuty that took Batavia, the leading Dutch position in the East Indies, in 1811. The British landed on 4 August and the Dutch governor abandoned Batavia, a vulnerable position which the British occupied on 8 August. Instead, the Dutch concentrated on holding the well-fortified lines of Cornelis, but they fell on 28 August: strongly defended, the lines only fell after an out-flanking British force attacked them from the rear. After another defeat at Samarang on 8 September, the Dutch surrendered. The following year, Brigadier-General Robert Gillespie deposed the Sultan of Palembang on Sumatra and stormed the Sultan of Yogyakarta's *kraton* (royal residence), despite its far larger garrison and numerous cannon. The treasury was seized as booty. Pangeran Arya Panular, a Sumatran whose diary covered the assault, was impressed by the British combination of discipline, bravery and determination.[31]

Yet the use of Indian military resources cannot alone explain British success. Ambitious, determined and skilful leadership was also crucial. Under Sir John Shore, the Governor-General who succeeded Cornwallis in 1791 and was in India in 1793–8, there was an emphasis on trade rather than territorial expansion. Shore used the army under the Commander-in-Chief, Sir Alured Clarke, to depose and replace the ruler of Oudh, but he otherwise adopted a cautious approach. The Maratha leaders and the Nizam of Hyderabad were able to develop their military power, and Shore did not take vigorous steps against Tipu Sultan. The situation was very different under Shore's successor, Richard Wellesley. He pressed for war with Tipu in 1799 against the wishes of the Madras government, and later for war with the Marathas.

British generalship was also crucial. At Assaye, Wellesley's brother, Arthur, had one horse shot from under him and another piked. His coolness under fire was impressive, but so also was his ability to respond immediately, boldly and flexibly to a confusing battle that did not conform to any plan and in which the Marathas fought well and hard. Lake was another brave and bold general. He had two horses killed under him at Laswari and headed a decisive charge there. Lake's second son, George, a Lieutenant-Colonel, was wounded by Maratha cannon shot in the same battle.

Aside from bold leadership, the British also benefited from the degree to which they were less willing than earlier conquerors to absorb Indian political and military values,[32] and from their high degree of military preparedness in the Revolutionary and Napoleonic period. The increase in British commitments led to an expansion in the military and to greater willingness to consider a resort to force. This was particularly apparent in India. The commercial values of the East India Company were placed under great pressure. The Company was nearly bankrupted by the campaigns of 1803–4 and recalled Richard Wellesley, replacing him with Cornwallis, who was instructed to ensure peace with the Marathas. Cornwallis, however, died soon after his arrival in 1805, and it was Lake who forced Holkar to terms in December 1805. Nevertheless, the cost of the war to the British and the terms they negotiated with their opponents, were such that Maratha power was not crippled.

Cornwallis was succeeded as acting governor by the pacific Sir George Barlow, but in 1807 he was replaced by Gilbert Elliot, Lord Minto. Minto (1751–1814), who had taken a vigorous role in the Mediterranean – at Toulon and Corsica – in 1793–6, gave a forward direction to British policy in India, where he was Governor until 1813. The British campaigned around Agra in 1812.

Minto's successor, Francis Hastings, 2nd Earl of Moira, had fought well in the War of American Independence, defeating Greene at Hobkirk's Hill (1781), and he also campaigned in the Low Countries in the 1790s. In India he adopted a vigorous approach. War was declared against the Gurkhas of Nepal in 1814. Initial failures in 1814–15, owed much to poor British generalship, unfamiliarity with mountain warfare, and the Gurkha combination of defensive positions, especially hill forts and stockades, with attacks on British detachments. British victories at Almora (1815), Malaun (1815) and Makwanpur (1816) eventually brought the conflict to a successful conclusion in March 1816. The victories owed much to the effective use of bayonet attacks. They also reflected luck, the skill of some commanders, especially Major-General David Ochterlongy, and the failure of the Sikhs and Marathas to suport the Gurkhas. British victory was far from inevitable.[33]

The Marathas were more rapidly crushed in 1817–18, thanks to victories at Kirkee, Sitabaldi, Mahidpur, Koregaon and Satara. At Mahidpur (21

December 1817) the British infantry under Brigadier-General Sir John Malcolm, advanced under heavy fire from the Maratha artillery. The Maratha infantry mostly retreated, but the gunners continued to fire until bayoneted beside their cannon. The infantry advance was supported by a cavalry attack on the left before which the Maratha cavalry and infantry retreated. The British horse was supported by 3,000 Mysore cavalry. The subsequent treaties led to major acquisitions of territory, and the remaining Maratha leaders had to accept treaties that brought them under British protection.

These victories brought to an end the challenge posed by one of the most dynamic elements in Indian society. The Marathas had successfully resisted and eventually overcome the Mughals, but could not do the same to the British. Between 1799 and 1818, Mysore, Nepal and the Marathas had all been humbled. There were other powerful rulers and states that were now increasingly coming into the focus of British attention, especially Burma (Myanmar) and the Sikhs. However, more of India was now under a greater degree of British power than hitherto, and this provided the British with a secure basis of manpower, although there was a sepoy mutiny at Vellore in 1806 in response to instructions to shave beards and moustaches. The British had come to dominate the market for military manpower.[34] The importance of doing so, and the need to retain the military initiative, had been recognized by Wellesley in 1800. He had written to Colonel Thomas Munro:

> I am sadly pressed for troops for all our extensive objects, and I must draw copiously upon Kanara in order to be able to make up a detachment at all equal to taking possession of the ceded countries . . . I recommend it to you therefore to keep in employment in Kanara all your peons – you will then have plenty of troops and no enemy. After all my efforts to provide a proper detachment for the ceded districts I shall be able to collect only one regiment of Europeans one battalion and eight companies of sepoys with as many guns as they please. I should recommend that this detachment should be kept together in one body to be thrown on any point where their assistance may be wanted, and that the common business should be done by peons till more troops can be spared from other services. You will then have no enemy. This is expensive I acknowledge but if you are determined to conquer all India at the same moment you must pay for it.[35]

During the remainder of the nineteenth century, other European powers would try to create empires comparable to that of the British in India. None would succeed. The British had gained an unassailable position in the imperial stakes. This did not mean that the British could expect their will to prevail elsewhere. Indeed, Cornwallis' refusal to help Nepal against the

The Capture of Saint Paul near the Isle de Bourbon, 21 September 1809 by Thomas Whitcombe. The range and extent of British naval power was truly impressive and indicated the capability of Britain's military-industrial complex. Progress in British metallurgy improved British gunnery, so that the impact of British naval gunfire on enemy hulls and crews markedly increased in the war period 1793–1815. Enemy ships were reduced to wrecks in a comparatively short time compared to earlier conflicts. The growing British naval and mercantile presence in the Indian Ocean owed much to shipyards in India. *National Maritime Museum, London.*

Chinese in 1792 registered an important limit to British capability. Nevertheless, by 1815 Britain was the strongest power on the shores of both the Atlantic and the Indian Ocean, as well as on the oceans themselves. The defeat of France was crucial to this achievement, but success in a holding war in Canada and repeated victories in India were also vital.

CHAPTER TEN

Conclusion: Britain as a military power

In 1815 Britain was the strongest state in the world, a bold statement that it is, nevertheless, difficult to challenge. The situation had certainly been different 70 years earlier as Jacobite forces under Bonnie Prince Charlie advanced on Derby, out-manoeuvring the armies sent to defeat them, and the British government feared a supporting French invasion of southern England. In 1746 the British had lost Madras to the French; by 1815 Britain was the dominant military force in India: many of the Indian powers had been defeated or overawed and the French had been reduced to a scatter of inconsequential trading positions that they had lost in 1793 as soon as war had broken out.

Chronology and causation are closely related when discussing this shift. This is especially the case in querying the interpretation that is most commonly advanced, that which involves the demilitarization of military history. In essence, the assertion of "structural" factors, whether, for example, of resource availability, domestic political system or geopolitics, leads to a down-playing of the role of what are generally, if more narrowly, construed as military factors, such as tactics, strategy, leadership and morale. An emphasis on structural factors also leads to a down-playing of the contingent and the conjunctural, and thus of the operational dimension of military history.

John Brewer's influential approach in *The sinews of power* conflates that of resource availability with a particular interpretation of the nature of the British political system. Brewer emphasizes the political institutions and culture of Britain after the "Glorious Revolution" of 1688–9. The system took some years to overcome initial difficulties, and was particularly precarious in the 1690s, but by the mid-eighteenth century it was working with great success, enabling the British government to borrow substantial sums at a lower rate of interest than their rivals, a situation that in part reflected the comparative appeal of the British financial system to foreign investors.[1]

More generally, Parliament bridged the two major social interests in the country: the landed and urban elites. This both eased the operation of the British political system, and ensured that, at least in part, it functioned in a fashion that was acceptable, if not efficient, from the perspective of developing mercantile and industrial interests. It was repeatedly and predictably possible to obtain national public support for the government's fiscal needs. Much of the resulting taxation and borrowing flowed into the military: funds were translated into flintlocks and frigates. In Britain, Parliament, indeed, supported the raising of substantial sums, and sums that were seen as such by contemporaries. Wartime public spending in real terms rose from an average annual expenditure in millions of pounds of 7.3 in 1701–13 to 8.9 (1739–48), 14.8 (1756–63), 17.4 (1777–83) and 29.2 in 1793–1815.[2] A variant on this thesis, again emphasizing resources, suggests that British success in India was substantially due to the relatively early conquest of Bengal, the best tax-paying region of India, which gave the British superior credit with local money sources.

War was expensive and cost the British state more than anything else. There were repeated problems during each conflict. In 1758 the Board of Ordnance observed "the expence of powder in His Majesty's navy is so great that we are apprehensive of not being able to supply the demands of it".[3] In the Napoleonic War massive amounts were expended on the forces of Britain and her allies, and the administrative system had to respond rapidly to many and varied demands. In late 1805 Lord Castlereagh, the Secretary of State for War, noted that the Ordnance was to provide 10,000 muskets to the Hanoverians; three years later, his correspondence covered such items as the dispatch of 300 artillery horses to the British army in Portugal and the "half-yearly delivery of shoes to the army at home".[4] The burden of the Peninsular War was considerable. Supplies dispatched in 1811 included 1,130 horses at the beginning of the year, clothes for 30,000 Portuguese troops, 46,756 pairs of shoes in July and August, and two portable printing presses. The costs of the Peninsular commitment mounted from £2,778,796 in 1808, to £6,061,235 in 1810, plus another £2 million in ordnance stores and in supplies in kind. Rising costs reflected increased commitments and the dispatch of more troops, and led to pressure for victory, or for the cutting or withdrawal of British forces. The Portuguese army was recreated with British assistance and leadership. Obliged to fight in allied countries, and, thus, unable to requisition supplies, Wellington needed hard cash, but by 1812 his shortage of money was a serious problem: the troops had not been paid for five months. When campaigning abroad it was necessary to pay troops and foreign suppliers in British bullion, the reserves of which fell rapidly. The government faced difficulties in meeting Wellington's demands for funds.[5]

Nevertheless, despite the complaints of officials, the system held and the capacity to supply grew. The burgeoning economy of Britain and of the

British oceanic trading system, and the strength of her public finances, were crucial to the war effort. The introduction of income tax from 1799 increased tax revenues dramatically. These rose from £18.8 million in 1793 to £39.1 million in 1802 and £77.9 million in 1815; in contrast, those of Austria rose from £8.7 million in 1792 to a maximum of £16.2 million in 1808. As a result of her financial strength, Britain was able to provide crucial subsidies to her allies: £23.25 million in 1803–12, £39.5 million in money and armaments in 1813–15.[6] In 1809 Britain was described as the "financial resource of all those who no longer have money".[7] Thanks to her economic and financial resilience, Britain was able to survive Napoleon's Continental System: his attempt to exclude her from trade with the Continent and thus to cripple the British economy and Britain's ability to sustain military opposition to France.

This analysis and emphasis, however, neglects or underplays the problems created by Parliament's position, and exaggerates the role of resources in warfare, important as they obviously are. Furthermore, British confidence in the financial system was not boundless. Ministers argued in 1755 that Britain could not afford to play a role in a major Continental war.[8] In 1807 Colonel J. W. Gordon, the Commander-in-Chief's military secretary, wrote:

> We have had a new plan of finance sprung upon us . . . it gives time, which, under present circumstances, is everything. It proclaims, however, pretty evidently that taxation is at an end, and I remain still of opinion that if the war goes on, and our establishments increase, that no system can long evade some attack upon the funds.[9]

The availability of resources was affected by bureaucratic practices and possibilities. These were not static. Thus, the rise of the War Office, under the Secretary at War, from 1783 and the Secretary of State for War after 1793, especially under Palmerston from 1809, provided a larger and more effective bureaucracy for the conduct of overseas operations. This process of administrative reform was taken further from 1806 with the appearance of the first of a number of reports by the newly established Commission of Military Enquiry.

The availability of greater resources was directly beneficial in many circumstances, but that does not imply that victory was therefore inevitable. Skilful strategy on both land and sea often entailed the gain of local numerical superiority in a less propitious wider context, and this was true throughout the period. Although he fought when outnumbered, Wellington's withdrawals in Iberia in 1809, 1810, 1811 and 1812 reflected his desire to avoid a potentially disastrous situation, and the limited manpower at his disposal. Whatever the odds, effective generals learned to co-ordinate infantry and artillery on the battlefield. In naval engagements a greater number of warships permitted an extension of the line, and smaller fleets often sought to avoid battle. This did not, however, mean that they lacked strategic value. The ability of the French to maintain a fleet "in being" in their principal naval ports, particularly Brest, obliged the British to maintain large blockading squadrons, exposing their fleet to the ravages of wind and wave and ensuring that it was essentially reactive. From the British perspective, it was just as well that their Indian opponents lacked any significant naval capability, because the British could spare few warships from shadowing the naval power of France and her European allies.

On both land and sea, the presence of more units could permit recovery from defeat and could enable the pursuit of more objectives. Both were evident in the British conquest of Canada in 1758–61. Thanks to far more numerous forces, the British were able to attack in a number of different places in 1758. More to the point, the failure of their main assault – on Carrillon – was matched by success elsewhere, especially at Louisbourg, and the following year the French were obliged to pull back from the Lake Champlain–Hudson axis in order to confront a more numerous British advance up the St. Lawrence.

However, this imbalance in regular forces in North America was a product of choice, not resources: in 1755 the French had chosen to send a relatively small force to North America, although the shipping was available to transport more troops. In contrast, in 1757, they sent substantial forces into Germany. The French invaded Minorca in 1756; not England. Apparent differences in resources were often explained by political and military choices in expenditure, allocation and use, rather than by intrinsic economic and financial characteristics. The British painfully learned this in 1778 and 1781 as the government faced difficult decisions over the stationing of warships. Similarly, Britain's opponents in that conflict had a choice of strategic options, as the French showed at sea and the Americans on land.[10]

Resources alone were not crucial to the character or success of the British military system. British expansion and victories were not simply a triumph for parliamentary finance or, later, for the Industrial Revolution. It is misleading to assume that comparisons can readily be made across the centuries, but superior resources, or for that matter technological skill, no more guaranteed the British success in 1688–1815 than it did their descendants against the Afghans in the nineteenth century or other great powers against their rivals in the twentieth.[11]

An emphasis on the interaction of parliamentary government and resource-fuelled military success can also be challenged by considering the chronology of British military development. It is unclear that it is appropriate to begin in 1689. To do so suggests a relationship that is misleading, not least because it presumes that the "Glorious Revolution", and such a Revolution on a British scale, were necessary to the development of military capability. Instead, other and earlier periods can be regarded as crucial.

One such is the reign of Henry VIII (1509–47), not least because of shifts in the British context and the rise of English naval power. Another is the 1590s, when the English under Elizabeth I fought in Ireland, Brittany, the Low Countries and the Caribbean, deploying trans-oceanic power as never before. A third, possibly the best, is the expansion of naval and land forces and public finance in the mid-seventeenth century, during and after the Civil War (1642–6).[12]

If war is seen as a cause of modernity, then such a process can be traced not to the Glorious Revolution, but civil conflict and to the unpopular Interregnum (1649–60) minority governments. In addition, the period of restored Stuart monarchy in 1660–88 was one of greater military capability and improved effectiveness, especially, but not only, in the navy.[13]

However, it is by no means clear that military effectiveness should be linked to modernity. Nor is it appropriate to ignore the political context of such effectiveness. The increase in army size and capability produced by Oliver Cromwell and James II entailed domestic consequences that were unwelcome to most.

The notion of a parliamentary-based trajectory of military development can also be challenged from another direction. The role of Parliament after 1689 should not be exaggerated. Its executive and regulatory functions were both limited. Parliamentary inquiries into accounts lapsed after 1714, estimates of annual military expenditure were generally passed without detailed scrutiny, and successive ministries ignored appropriation clauses. The ability of Parliament to overthrow ministries was limited. Parliamentary criticism of individual generals and admirals was often ill informed and partisan, and decided by political considerations. There is scant sign that it led to any improvement in military effectiveness.[14]

Resources *per se* did not guarantee success, either prior to the "Glorious Revolution" or subsequently. Furthermore, the British were not necessarily superior in them. Thanks to a relatively small population, to the demands of naval service, and to traditional and continuing hostility to a large standing army, the British lacked a substantial army. The Revolution Settlement ensured that parliamentary approval was necessary for the maintenance of a standing army,[15] and this requirement helped to discourage ministries from seeking a large peacetime standing army. Due to substantial differences between authorized establishments and actual unit strengths, it is impossible to be precise about the number of troops under arms, but figures were below those for Austria, France and Russia.

The need for parliamentary approval provided opposition politicians with annual opportunities to criticize the size and use of the army. On 2 December 1697, William III told Parliament that the maintenance of a standing force was essential. Nine days later, the Commons decided to reduce the English establishment to 7,000 and its Irish counterpart to 12,000, and to restrict the army to native troops, a blow to William which he tried without success to reverse. In contrast, the Dutch army was kept at 45,500. There was little doubt where William's views were more influential. On 8 March 1701, at a time of mounting international tension, the Commons refused to support an army big enough to fulfil their promise of troops to help the Dutch. In the Commons debate on the Address of Thanks on 13 January 1732, Joseph Danvers declared that his Leicestershire neighbours would argue "that a peace attended with a continuance of all the taxes, and a keeping on foot the standing army, did not deserve any thanks from the nation". Thirteen days later, opposition parliamentarians moved a motion to cut the army to 12,000 effectives, although the Commons threw it out. Opposition to an army was even expressed during the confrontation with Napoleon, Sheridan telling the Commons in December 1802 that as Britain could not hope to match the French army it should not seek to do so. More generally, criticism of war with America and with Revolutionary France led to the growth of anti-war sentiment.[16]

Widespread conscription on the model of Austria, Prussia or Russia was unacceptable. Indeed, the very fact that Continental states resorted to such a system established it as unacceptable, although there was impressment of the unemployed during some periods of wartime acute manpower shortage, as in the War of the Spanish Succession. In 1756 a Press Act made possible the compulsory enlistment of "such able-bodied Men as do not follow any lawful Calling or Employment, or have not some other lawful and sufficient support and Maintenance". The Act, however, disappointed expectations. It proved difficult for officials to raise sufficient men, their quality was low and desertion was a major problem. The system fell into disuse in 1758. Britain lacked a regulatory regime and social system akin to that of Prussia or Russia, and, without them, it was difficult to make a success of conscription or to control desertion. The army remained a largely volunteer force, and, as such, was affected by the growth of the civilian economy, which increasingly provided attractive job opportunities. In 1780 Charles Jenkinson, the Secretary of War, wrote to Amherst[17]

> I am convinced that any plan of compulsion in a greater extent is not only contrary to the nature of the government of this country, but would create riots and disturbances which might require more men for the purpose of preserving the peace, than would be obtained by the plan itself . . . besides, that men who are procured in this way almost constantly desert, or at best make very indifferent soldiers.

Plans for large-scale conscription were drawn up in 1803, but not introduced.

Although hostility to a large standing army owed much to seventeenth-century British history, especially the experience of military rule during the Interregnum, it was accentuated by the legacy of the War of the Spanish Succession, specifically criticism of the Whigs and the 1st Duke of

Marlborough for protracting the struggle. A pamphleteer of 1758 claimed, "it was his abuse of spinning out the war, that has transmitted to posterity in England, such a national aversion to continental connections; a prudent use whereof preponderates to all arguments against it".[18] That was an exaggeration – hostility to interventionism and land operations had many sources – but it was also a reminder that campaigns and wars influenced the political context of subsequent military decisions. Indeed, the argument that British public culture and institutions were conducive to military strength and success has to address the degree to which Britain was unusual as a great power in that it lacked a large army. Including the Irish establishment, the peacetime army was only about 30,000 strong in the first half of the century, and 45,000 strong in the 1760s.[19] Furthermore, rapid demobilizations at the end of conflicts lessened the effectiveness of the army.

There was also no adequate permanent force of naval personnel. The formation of a reserve of seamen was proposed without result in Britain: the Register Act of 1696, which provided for a voluntary register of seamen, proved unworkable and was repealed in 1710. Subsequent proposals for legislative action met resistance. The anonymous "Reasons against the Bill for the better manning the Navy etc." of 1758 claimed, with much reason:

> It is a fact which experience has proved to be true, that every seaman, who can avoid the service of the Navy, will, and, if they have no other method of doing it, but by deserting their own ship before she is moored, they will do it; and laws, which lay so many persons under an inconvenience, will by unanimous consent of the parties concerned be evaded.[20]

Although the enlistment of volunteers was important, and in mid-century landsmen, nearly all of whom were volunteers, composed nearly one-third of the navy's wartime strength, the navy continued to be dependent on impressment by the press gang. Although, by law, this applied only to professional seamen, it was both abused and arbitrary, and was extended in the 1790s by quota acts to include "landsmen". The system was only partially successful. On many occasions, naval preparations and operations were handicapped by a lack of sailors. Numbers, for example, were a serious problem in the crisis year of 1805, and the situation remained critical for the rest of the war. Possibly there was no better option, in the absence of any training system for the navy, and given the difficulty of making recruitment attractive when length of service was until the end of the war.

Recruitment was badly affected by the higher rates of pay provided by the merchant marine, James Wallace, an Under Secretary in the Northern Department, worrying in 1755, "our fleet is in admirable order; but our enormous extent of trade, and the high mercantile wages, make the manning go on more lazily, than I could wish". Desertion was a serious problem. Material conditions worsened in the second half of the century, helping prepare the way for the mutinies of 1797. Inflation reduced the value of naval wages, and the coppering of ships the possibility of frequent leave.[21] However, British governments never seriously considered paying sailors more; this was unsurprising given the size of the navy, and in light of concern over naval expenditure.

The Bourbon alternative – the French and Spanish registrations of potential sailors – was not obviously superior. They led to evasion and a shortage of sailors. The French were badly affected by the latter during the Seven Years' War and the War of American Independence.[22] Moreover, political support for impressment ensured that the British navy had the manpower to sustain a fleet that included numerous ships of the line. Furthermore, although not without many difficulties, manpower in large measure kept up with the rise in the number of British warships. Numbers of sailors in the Seven Years' War rose from 62,000 in June 1757 to 82,000 in the later stage of the war.[23] Nevertheless, the shortage of sailors helped to embitter relations with the newly independent USA. The impressment at sea of British-born American sailors contributed to poor relations in the 1790s and 1800s, provided opportunities for violent clashes that in turn led to further diplomatic complications,[24] and helped to lead Congress to declare war in 1812.

The issue of army size can be approached in a number of ways. Excluding the embodied militia, the army was 106,000 strong in the spring of 1780, but was less than that of the major Continental powers, and this discrepancy was to increase during the French Revolutionary and Napoleonic Wars. The contrast was also far greater in peacetime. It can be suggested that Britain became a great power despite lacking a large army, or that the absence of such a force directly assisted the process.

The latter argument can encompass the suggestion that a large army would have entailed fewer resources being available for the navy, especially men and money, and also that the navy would have enjoyed less political support. Secondly, it could be argued that a larger army would have led Britain to send more substantial forces to the European Continent in wartime, not least as a contribution to alliances, in order to satisfy domestic pressure for action, and in likely response to demands from the military. This would have exposed the British both to the general problems of amphibious operations and to engaging in campaigns in which their strength was deployed against the strongest aspects of their opponents' armed forces, for example invading northern France. Thirdly, the relatively small size of the British army did not pose serious problems for the labour market and the economy. Furthermore, pressure for troops and sailors did not mould society as it did in much of Continental Europe. Fewer troops were employed, and thus required, for operations in North America than was the case in Europe. Wolfe arrived on the Plains of Abraham with fewer than 4,500 men while in 1762 only 1,738 men were despatched against Manila, and that figure included French deserters and 100 lascars as a labour force. In contrast, a total of 89,000 men fought at Leuthen in 1757, and 62,000 at Rossbach the same year.

For these essentially "structural" reasons, the absence of a large army can be regarded not simply as benign, but also as a condition of British military strength. It can be argued that having smaller forces, the British could afford to have them well trained and equipped, at least in wartime. However, a less optimistic and "structural" approach can also be adopted, and it can be suggested that Britain became a great power despite the absence of a large army. Such an argument would concentrate on conjunctures and would draw attention to particular problems created by the absence of a substantial force. Thus, for example, the commitment of most of the British army to operations against Napoleon ensured that the war against the USA had to be waged on land in an essentially defensive fashion in 1812 and 1813. This left Canada vulnerable, and it was only thanks to the maladroitness of the American offensive in both years that Canada was preserved. Conversely, offensive operations against the Chesapeake in 1814 and against New Orleans in 1815 could only be mounted once Napoleon had abdicated; the failure of the second indicated that the Americans had no monopoly of maladroitness, and that there were important limits on the British military learning curve during the French Revolutionary and Napoleonic period.

More seriously, the lack of a large army made the British Isles more vulnerable to invasion, and thus both increased the need for naval superiority and limited the options available for naval strategy. This vulnerability was apparent in each of Britain's wars with France. Horatio Walpole wrote of the French invasion attempt in 1744:

> They began it so early hoping that we should not have got together a sufficient fleet to oppose to their Brest squadron nor a sufficient number of regular troops time enough together to resist the body which they should be able to land; and as to this last, they would have judged right, had not Providence interposed by a most seasonable storm; otherwise they would have got on shore above 14,000 men, when we should not have had together in one body above 6,000 men effective.[25]

The lack of a large standing army could be lessened by several means, principally the wartime expansion of the regular army, the use of militia and Volunteer forces for home defence;[26] reliance on forces raised within the Imperial system, most obviously, the large sepoy army raised by the East India Company, and also colonial militias, but also the black auxiliaries used against the Maroons on Jamaica in the 1730s and the Maroon auxiliaries employed against the Tacky Slave revolt on Jamaica in 1760;[27] by the hiring of forces in Europe and further afield; and by reliance on the armies of allies.[28] Although problems were encountered, as in Virginia in 1744–8, while there was widespread opposition in Britain to the hiring of foreign troops, all these methods were employed and they accounted for much of the manpower at the disposal of the British Crown. If this was true in the first half of the eighteenth century, it became even more the case thereafter, with the great expansion in the East India Company army and the growth of militia and Volunteer forces in the British Isles. In the Napoleonic Wars, Britain also subsidized or otherwise supported hitherto unmatched numbers of European troops, and the British alliance system was more powerful than ever before. Thus empire and trade served as substitutes for army.

An approach that emphasizes the degree to which Britain was able to raise troops risks the danger that it can be somewhat mechanistic, teleological, optimistic and even benign, if the last term is not inappropriate. The notion of some sort of political economy of effort by Britain, and acting to the benefit of her military strength, is one that has been recently advanced by Peter Taylor in his *Indentured to liberty: peasant life and the Hessian military state, 1688–1815* (Ithaca, NY, 1994). This was an interesting, although problematic, attempt to use the long-standing and often important Anglo-Hessian military subsidy relationship as a means to approach the development of both powers. Instead of studying subsidy treaties as diplomatic devices or in terms of their impact on the recipient's policies and finances, Taylor considered the socio-political resonances of the relationship and the extent to which it should be seen as dynamic product and cause of differential state development.

Adopting Brewer's notion of Britain as a "fiscal–military state", Taylor sought to integrate the role of subsidy troops by arguing that the importance of such troops and the cost of such treaties helped to drive the creation of such a state. Taylor also claimed that the availability of the troops enabled Britain to have a freer use of its own labour and to preserve better its own liberties, but that this was achieved at the cost of an opposite process occurring in Hesse Cassel.

This thesis was a variation on Immanuel Wallenstein's core-periphery model of early modern economic development, and offered an interesting approach to the spatial and dynamic nature of British military power. Indeed, Taylor's model could be extended to include a discussion of the socio-political consequences of the extensive recruiting for the British army in the Scottish Highlands after the suppression of the '45 and, on a similar scale, in Ireland later in the century, as well as the results of the massive expansion of the recruitment of sepoys for the East India Company from mid-century.

In 1708 Lord Tyrawly had pressed the case for raising Irish Catholics: "I know the common arguments against it, as the danger of training the Irish in arms, that were something if we could prevent it, but the people have a genius that way" and many of the best French troops were Irish. The recruitment of Irish Catholics would therefore weaken an important source of men for the French army. "Hints offered towards raising men for His Majesty's Land and Sea Service, January 1757" included, besides a free pardon for smugglers, a tax on footmen, the recruitment of jailed debtors and the proposal that each port be obliged to provide sailors, a suggestion that Scots be used:

> It has been often urged, how useful, in various shapes, those of His Majesty's subjects might be rendered, who occupy the Highlands and Islands of Scotland, whence very little advantage has hitherto accrued to the nation . . . how many thousands may be collected throughout the Scotch Isles and Continent, provided they are taken but for a term of years, not sent into the burning climes, well paid, and in all other respects, well treated.[29]

Many Scots were indeed recruited and their service lessened suspicion about Jacobitism. The *Briton* of 19 June 1762 claimed,

> the survivors have since literally washed away their offences with their blood; witness their bones now bleaching in almost every quarter of the globe – at Cape Breton, Ticonderoga, Fort du Quesne, and Quebec, in Guadaloupe and Martinique, before the walls of Pondicherry, and in the plains of Westphalia.

The same process affected Ireland after the 1798 rising. The Connaught Rangers played a major role in Wellington's storming of Badajoz in 1812. Irish recruiting in the 15 years before Waterloo exceeded 90,000.[30]

Taylor's thesis is a functionalist argument akin to the notion that the navy was supported to produce trade revenues that could finance subsidy forces. Aside from the degree to which such arguments are unduly simplistic, it is also the case that they neglect the drawbacks of such a strategy. Foreign troops, whether subsidized or allied, did not necessarily act in accordance with British interests, as the British government discovered when they tried to use Dutch and Hessian troops to suppress the '45. The future Frederick II of Hesse Cassel, one of George II's sons-in-law, proved reluctant to attack without the prisoner cartel (agreement to exchange) that Cumberland refused to allow him to negotiate, and he did not wish to expose his troops to the risk of ambush. Furthermore, and, more generally, the potential use of non-regular domestic and imperial forces was also limited. For example, militia and Volunteer units were generally unwilling to serve abroad, and their conditions of service were otherwise more limited than those of regular units; they were also less effective soldiers. Most of the colonial militia proved as unsuited as the regulars to North American frontier warfare. A lack of sufficient regulars in Britain led to anxieties about invasion, as in 1756, forcing reliance on inadequate militia and Volunteer units and a search for foreign troops. Thus, the relatively small size of the regular army did pose important problems for Britain as a military power.[31]

Manpower was not the sole resource in which there were shortages. Complaining of inaction after the fall of Louisbourg in 1758, Wolfe wrote, "Our fleet, it seems, wants anchors, and cables, and provisions and pilots, pretty essential articles you will say".[32] Studholme Hodgson was not the only general who remonstrated bitterly about a shortage of ordnance supplies. He wrote from Belle Isle in 1761:

> For this week past I have been reduced to fire only twenty-four rounds a day. Lord Ligonier has been pressed over and over to send me a supply of ammunition; instead of which, his Lordship sent me, last week, two ordnance ships, laden with wheel-barrows and empty shells. He has wrote me a letter . . . that I used too much ammunition in taking the redoubts . . . as powder is very expensive.

The dispatch of gunpowder to units in the field was often haphazard and inefficient, but greatly fluctuating demands created problems both for gunpowder makers and for the Ordnance. At the outset of the Seven Years' War the makers failed to provide the required and agreed amount. There were major problems in supplying units in North America: distance, difficult terrain and problems in the relationship with colonial governments. In addition, whether in government or in opposition, British politicians were unwilling to extend the powers of government in the crucial field of gunpowder production and distribution, even though they were aware of their inadequacy.[33]

Provisions often had to be largely obtained in the field. Visiting Marlborough's army in 1707, Joseph Taylor "saw all the foragers come in . . . You will scarce believe what vast quantities of corn, hay, clover and other things they brought in". He also passed a village burned down by the British "for refusing to pay contributions".[34]

Shortages were exacerbated by the consequences of administrative complexity. The field army – cavalry, Guards and infantry – was administered by the War Office, the Ordnance – artillery and, after 1787, engineers – by the Board of Ordnance. This created problems of co-ordination and supply that were enhanced because logistics as such were under the control of the Treasury. In addition, there were separate "establishments", housing British regiments in Ireland (to 1801) and India (after 1782).

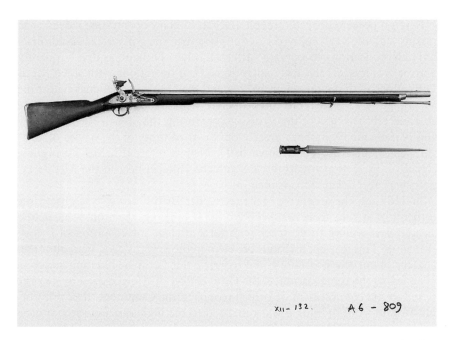

Flintlock Military Musket. English, c.1803. New Land Pattern, with bayonet. The first pilot group of barrels for this musket had been produced in 1801 but, like the earlier Short Land Pattern Musket and "The Duke of Richmond's Pattern", this proved too costly and elaborate to produce and the Board of Ordnance preferred the simplified design of the India Pattern Musket produced for the East India Company. Big deliveries of the last to the Ordnance began in 1797 and in 1795–1815 nearly 3 million were produced. *By kind permission of The Board of Trustees of the Royal Armouries.*

The demands of the British frequently proved unwelcome to their allies: British ability to purchase did not necessarily ensure supplies. This was an important aspect of the operational problem of alliances. The deficiencies of allied and subsidized troops related not so much to their training and fighting effectiveness, as to the difficulties of ensuring that foreign states conformed to British expectations. This was repeatedly an issue in Anglo-Austrian alliances, sufficiently so for the term "strategic planning" to be particularly misleading. Marlborough had to be a diplomat as much as a general. Later, Frederick the Great did not co-operate with the British forces in Germany in 1758–62; instead, it was as if two separate wars were being conducted. This owed much to the pressures Frederick was subject to, but also to his unwillingness to consider British interests; furthermore, although at war with France, Britain was not at war with Austria, Russia or Sweden as Prussia was, and had no wish to be so in order to help Frederick. Coalitions against Revolutionary France and Napoleon repeatedly collapsed. Similar problems affected the British in India and North America.

279

Foreign powers proved difficult allies in military operations; indeed, one reason why the navy enjoyed a better press than the army was that admirals only had to learn to co-operate with each other. Difficult as that frequently was, it was less so, and less contentious, than operations with allied fleets. Difficulties with the French in 1672–4 and the Dutch in 1690 make clear the advantage of rarely having to co-operate with allied fleets after 1748. The size and effectiveness of the British navy during the French Revolutionary and Napoleonic Wars both greatly outweighed those of the navies of Britain's allies, and they contributed little. Nelson referred to the Portuguese squadron in 1798 as totally useless and the Russian fleet in the Mediterranean was also deemed inadequate.

In addition, the absence of a large regular British army exacerbated the difficulties arising from the willingness of allies to abandon wars before Britain was willing to do so or without sufficient consideration of British war aims. This was not a serious problem in the Seven Years' War, although anxiety about the possibility of Frederick the Great negotiating peace in 1758 led to the renunciation of the Convention of Klosterseven by George II and to the commitment of British troops to the Continent, thus preventing Britain from fighting a war restricted to the high seas and the colonies.

Her next conflict with a "European" people was, indeed, such a war, but, as Britain lacked European allies during the War of American Independence, it was not necessary to consider the consequences of any unilateral negotiations they might make. The situation was very different during the French Revolutionary and Napoleonic Wars. Britain was then repeatedly exposed to the strains of coalition warfare: her allies were converted into opponents, a serious development in the case of naval powers, particularly Spain and the Dutch, and, more generally, a major problem when states conformed to the Napoleonic Continental System of commercial blockade. As late as early 1814, there was a serious danger that Britain's allies would make peace without securing Britain's war goals. Only Napoleon's stubborn folly prevented such an outcome.

Aside from differences with allies over political and military objectives, the British also encountered difficulties arising from the fate of war, and, more specifically, the vulnerability of some of their allies. This was a particular problem in the Low Countries. British politicians, diplomats, generals and commentators referred often to the poor state of defences in the region, and these served as an equivalent to notions of naval unpreparedness arising from insufficient ships. Concern, however, was not restricted to this region. Whenever Britain was obliged to go to the assistance of Portugal, similar fears were expressed. Lieutenant-Colonel Guard, put in command of Almeida in Portugal in the winter of 1808–9, complained that he was short of nails, wood, fascines and pallisades, that the gun carriages were in a very bad state, and that the Portuguese Governor claimed that he had no right or means to help.[35] Hanover was a diplomatic and strategic encumbrance for much of the period, leading, for example, to the negotiation of an expensive and politically controversial subsidy treaty with Hesse Cassel in 1726.

The problems of alliance strategy serve to underline the danger of arguing either that the absence of a large army able to campaign in Europe was not a serious disadvantage or that Britain "conquered America in Germany", in short that, thanks to her politico-military strategy, the British were able to achieve colonial hegemony by forcing the French to commit the bulk of their forces to Continental conflict. The latter is generally held to have arisen from British alliance strategy and is also a benign way of discussing both the Hanoverian connection and the commitment of troops to the Continent.[36]

The military history of the period suggests that a less optimistic account should be offered. In 1741 a French advance towards Hanover had led to a Hanoverian neutrality that compromised British attempts to rally support for Austria, and weakened the domestic position of the British government. In 1748 Britain had to restore Cape Breton, again a measure that was unpopular, as part of a peace settlement that included a French evacuation of the Austrian Netherlands and part of the United Provinces. In 1757 a French invasion of Hanover led to another compromising Hanoverian neutrality. Britain's ability to retain colonial gains at the eventual peace was threatened later in the war by French occupation of Prussia's Rhineland provinces and by the French-backed Spanish invasion of Portugal in 1762.

The situation was even more serious during the French Revolutionary and Napoleonic Wars. In the Peace of Amiens of 1802, France was able to reverse colonial losses, for example regaining Minorca and Cape Town for her allies, Spain and the Dutch, and obliging Britain to agree to evacuate Malta, and, subsequently, there was the danger that any peace with France would entail the loss of colonial gains. Napoleon's Continental System dramatized the danger of exclusion from the Continent, but was also the product of Britain's failure to prevent French dominance.

There was therefore no British system or way of warfare or politico-military state that guaranteed success. The economic growth of the 1780s, the parliamentary strength of the Pittite system and the availability of allies, did not prevent the total collapse of British intervention at Toulon in 1793 and of the British commitment to the Low Countries in 1794–5. Any questioning of structural factors necessarily directs attention to conjunctures and contingencies. The extension of British interests led to a greater range of possible military commitments. Thus in 1764 the Council at Fort William referred to the "necessity of keeping up a respectable" force "which is the only method of preserving tranquility" in light of the disposition of neighbouring powers.[37]

The extent and nature of challenges and commitments is central to the questions of the effectiveness of the British military system and the chronology of its success, because the latter can best be considered in this context and, indeed, as part of an investigation of relative power. The domestic changes that stemmed from the "Glorious Revolution" were clearly important, but largely in interaction with subsequent shifts in challenge and commitment. In the 1690s, 1700s and 1740s it appeared crucial to challenge France in Europe, but thereafter there was a process of diseng-agement. No British troops accompanied Cumberland to Germany in the early stages of the Seven Years' War and, although an army was sent in 1758, land warfare on the Continent was relatively less important to the British war effort than in previous wars. This was even more the case in the War of American Independence.

There were also shifts in the interests of other powers. France chose to fight Britain in the War of American Independence rather than to engage in the War of the Bavarian Succession (1778-9), a struggle between Prussia and France's ally Austria for dominance in Germany. This decision helped to create the crisis in British power that proved fatal to Britain's North Atlantic empire: although the British retained Newfoundland, Nova Scotia and Canada, their loss of the Thirteen Colonies, West and East Florida and the "Old Northwest", and the strength of the new American state were such that British control or domination of the future of the continent was unlikely.

By 1783 the success of Britain as a military power was far from clear. Britain had failed to suppress rebellion in North America and had been hard pressed by the Bourbons at sea. Furthermore, the Marathas had made the Bombay army accept terms at Wadgaon, and Mysore had been able to invade the Carnatic. The possibility that France and her allies would suc-ceed in subverting the British position seemed strong in the mid-1780s, especially prior to the overthrow of French influence in the United Provinces in 1787. Thus, it was the years of struggle from 1793 to 1815 that were decisive to Britain's success, rather than the "Glorious Revolution". British economic growth in those years was important, but so also was the concentration of French resources on conflict in Europe, and the role of contingency outside Europe, not least the absence of co-operation between Britain's opponents in India, the unwillingness of the USA to try to export its revolution to the remainder of the British New World and the failure of the American attack on Canada.

These years were also a period of the development of a more effective system of government in Britain, one better suited to the effective prosecu-tion of war. The Cabinet developed as the discussions and decisions of the inner core of ministers became more formal. Collective responsibility and loyalty to the leading minister increased, and this strengthened the Cabinet's ties with that minister and increased his power with reference to the monarch. Greater Cabinet cohesion and influence and consistent united Cabinet initiation of policy and control of policy-making were increasingly features of government from the 1790s.[38]

Military challenges were a product of international rivalry and of domestic hostility leading to rebellion. There was no real sense that the British armed forces and military system were under pressure from technological improvements by potential and actual rivals, no equivalent to the ratchet-like competitive emulation in developments in steamships, armour plating, steel artillery, rifles and machine guns of the last three quarters of the nineteenth century. Neither the first working submarine in the 1770s nor balloons and rockets in the 1790s posed comparable challenges. None was sufficiently accurate nor available in large enough quantities to undermine conventional means of waging war. Pressing the British government to finance his work in submarine warfare, Robert Fulton claimed in 1806 that "every year exhibits new combinations and effects: steam engines, cotton mills, telegraphs, balloons and submarine navigation and attack have all appeared almost within our memory: and only vulgar minds harbour the thought that a physical possibility is impracticable because it has not already been done".[39]

The government was less impressed. Indeed, in comparison with the following century, the process of military challenge was essentially static. Instead, the British had to come to understand methods of warfare in particular environments and had to respond to political agendas of confrontation and war. The environments were often harsh. Colonel Dudley reported from Massachusetts in 1707 that his forces, in operations against the French-backed Native Americans, "have with the greatest hardship in winter marches for twenty days at a time carrying their provisions on their backs in the depths of the snow, followed the enemy and driven them from all their ancient seats to their terror and starving". Oakes wrote from Egypt in 1801, "we shall shortly have the severity of the climate to encounter, a still greater enemy, and which I should think must prevent our entering or at any rate continuing the siege of Alexandria".[40]

There were of course developments in warfare in particular areas. This was true in weaponry, not particularly at sea, although the carronade did enhance firepower capability, but to a greater extent on land both in Europe, where the bayonet replaced the pike, and outside. Just as the Native Americans had adopted firearms to deadly effect in the seventeenth century, so the Marathas made increased and effective use of field artillery from the close of the eighteenth. Wellesley's army suffered grievously as a consequence at the battle of Assaye in 1803. The British were not necessarily technologically superior to their rivals. Their artillery could be outmatched, as in India both by the Marathas, and by the Gurkhas. The development or adoption of more effective weapons represented a challenge for British forces.

There were also some threatening developments in tactics. The emphasis the Revolutionary French placed on *l'ordre mixte*, on column attacks preceded by a swarm of sharpshooters, created a serious challenge. Nevertheless,

283

in general, warfare changed less in individual military environments than was to be the case over the following century.

Despite this, the variety of military environments was such as to pose a major challenge to the British military system. Insofar as military roles were primarily fulfilled by regular forces, these forces and their commanders had either to adapt to very different tasks, or remain in a given location for a long period and run the risk of losing flexibility. There was also the issue of the reliance to be placed on local forces and the control that could be exercised over them. Varied challenges and requirements obliged the British military to have a multiple capability and to have a positive synergy between the army and the navy, and these were at least as important as the crude resource level available.

As a military power, the British state operated frequently and effectively in a number of spheres. The first was in opposition to public disorder and rebellion, both in the British Isles and in British overseas possessions. The most prominent instances were the Irish rising of 1798 and, far less effectively, the American War of Independence. With the major exception of the initial failures in Scotland in 1745 and the more serious failure in America, the British military was successful in this sphere, crucially so in the British War of Succession in 1689–91. Furthermore, the suppression of the '45 and the '98 (and indeed of the naval mutinies in 1797) was vital to the continued political and military strength of the state. Law and order was also a major responsibility and lawlessness could involve an important commitment of military resources, as against the Luddite riots of 1812. Defending a forthcoming English establishment of 18,800 troops, against an opposition proposal that it be reduced to 15,000 men, Lord Barrington, the Secretary-at-War, told the Commons in November 1754 that:

> the licentiousness of the capital, the mutinous miners and colliers, the smugglers, the destroyers of turnpikes, all the outlaws that increase of riches and licence produces and encourages, all were to be kept in awe.[41]

The second sphere was as a land power fighting other land powers in Europe. British effectiveness in this sphere depended heavily on co-operation with other powers, especially in the case of sustained operations. The British were most successful in 1704–11, 1743, 1759 and 1813–15, and least in 1745–8 and 1793–9.

The third sphere was naval. Whether in home, European or extra-European waters, this was overwhelmingly against the naval forces of other European powers. There were exceptions, especially in the war of 1812 with the USA, but relatively little naval effort had to be employed against non-European powers, although the navy was required to assist amphibious operations against such powers and to secure the movement of military resources. Furthermore, there were operations against those deemed

The Sacking of Ras-ul-Khymah, 13 November 1809. From their base in the Persian Gulf, the Wahabi pirates had attacked East Indiamen and British warships in the Arabian Sea. The punitive expedition launched in 1809 freed British trade from attack until a fresh pirate campaign began in 1816. British sensitivity about the region had been increased by the Franco-Persian alliance of 4 May 1807 in which Napoleon promised to support Persia against Britain. French strategic interest in the Middle East had led to greater British concern from the mid-1780s. *National Maritime Museum, London.*

pirates. The range of such activities increased, itself a testimony to the expanded interests of British commerce and the more far-flung commitments of British power. Whereas anti-piratical operations in the 1750s had been directed against the Angria strongholds on the west coast of India, in 1809 the Wahabi base of Ras-ul-Khymah in the Persian Gulf was successfully stormed, and in 1813 pirates were attacked off Borneo. In 1816, in the most effective display of power hitherto against the North African pirate states, Algiers was bombarded by an Anglo-Dutch fleet and the Bey forced to release Christian slaves.[42]

The fourth sphere was trans-oceanic land conflict. The British generally took the initiative in warfare with European-composed or commanded land forces, a consequence of political choices as much as strategic possibilities. Thus, three expeditions were mounted against Québec, but no comparable French strokes were launched against Boston. In India, North America and, in 1762-3, the Philippines there was an important interaction between two sets of Europeans and a wide range of natives with their own changing aims and fears, an interaction complicated by such preconceptions as British confidence of native support against Popery. From 1775, this interaction was complicated by the role of newly independent peoples, first in North America, then in Haiti and, eventually, in South America.

The nature of the military challenge from non-European peoples varied. Hostile Indian rulers could threaten the leading British bases – the Marathas, Bombay, and Mysore, Madras – although not their maritime links, unless in alliance with the French. Furthermore, although the great distances between the Company's Presidencies in India was a weakness, most obviously in 1756, it could also be a strength: Bengal was virtually invulnerable in Hastings' and Wellesley's time to the Indian powers fighting Madras and Bombay, so that Bengal's massive resources were always at the disposal of the more exposed sister presidencies, provided that co-operation could be secured. In 1782 Madras pressed Bengal to send troops to cover the Northern Circars.[43] Similarly, during Pontiac's War, the Native Americans could not threaten New York or Boston. In contrast, European Americans posed a much greater political and military threat in 1775.

Thanks to the dispatch of regulars to North America and India, Britain's trans-oceanic presence increasingly took on an official military dimension. It would have been unlikely that the East India Company would have made much headway territorially in the period without the occasional substantial support of Crown forces. In 1749 the government appointed an army officer, Captain Robert Hodgson, the first Superintendent of the Mosquito Shore and thus the first British official on the Latin American mainland. The British imperial system gave rein to and, albeit with many difficulties, reconciled local initiatives and a large measure of central allocation of resources.[44]

British military capability developed in response to challenges and threat, although only European opponents had the capability to threaten the British Isles. Henry Fielding was being satirical when he had "Politic" declare in his play *Rape upon rape or the coffee-house politician* (1730):

> Suppose we should see Turkish galleys in the Channel? We may feel them, yes, we may feel them in the midst of our security. Troy was taken in its sleep, and so may we . . . he can come by sea to us.[45]

Gibbon was more typical in thinking such an overthrow very unlikely.

The British were crucially helped by the timing of challenge. When these coincided, they indeed faced crisis, most obviously in 1779–83. Then war with American Patriots (1775–83), France (1778–83), Spain (1779–83), the Dutch (1780–3), the Marathas (1778–82) and Mysore (1780–4), threatened the dissolution of the empire. In 1795–1802 the British had to face France (1795–1802), Spain (1796–1802), the Dutch (1795–1802), Denmark (1801), Mysore (1799), an Irish rebellion (1798) and naval mutinies (1797). Although the situation was less threatening, in 1760–5, the British had had to fight France, Spain, and a host of opponents in India and North America.

Yet both then and at other times the British were fortunate. Spain did not enter the Seven Years' War until 1762, by which time the French navy had been defeated, and much of the French empire conquered. In 1778 the British did not also have to face Spain at sea and in North America. That year, there was an opportunity for the British to take on the French fleet alone, although they were unable to achieve any naval victories. Indeed, there was no major victory until 1782, by when the British had to confront the French, Spanish and Dutch fleets.

The challenges of 1795–1802 did not all coincide. Similarly, when Britain faced the Bourbons in the Falkland Islands crisis of 1770, the Thirteen Colonies (and Ireland) were quiescent. America rebelled in 1775 at a time when Britain did not face conflict elsewhere, and, indeed, this offered a rare and, as it turned out, unfortunate opportunity for military firmness. The War of 1812 broke out after the Irish rising of 1798 had been suppressed, and when Napoleon had his naval strategy greatly affected by defeat at Trafalgar and was deeply engaged in conflict with Russia.

Combinations and chronology also affected the capacity of the British imperial congeries to act as a military system, providing mutual support. Thus, an absence of challenge in one area or sphere could enable a movement of resources or a necessary change in priorities. The importance of interdependence was increasingly grasped in this period, as was an ability to secure and sustain it. Colonel John Stewart reflected on the failure of the Cartagena expedition in 1741, not least the absence of adequate co-operation between army and navy:

> if ever Britain strikes any considerable stroke in this part of the world the blow must come from the North American colonies not by bringing raw men from thence like those we had last, but by sending officers of experience and good corps to incorporate with and discipline the men to be raised there. These troops as the passage from thence is much shorter might be transported directly to any part of the Spanish West Indies and arrive there with the health and vigour necessary for action, whereas troops sent from home as our own experience has taught us, are by the length of the passage one half disabled with the scurvy and the other laid up with diseases contracted by confinement and the feeding on salt provisions.[46]

Movements of troops and warships posed administrative problems and faced the stresses of distance and weather, but such transfers became increasingly common and predictable. In November 1809 reports of an imminent mutiny of troops at Madras led to preparations at the Cape to send troops.

Any stress on combinations and chronology invites the rejoinder that surely more was at stake. Clearly this was indeed the case, but the emphasis on chronology and combinations prevents any simple reading from structural strengths to inevitable victory. It also serves as a reminder that success was neither a constant nor an absolute, but a finely balanced situation that was open to extension, challenge and re-definition, as in debates over the role of maritime interests and power.[47]

This process of redefinition was readily apparent in the Seven Years' War. British war goals expanded greatly during the conflict. Victory both sustained political and financial support for the conflict and encouraged a widening of its scope that made peace more difficult to negotiate. There was also a marked shift in perception about British military capabilities. Victory at Minden in 1759 reversed the impact of defeats at Fontenoy, Roucoux and Lawfeldt in the latter half of the War of Austrian succession, and the resulting confidence in the army was sustained by success at Warburg (1760), Fellinghausen (1761), Gravenstein (1762) and Wilhelmstahl (1762). The army became more popular.

However, although continental interventionism became credible militarily, the domestic, political and international conjunctures shifted against the policy. A sharp reaction against interventionism from 1761 reshaped the parameters of foreign policy and thus military attitudes. This interacted with a shift in international relations such that Britain was more truly isolated from European diplomacy than it had been for over a century. As a consequence, there was no Continental dimension to the War of American Independence: then the French were resisted in Virginia and the Carnatic, not the Low Countries and Westphalia.

The situation was very different in Britain's next war. The British contested the French advance and presence on the European mainland, most obviously, although not only, in the Low Countries (1793–5), Southern Italy (1806) and Iberia (1808–13). There was no military need for such a policy, but successive ministries felt it necessary to demonstrate to actual and potential allies that the British could challenge the French on land. Naval success insulated Britain from invasion, but that was not enough. As a consequence, the percentage of defence spending devoted to land services rose from an average of 32 per cent in 1784–92 to 51 per cent in 1793–1802 and 57 per cent in 1803–1815,[48] although, in part, this reflected the limited possibilities for expanding expenditure on the navy, given the number of sailors that could be raised and the absence of a naval equivalent of the large forces in British pay.

Clearly, these shifting expectations affect the question of relative success. Had the British armed forces in 1793–1815 been expected simply to preserve the integrity of the British Isles, to defeat the French at sea and to conquer the French colonies, then success would have been more obviously and rapidly achieved. Napoleon's concentration on Continental hegemony and the limited interchangeability of French military resources provided the British with an opportunity to adopt this policy. Had Napoleon not invaded Russia he would have had more troops to spare for Spain in 1812, but he would not necessarily have been in a better position to invade Britain. Furthermore, between 1792 and 1815 the British fought the French for longer than any other major combatant, but this was not necessary. Other states were able to accommodate themselves to a degree of French success, sometimes, as with Russia, to their own profit in terms of the economy of territorial gains: the Russians made gains at the expense of Sweden and the Turks.

Thus, an assessment of military effectiveness has to consider political contexts and requirements, and the contentious nature of the latter made it difficult to establish a widely accepted level of military preparedness. In 1763 Bute observed "I certainly wished to render the Peace Establishment as agreeable as possible to the nation; in forming it I had two things principally in view: security and economy",[49] apparently reasonable, but security against whom and with what guarantees of strength and operational flexibility?

At the most stark, in 1792 the British chose not to respond to a Nepalese request for assistance against China; yet, the same year, the government decided that French moves in the Low Countries, especially the opening of the Scheldt, were sufficient cause for the war that broke out early the following year. As with Poland and British entry into World War Two, the British were, in practice, unable to do little over the area that led to initial hostilities. The French were in reasonably secure control of the Low Countries from 1795 until 1814. British challenges, in Holland in 1799 and in the Scheldt estuary in 1809, were both short lived and unsuccessful. In 1802, by the Peace of Amiens, the British had to accept what they were unwilling to tolerate in 1792–3. Nevertheless, the logic of domestic politics and foreign policy both pointed to confrontation and war in 1792–3.

Defeat in the Low Countries may appear part of a pattern of British military failure and insignificance, a pattern that some Napoleonic scholars are apt to discern. British forces were not only driven from their traditional sphere of operations in the Low Countries, by French forces that operated far more successfully and dynamically than those of their *ancien régime* forebears; in addition, success came faster for the French than it had done in 1745–8. Furthermore, many of the subsequent British amphibious operations were unsuccessful, as at Ferrol and Cadiz in 1800. It was as if, having shown in 1775–83 that it could no longer handle North American warfare successfully, the army was now demonstrating afresh its inadequacies in European conflict.

Yet these deficiencies should not be exaggerated. Much of the army fought creditably in 1793–4. The victories in Egypt in 1801 and at Maida in 1806 were not bolts from the blue. Wellington did not reform the army; instead, he knew how to use the reformed army. Although not at the level of effectiveness of Marlborough's forces, the army after York's reforms was in a better state than had been the case in the 1730s and early 1740s. In 1742 the Earl of Stair, commander of the troops sent to the Austrian Netherlands, wrote

> I am endeavouring to establish rules, and to settle many things
> upon a regular foot that want to be regulated here, to establish
> order and discipline, things very much wanted here, in an army
> where nobody has been in use to have any authority, and where
> every corps has been in use to be a kind of republic, depending
> on the ministry, for whose use only preferments were calculated.
> If His Majesty is not disposed to give his General the authority
> requested, I foresee it will be quite needless to endeavour to do
> any good.[50]

Although the process was far from smooth, ministerial patronage was less insistent by the 1800s and Wellington had more power than Stair, although Wellington was no radical consolidator in military administration.

Furthermore, the British, and their Iberian allies, did make an important contribution in the Peninsula, both in 1808–13, and indeed, earlier, during the War of the Spanish Succession. Although the British advances into Spain were chased back by the advance of larger French forces in 1808, 1809, 1811 and 1812, the French both had to deploy such forces, thus weakening their hold elsewhere in Spain, and did so without crushing their British opponents: the British avoided heavy defeats such as those inflicted on the Spaniards, and, elsewhere, on the Austrians and Prussians. Corunna and Albuera were neither Ulm nor Jena, nor, indeed, Yorktown.

The British army did not have to face the ultimate challenge: the defence of Britain against a major French invasion; but that, in part, was because the army and the navy were complementary facets of British military effectiveness, while, had Napoleon or his predecessors landed, they would probably have faced considerable difficulties.[51] During the Napoleonic War, thanks to successive naval victories by Nelson and his colleagues, and much additional effort unattended by victory, the army was able, subsequently, to move into a major role, both defensive and offensive, in Iberia. The defensive function had been fulfilled as far as Britain was concerned, although vigilance was required while the war lasted. Thanks to the army, the British were able to take the war to French Europe, by playing the major role in preventing Napoleon from successfully integrating Iberia into his system. The army, and all ancillary services, developed and improved throughout the course of the war.

It is common among Napoleonic scholars to treat Napoleon as a better general than Wellington. He was certainly a different general with many of the commitments and opportunities that came from being a head of state. As Frederick the Great had shown, this was very valuable. Yet Napoleon's opportunistic generalship proved of limited value when opposed to the formidable military resources deployed against him in 1812–15. Furthermore, his one excursion into the extra-European world, that of 1798–9, brought Napoleon against an anachronistic army, that of the Mamelukes.

At Shubra Khit and Embabeh he was able to rely on cannon and musket fire to repel attacks by Mameluke cavalry. Napoleon was also successful against Turkish forces in 1799, but neither opponent posed a challenge comparable to that of the Marathas with their numerous well-aimed cannon at Assaye in 1803.

Although Wellington came close to defeat on occasion, as at Assaye and Talavera, he never lost a battle or an army. His understanding of, and ability in, strategy, tactics and organization made him the best general the British had, although, without the troops, these qualities would have been of scant value. They fought well, and went on fighting, despite heavy casualties. Unit cohesion and a sense of duty helped to carry the troops through many difficult encounters: Thomas Howell recorded of his first engagement, near Montevideo in 1806, "I heard an old soldier answer, to a youth like myself, who inquired what he should do during the battle, 'Do your duty'". Subsequently, he took part in the attack on Buenos Aires on 5 July 1807, recording "'Mind your duty, my lads; onwards, onwards, Britain for ever', were the last words I heard our noble Captain Brookman utter".[52]

Wellington's dispatch from Assaye, printed in the *London Gazette* of 31 March 1804, noted:

> the troops advanced under a very hot fire from cannon, the execution of which was terrible . . . I cannot write in too strong terms of the conduct of the troops, they advanced in the best order, and with the greatest steadiness under a most destructive fire, against a body of infantry far superior in numbers, who appeared determined to contend with them to the last, and who were driven from their guns only by the bayonet.

The glory was often hard won. Skelly recorded of the British troops hard attacked in a redoubt outside Seringapatam on 7 February 1792:

> the enemy now brought three field pieces against us from which, as well as with their musketry and rockets . . . our loss soon became serious . . . the want of water was severely felt . . . these different attacks were still attended with loss on our side, and the redoubt was now become a horrid scene of carnage – many had fallen, and the rest, through heat, exertion, and thirst were almost exhausted most of them, however, stood gallantly to their duty, though in a few signs of despondency began to appear.[53]

Warfare in Europe could be equally debilitating and horrific.[54] John Hill wrote to his brother-in-law after Waterloo:

> The front wound still continues to discharge very much, he is a most confounded ugly fellow . . . as big as a tea-cup . . . I got the grape shot in my shoulder and five other wounds in my face . . . Honesty [his horse] got three shot . . . he bled to death.[55]

An emphasis on fighting quality and generalship again detracts from any simple focus on resources, and leads to further emphasis on contingency. This was also pertinent in India. The use of Indian military resources cannot alone explain British success, although it was important, and also helped provide the momentum for territorial growth.[56] Indeed, the process of the formation of the Company's army provided the momentum for the territorial expansion west from Bengal.[57] The discovery that Indians could be trained to fight effectively in the European manner was critical to the sustained penetration and "pacification" of India.

Even so, British field armies in eighteenth-century India (whether solely Company or Crown and Company) were always greatly outnumbered in the field. Nevertheless, they won in the end, in part because of tactical advantages. The discipline of British units under fire was superior. This was not a matter of Indian cowardice or not, but of controlled British evolutions on the battlefield, including withheld fire. Furthermore, the British benefited against many opponents from their heavy reliance on firepower, especially from light field guns firing grape and case, as opposed to shock: cavalry hardly figured in the British line. Storming did play an important role in the capture of fortified positions, but it generally followed the use of firepower to create breaches. Efficient artillery had shifted the balance between attack and defence, to the benefit of those who sought change, especially the British. The incorporation of South Asian light horse, both manpower and tactics, was also important, adding valuable flexibility to the British forces.[58]

Ambitious, determined and skilful leadership was also crucial, both on land and at sea. This can be seen clearly by comparing the differing achievements of particular admirals and of Governor Generals of India, and also in noting the benefit the French derived during the War of American Independence from the effective military and political leadership of Sartine and Castries as naval ministers, Ségur as war minister and Necker as finance minister. British policy- and decision-making processes could be impressive, but they faced numerous problems, not least the impact of the weather on naval operations and the, often understandable, unwillingness of allies to accept British requirements. Furthermore, these processes did not prevent numerous failures, not only in the War of American Independence, but also in wars generally seen as successful. The Walcheren debacle of 1809 scarcely encourages strong confidence in British decision-making, but, as Piers Mackesy has pointed out, there was not a "right" strategy for a British government to pursue.[59] Any emphasis on leadership and political

Edward Hodges Bailey completing the statue of Nelson in his studio, 1842. Nelson's death at Trafalgar was a potent symbol of self-sacrifice that came to play a major role in national identification. A national day of thanksgiving was followed by a funeral in 1806. Trafalgar Square, begun in the 1820s, soared with Nelson's column, which was topped by Bailey's eighteen foot high statue. The bronze lions followed in 1867. The heart of empire was complete. Nelson monuments were also erected in Dublin and Edinburgh. Nelson's death was also commemorated on canvas, most famously with Arthur William Devis' *Death of Nelson in the Cockpit of H.M.S. Victory*, which was reproduced in a popular engraving. Robert Southey's popular *Life of Nelson* (1813) helped develop the patriotic ideal. *British Architectural Library, RIBA, London.*

context also acts as another reminder that military success is open to multiple interpretations and that these affect the judgement of capability and effectiveness.

Failure at Rosetta in 1807 and the Chinese rejection in 1809 of Minto's suggestion of a British presence in Macao, to protect the Portuguese colony against possible French attack, were reminders of fresh challenges and opportunities; Egypt was not to be invaded successfully until 1882, Hong Kong was not occupied until 1841. Nevertheless, by 1815 Britain was the leading world power. Resources were important to this process but they were not sufficient. Military history is more than the account of the accountants.

Notes

The following abbreviations are used:

Add.	Additional Manuscripts
AE	Paris, Ministère des Affaires Etrangères
Beinecke	New Haven, Beinecke Library
BL	London, British Library
CP	Cumberland papers
CRO	County Record Office
Eg.	Egerton Manuscripts
IO	India Office Library
HL	San Marino, California, Huntington Library
Lo.	Loudoun papers
MM	*Mariner's Mirror*
PRO	London, Public Record Office
PRONI	Belfast, Public Record Office of Northern Ireland
RA	Windsor, Royal Archives
SP	State Papers
WO	War Office

Unless otherwise stated, all books are published in London.

Preface

1. BL. Add. 9872 f. 99, 36747 C f. 31.

Chapter 1: Introduction

1. Dudley to John, 1st Duke of Marlborough, 28 Dec. 1703, BL Add. 61306 f. 144.
2. Cumberland to the diplomat Onslow Burrish, 29 May 1757, PRO SP 110/6.
3. This is a major theme of J. M. Black, *America or Europe? British foreign policy 1739–63* (1998).

Chapter 2: The suppression of rebellion

1. D. Davies, "James II, William of Orange, and the Admirals", in E. Cruickshanks (ed.), *By force or by default? The revolution of 1688–89* (Edinburgh, 1989), pp. 82–108; A. Pearsall, "The Invasion Voyage: some nautical thoughts", in C. Wilson and D. Proctor (eds), *1688. The Seaborne Alliance and diplomatic revolution* (1989), pp. 166–71.
2. J. Childs, *The army, James II and the Glorious Revolution* (Manchester, 1980).
3. A. M. Scott, *Bonnie Dundee, John Graham of Claverhouse* (Edinburgh, 1989).
4. P. Hopkins, *Glencoe and the end of the Highland War* (Edinburgh, 1986).
5. J. G. Simms, *Jacobite Ireland, 1685–1691* (London, 1969); P. Wauchope, *Patrick Sarsfield and the Williamite War* (Blackrock, 1992); B. Whelan (ed.), *The last of the great wars. Essays on the War of the Three Kings in Ireland 1688–91* (Limerick, 1995); J. Childs, "The Williamite War, 1689–1691", in T. Bartlett and K. Jeffery (eds), *A military history of Ireland* (Cambridge, 1996), pp. 188–210.
6. J. Gibson, *Playing the Scottish card. The Franco-Jacobite invasion of 1708* (Edinburgh, 1988).
7. L. Gooch, *The desperate faction? The Jacobites of north-east England 1688–1745* (Hull, 1995).
8. I. G. Brown and H. Cheape (eds), *Witness to rebellion. John Maclean's journal of the 'Forty-Five and the Penicuik drawings* (Edinburgh, 1996), pp. 35–7; J. Prebble, *Culloden* (1961); K. Tomasson and F. Buist, *Battles of the '45* (1962); W. A. Speck, *The Butcher, the Duke of Cumberland and the suppression of the '45* (Oxford, 1981); F. J. McLynn, *The Jacobite Army in England* (Edinburgh, 1983) and *Charles Edward Stuart* (1988); J. Black, *Culloden and the '45* (Stroud, 1990); S. Reid, *1745. A military history of the last Jacobite rising* (Staplehurst, Kent, 1996).
9. E. H. Stuart Jones, *The last invasion of Britain* (Cardiff, 1950).
10. T. Pakenham, *The year of liberty: The great Irish Rebellion of 1798* (1969); K. Ferguson, "The army and the Irish Rebellion of 1798", in A. J. Guy (ed.), *The road to Waterloo. The British army and the struggle against Revolutionary and Napoleonic France, 1793–1815* (Stroud, 1990), pp. 88–100; D. Gahan, *The people's rising, Wexford 1798* (Dublin, 1995); A. T. Q. Stewart, *The summer soldiers. The 1798 rebellion in Antrim and Down* (Belfast, 1995); D. Keogh and N. Furlong (eds), *The mighty wave. The 1798 rebellion in Wexford* (Blackrock, 1996).
11. C. Esdaile, *The Spanish army in the Peninsular War* (Manchester, 1988), and "Wellington and the Spanish guerrillas: the campaign of 1813", *Consortium on Revolutionary Europe. Proceedings* (1991), pp. 298–306.
12. M. Finley, *The most monstrous of Wars. The Napoleonic guerrilla war in southern Italy, 1806–11* (Columbia, SC, 1994), p. 133.
13. J. A. Lowe (ed.), *Records of the Portsmouth Division of Marines 1764–1800* (Portsmouth, 1990), pp. l–li.
14. A. Charlesworth (ed.), *An atlas of rural protest, 1549–1900* (1983); P. Muskett, "Military operations against smugglers in Kent and Sussex, 1698–1750", *Journal of the Society for Army Historical Research*, **52**, 1974, pp. 89–110.
15. Thomas Waite to Sir Robert Wilmot, 22 May 1762, Matlock, Derbyshire CRO D3155 WH3461; Exeter, Devon CRO 64/12/29/1/1; Lieutenant W. A. Oliver to . . . , 30 Dec. 1789, Gloucester, CRO D214 F1/93.
16. *Bonner and Middleton's Bristol Journal*, 11 April 1801.

17. C. Bridenbaugh and R. Bridenbaugh, *No peace beyond the line* (1972); R. C. Ritchie, *Captain Kidd and the war against the pirates* (1987); D. Cordingley (ed.), *Pirates* (1966).

18. T. Hayter, *The army and the crowd in mid-Georgian England* (1978); S. H. Palmer, "Calling out the troops. The military, the law, and public order in England, 1650–1850", *Journal of the Society for Army Historical Research*, **56**, 1978, pp. 198–214.

19. R. Wells, *Insurrection. The British experience, 1795–1803* (Gloucester, 1986) and *Wretched faces: famine in wartime England, 1793–1800* (Gloucester, 1988).

20. J. R. Breihan, "Barracks in Dorset during the French Revolutionary and Napoleonic Wars", *Proceedings of the Dorset Natural History and Archaeological Society*, **111**, 1989, pp. 9–14, "Army barracks in the north-east in the era of the French Revolution", *Archaeologiana Aeliana*, *5th series*, **18**, 1990, pp. 165–76, "Army barracks in Devon during the French Revolutionary and Napoleonic Wars", *Devon Association Report and Transactions*, **122**, 1990, pp. 133–58; A. Ruderman, *A history of Ashford* (Chichester, 1994), pp. 63–4.

21. M. I. Thomas, *The Luddites* (1970); J. Stevenson, *Popular disturbances in England 1700–1870* (1971), pp. 155–61.

22. J. R. Western, "The Volunteer movement as an anti-revolutionary force, 1793–1801", *English Historical Review*, **71**, 1956, pp. 603–14; C. Emsley, "The military and popular disorder in England, 1790–1801", *Journal of the Society for Army Historical Research*, **61**, 1983, pp. 10–21, 96–112.

23. Wade to Duke of Newcastle, Secretary of State for the Southern Department, 29 Aug. 1729, PRO SP 54/19.

24. Albemarle to Newcastle, 9 Feb. 1747, PRO SP 54/35.

25. P. Luff, "The noblemen's regiments: politics and the 'forty-five'", *Historical Research*, **65**, 1992, pp. 54–73.

Chatper 3: Conflict in Europe, 1688–1763

1. R. Martin, "The army of Louis XIV", in P. Sonnino (ed.), *The reign of Louis XIV* (1990), pp. 111–26.

2. J. Childs, *The British army of William III* (Manchester, 1987), pp. 209–39.

3. J. Childs, *Army of William III*, pp. 268, 153, 210 and *The Nine Years' War and the British army. The operations in the Low Countries* (Manchester, 1991).

4. D. W. Jones, *War and economy in the age of William III and Marlborough* (Oxford, 1988), p. 240.

5. J. Childs, *Army of William III*, pp. 171–2.

6. J. Childs, *Nine Years' War*, p. 76.

7. W. Roosen, "The origins of the War of the Spanish Succession", in J. Black (ed.), *The origins of war in early modern Europe* (Edinburgh, 1987), pp. 151–75.

8. Colonel Ross to Marlborough, 25 July, Lieutenant-Colonel Holcroft Blood to Marlborough, 28 Aug. 1702, BL Add. 61306 f. 25, 36.

9. Blood to Marlborough, 2 Aug. 1706, BL Add. 61310 f. 3–4.

10. D. Chandler, *The art of warfare in the age of Marlborough* (1976), *Marlborough as military commander* (1973) and, most recently, "The Great Captain-General 1702–1714", in D. Chandler and I. Beckett (eds), *The Oxford illustrated history of the British army* (Oxford, 1994), pp. 69–91. C. C. Sturgill, *Marshal Villars and*

the War of the Spanish Succession (Lexington, Kentucky, 1965); J. R. Jones, *Marlborough* (Cambridge, 1993). The Duke's views can be approached through George Murray (ed.), *The letters and dispatches of John Churchill, First Duke of Marlborough, from 1702 to 1712* (5 vols, 1845) and H. L. Snyder (ed.), *The Marlborough–Godolphin Correspondence* (3 vols, Oxford, 1975). The army can be approached via R. E. Scouller, *The armies of Queen Anne* (Oxford, 1966). For the French, see, most recently, J. A. Lynn, *Giant of the Grand Siècle. The French army, 1610–1715* (Cambridge, 1997). For French defensive lines, see C. J. Duffy, *The fortress in the age of Vauban and Frederick the Great, 1660–1789* (1985), p. 34.

11. A. D. Francis, *The First Peninsular War, 1700–1713* (1975); J. Hattendorf, *England in the War of the Spanish Succession: a study of the English view and conduct of grand strategy, 1702–1712* (1987) and "Alliance, encirclement and attrition: British grand strategy in the War of the Spanish Succession, 1702–1713", in P. L. Kennedy (ed.), *Grand strategies in war and peace* (New Haven, 1990), pp. 11–29.

12. Galway to Lord Rivers, 24 Oct. 1706, BL Add. 61310 f. 102.

13. Colonel John Richards to Marlborough, 12 Oct. 1704, 29 June 1707, BL Add. 61307 f. 157–8, 61310 f. 247–8.

14. Wightman to Marlborough, 13 June 1704, BL Add. 61307 f. 53–4.

15. Queen Anne.

16. Cambridge, University Library, Add. 6570.

17. H. Davis *et al.* (eds), *The prose works of Jonathan Swift* (16 vols, Oxford, 1939–68), vol. VI, 15–16, 23. See, more generally, J. A. Downie, *Robert Harley and the press. Propaganda and public opinion in the age of Swift and Defoe* (Cambridge, 1979).

18. Correspondence of Henry Worsley, BL Add. 15936 f. 256, 265, 270.

19. Reverend Henry Etough to Horatio Walpole, 26 Aug. 1756, BL Wolterton deposit, vol. 187; Colonel Montagu to Duke of Newcastle, 5 June 1729, PRO SP 43/78.

20. A. Guy, *Oeconomy and discipline. Officership and administration in the British army 1714–63* (Manchester, 1985); G. W. Morgan, "The impact of War on the administration of the army, navy and ordnance in Britain 1739–1754", PhD thesis, Leicester, 1977 (unpublished).

21. Old style, the calendar then used by the British.

22. John Royland Hughes to Burland, Taunton, Somerset CRO, Trollop-Bellow papers, DD/TB 16 FT18; M. Orr, *Dettingen 1743* (1972).

23. Lieutenant-Colonel Charles Russel to his wife Mary, 5, 13 July 1743, BL Add. 69382; Orr, *Dettingen*, pp. 59–60.

24. Using triple rolling fire.

25. Barbara Andrews to Elizabeth Baker, Aylesbury, Buckinghamshire CRO, D/X 1069/2/115. This complements the letters from Cornet Philip Brown to his brother Thomas, published in the *Journal of the Society for Army Historical Research*, **V**, 1926; Leonard to Molly Robinson, 18 June 1743, Warwick, The Queen's Own Hussars Regimental Museum.

26. Cobham to Duke of Newcastle, 9 Dec. 1743, BL Add. 35587 f. 205.

27. Wade to Lord Carteret, Secretary of State for the Northern Department, 10 June 1744, Oxford, Bodleian Library, Ms. Eng. Hist. c314 f. 15.

28. C. Grant, *The Battle of Fontenoy* (1975).

29. Philip Brown to Richard Andrews[?], 30 Ap. 1745, Aylesbury, D/X 1069/2/ 116.

30. F. H. Skrine, *Fontenoy and Great Britain's share in the War of the Austrian Succession* (1906), pp. 197–8.

31. For a contemporary account of the hard fighting for the village, see BL Add. 71172 f. 13.

32. R. Butler, *Choiseul I* (Oxford, 1980), pp. 689–95.

33. E. E. Charteris, *William Augustus, Duke of Cumberland, his early life and times* (1913); A. W. Massie, "Great Britain and the defence of the Low Countries, 1744–1748", PhD thesis, London, 1988 (unpublished).

34. Cumberland to Pelham, 31 July 1747, Nottingham, University Library, Clumber papers 471.

35. J. Black, *America or Europe? British foreign policy 1739–63* (1998), pp. 17–23.

36. E. E. Charteris, *William Augustus, Duke of Cumberland and the Seven Years' War* (1925), pp. 251–309.

37. Hatton to Earl of Holdernesse, 18 July, 13 Aug. 1758, BL Eg. 3443 ff. 34, 42, 48.

38. Lieutenant-General Henry Conway to Charles Townshend, Secretary at War, 5 May 1761, PRO WO 1/165 p. 39.

39. *Ibid.*, 20 Sept. 1762, p. 182.

40. P. Mackesy, *The Coward of Minden* (1979).

41. R. A. Savory, *His Britannic Majesty's Army in Germany during the Seven Years' War* (Oxford, 1986); C. T. Atkinson, "British strategy and battles in the Westphalian Campaign, 1758–62", *Journal of the Royal United Services Institute*, **79**, 1934, pp. 733–40.

42. I would like to thank Richard Harding for sending me a copy of an unpublished paper on this expedition.

43. W. K. Hackman, "English military expeditions to the coast of France 1757–1761", PhD thesis, Ann Arbor, MI, 1968 (unpublished) and "The British raid on Rochefort, 1757", *MM*, **64**, 1978, pp. 263–75. I would like to thank Professor Hackman for providing me with a copy of his thesis.

44. Account of expedition by Lieutenant-Colonel Charles Hotham, Hull, University Library, DDHO/4/172; A. W. H. Pearsall, "Naval aspects of the landings on the French coast, 1758", in N. A. M. Rodger (ed.), *Naval Miscellany* (1984), vol. V, pp. 207–43.

45. F. J. Hebbert, "The Belle Ile expedition of 1761", *Journal of the Society for Army Historical Research*, **64**, 1986, pp. 81–93.

46. T. Keppel, *The life of Augustus, Viscount Keppel* (2 vols, 1842), vol. I, pp. 299, 320.

47. Bedford to Bute, 9 July 1761, Mount Stuart, Bute, papers of the 3rd Earl, 1761 correspondence No. 478.

48. Marlborough to his wife, 30 June 1758, BL Add. 61667 f. 22; Hodgson to Lord Barrington, Secretary at War, 29 Ap. 1761, PRO WO 1/165 p. 340.

49. HL Lo. 10125.

50. *Ibid.*, 8607, 8604, 8608.

51. Tyrawly to Pombal, Portuguese First Minister, 24 July 1762, PRONI T 2812/ 8/48.

52. R. Whitworth (ed.), *Gunner at large. The diary of James Wood R. A. 1746–1765* (1988), pp. ix–x.

Chapter 4: Naval triumph, 1688–1763

1. D. Loades, *The Tudor navy: An administrative, political and military history* (Aldershot, 1992); K. R. Andrews, *Ships, money and politics: seafaring and naval enterprise in the reign of Charles I* (Cambridge, 1991); B. S. Capp, *Cromwell's navy: the fleet and the English revolution, 1648–60* (Oxford, 1989); M. Baumber, *General-at-sea: Robert Blake and the seventeenth century revolution in naval warfare* (1989); S. Hornstein, *The restoration navy and English foreign trade, 1674–1688. Study in the peacetime use of seapower* (Aldershot, 1991); J. Glete, *Navies and nations. Warships, navies and state building in Europe and America, 1500–1860* (Stockholm, 1994), p. 192. The best introduction is R. Harding, *Seapower and naval warfare 1650–1850* (1999).

2. J. Ehrman, *The navy in the war of William III* (Cambridge, 1953); E. B. Powley, *The naval side of King William's war* (1972); P. Aubrey, *The defeat of James Stuart's armada 1692* (Leicester, 1979).

3. G. Symcox, *The crisis of French naval power, 1688–1697* (The Hague, 1974).

4. J. G. Coad, *The Royal dockyards 1690–1850* (Aldershot, 1989), pp. 7–10, 92–7; M. Duffy, "The establishment of the Western Squadron as the linchpin of British naval strategy", in M. Duffy (ed.), *Parameters of British naval power 1650–1850* (Exeter, 1992), pp. 61–2 and "The creation of Plymouth Dockyard and its impact on naval strategy", in *Guerres maritimes 1688–1713* (Vincennes, 1990), pp. 245–74.

5. S. F. Gradish, "The establishment of British seapower in the Mediterranean, 1689–1713", *Canadian Journal of History*, **10**, 1975, pp. 1–16.

6. Marquis of Carmarthen to Marlborough, 3 Ap. 1705, BL Add. 61308 f. 36.

7. Colonel John Richards to Marlborough, 10 May 1706, BL Add. 61309 f. 50.

8. Shovell to Earl of Sunderland, 10 Aug. 1707, BL Add. 61311 f. 50.

9. Richards to Marlborough, 15 Aug. 1706, BL Add. 61310 f. 44.

10. Norris to Marlborough, 27 July 1710, BL Add. 61314 f. 79–80.

11. J. S. Bromley, "The French privateering war, 1702–13", in H. F. Bell and R. L. Ollard (eds), *Historical Essays Presented to David Ogg* (1963), pp. 203–31, and "The North Sea in wartime, 1688–1713" *Bijdragen en Mededelingen Betreffende de Geschiedenis der Nederlanden*, **92**, 1977, pp. 270–99.

12. Ellis to Stepney, 17 Oct. 1701, BL Add. 7074 f. 49.

13. Blathwayt to Stepney, 28 Feb. 1702, Beinecke, Osborn Shelves.

14. *Ibid.*, 6 Aug. 1703, Beinecke, Osborn, Blathwayt Box 21.

15. H. C. Owen, *War at sea under Queen Anne* (Cambridge, 1934).

16. J. Hattendorf, "Admiral Sir George Byng and the Cape Passaro incident, 1718: A case study in the use of the Royal Navy as a deterrent", in *Guerres et Paix* (Vincennes, 1987), pp. 19–38; J. D. Harbron, *Trafalgar and the Spanish navy* (1988), p. 31.

17. Anon., *An account of the expedition of the British fleet to Sicily, in the years 1718, 1719 and 1720* (3rd edn, 1739), p. 88.

18. Du Bourgay, envoy in Berlin, to Viscount Townshend, Secretary of State for the Northern Department, 9 Ap., Townshend to Du Bourgay, 31 May 1726, PRO SP 90/20; Richelieu to Marquis de Silly, 25 May, St Saphorin, British envoy in Vienna, to Lord Glenorchy, envoy in Copenhagen, 1 June 1726, Paris, Bibliothèque Victor Cousin, Fonds Richelieu 31 f. 63, 65.

19. Craggs to Duke of Newcastle, 10 Aug. 1719, BL Add. 32686 f. 137.

20. Davenant to Lord Carteret, Secretary of State, 23 Dec. 1721, Hedges to Charles Delafaye, Undersecretary, 8 Feb. 1727, Tyrawly to Newcastle, 17 July 1729, PRO SP 79/14, 92/32 f. 128, 89/35 f. 188.

21. Townshend to William Stanhope, 11 Aug. 1726, PRO SP 94/98.

22. Newcastle to Wager, 12, 18 July, 12 Sep., Townshend to Wager, 6 Aug. 1727, PRO SP 47/78 f. 95, 98, 104–6, 101–2.

23. Newcastle to Townshend, 13 June 1729, PRO SP 43/77.

24. *Wye's Letter*, 24, 26, 29 July, 12 Aug. 1729.

25. Horatio Walpole to Newcastle, 26 June 1726, BL Add. 32746 f. 296; Townshend to Chesterfield, 12 July 1729, PRO SP 84/304 f. 217; Townshend to Chesterfield, 1 July, Townshend to Horatio Walpole, 1 July 1729, BL Add. 48982 f. 166, 160; Lord Chancellor, Lord King, "Notes", appendix to P. King, *Life of John Locke* (2 vols, 1830), vol. II, pp. 90–1.

26. Newcastle to Horatio Walpole, 23 May 1726, BL Add. 32746 f. 136; Townshend to Stephen Poyntz, envoy in Stockholm, 1 Aug. 1727, PRO SP 95/47 f. 313.

27. Du Bourgay to Townshend, 17 May 1726, PRO SP 90/20.

28. Horatio Walpole to Newcastle, 6 July 1728, BL Add. 32756 f. 419.

29. Charles Caesar to "James III", 20 Feb. 1726, Windsor Castle, RA, Stuart Papers 90/133.

30. J. Black and A. Reese, "Die Panik von 1731", in J. Kunisch (ed.), *Expansion und Gleichgewicht. Studien zur europäischen Mächtepolitik des ancien régime* (Berlin, 1986), pp. 69–95.

31. Anon., *A letter from a by-Stander to a member of parliament: wherein is examined what necessity there is for the maintenance of a large regular land force in this island* (1742), pp. 19, 23–5.

32. W. Cobbett, *A parliamentary history of England* (36 vols, 1806–20), vol. XI, p. 190; Waldegrave to Newcastle, 8 June, Newcastle to Waldegrave, 12 June 1740, PRO SP 78/223 f. 61, 111.

33. Titley to Edward Weston, 21 Ap. 1744, Farmington, Connecticut, Lewis Walpole Library, Weston papers vol. 14.

34. Hay, Northampton, CRO L(C) 1734.

35. Newcastle to Sandwich, 2 Oct. 1747, BL Add. 32810 f. 111.

36. P. A. Luff, "Mathews *v.* Lestock: Parliament, politics and the navy in the mid-eighteenth century England", *Parliamentary History*, **10**, 1991, pp. 45–62.

37. Meeting of Lords Justices, 24 July 1745, PRO SP 43/111.

38. Newcastle to Viscount Lonsdale, 3 Oct. 1745, Carlisle, CRO D/Pen Acc. 2689.

39. Stone to Edward Weston, 2 Aug., Stephen to Edward Weston, 25 Dec. 1745, Farmington, Weston Papers 16.

40. Newcastle to Cumberland, 12 Dec. 1745, RA CP 8/9.

41. For differing views, see H. W. Richmond, *The navy in the war of 1739–1748* (3 vols, Cambridge, 1920), vol. II, pp. 154–89; F. McLynn, "Sea power and the Jacobite rising of 1745", *MM*, **67**, 1981, pp. 163–72.

42. Leigh to Lydia, Dowager Duchess of Chandos, 5 July 1747, Oxford, Balliol College, Mss. 403 f. 27.

43. Stephen to Edward Weston, 28 June 1746, Farmington, Weston papers vol. 18; Newcastle to Cumberland, 3 July 1746, BL Add. 32707 f. 390.

44. S. W. C. Pack, *Admiral Lord Anson* (1960), pp. 153–60.

45. R. Mackay, *Admiral Hawke* (Oxford, 1965), pp. 69–88.
46. Newcastle to Cumberland, 27 Oct. 1747, RA CP 29/145; Newcastle to Lieutenant-General Bland, 30 Oct. 1747, PRO SP 54/37 f. 14.
47. Yorke to Grey, 27 Oct. 1747, Bedford, CRO Lucas papers 30/9/102/12.
48. Lady Finch to Earl of Malton, 19 Aug. 1740, Sheffield, City Archives, Wentworth Woodhouse Muniments, M3 73.
49. Sandwich to Anson, 14 Nov. 1747, BL Add. 15957 f. 29.
50. Newcastle to Cumberland, 11 Mar. 1748, RA CP 32/245.
51. D. J. Starkey, *British privateering enterprise in the eighteenth century* (Exeter, 1990).
52. C. Swanson, *Predators and prizes: American privateering and imperial warfare, 1739–1748* (Columbia, SC, 1991).
53. D. Crewe, *Yellow Jack and the worm: British naval administration in the West Indies, 1739–1748* (Liverpool, 1993).
54. Holdernesse to Rochford, 4 Oct. 1751, PRO SP 92/59 f. 170.
55. Newcastle to Keith, 22 Oct., Keith to Newcastle, 3 Nov. 1753, PRO SP 80/192.
56. Puysieulx to Richelieu, 22 July 1748, Paris, Archives Nationales, KK1372; J. G. Droysen *et al.* (eds), *Politische Correspondenz Friedrichs des Grossen* (46 vols, Berlin, 1879–1939), vol. VI, p. 218; Hanbury-Williams to Newcastle, 30 July 1749, PRO SP 88/70.
57. *Sbornik Imperatorskogo Russkogo Istoricheskogo Obshchestva* (148 vols, St Petersburg, 1867–1916), vol. C111, pp. 259–60, 275; D. Aldridge, "The Royal Navy in the Baltic 1715–1727", in W. Minchinton (ed.), *Britain and the northern seas* (Pontefract, 1988), pp. 75–9.
58. *Polit. Corresp.* **IX**, 345.
59. C. Baudi di Vesme, *La politica Mediterranea inglese nelle relazioni degli inviati italiani a Londra durante la cosidetta Guerra di successione d'Austria* (Turin, 1952); J. Black, "The development of Anglo-Sardinian relations in the first half of the eighteenth century", *Studi Piemontesi*, **12**, 1983, pp. 48–60.
60. *Craftsman*, 19 Nov. 1748; *Westminster Journal*, 18 Mar. 1749; *Remembrancer*, 9 Sept. 1749; *Old England*, 9 June, 16 June, 6 Oct. 1750.
61. Vernon to Sir Francis Dashwood, 29 July 1749, Oxford, Bodleian Library, Ms. D. D. Dashwood B11/12/6.
62. Duke of Bedford, Secretary of State for Southern Department, to Earl of Albemarle, envoy in Paris, 5 Apr. 1750, London, Bedford Estate Office, vol. 23; J. Black, "British intelligence and the mid-eighteenth century crisis", *Intelligence and National Security*, **2**, 1987, pp. 209–29.
63. Newcastle to Yorke, 26 June 1753, PRO SP 84/463.
64. Rochford to Bedford, 1 Oct. 1749, PRO SP 92/58 f. 177–8; Newcastle to Hardwicke, 10 Sept. 1749, BL Add. 35410 f. 153–4.
65. Cumberland to Holdernesse, 31 May, 18 June, Holdernesse to Cumberland, 13 May 1757, BL Eg. Mss. 3442 f. 99–100, 122, 74–5.
66. R. Middleton, "British naval strategy, 1755–1762: the Western Squadron", *MM*, **75**, 1989, pp. 349–67; M. Duffy, "Western Squadron", in M. Duffy (ed.), *Parameters*, pp. 60–81.
67. Hardwicke to Newcastle, 4 Aug. 1755, BL Add. 32857 f. 571.
68. H. W. Richmond (ed.), *Papers relating to the loss of Minorca* (1915); B. Tunstall, *Admiral Byng and the loss of Minorca* (1928).

69. Diary of George Paterson, May 1770, IO Mss. Eur. E379/1, pp. 190–1.

70. J. Hitsman and C. Bond, "The assault landing at Louisbourg, 1758", *Canadian Historical Review*, **35**, 1954, pp. 374–40.

71. P. Padfield, *Guns at sea* (1973), pp. 90–2, 100.

72. G. J. Marcus, *Quiberon Bay: The campaign in home waters, 1759* (1960).

73. J. F. Bosher, "Financing the French navy in the Seven Years' War: Beaujon, Goosens et Compagnie in 1759", *Business History*, **28**, 1986, pp. 115–33; J. Pritchard, *Louis XV's navy, 1748–1762. A study in organisation and administration* (Quebe, 1987), pp. 185–202.

74. J. Cresswell, *British admirals of the eighteenth century* (1972), p. 254; M. A. J. Palmer, "The 'military revolution' afloat: the era of the Anglo-Dutch wars and the transition to modern warfare at sea", *War in History*, **4**, 1997, pp. 147–8. The social dimension can be approached best through N. A. M. Rodger's excellent *The wooden world. An anatomy of the Georgian navy* (1986).

Chapter 5: The conquest of Empire, 1688–1763

1. P. M. Malone, *The skulking way of war. Technology and tactics among the New England Indians* (Baltimore, 1993), pp. 105–28. For the general background, A. Starkey, "European–Native American Warfare in North America 1513–1815", in J. Black (ed.), *War in the early modern world* (1998), pp. 237–61, and *European–Native American warfare, 1675–1815* (1998).

2. W. E. Washburn, *The Governor and the rebel: a history of Bacon's rebellion in Virginia* (Chapel Hill, 1957); S. S. Webb, *1676: The end of American independence* (New York, 1984).

3. B. P. Lenman, "The East India Company and the Emperor Aurangazeb", *History Today*, **33**, 1982, pp. 36–42. For the Indian military background, J. Gommans, "Warhorse and gunpowder in India *c.*1000–1850", in J. Black (ed.), *War in the early modern world*, pp. 105–28.

4. W. J. Eccles, *Canada under Louis XIV, 1663–1701* (Toronto, 1964); J. Verney, *The good regiment: the Carignan-Salières Regiment in Canada 1665–1668* (Montréal, 1991).

5. F. Jennings, *The ambiguous Iroquois Empire* (New York, 1984).

6. Journal of Captain Michael Richards, 1697, BL Stowe 463; J.-C. Marsan, *Montréal en Evolution* (2nd edn, Montréal, 1974); A. Charbonneau, Y. Desloges and M. Lafrance, *Québec, Ville fortifiée du XVIIe Siècle* (Québec, 1982).

7. W. T. Morgan, "The British West Indies during King William's war, 1689–97", *Journal of Modern History*, **2**, 1930, pp. 378–409 and "The expedition of Baron de Pontis against Cartagena", *American Historical Review*, **37**, 1932, pp. 237–58; N. H. Moses, "The British navy and the Caribbean, 1689–1697", *MM*, **52**, 1966, pp. 13–40.

8. Rivers to Marlborough, 19 June 1703, BL Add. 61306, f. 106; R. Bourne, *Queen Anne's navy in the West Indies* (New Haven, 1934); C. T. Atkinson, "Queen Anne's war in the West Indies", *Journal of the Society for Army Historical Research*, **24**, 1946, pp. 100–9, 183–97; I. K. Steele, *Politics of colonial policy. The Board of Trade in Colonial Administration 1696–1720* (Oxford, 1968), pp. 101–6.

9. C. W. Arnade, *The Siege of St Augustine in 1702* (Gainesville, 1959).

10. J. H. Hann, *Apalachee: the land between the rivers* (Gainesville, 1988), pp. 264–83.
11. R. I. Melvoin, *New England outpost: war and society in colonial Deerfield* (New York, 1989).
12. Dudley to Marlborough, 28 Dec. 1703, BL Add. 61306 f. 144.
13. Dudley to Marlborough, 29 Sept. 1706, BL Add. 61310 f. 82.
14. J. D. Alsop, "Samuel Vetch's 'Canada Survey'd': the formation of a colonial strategy, 1706–1710", *Acadiensis*, **12**, 1982, pp. 39–58; F. Nicholson, *Journal of an expedition for the reduction of Port Royal* (1711).
15. G. S. Graham (ed.), *The Walker expedition to Quebec, 1711* (1953); R. H. Harding, "The expeditions to Quebec, 1690–1711: the evolution of British trans-Atlantic amphibious power", *Guerres maritimes, 1688–1713* (Vincennes, 1996), pp. 197–212.
16. G. Metcalf, *Royal goverrment and political conflict in Jamaica 1729–1783* (1965), pp. 33–79; O. Patterson, "Slavery and slave revolts: a socio-historical analysis of the First Maroon War – Jamaica, 1655–1740", *Social and Economic Studies*, **19**, 1970; M. Craton, "The passion to exist: slave rebellions in the British West Indies, 1650–1832", *Journal of Caribbean History*, **13**, 1980 and *Testing the Chains. Resistance to slavery in the British West Indies* (1982), pp. 61–96; M. Campbell, *The Maroons of Jamaica, 1655–1796: A history of resistance, collaboration and betrayal* (Trenton, NJ, 1990).
17. P. H. Wood, *Black majority: negroes in colonial South Carolina from 1670 through the Stono Rebellion* (New York, 1974), pp. 314–23.
18. R. Law, "'Here is no resisting the country'. The realities of power in Afro-European relations on the West African 'Slave Coast'", *Itinerario*, **18**, 1994, pp. 55–6.
19. A. Deshpande, "Limitations of military technology. Naval warfare on the West Coast, 1650–1800", *Economic and Political Weekly*, **25**, 1992, pp. 902–3.
20. C. Calloway, *The Western Abenakis of Vermont, 1600–1800* (Norman, 1990).
21. D. W. Boyce, "'As the wind scatters the smoke': the Tuscarora in the eighteenth century", in D. K. Richter and J. H. Merrell (eds), *Beyond the covenant chain: the Iroquois and their neighbors in Indian North America, 1600–1800* (Syracuse, 1987), pp. 151–63; I. K. Steele, *Warpaths. Invasions of North America* (Oxford, 1994), pp. 159–67.
22. J. L. Wright, Jr, *The only land they knew: the tragic story of the American Indians in the Old South* (New York, 1981).
23. W. J. Eccles, *The Canadian frontier, 1534–1760* (New York, 1969).
24. W. S. Sorsby, "The British superintendency of the Mosquito Shore 1749–1787", PhD thesis, London, 1969, pp. 47–8 (unpublished).
25. L .E. Ivers, *British drums on the southern frontier: the military colonization of Georgia* (Chapel Hill, 1974); P. Spalding, *Oglethorpe in America* (Chicago, 1977).
26. J. J. Tepaske, *The governorship of Spanish Florida, 1700–1765* (Durham, NC, 1964).
27. K. Wilson, "Empire, trade and popular politics in mid-Hanoverian Britain: the case of Admiral Vernon", *Past and Present*, **121**, 1988, pp. 74–109; G. Jordan and N. Rogers, "Admirals as heroes: patriotism and liberty in Hanoverian England", *Journal of British Studies*, **28**, 1989, pp. 201–24.
28. R. H. Harding, *Amphibious Warfare in the Eighteenth Century. The British Expedition to the West Indies 1740–1742* (Woodbridge, 1991), pp. 83–122.

29. P. L. Woodfine, "The War of Jenkins' Ear: a new voice in the Wentworth–Vernon debate", *Journal of the Society for Army Historical Research*, **65**, 1987, pp. 67–91.

30. J. C. M. Oglesby, "British attacks on the Caracas coast, 1743", *MM*, **78**, 1972, pp. 71–9.

31. Sorsby, *British superintendency*, pp. 56–7.

32. G. A. Rawlyk, *Yankees at Louisbourg* (Orono, MN, 1967).

33. J. Pritchard, *Anatomy of a naval disaster: The 1746 French naval expedition to North America* (Montréal, 1995).

34. W. Barr and G. Williams (eds), *Voyages to Hudson Bay in search of a northwest passage 1741–1747, i, The voyage of Christopher Middleton 1741–1742* (1995).

35. B. P. Lenman, "The transition to European military ascendancy in India, 1600–1800", in J. A. Lynn (ed.), *Tools of war. Instruments, ideas, and institutions of warfare, 1445–1871* (Urbana, IL, 1990), p. 117.

36. G. J. Bryant, "The military imperative in early British expansion in India, 1750–1785", *Indo-British Journal*, 1996, p. 20; H. H. Dodwell, *Dupleix and Clive* (1920).

37. Robert, 4th Earl of Holdernesse, Secretary of State for the Northern Department, to Colonel Adlercron, 4 Ap., and to Robert Orme, 4 Ap. 1755, Watson to Holdernesse, 7 Oct. 1755, 15 Feb., 10 Mar. 1756, George Thomas to Mr Thomas, 15 Feb. 1756, BL Eg. 3488 f. 65–6, 70, 81–2, 140–1, 157–8, 216–17; Deshpande, *Limitations*, p. 903.

38. P. Spear, *Master of Bengal: Clive and his India* (1976); M. Edwardes, *The Battle of Plassey and the conquest of Bengal* (1963).

39. Carnac to Clive, 24 Jan. 1761, IO Mss. Eur. G37, Box 29.

40. Coote to Clive, 25 July 1757, IO Mss. Eur. G37, Box 5.

41. Thomas Cochran to Clive, 2 Jan., Caillaud to Clive, 20, 28 Jan. 1760, IO Mss. Eur. G37, Box 28.

42. Ironside to John Holwell, 23 Feb. 1760, IO Mss. Eur. G37, Box 28 f. 58.

43. Carnac to Clive, 26 Ap. 1763, IO Mss. Eur. G37, Box 30 f. 56.

44. Journal of Colonel Alexander Champion, IO H/Misc/198, pp. 35–6; journal of Captain Harper, IO Mss. Eur. Orme OV 219, pp. 26–30.

45. Champion, pp. 99–107, Harper, pp. 39–44.

46. L. H. Gipson, *Zones of international friction: North America, south of the Great Lakes region, 1748–1754* (New York, 1939).

47. G. Williams, "The Hudson's Bay Company and the fur trade: 1670–1870", *The Beaver*, Autumn, 1983, p. 14.

48. W. P. Bell, *The "Foreign Protestants" and the settlement of Nova Scotia* (Toronto, 1961).

49. I. K. Steele, *Betrayals. Fort William Henry and the "Massacre"* (Oxford, 1990), pp. 26–7.

50. "A scheme for the improvement and employment of His Majesty's Forces in America", sent by Townshend to Newcastle, 13 Sept. 1754, BL Add. 32736 f. 515.

51. D. Graham, "The planning of the Beauséjour operation and the approaches to war in 1755", *New England Quarterly*, **61**, 1968, pp. 551–66; T. R. Clayton, "The Duke of Newcastle, the Earl of Halifax, and the American origins of the Seven Years' War", *Historical Journal*, **24**, 1981, pp. 571–603.

52. N. E. S. Griffiths, *The Acadian deportation: deliberate perfidy or cruel necessity?* (Toronto, 1969).

53. T. Keppel, *The life of Augustus Viscount Keppel* (2 vols, 1842), vol. I, pp. 209–21; Sackville to Sir Robert Wilmot, 6 Aug. 1755, Derby, Public Library, Catton Collection WH 3448; De Lancey to Sir Thomas Robinson, Secretary of State, 7 Aug. 1755, BL Add. 32858 f. 25; L. McCardell, *Ill-starred General: Braddock of the Coldstream Guards* (Pittsburgh, 1958); C. Hamilton (ed.), *Braddock's defeat* (Norman, Oklahoma, 1959); P. E. Kopperman, *Braddock at the Monongahela* (Pittsburg, 1977); R. L. Yaple, "Braddock's defeat: the theories and a reconsideration", *Journal of the Society for Army Historical Research*, **46**, 1968, pp. 194–201; M. C. Ward, "'The European Method of Warring is not practiced here': The failure of British military policy in the Ohio Valley, 1755–1759", *War in History*, **4**, 1997, pp. 247–63.

54. Pitt to Earl of Loudoun, 4 Feb. 1757, HL Lo. 2765A.

55. G. S. Kimball (ed.), *Correspondence of William Pitt when Secretary of State with colonial governors and military and naval commissioners in America* (2 vols, 1906), vol. I, p. 143.

56. Pitt to Abercromby, 30 Dec. 1757, Kimball, vol. I, pp. 143–9.

57. J. S. McLennan, *Louisbourg from its foundation to its fall* (1918).

58. John Calcraft to Lt Colonel Hale, 27 Aug. 1758, BL Add. 17494 f. 17.

59. J. R. Cuneo, *Robert Rogers of the Rangers* (New York, 1959); P. Russell, "Redcoats in the wilderness: British officers and irregular warfare in Europe, 1740 to 1760", *William and Mary Quarterly, 3rd series*, **35**, 1978, pp. 629–52; D. J. Beattie, "The adaption of the British army to wilderness warfare, 1755–1763", in M. Ultee (ed.), *Adapting to conditions: war and society in the eighteenth century* (Tuscaloosa, 1986), pp. 56–83. The most detailed recent study, emphasizing the importance of "irregular" conflict, is S. Brumwell, "The British soldier in the Americas, 1755–1763", PhD thesis, Leeds, 1998 (unpublished).

60. S. Pargellis, *Military affairs in North America 1748–1765* (New York, 1936), pp. xviii–xxi.

61. R. Wright, *The life of Major-General James Wolfe* (1864); B. Wilson, *The life and letters of James Wolfe* (1909); T. Waught, *James Wolfe: man and soldier* (Montréal, 1928).

62. Journal, possibly by Henry Fletcher, Providence, John Carter Brown Library, Codex Eng. 41; G. Frégault, *La Guerre de la Conquête* (Montréal, 1955); C. P. Stacey, *Quebec 1759: The siege and the battle* (Toronto, 1959).

63. S. Pargellis (ed.), *Military affairs in North America 1748–1765*, p. xx.

64. S. Schama, "The many deaths of General Wolfe", *Granta*, **32**, 1990, pp. 13–56.

65. Leland to Charles Hotham, 28 Ap. 1760, Hull, University Library, DDHo/4/11(60).

66. R. L. Meriwether, *The expansion of South Carolina, 1729–1765* (Kingsport, TN, 1940), pp. 213–40; D. H. Corkran, *The Cherokee Frontier: conflict and survival, 1740–1762* (Norman, OK, 1962); T. Hatley, *The dividing paths: Cherokees and South Carolinians through the era of revolution* (New York, 1993).

67. G. M. Day, "Rogers' raid in Indian tradition", *Historical New Hampshire*, **17**, 1962, pp. 3–17; Calloway, *Abenakis*, pp. 174–80.

68. A. J. Marsh, "The taking of Goree, 1758", *MM*, **51**, 1965, pp. 117–30.

69. Michael Becher to Edward Southwell MP, 31 Mar. 1744, Richard Henvill, Master of the Incorporated Society of Merchants at Bristol, to Board of Trade, 12 Sep. 1744, Bristol, City Library, Southwell papers vol. 8.

70. Accounts received from Africa, 10 June 1758, BL Add. 32880 f. 393; J. L. A. Webb, "The mid-eighteenth century gum arabic trade and the British conquest of Saint-Louis du Sénégal, 1758", *Journal of Imperial and Commonwealth History*, **25**, 1997, pp. 49–50.

71. M. Smelser, *The campaign in the Sugar Islands, 1759* (Chapel Hill, 1955).

72. K. Datta, *The Dutch in Bengal and Bihar, 1740–1825* (Delhi, 1968), pp. 45–6; Call to –, 21 Feb. 1760, IO Mss. Eur. G37, Box 28 f. 53.

73. Call to Colonel Draper, 15 July 1760, IO H/Misc/96, pp. 28–9.

74. B. Malleson, *The career of Count Lally* (1865).

75. Francis to Jeremy Browne, 26 Oct. 1762, BL RP 3284.

76. D. Syrett, "The British landing at Havana: an example of eighteenth-century combined operations", *MM*, **55**, 1969, pp. 325–31, and *The siege and capture of Havana* (1970).

77. Monson to Charles Townshend, Secretary at War, 30 Oct. 1762, PRO WO 1/319, p. 392.

78. A. Harfield, "The British expedition to Manila, 1762–1763", *Journal of the Society for Army Historical Research*, **66**, 1988, pp. 101–11; N. Tracy, *Manila ransomed. The British assault on Manila in the Seven Years' War* (Exeter, 1995).

79. Durand to Puysieulx, 13 July 1750, Paris, AE Correspondance Politique Angleterre 429 f. 15.

80. Keppel, *Keppel*, vol. I, p. 322.

81. Newcastle to Hardwicke, 4 Aug. 1755, BL Add. 32857 f. 568–9.

82. Richards to Lieutenant-General Erle, 15 Ap. 1707, BL Stowe 474 f. 7.

Chapter 6: Rebellion successful: the American War of Independence

1. H. M. Scott, "The importance of Bourbon naval reconstruction to the strategy of Choiseul after the Seven Years' War", *International History Review*, **1**, 1979, pp. 17–35.

2. F. Parkman, *The conspiracy of Pontiac* (Boston, 1851); H. H. Peckham, *Pontiac and the Indian uprising* (Princeton, NJ, 1947); B. Knollenberg, "General Amherst and germ warfare", *Mississippi Valley Historical Review*, **41**, 1954–5, pp. 489–94; J. M. Sosin, *Whitehall and the wilderness* (Lincoln, 1961); G. E. Dowd, *A spirited resistance: The North American struggle for Indian unity 1745–1815* (Baltimore, 1992); I. K. Steele, *Warpaths*, pp. 233–47; D. Daudelin, "Numbers and tactics at Bushy Run", *Western Pennsylvania Historical Magazine*, **68**, 1985, pp. 153–79.

3. Documents for the campaign are in PRO WO 1/57.

4. Call to Clive, 25 May 1763, John Pybus to Clive, 22 Mar. 1763, IO Mss. Eur. G37 Box 30 f. 70–1, 37; S. C. Hill, *Yusuf Khan: the rebel Commandant* (1914).

5. Anon. to –, 7 Sep. 1768, IO Mss. Eur. Orme 197, pp. 119–20.

6. Major Skelly, narrative, BL Add. 9872 f. 113; G. Bryant, "Pacification in the early British Raj, 1755–85", *Journal of Imperial and Commonwealth History*, **14**, 1985, pp. 3–19.

7. Diary of George Paterson, May 1770, IO Mss. Eur. E379/1, p. 184.

8. Baugh, "Seapower and science: the motives for Pacific exploration", and G. Williams, "The achievement of the English voyages, 1650–1800", in D. Howse

(ed.), *Background to discovery: Pacific exploration from Dampier to Cook* (Berkeley, 1990), pp. 1–80.

9. N. Tracy, "The Falkland Islands crisis of 1770: use of naval force", *English Historical Review*, **90**, 1975, pp. 40–75; H. M. Scott, *British foreign policy in the age of the American Revolution* (Oxford, 1990), pp. 141–55.

10. N. Tracy, "Parry of a threat to India, 1768–1774", *MM*, **59**, 1973, pp. 35–48; M. Turlotte, "La mission militaire Française auprès des Nababs du Mysore à la fin de l'ancien régime", *Revue Historique des Armées*, **190**, 1993, pp. 4–5.

11. J. Glete, *Navies and nations. Warships, navies and state building in Europe and America, 1500–1860* (Stockholm, 1993), pp. 272–3.

12. J. Shy, *Towards Lexington: the role of the British army in the coming of the American Revolution* (Princeton, NJ, 1965); N. R. Stout, *The Royal Navy in America, 1760–1775* (Annapolis, 1973); P. D. G. Thomas, "The cost of the British army in North America, 1763–1775", *William and Mary Quarterly*, **45**, 1988, p. 516.

13. P. D. G. Thomas, *Tea Party to Independence: the third phase of the American Revolution, 1773–1776* (Oxford, 1991). For a recent approach from a wider perspective, L. D. Langley, *The Americas in the age of revolution 1750–1850* (New Haven, CT, 1996), pp. 14–34.

14. G. F. G. Stanley, *Canada invaded 1775–1776* (Toronto, 1973); R. M. Hatch, *Thrust for Canada: the American attempt on Quebec in 1775–1776* (Boston, 1979).

15. A. G. Bradley, *Sir Guy Carleton* (Toronto, 1926).

16. Congreve to Reverend Richard Congreve, 4 Sep. 1776, Stafford CRO D1057/M/F/30; I. Gruber, "America's first battle: Long Island, August 27, 1776", in C. Heller (ed.), *America's first battles, 1776–1965* (Lawrence, KS, 1986), pp. 1–32.

17. S. S. Smith, *The Battle of Trenton* (Monmouth Beach, 1965).

18. M. Mintz, *The Generals of Saratoga. John Burgoyne and Horatio Gates* (New Haven, CT, 1990).

19. J. R. Dull, *A diplomatic history of the American Revolution* (New Haven, CT, 1985).

20. M. V. Kwasny, *Washington's partisan war 1775–1783* (Kent, OH, 1996).

21. J. J. Crow and L. E. Tise (eds), *The southern experience in the American Revolution* (Chapel Hill, 1978); T. W. Tate and P. J. Albert (eds), *An uncivil war. The southern backcountry during the American Revolution* (Charlottesville, 1985).

22. H. Selesky, *War and society in colonial Connecticut* (New Haven, CT, 1990).

23. J. Hutson, *Logistics of liberty. American services of supply in the Revolutionary War and after* (Newark, 1991); E. Risch, *Supplying Washington's army* (Washington, 1981); E. W. Carp, *To starve the army at pleasure: Continental army administration and American political culture, 1775–1783* (Chapel Hill, 1984).

24. F. Wickwire and M. Wickwire, *Cornwallis and the War of Independence* (1971).

25. P. Mackesy, *The War for America 1775–1783* (1964, 2nd edn, Lincoln, Nebraska, 1993); D. Higginbotham, *The War of American Independence* (New York, 1971); J. Black, *War for America* (Stroud, 1991); S. Conway, *The War of American Independence 1775–1783* (1995).

26. J. Black, "Could the British have won the American War of Independence?", *Journal of the Society for Army Historical Research*, **74**, 1996, pp. 145–54. I have benefited from discussing this issue with John Murrin.

27. J. Gwyn, "The Royal Navy in North America, 1712–1776", in J. Black and P. L. Woodfine (eds), *British navy*, pp. 144–5.

28. D. Syrett, *The Royal Navy in American waters 1775–1783* (Aldershot, 1989), pp. 26–7.

29. C. W. Stephenson, "The supply of gunpowder in 1776", *American Historical Review*, **30**, 1925, pp. 271–81.

30. W. B. Clark, *George Washington's navy* (Baton Rouge, LA, 1960); W. M. Fowler, *Rebels under sail: the American navy during the Revolution* (New York, 1976).

31. W. H. Whiteley, "The British navy and the siege of Quebec, 1775–6", *Canadian Historical Review*, **61** (1980).

32. J. Shy, "Logistical crisis and the American Revolution: a hypothesis", in J. Lynn (ed.), *Feeding mars. Logistics in western warfare from the Middle Ages to the present* (Boulder, CO, 1993), pp. 161–79.

33. E. Robson, "The expedition to the southern colonies, 1775–1776", *English Historical Review*, **66** (1951).

34. Anon., *Reflections on the present state of the American War* (1776), p. 5.

35. On rivalry N. A. M. Rodger, *The insatiable Earl. A life of John Montagu, 4th Earl of Sandwich* (1993), pp. 221–3; on strategy, pp. 266–79.

36. I. D. Gruber, *The Howe brothers and the American Revolution* (New York, 1972), pp. 281–5; D. Syrett, "Home waters or America? The dilemma of British naval strategy in 1778", *MM*, **77**, 1991, pp. 365–77.

37. W. Cobbett, *Parliamentary history*, vol. XX, p. 332.

38. Blankett to Earl of Shelburne, 29 July 1778, BL Bowood papers S11 f. 9–11.

39. A. T. Patterson, *The other Armada: the Franco-Spanish attempt to invade Britain in 1779* (Manchester, 1960).

40. D. Gregory, *Minorca, the illusory prize. A history of the British occupations of Minorca between 1708 and 1802* (1990), pp. 187–93.

41. K. Breen, "Graves and Hood at the Chesapeake", *MM*, **66**, 1980, pp. 53–65, and "Divided command: the West Indies and North America, 1780–1781", in J. Black and P. L. Woodfine (eds), *British navy*; J. H. Owen, "Operations of the Western Squadron, 1781–82", *Naval Review*, **15**, 1927, pp. 33–53; Pritchard, "French strategy and the American Revolution: a reappraisal", *Naval War College Review*, **47**(4), 1994, pp. 83–108.

42. Dull, *The French navy and American Independence, 1774–87* (Princeton, NJ, 1975).

43. P. Padfield, *Guns at sea*, pp. 111–16; Anon. account of reception in Bristol, Bristol Record Office, Mss. 17839.

44. Rockingham to Earl of Hardwicke, *c.* Ap. 1781, Sheffield, City Archive, Wentworth Woodhouse Mss. R1-1962; J. E. Talbott, "Copper, salt, and the worm", *Naval History*, **3**, 1989, p. 53.

45. J. E. Talbott, "The rise and fall of the carronade", *History Today*, **39**(8), 1989, pp. 24–30. See, more generally, R. J. W. Knight, "The Royal Navy's recovery after the early phase of the American Revolutionary War", in G. J. Andreopoulos and H. E. Selesky (eds), *The aftermath of defeat. Societies, armed forces, and the challenge of recovery* (New Haven, CT, 1994), pp. 10–25.

46. W. S. Coker and R. R. Rea (eds), *Anglo Spanish confrontation on the Gulf Coast during the American Revolution* (Pensacola, 1982).

47. J. A. Lewis, *The final campaign of the American Revolution: rise and fall of the Spanish Bahamas* (Columbia, SC, 1991).

48. Hughes' journal, IO Mss. Eur. F29; Hughes' account of battle on 3 Sep. 1782, BL Add. 22422 f. 61–3; R. Cavaliero, *Admiral Satan. The life and campaigns of Suffren* (1994).

49. P. Nightingale, *Trade and empire in Western India 1784–1806* (Cambridge, 1970), pp. 5, 12; Council of Bombay to Warren Hastings, 12 Dec. 1778, BL Add. 38402 f. 13–15.

50. Cockburn to Council of Bombay, 13 Feb. 1779, IO Mss. Eur. Orme 197, pp. 55–7.

51. G. J. Bryant, "The cavalry problem in the early British Indian army, 1750–1785", *War in History*, **2**, 1995, pp. 1–21.

52. Carnac to Clive, 24 Jan. 1761, IO Mss. Eur. G.37 Box 29.

53. Paterson diary, July 1770, IO Mss. Eur. E379/1 p. 268.

54. Narrative of the proceedings of Colonel Leslie and his detachment, letters from Goddard, General Orders by Goddard, BL Add. 28215, 29119, 38402.

55. Extract from a letter from an officer in Goddard's force, 25 Feb. 1780, IO Mss. Eur. Orme 197, pp. 95–100.

56. Kirkpatrick to Colonel Alexander Champion, 30 Aug. 1780, Colonel Giles Stibbert to Robert Orme, 30 Nov. 1781, IO Mss. Eur. Orme 197, pp. 24–38; M. H. Fisher (ed.), *The travels of Dean Mahomet* (Berkeley, CA, 1997), pp. 115–19.

57. G. J. Bryant, "Military imperative", p. 27; Cosby to –, 15 Oct. 1780, IO Mss. Eur. Orme 197, p. 148.

58. Anon., "A short review of the past and present state of the British empire in India", BL Add. 29209 f. 214–16.

59. Report by Lieutenant Salmon, 19 Feb. 1782, BL Add. 22419, pp. 901–5.

60. Kirkpatrick to Champion, 30 Aug. 1780. IO Mss. Eur. Orme 197, pp. 21–2.

61. G. A. Billias (ed.), *George Washington's opponents: British generals in the American Revolution* (New York, 1969).

62. Proceedings of the Secret Committee of Fort St George, BL Add. 22422 f. 11.

Chapter 7: Conflict in Europe, 1793–1815

1. M. Duffy, "A particular service: the British government and the Dunkirk expedition of 1793", *English Historical Review*, 1976, pp. 529–44; A. H. Burne, *The Noble Duke of York: the military life of Frederick, Duke of York and Albany* (1949); R. N. W. Thomas, "Wellington in the Low Countries, 1794–1795", *International History Review*, **11**, 1989, pp. 14–30.

2. J. Holland Rose, *Lord Hood and the defence of Toulon* (Cambridge, 1922); S. Wilkinson, *The rise of General Bonaparte* (Oxford, 1930), pp. 21–4; D. Gregory, *Minorca, the illusory prize*, pp. 196–9.

3. P. Mackesy, *Statesmen at war. The strategy of overthrow, 1798–1799* (1974), pp. 184–314; C. O. Williams, "The Royal Navy and the Helder Campaign, 1799", *Consortium on Revolutionary Europe. Proceedings 1986*, pp. 235–47.

4. Dundas to Maitland, 16 June 1800, PRO WO 6/21, p. 21. More generally, see P. Mackesy, "Problems of an amphibious power: Britain against France, 1793–1815", *Naval War College Review*, **30**(4), 1978, pp. 16–25; R. Harding, "Sailors and gentlemen of parade: some professional and technical problems concerning the conduct of combined operations in the eighteenth century", *Historical Journal*, **32**, 1989, pp. 45–52; P. C. Krajeski, "The foundation of British amphibious

warfare methodology during the Napoleonic era, 1793–1815", *Consortium on Revolutionary Europe 1750–1850. Proceedings* (1996), pp. 191–8.

5. William to Anne Young, 30 Aug., 22 Sep. 1800, BL Add. 46712 f. 8–9, 12.

6. Philip, 5th Earl of Stanhope, Notes of conversations with the Duke of Wellington (1889), p. 182; Moore diary, BL Add. 57326 f. 11.

7. R. Williams to Marquess of Buckingham, 11 May 1793, BL Add. 59279 f. 23–4; J. A. Lynn, *The bayonets of the Republic. Motivation and tactics in the army of Revolutionary France, 1791–1794* (Urbana, IL, 1984).

8. J. Glenie, *A short essay on the modes of defence best adapted to the situation and circumstances of this island* (1785); O'Hara to Sir Evan Nepean, – Oct. 1787, PRONI, T.2812/8/50.

9. Hill to his mother, 10 Aug. –, Hill papers; R. Glover, *Peninsular preparation: the reform of the British army, 1795–1809* (Cambridge, 1963); R. H. Thoumine, *Scientific soldier: a life of General Le Marchant 1766–1812* (Oxford, 1968); G. A. Steppler, "The British army on the eve of war", in A. J. Guy (ed.), *The road to Waterloo. The British army and the struggle against Revolutionary and Napoleonic France, 1793–1815* (1992), pp. 4–15; J. L. Pimlott, "The administration of the British army, 1783–1793", PhD thesis, Leicester, 1975 (unpublished); D. Gates, *The British light infantry arm c. 1790–1815: its creation, training, and operational role* (1987).

10. R. Glover, *Britain at bay: defence against Bonaparte, 1803–14* (1973); *Bristol Gazette and Public Advertiser*, 26 Apr., 12 Jan. 1804.

11. J. A. Lochet, "The Battle of Maida revisited: column versus lines", *Proceedings of the Consortium on Revolutionary Europe*, **27** (1997), pp. 307–15.

12. Lieutenant-Colonel Hudson Lowe to General Fox, 12 Aug. 1806, BL Add. 20107 f. 151.

13. D. Gregory, *Sicily. The insecure base: a history of the British occupation of Sicily, 1806–1815* (1988).

14. C. T. Atkinson, "Gleanings from the Cathcart Mss: Part VI – The 'Conjoint' expedition to Copenhagen, 1807", *Journal of the Society for Army Historical Research*, **30**, 1952, pp. 80–7; P. W. Schroeder, *The transformation of European politics 1763–1848* (Oxford, 1994), p. 329.

15. G. C. Bond, *The grand expedition. The British invasion of Holland in 1809* (Athens, GA, 1979).

16. C. Oman, *Wellington's army* (1912), p. 79.

17. M. Glover, *Britannia sickens: Sir Arthur Wellesley and the convention of Cintra* (1970).

18. Colonel Gordon to General Dundas, 15 Oct. 1808, BL Add. 49512 f. 33; Carola Oman, *Sir John Moore* (1953); D. W. Davies, *Sir John Moore's Peninsular Campaign, 1808–1809* (The Hague, 1974).

19. D. D. Horward, *Napoleon and Iberia, the twin sieges of Ciudad Rodrigo and Almeida, 1810* (Tallahassee, 1984) and *The Battle of Bussaco: Masséna vs. Wellington* (Tallahassee, 1965).

20. D. D. Horward, "Wellington and the defence of Portugal", *International History Review*, **11**, 1989, pp. 39–54 and "Masséna and Wellington on the Lines of Torres Vedras", in A. Berkeley (ed.), *Select Papers of the International Congress on the Iberian Peninsula* (Lisbon, 1991), pp. 119–29.

21. Hill to his mother, 11 Nov. 1810, Hill papers.

22. Horward, "Masséna and Napoleon: abandonment in Portugal", *Military Affairs*, **37**, 1973, pp. 84–8.
23. B. H. Liddell Hart (ed.), *The letters of Private Wheeler 1809–1828* (London, 1951), p. 87.
24. Hill to his mother, 22, 18 May 1811, Hill papers.
25. Among the numerous books on the subject, it is worth looking at the following, Oman, *A history of the Peninsular War* (7 vols, Oxford, 1902–30); M. Glover, *Wellington's Peninsular victories* (1963), *Wellington as a military commander* (1973) and *Wellington's army in the Peninsula, 1808–1814* (Newton Abbot, 1977); P. Young and J. P. Lawford, *Wellington's masterpiece: the Battle and Campaign of Salamanca* (1973); D. Gates, *The Spanish ulcer: a history of the Peninsular War* (1986); D. D. Horward, "Wellington as a strategist, 1808–1814", in N. Gash (ed.), *Wellington: studies in the military and political career of the First Duke of Wellington* (Manchester, 1990), pp. 87–116; C. Esdaile, *The Duke of Wellington and the command of the Spanish army, 1812–1814* (Basingstoke, 1990); C. Hall, *British strategy in the Napoleonic War, 1803–1815* (Manchester, 1992). R. Muir, *Britain and the defeat of Napoleon 1807–1815* (New Haven, CT, 1996). The face of battle is covered in R. Muir, *Tactics and the experience of battle in the age of Napoleon* (New Haven, 1998).
26. P. Griffith, "The myth of the thin red line – Wellington's tactics", in P. Griffith (ed.), *Wellington commander. The Iron Duke's Generalship* (Chichester, 1985), pp. 147, 149, and *Forward into battle* (Chichester, 1981).
27. Wellington to Lord Stewart, later 3rd Marquis of Londonderry, 8 May 1815, BL Loan 105 f. 9.
28. E. E. Kraehe, "Wellington and the reconstruction of the allied armies during the Hundred Days", *International History Review*, **11**, 1989, pp. 84–97.
29. J. Brewster, "Battle within a battle", *Napoleon*, **7**, 1997, p. 9.
30. C. Hibbert (ed.), *The Wheatley diary* (1964), p. 65; J. Weller, *Wellington at Waterloo* (1967); D. Howarth, *A near run thing* (1968); D. G. Chandler, *Waterloo, the hundred days* (1980). For a recent view, F. Bauer, "Die Schlacht von Waterloo", *Militargeschichte*, **29**, 1990, pp. 275–84. For a very critical assessment of Wellington, P. Hofschröer, *1815. The Waterloo campaign. Wellington, his German allies and the Battles of Ligny and Quatre Bras* (1998).
31. Lord Keith to Hotham, 10 July 1815, Hull, DDHO/7/8.
32. Anon. to Sir Thomas Acland, undated, Exeter, Devon CRO 1148 Madd/36/91.
33. S. G. P. Ward, *Wellington's headquarters: a study of the administrative problems in the Peninsula, 1809–1814* (Oxford, 1957).
34. T. Cornell, "The military revolution, effectiveness, innovation, and the Duke of Wellington", *Consortium on Revolutionary Europe 1750–1850. Proceedings* (1996), pp. 250–9, esp. 258–9.

Chapter 8: Naval success, 1793–1815

1. G. Mowbray, *Remarks on the conduct of opposition during the present Parliament* (1798), p. 115.
2. A. T. Mahan, *The influence of sea power upon the French Revolution and Empire, 1793–1812* (2 vols, Boston, 1892) , vol. I, pp. 131–47; W. S. Cormack, *Revolution*

and political conflict in the French navy 1789–1794 (Cambridge, 1995), pp. 279–85.

3. M. A. J. Palmer, "Sir John's victory: the Battle of Cape St Vincent reconsidered", *MM*, **67**, 1991, pp. 31–46.

4. C. Lloyd, *St Vincent and Camperdown* (1963); R. Saxby, "The blockade of Brest in the French Revolutionary War", *MM*, **78**, 1992, pp. 25–35; R. Gardiner (ed.), *Fleet battle and blockade: The French Revolutionary wars, 1793–1797* (1996).

5. A. T. Mahan, *The life of Nelson. The embodiment of British sea power* (1898); O. Warner, *Nelson's battles* (Newton Abbot, 1965); D. Howarth, *Trafalgar: the Nelson touch* (1969); G. J. Marcus, *The age of Nelson* (1971); C. N. Parkinson, *Britannia rules. The classic age of naval history 1793–1815* (1977); D. Howarth and S. Howarth, *Nelson: the immortal memory* (1988); M. A. J. Palmer, "Lord Nelson: master of command", *Naval War College Review*, **41**, 1988, pp. 105–16; B. Lavery, *Nelson's navy. The ships, men and organisation, 1793–1815* (1989); E. Ingram, "Illusions of victory: the Nile, Copenhagen and Trafalgar revisited", *Military Affairs*, **48**, 1984, pp. 140–3; C. White (ed.), *The Nelson companion* (Stroud, 1997).

6. *Bonner and Middleton's Bristol Journal*, 25 Apr. 1801.

7. Dundas to General Sir Ralph Abercromby, 5 May 1800, PRO WO 6/21 p. 28.

8. Nelson to Addington, 19 Mar. 1804, Exeter CRO 152M C 1804 ON33.

9. N. Tracy, "Sir Robert Calder's action", *MM*, **77**, 1991, pp. 259–69.

10. J. S. Corbett, *The campaign of Trafalgar* (1910).

11. P. Crowhurst, *The French war on trade: privateering, 1793–1815* (Aldershot, 1989).

12. P. Mackesy, *The war in the Mediterranean, 1803–1810* (1957), pp. 158–81.

13. A. N. Ryan, "The navy at Copenhagen in 1807", *MM*, **39**, 1953, pp. 201–10.

14. Hewes to his father, 30 Nov. 1807, Bristol, Record Office 12571 (8).

15. A. Ryan, "An Ambassador afloat: Vice-Admiral Sir James Saumarez and the Swedish court, 1808–1812", in J. Black and P. L. Woodfine (eds), *British navy*, pp. 237–58.

16. W. M. P. Hornby, "Letters describing the Battle of Lissa 1811", *MM*, **52**, 1966, pp. 193–8; J. Henderson, *The frigates . . . 1793 to 1815* (1970), pp. 127–37.

17. A. Ryan, "In search of Bruix, 1799", in *Français et Anglais en Méditerranée 1789–1830* (Paris, 1991), pp. 83–90.

18. P. Webb, "Construction, repair and maintenance in the battle fleet of the Royal Navy, 1793–1815", in Black and Woodfine (eds), *British navy*, pp. 207–19.

19. J. S. Corbett, "Napoleon and the British navy after Trafalgar", *Quarterly Review*, **237**, 1922, pp. 238–55; P. Mackesy, *War in the Mediterranean*; D. Syrett, "The role of the Royal Navy in the Napoleonic Wars after Trafalgar, 1805–1814", *Naval War College Review*, Sep.–Oct. 1977, pp. 71–84; P. Crimmin, "A community of interest and danger: British naval power in the eastern Mediterranean and the Levant, 1783–1815", in W. Cogar (ed.), *New interpretations in naval history* (Baltimore, 1990), pp. 61–73.

20. Aberdeen to Wellesley, 15 Feb. 1810, BL Add. 37309 f. 344.

21. D. D. Horward, "British seapower and its influence on the Peninsular War, 1810–1814", *Naval War College Review*, **21**, 1978, pp. 54–71; C. D. Hall, "The Royal Navy and the Peninsular War", *MM*, **79**, 1993, pp. 403–18; B. M. De Toy, "French invasions: George Berkeley and Defense, 1779–1811", *Consortium on Revolutionary Europe. Proceedings 1996*, pp. 188–90.

22. A. T. Mahan, *Sea power in its relations to the War of 1812* (2 vols, Boston, 1905); L. Maloney, "The War of 1812: what role for sea power?", in K. J. Hagan (ed.), *This people's navy: the making of American sea power* (New York, 1991), pp. 46–62; R. Morriss, *Cockburn and the British navy in transition: Admiral Sir George Cockburn 1772–1853* (Exeter, 1997), pp. 83–120.

23. J. R. Breihan, "The Addington party and the navy in British politics, 1801–6", in C. L. Symonds, *New aspects of naval history* (Anapolis, 1981), pp. 163–89; R. A. Morriss, "St Vincent and reform, 1801–4", *MM*, **69**, 1983, pp. 269–90, and "Samuel Bentham and the management of the royal dockyards, 1796–1807", *Bulletin of the Institute of Historical Research*, **54**, 1981, pp. 226–40.

24. C. Gill, *The naval mutinies of 1797* (1918); G. E. Mainwaring and B. Dobrée, *Mutiny; the floating republic* (1935); R. Wells, *Insurrection: the British experience, 1795–1803* (Gloucester, 1983), pp. 79–109.

25. M. Steer, "The blockade of Brest and the victualling of the Western Squadron, 1793–1805", *MM*, **76**, 1990, pp. 307–16.

26. P. MacDougall, "The formative years: Malta dockyards, 1800–1815", *MM*, **76**, 1990, pp. 205–13.

27. R. Morriss, *The royal dockyards during the Revolutionary and Napoleonic Wars* (Leicester, 1983).

Chapter 9: Britain the world power, 1783–1815

1. R. N. Buckley, *Slaves in red coats: the British West India Regiments, 1793–1815* (New Haven, CT, 1979); D. Geggus, *Slavery, war and revolution: the British occupation of Saint Domingue 1793–1798* (Oxford, 1981); M. Duffy, *Soldiers, sugar and seapower: the British expeditions to the West Indies and the war against Revolutionary France* (Oxford, 1987).

2. Moore diary, BL Add. 57326 f. 11.

3. Blankett to Shelburne, 23 Aug. 1799, 30 Nov. 1800, BL Bowood S11 f. 211, 217.

4. Lowe to father, also Hudson, 29 Mar., Moore to his father, 25 Mar., Oakes to –, 17 Mar. 1801, BL Add. 36297C f. 12–13, 59281 f. 74–5, 36747 C f. 44–5; P. Mackesy, *British victory in Egypt, 1801* (1995).

5. R. N. Buckley (ed.), *The Napoleonic War Journal of Captain Thomas Henry Browne* (1987), pp. 106–7; W. Y. Carman, "The capture of Martinique, 1809", *Journal of the Society for Army Historical Research*, **20**, 1941, pp. 1–4.

6. H. W. Jackson, *A County Durham man at Trafalgar. Cumby of the Bellerophon* (Durham, 1997), pp. 22–3.

7. C. Hibbert (ed.), *A soldier of the Seventy-first* (1975), pp. 1–13; I. Fletcher, *The waters of oblivion. The British invasion of the Rio de la Plata, 1806–1807* (Tunbridge Wells, 1991); J. Archer, "General Whitelocke – vanquished at Buenos Aires in 1807", *British Army Review*, **104**, 1993, pp. 37–44; J. D. Grainger (ed.), *The Royal Navy in the River Plate, 1806–1807* (1996).

8. G. Douin and E. C. Fawtier-Jones, *L'Angleterre et L'Egypte. La Campagne de 1807* (Cairo, 1928); J. Dunn, "All Raschid al-Kebir. Analysis of the British defeats at Rosetta", Paper read at the conference of the Consortium on Revolutionary Europe, Baton Rouge, 1997.

9. J. Hitsman, *The incredible war of 1812: a military history* (Toronto, 1965); P. Berton, *The invasion of Canada, 1812–1813* (Toronto, 1980) and *Flames across the border, 1813–1814* (Toronto, 1981); G. F. G. Stanley, *The war of 1812: the land operations* (Toronto, 1983); D. Carter-Edwards, "The war of 1812 along the Detroit frontier: a Canadian perspective', *Michigan Historical Review*, **13**, 1987, pp. 25–50. For battle of New Orleans, see P. Griffith, *Forward into battle*, pp. 57–9.

10. R. Callahan, *The East India Company and army reform, 1783–1798* (Cambridge, MA, 1972); F. Wickwire and M. Wickwire, *Cornwallis. The imperial years* (Chapel Hill, NC, 1980), pp. 98–173.

11. Cornwallis to Henry Dundas, President of the Board of Control, 4 Ap. 1790, PRO 30/11/151 f. 40.

12. Colonel Agnew to Lord Buckinghamshire, 18 Oct. 1806, Exeter, CRO 152M C 1806 OC4.

13. Wellesley to Secretary of the Military Board, 7 May 1800, BL Add. 29238 f. 3.

14. Shore to Cornwallis, 4 Oct. 1787, PRO 30/11/122 f. 34.

15. Cornwallis to Medows, 4 Jan. 1791, PRO 30/11/173 f. 43, 45.

16. Cornwallis to Medows, 15 Dec. 1790, PRO 30/11/173 f. 11–12.

17. Skelly, narrative, anon., narrative, BL Add. 9872 f. 97–8, 36747C f. 28–30.

18. Anon. narrative, BL Add. 36747C f. 35–41.

19. Cornwallis to Court of Directors of the East India Company, 26 Dec. 1791, PRO 30/11/155 f. 134–8; Skelly, narrative, BL Add. 9872 f. 114–16, 125.

20. Skelly, f. 134.

21. S. Gordon, *Marathas, marauders and state formation in eighteenth-century India* (Delhi, 1994).

22. R. G. S. Cooper and N. K. Wagle, "Maratha artillery: from Dalhoi to Assaye", *Journal of the Ordnance Society*, **7** (1995). For a less complimentary account of Tipu's artillery, BL Add. 36747C f. 42.

23. J. Weller, *Wellington in India* (1972), p. 192.

24. P. Griffith, "The myth of the thin red line – Wellington's tactics", in P. Griffith (ed.), *Wellington commander*, p. 149.

25. R. G. S. Cooper, "Wellington and the Marathas in 1803", *International History Review*, **11**, 1989, pp. 36–8.

26. Lord Wellesley to Addington, 1 Mar. 1804, Exeter, CRO 152 M C 1804 OC3; A. S. Bennell, *The making of Arthur Wellesley* (1997).

27. G. J. Alder, "Standing alone: William Moorcroft plays the great game, 1808–1825", *International History Review*, **2**, 1980, pp. 176–88.

28. J. Weller, *Wellington*, pp. 275–6.

29. R. G. S. Cooper, "Cross-cultural conflict analysis: the 'reality' of British victory in the second Anglo-Maratha War 1803–1805", PhD thesis, Cambridge, 1992 (unpublished); D. D. Khanna (ed.), *The Second Maratha Campaign 1804–1805: diary of James Young Officer, Bengal Horse Artillery* (New Delhi, 1990).

30. Carnac to Clive, 24 Jan. 1761, IO Mss. Eur. G. 37, Box 29.

31. P. Carey (ed.), *The British in Java 1811–1816: a Javanese account* (Oxford, 1992).

32. C. A. Bayly, "The British military–fiscal state and indigenous resistance. India 1750–1820", in L. Stone (ed.), *An imperial state at war. Britain from 1689 to 1815* (1994), pp. 324–49; S. Alavi, *The Sepoys and the Company. Tradition and transition in northern India 1770–1830* (Delhi, 1995), p. 4.

33. J. Pemble, *The invasion of Nepal. John Company at war* (Oxford, 1971), p. 356.
34. D. H. A. Kolff, "The end of an *ancien régime*: colonial war in India 1798–1818", in J. A. de Moor and H. L. Wesseling (eds), *Imperialism and war. Essays on colonial wars in Asia and Africa* (Leiden, 1989), pp. 22–49, and, more generally, *Naukar Rajput and Sepoy: the ethnohistory of the military labour market in Hindustan, 1450–1850* (Cambridge, 1990).
35. Wellesley to Munro, 10 Oct. 1800, BL Add. 29239 f. 14.

Chapter 10: Conclusion: Britain as a military power

1. See also, P. K. O'Brien, "The political economy of British taxation, 1660–1815", *Economic History Review, 2nd series,* **41**, 1988, pp. 1–32; P. K. O'Brien and P. A. Hunt, "The rise of a fiscal state in England, 1485–1815", *Historical Research,* **66**, 1993, p. 170; M. Levi, *Of Rule and Revenue* (Berkeley, CA, 1988), pp. 95–121; T. Ertman, *Birth of the Leviathan. Building states and regimes in medieval and early modern Europe* (Cambridge, 1997), pp. 208–23.
2. P. Harling and P. Mandler, "From 'fiscal–military' state to laissez-faire state, 1760–1850", *Journal of British Studies,* **32**, 1993, p. 48.
3. Board of Ordnance to Lords of Admiralty, 21 Feb. 1758, PRO ADM. 1/4011 f. 158.
4. Castlereagh to Colonel J. W. Gordon, 17 Oct. 1805, 20 Nov. 1808, BL Add. 49480 f. 6, 58–9.
5. PRO WO 6/35, pp. 118–19, 5, 17, 331, 54–9, 75–9; C. D. Hall, *British strategy in the Napoleonic War 1803–1815* (Manchester, 1992), pp. 20–1; F. O. Cetre, "Beresford and the Portuguese army, 1809–1814", in A. D. Berkeley (ed.), *New lights on the Peninsular War* (Almada, 1991), pp. 149–56.
6. M. Duffy, "British diplomacy and the French wars 1789–1815", and P. K. O'Brien, "Public finance in the wars with France 1793–1815", in H. T. Dickinson (ed.), *Britain and the French Revolution 1789–1815* (1989), pp. 139, 142, 165–87, 270; J. M. Sherwig, *Guineas and gunpowder. British foreign aid in the wars with France, 1793–1815* (Cambridge, MA, 1969); O. W. Johnston, "British pounds and Prussian patriots", *Consortium on Revolutionary Europe. Proceedings 1986,* pp. 294–305.
7. Anon., memorandum, Reflexions sur quelques imputations dirigées contre l'Angleterre, Vienna, Haus-, Hof-, und Staatsarchiv, Staatskanzlei, England, Varia 13.
8. Robert, 4th Earl of Holdernesse, Secretary of State, to Duke of Newcastle, 6 Aug. 1755, BL Add. 32858 f. 9.
9. Gordon to Lord Hutchinson, 1 Feb. 1807, BL Add. 49512 f. 4.
10. Pritchard, "French strategy and the American Revolution: a reappraisal", *Naval War College Review,* **47**, 1994, pp. 83–108.
11. J. Black, *War and the world 1450–2000* (New Haven, CT, 1998).
12. M. J. Braddick, "An English military revolution?", *Historical Journal,* **36**, 1993, pp. 965–75; G. Parker, "The *Dreadnought* revolution of Tudor England", *Mariner's mirror,* **82**, 1996, pp. 269–300; P. K. O'Brien and P. Hunt, "The emergence and consolidation of excises in the English fiscal system before the Glorious Revolution", *British Tax Review,* **1**, 1997, pp. 35–58. I have benefited from

reading J. S. Wheeler's unpublished study, *War and the military revolution in seventeenth-century England*. See also, *re.* the 1620s, L. J. Reeve, "The politics of war finance in an age of confessional strife: a comparative Anglo-European view", *Parergon*, **14**, 1996, pp. 85–109.

13. H. C. Tomlinson, *Guns and government: the Ordnance Office under the later Stuarts* (1979).

14. P. A. Luff, "Mathews *v.* Lestock: parliament, politics and the navy in mid-eighteenth-century England", *Parliamentary History*, **10**, 1991, pp. 45–62.

15. L. G. Schwoerer, *No standing armies: the antiarmy ideology in seventeenth-century England* (Baltimore, 1974).

16. H. Horwitz, *Parliament, party and politics in the reign of William III* (Manchester, 1977), pp. 226–7, 248–55; J. Childs, *British army of William III*, pp. 191–206; J. E. Cookson, *The friends of peace. Anti-war liberalism in England, 1793–1815* (Cambridge, 1982); M. Ceadel, *The origins of war prevention. The British peace movement and international relations, 1730–1854* (Oxford, 1996).

17. T. Hayter, "England, Hannover, Preussen, gesellschaftliche und wirtschaftliche Grundlagen der britischen Beteiligung an Operationen auf dem Kontinent während des Siebenjährigen Krieges" [England, Hanover, Prussia, social and economic conditions of the British participation in Continental operations during the Seven Years' War], in B. R. Kroener (ed.), *Europa im Zeitalter Friedrichs des Grossen. Wirtschaft, Gesellschaft, Kriege* (Munich, 1989), pp. 171–92; Jenkinson to Amherst, 24 Oct. 1780, PRO WO 34/127 f. 155.

18. Anon., *Things set in a proper light* (1758), pp. 40–1.

19. J. A. Houlding, *Fit for service: the training of the British army, 1715–1795* (Oxford, 1981), pp. 9–11.

20. Bristol, Record Office, papers of Jarrit Smith MP, AC/JS 102(8)b; J. S. Bromley (ed.), *The manning of the Royal Navy. Selected public pamphlets 1693–1873* (1974); N. A. M. Rodger, *The wooden world. An anatomy of the Georgian navy* (1986), pp. 145–204, 346.

21. N. Rogers, "Liberty Road: opposition to impressment in Britain during the American War of Independence", in C. Howell and R. Twomey (eds), *Jack Tar in history* (Fredericton, NB, 1991), pp. 55–75; Wallace to Burrish, 4 Feb. 1755, PRO SP 110/6.

22. J. Pritchard, *Louis XV's navy: a study of organisation and administration* (Montréal, 1987), pp. 71–88; J. Dull, *French navy*, pp. 286–7.

23. S. F. Gradish, *The manning of the British navy during the Seven Years' War* (1980).

24. S. Tucker, *Injured Honor: The Chesapeake–Leopard affair of June 22, 1807* (Annapolis, 1996).

25. Horatio Walpole to Reverend Milling, 26 Mar. 1744, BL. Wolterton deposit, vol. 187.

26. J. R. Western, *The English militia in the eighteenth century* (1965); L. J. Colley, *Britons. Forging the nation 1707–1837* (New Haven, CT, 1992), pp. 283–319.

27. F. Anderson, *A people's army. Massachussetts soldiers and society in the Seven Years' War* (Chapel Hill, NC, 1984); D. Higginbotham, "The military institutions of colonial America: the rhetoric and the reality", in J. Lynn (ed.), *Tools of War*, pp. 131–53; M. Craton; *Testing the chains*, pp. 135–6.

28. C. W. Eldon, *England's subsidy policy towards the Continent during the Seven Years' War, 1756–1763* (Philadelphia, 1938); G. Symcox, "Britain and Victor Amadeus

II: or, the use and abuse of allies", in S. B. Baxter (ed.), *England's rise to greatness, 1660–1763* (Berkeley, CA, 1983), pp. 151–84.

29. Tyrawly to Marlborough, 12 Nov. 1708, BL Add. 61312 f. 168; Bristol, Record Office, papers of Jarrit Smith MP, AC/JS 102(7).

30. E. M. Spiers, "Army organisation and society in the nineteenth century", in T. Bartlett and K. Jeffery (eds), *Military history of Ireland*, p. 335.

31. E. Ingram, "Great Britain's great game: an introduction", *International History Review*, **2**, 1980, pp. 163–4.

32. Wolfe to Colonel Charles Hotham, 9 Aug. 1758, Hull, Hotham papers, DDHo/4/7.

33. Keppel, *Keppel*, vol. I, pp. 321–2; J. West, *Gunpowder, government and war in the mid-eighteenth century* (Woodbridge, 1991).

34. J. Taylor, *A relation of a voyage to the army*, ed. by C. D. van Strien (Leiden, 1997), pp. 74–5.

35. Memorandum by Lieutenant-Colonel Guard, 17 Dec. 1808, Guard's letterbook, Exeter, CRO 49/33 f. 10.

36. J. Black, *America or Europe? British foreign policy 1739–1763* (1998).

37. Council report, 19 Mar. 1764, IO E/4/7, p. 132.

38. A. Aspinall, "The Cabinet Council 1783–1885", *Proceedings of the British Academy*, **38**, 1952, pp. 145–252; R. Pares, *King George III and the Politicians* (Oxford, 1953), pp. 143–81; C. R. Middleton, "The impact of the American and French revolutions on the British constitution: a case study of the British Cabinet", *Consortium on Revolutionary Europe. Proceedings* (1986), pp. 317–26.

39. Fulton to Lord Grenville, 2 Sep. 1806, BL Add. 71593 f. 134.

40. Dudley to Marlborough, 10 Nov. 1707, BL Add. 61311 f. 97; Oakes to –, 17 Mar. 1801, BL Add. 36747 C f. 45.

41. Horace Walpole, *Memoirs of King George II*, ed. by John Brooke (3 vols, New Haven, CT, 1985), vol. II, p. 26.

42. C. E. Davies, *The blood-red Arab flag. An investigation into Qasimi piracy 1797–1820* (Exeter, 1997).

43. Secret Committee at Fort St George to Warren Hastings and Council at Fort William, 11 Sep. 1782, BL Add. 22422 f. 90.

44. J. T. Alsop, "The age of the projectors: British imperial strategy in the North Atlantic in the War of Spanish Succession", *Acadiensis*, **21**, 1991, pp. 52–3.

45. Vol. II, p. xi; see, more generally, J. Black, "Political allusions in Fielding's 'Coffee-House Politician'", *Theoria*, **62**, 1984, pp. 45–56.

46. Stewart to Earl of Stair, 10 Sep. 1741, Beinecke, Osborn Shelves, Stair Letters, No. 70.

47. D. Baugh, "Great Britain's blue water policy, 1689–1815", *International History Review*, **10**, 1988, pp. 33–58, and "Maritime strength and Atlantic commerce: the uses of a grand maritime empire", in L. Stone (ed.), *An imperial state at war*, pp. 185–233. See also T. J. Denman, "The political debate over strategy, 1689–1712", PhD thesis, Cambridge, 1985 (unpublished).

48. D. French, *The British way in warfare 1688–2000* (1990), pp. 91, 117.

49. Bute to Sir John Philipps, 23 Feb. 1763, BL Add. 36797 f. 34.

50. Stair to Loudoun, 14 Nov. 1742, HL Lo. 7615.

51. D. G. Chandler, "Fire over England: threats of invasion that never came", *Consortium on Revolutionary Europe. Proceedings* (1986), p. 443. A less optimistic

view of British capabilities is offered by E. N. Renn, "England faces invasion: the land forces, 1803–1805", *Consortium on Revolutionary Europe. Proceedings 1974*, pp. 129–40. See also, F. Beaucour, "Le grand projet Napoléonien d'expédition en Angleterre: mythe ou réalité, *ibid.*, 1982, pp. 225–45.

52. C. Hibbert (ed.), *A soldier of the Seventy-first* (Moreton-in-Marsh, 1996), pp. 2, 9.
53. Skelly narrative, 7 Feb. 1792, BL Add. 9872 f. 136–7.
54. Black, *European warfare 1660–1815* (1994), pp. 229–31.
55. Hill to Rev. Jacob Ley, 7 July 1815, Hill papers.
56. R. Mukherjee, "Trade and empire in Awadh, 1765–1804", *Past and Present*, **94**, 1982, pp. 85–102.
57. S. Alavi, *Sepoys and the Company*, p. 292.
58. S. Gordon, *Marathas, marauders, and state formation in eighteenth-century India* (Delhi, 1994), pp. 20–1; R. G. S. Cooper, *Cross-Cultural Conflict*, p. 109.
59. P. Mackesy, "Strategic problems of the British war effort", in H. T. Dickinson (ed.), *Britain and the French Revolution 1789–1815* (1989), p. 159.

Index

Abenaki 118, 120, 124–5, 128–9, 136, 145, 157
Abercromby, General James 140, 142
Abercromby, Major-General John 249
Abercromby, Major-General Sir Ralph 196, 242–3, 245–7
Abercromby, Sir Robert 258–9
Aberdeen 14, 22, 28
Acadia 118, 121, 129, 137
Acadians 137
Acre 227, 245
Adams, Major John 134
Adriatic 85, 234, 237
Ahmadabad 185–6
Ahmadnagar 260
Aire 54–5
Aix-la-Chapelle, Peace of (1748) 100, 130, 135
Albany 117, 122, 128, 136, 139, 143
Albemarle, George, 3rd Earl of 44, 149
Alexandria, Virginia 238
Alexandria, Egypt 246–7, 251–2, 283
Alicante 84, 152, 211
Allahabad, Treaty of (1765) 135
Almeida 208
Alsace 65
American Independence, War of (1775–83) 30, 33–4, 101, 159, 164–8, 199, 214, 222, 284
Amherst, General Jeffrey 140, 143–5, 158–9, 200, 272
amphibious operations 85, 87, 127–8, 131, 146–7, 152, 193–7, 202–4, 244–8, 289
Anglo-Dutch wars 79
Angrias 123, 132, 285

Annapolis Royal 129
Anne, Queen 12, 21, 49
Anson, Admiral George, Lord 1, 97–8, 107
Anstruther, Brigadier-General Robert 219
Antigua 100, 151
Antwerp 9, 31, 52, 66, 68, 203–4, 231
Apalachees 120
Arcot 131–2, 148
Argentina 220
Argyll, John, 2nd Marquis of 22–4, 57
Arnold, Benedict 165–7, 172
artillery 26, 28, 30, 37, 39, 55, 72–3, 84, 117, 119–20, 133–5, 138–9, 148–9, 157, 185–6, 199, 210, 248–9, 262, 283, 291–2
Asiento 48
Athlone 17, 19–20
Atterbury Plot (1722) 25
Auchmuty, General Samuel, 247, 250, 263
Aurangzeb, Mughal Emperor 117
Australia 162–3
Austrian Netherlands 3, 26, 62, 68, 71, 89, 96, 289
Austrian Succession (1740–8), War of the 6, 31, 45, 62–70, 77, 92–100, 106, 147, 149

Bacon's Rebellion 116–17
Badajoz 208–9, 277
Bahamas 182
Baillie, Colonel William 187
Baird, Sir David 247–8
Ballinamuck 38
Ballyneety 18
Baltic 6, 87–90, 99, 102–3, 105, 193, 233

Baltimore 254
Bangalore 257–8
Bank of England 1, 38
Bantry Bay 36, 40
Barbary states 83, 88
Barbados 116, 119, 147, 229, 239
Barcelona 56–7, 84, 236
Barlow, Sir George 264
Barnett, Commodore Curtis 98
Barnwell, Colonel John 124
barracks 35, 43
Bass Rock 14
Batavia 248–9, 263
Bath 22
Baton Rouge 182
battles
  Aboukir Bay (1801) 245–6 Aig (1803)
    262 Albuera (1811) 208, 211, 220,
    290 Alexandria (1801) 246–7
    Almanza (1707) 56–7 Almenara
    (1710) 56 Almora (1815) 264
    Andwanala (1763) 134 Aragon
    (1803) 261 Argaum (1803) 220
    Arklow (1798) 37 Arní (1751) 132
    Arrakerry (1800) 260 Assaye (1803)
    134, 220, 260–1, 264, 283, 291
    Aughrim (1691) 19–20 Austerlitz
    (1805) 202 Bahur (1752) 132
    Ballyellis (1798) 39 Ballynahinch
    (1798) 38 Bantry Bay (1689) 15, 80
    Barfleur (1692) 6, 20, 80–2, 84, 119
    Barossa (1811) 211 Basque Roads
    (1809) 234, 237 Battina (1794) 259
    Beachy Head (1690) 19, 80, 119
    Beaver Dams (1813) 253 Bemis
    Heights (1777) 168 Bennington
    (1777) 168 Bidassoa (1813) 210
    Bladensburg (1814) 254 Blenheim
    (1704) 6, 49–50, 52, 55, 151
    Blouberg (1806) 248 Borodino
    (1812) 54 Boyne (1690) 17–20
    Brandywine (1777) 167, 172
    Brihuega (1710) 56 Buenos Aires
    (1807) 251 Bunker Hill (1775) 165,
    167 Bushy Run (1763) 156–7
    Bussaco (1810) 208, 214 Buxar
    (1764) 8, 135, 187 Camden (1780)
    169 Camperdown (1797) 40, 224–5
    Cape Finisterre (1747) 33, 97, 99
    Cape Finisterre (1805) 229 Cape
    Passaro (1718) 24, 60, 87–8 Cape St
    Vincent (1780) 181 Cape St Vincent
    (1797) 223, 225 Castalla (1813) 211
    Castine (1779) 176 Castlebar (1798)
    38 Castricum (1799) 196 Cáveripák
    (1751) 132 Chateauguay (1813) 253

  Chelambakam (1781) 188 Chippawa
    (1814) 254 Chrysler's Farm
    (1813) 253 Condore (1759) 148
    Copenhagen (1801) 228 Corunna
    (1809) 195, 207, 211, 290 Cowpens
    (1781) 169, 171–2 Cromdale (1690)
    14 Culloden (1746) 13–14, 25,
    28–32, 142 Dalmau (1793) 259 Delhi
    (1803) 262 Denain (1712) 55, 59
    Dettingen (1743) 3, 26, 62–5, 67,
    70, 72, 96, 142, 147, 158 Dogger
    Bank (1781) 181 Dromore (1689)
    15 Elixheim (1705) 51 Falkirk (1746)
    28, 31, 33 Farruckhabad (1804) 262
    Fellinghausen (1761) 73, 288
    Fontenoy (1745) 31, 33, 66–8, 70,
    72, 147, 158, 288 Fuentes de Oñoro
    (1811) 208 Germantown (1779)
    167–8 Gheriah (1763) 134–5
    Glenshiel (1719) 25 Glorious First of
    June (1794) 222–3 Golden Rock
    (1753) 132 Grand Port (1810)
    249–50 Gravenstein (1762) 73, 288
    Grenada (1779) 180 Guilford Court
    House (1781) 169 Hastenbeck (1757)
    33, 71, 87 Hohenfriedberg (1745)
    31 Hondschoote (1793) 195 Île de
    Groix (1795) 223 Île de Hyères
    (1795) 223 Jena (1806) 290 Jutland
    (1916) 111 Kesseldorf (1745) 31
    Kilcullen (1798) 39 Killiecrankie
    (1689) 13–14, 27 King's Mountain
    (1780) 169, 171–2 Kjöge (1807) 203
    Lagos (1759) 109, 111–12, 180
    Laswari (1803) 262 Lawfeldt (1747)
    69–70, 142, 147, 158, 288 Leipzig
    (1813) 204 Leuthen (1757) 275
    Ligny (1815) 215–16 Lissa (1811)
    234 Long Island (1776) 166, 171–2,
    176 Lundy's Lane (1814) 254
    Mahidpur (1817) 264–5 Maida
    (1806) 202–3, 218, 289 Makwanpur
    (1816) 264 Malaga (1704) 84 Malaun
    (1815) 264 Malavelly (1799) 259
    Malplaquet (1709) 3, 22, 53–5
    Mandara (1801) 246 Manoli (1800)
    260 Merksem (1814) 204 Minden
    (1759) 72–3, 77–8, 288 Minorca
    (1756) 108–9 Monongahela (1755)
    138 Narva (1700) 59 Neerwinden
    (1693) 46–7 Negapatam (1782) 183
    New Orleans (1815) 252, 254 New
    Ross (1798) 37 Nile, the (1798)
    226–7, 245 North Point (1814) 254
    Ocana (1809) 207 Orthez (1814) 211
    Oudenaarde (1708) 22, 53 Oulart

Hill (1798) 37 Patna (1764) 135 Perumbakam (1780) 187 Plassey (1757) 133–4 Porto Novo (1781) 188 Preston (1648) 23 Preston (1715) 23–4 Prestonpans (1745) 26–7, 31, 33 Princeton (1777) 171 Providien (1782) 183 Quatre Bras (1815) 215 Québec (1759) 142–3 Queenston (1812) 253 Quiberon Bay (1759) 109, 111–12, 180 Raisin River (1813) 253 Ramillies (1706) 22, 52, 55 Rossbach (1757) 275 Rosetta (1807) 252 Roucoux (1746) 33, 68–70, 158 Sadras (1782) 183 Sahaguan (1808) 206 St Pierre d'Irube (1813) 211 Sainte-Foy (1760) 144 Saints (1782) 180–1, 191 Salamanca (1812) 209, 212, 220 Samarang (1811) 263 San Marcial (1813) 210 Santa Marta (1702) 86 Saragossa (1710) 56 Saratoga (1777) 168, 172 Schellenberg (1704) 50 Sedgemoor (1685) 32, 49 Seringapatam (1791) 257–9, 291 Sheriffmuir (1715) 22–4, 27, 54, 57 Soor (1745) 31 Sorauren (1813) 210 Springfield (1780) 172 Staffarda (1690) 59 Steenkirk (1692) 46–7 Stoney Creek (1813) 253 Stono Ferry (1779) 175 Sugarloaf Rock (1753) 132 Talavera (1809) 207, 209, 220, 291 The Meadows (1754) 137 The Nile (1798) 226–7 Toulon (1707) 59, 93–4 Toulouse (1814) 211 Tourcoing (1794) 195 Trafalgar (1805) 6, 9, 202, 219, 229–30, 236, 240, 287, 293 Trenton (1776) 167, 170–1 Trincomalee (1782) 183 Trois-Rivières (1776) 166 Ulm (1805) 290 Ushant (1778) 109, 178–9 Villaviciosa (1710) 56, 58 Valmy (1792) 33 Vimeiro (1808) 205, 212 Vinegar Hill (1798) 38–9, 261 Virginia Capes (1781) 180 Vitoria (1813) 210, 212–13, 220 Wandewash (1759) 148 Warburg (1760) 73, 288 Waterloo (1815) vii, 49, 194–5, 214–20, 277, 291–2 Wilhelmsthal (1762) 73, 288 Willems (1794) 195 Yorktown (1781) 38, 169, 172, 180, 190, 261, 290
Bavaria 31
Bavarian Succession (1778–9), War of the 33
bayonets 17, 28, 38, 47, 55, 59–60, 72, 143–4, 157, 194, 214–15, 243, 248, 265, 283, 291

Bayonne 211
Beckwith, Lieutenant-General Sir George 248–9
Bedford, John, 4th Duke of 74
Belfast 15
Belize 182
Belle Isle 74–5, 112, 152, 197, 278
Benares 161, 186
Benbow, Vice-Admiral John 86
Bengal 115, 132–5, 148, 184–8, 263, 268, 292
Bengal, Bay of 109, 117, 134, 183, 222
Benkulen 183
Beresford, General William 208, 211, 250
Bergen-op-Zoom 32, 69, 204
Berkeley, Sir William 116–17
Bertie, Vice-Admiral Sir Albemarle 249
Berwick, James, Duke of 56–7, 60
Béthune 54–5
Bharatpur 262
Bhonsle 261
Bihar 134–5
Birmingham 47
Blainville, Céleron de 135
Blair Castle 13
Blake, Admiral George 83
Blankett, Admiral John 178–9, 245
Blue Water strategy 91, 122
Bohemia 31
Bologna 89
Bombay 117, 135, 162, 184, 223, 259, 286
Bombay Marine 108–9, 223
Bonn 49
Bordeaux 75
Borneo 162, 248, 285
Boscawen, Admiral Edward 107–8, 131, 139–40
Boston 43, 118, 122, 160, 164–6, 173–4, 285–6
Boston Massacre 164
Boston Tea Party 164
Bouchain 54–5
Boulogne 33, 228
Bouquet, Lieutenant-Colonel Henry 157
Brabant 31, 51, 68
Braddock, Major-General Edward 137–8, 141, 156
Bradstreet, Lieutenant-Colonel John 141
Braithwaite, Colonel 188, 244
Bremen 195, 202
Brest 14, 19, 25, 33, 46, 68, 75, 80, 85, 94–5, 97, 108, 111–12, 127, 177, 180, 224–5, 229, 235–6, 270, 275
Brewer, John 1, 267, 276
Bristol 36, 41, 95, 181

Brittany 1, 39, 80, 92, 122, 196, 224, 271
Brock, Major-General Isaac 253
Brown, Philip 64–5, 67–8
Brownrigg, Sir Robert 263
Bruges 52–3, 68
Brussels 52, 68, 204, 215
Buchan, Major-General Thomas 14
Buenos Aires 250–2, 291
Bundelkhand 185
Burgos 209–10, 219
Burgoyne, General John 76, 167, 184, 190
Burma 265
Bute, John, 3rd Earl of 74, 108, 153, 289
Byng, Admiral Sir George 21, 87–8
Byng, Admiral John 61, 178
Byron, Vice-Admiral John 178, 180

Cadiz 24, 56, 83, 85, 90, 110, 197, 211, 222, 224, 229, 231, 235, 239, 289
Cadogan, Lieutenant-General William 24
Caillaud, Major John 134, 148, 160–1
Calabria 40, 193, 202, 237
Calais 33, 83, 92
Calcutta 132–3, 162, 187
Calder, Vice-Admiral Sir Robert 229
Call, John 148–9, 161
Calvi 196, 225
Canada 106, 108–9, 116, 118, 122, 129, 139–45, 158, 165–6, 168, 172, 189, 253–5, 275, 282
Cannon, Colonel Alexander 14
Cape Breton 96–8, 104, 129, 140, 277
Cape Coast Castle 122–3, 233
Cape Finisterre 24
Cape Town 192, 223, 244–5, 248, 250, 281, 287
Capri 203, 227
Caracas coast 128
Caribbean 83, 119–20, 126–8, 173, 180–1, 239, 248, 271
  see also West Indies
Carillon 139–40, 142–3
Carleton, Guy 115–16, 190
Carlisle 23, 27, 32
Carlow 37–8
Carnac, John 133–4, 184, 262
Carnatic 9, 130–2, 147–9, 160–1, 185–91, 256, 257, 263, 282, 288
Carpenter, Lieutenant-General George 23
Carrickfergus 15–17, 35
carronade 182
Cartagena, Colombia 86–7, 100, 119, 127, 130–1, 149, 287
Cartagena, Spain 109
Carteret, John Lord 3

Castile 56–7
Castine 121, 175
Castlereagh, Robert, Lord, 268
Catalonia 56–7
Catholics 39
cavalry 39, 55, 63–5, 72–3, 117, 133, 161, 184–6, 195, 209, 211, 255–6, 261, 265
Ceylon see Sri Lanka
Chanda Sahib 131–2
Chandernagore 133, 148, 244
Charlemont 16
Charleroi 31, 46, 68
Charles VI, Emperor, 'Charles III' 47, 56, 59
Charles II of England 47, 116
Charles of Lorraine 133, 148, 244
Charles XII of Sweden 59
Charleston 43, 116, 120, 124, 168–70, 172, 174, 238
Charnock, Job 117
Cherbourg 74–5, 109, 224, 237
Cherokee 124, 138, 145, 157
Chesapeake 33, 100, 116, 167, 169, 174, 238, 254, 275
Chester 27, 32
Chickasaw 124–5
China 8, 266, 289
Choiseul, Etienne-François, Duke of 111, 163, 286
Cintra, Convention of (1808) 206
Circars, Northern 148, 161, 187, 286
Ciudad Rodrigo 108–9
Civitàvecchia 89, 227, 237
Cleland, Lieutenant-Colonel William 14
Clinton, General Sir Henry 169, 171–2, 190
Clive, Robert 131–5, 148
Cobham, Richard Viscount 60, 65
Cochrane, Captain Thomas 236–8
Cockburn, Lieutenant-Colonel William 184
Codrington, Christopher 85, 119
Coesfeld 71–2
Collingwood, Admiral Lord 204, 236
column 198, 213–14, 283
Concord 164, 175
Conflans, Marquis de 111
Connacht 38, 41
Connecticut 4, 174
Continental Army 169
Continental System 280
Cook, Captain James 142, 162
Coote, General Sir Eyre 134, 148, 152, 187–8, 191, 196, 257
Cope, Lieutenant-General Sir John 26–7

Copenhagen 193, 203–4, 231–2
copper sheathing 181–2
Corfu 223, 236
Cork 18, 82
Cornish, Rear-Admiral Samuel 150
Cornwall 22, 41
Cornwallis, Charles, General, 2nd Earl
    and 1st Marquis 38, 123, 169–73,
    180, 190, 256–8, 263–5
corruption 61
Corsica 178, 196, 218, 225, 228, 264
Cotton, Admiral Sir Charles 236
Creek 120, 124
Cromwell, Oliver 20, 23, 30, 86
Crown Point 129, 138, 143–4
Cuba 6, 116, 120, 127, 151, 238, 243
Cuddalore 131, 148, 183, 188, 191
Cumberland 23
Cumberland, William, Duke of 5, 13,
    27, 32, 45–6, 61, 66–9, 71, 74, 77,
    87, 95, 97, 105, 149, 158, 277
Curaçao 243

Dabhoi 185
Dalnacardok 44
Dalrymple, Lieutenant-Colonel William
    159–60
Dalton, Captain John 132
Danes 17
Dardanelles 231–2, 235
Dartmouth, Admiral George, Lord 12
De Lancey, James 139
Delhi 263
Demerara 242, 248
demography 124, 151
Dendermonde 52, 68
Denmark 83, 87, 102, 163, 193, 203, 286
Deptford 83
Derby 12, 27, 44, 267
Despard, Edward 38–9
Detroit 119, 156–7, 253
Diplomatic Revolution 70–1
disease 100, 118–20, 123–4, 130, 151–2,
    243–4, 249, 287
Döhla, Johann Conrad 170
Dominica 142, 182, 229, 242
Douai 54–5
Douglas, Captain Charles 180–1
Douglas, Sir James 147
Draper, Colonel William 149–50
Dublin 14, 17, 20, 35, 37–8, 41, 61, 293
Duckworth, Vice-Admiral Sir John
    231–2, 234
Dudley, Colonel 4, 121, 282
Dumfries 23
Duncan, Admiral Adam 224

Duncannon Castle 82
Dundalk 16
Dundas, Colonel David 198
Dundee 13, 24
Dundee, John, Viscount 13
Dunkirk 7, 14, 20–1, 25, 33, 62, 65, 68,
    83, 92, 95, 189, 194–5, 219
Dunmore, John, 4th Earl of 160
Dupleix, Joseph, Marquis de 130–2
Durham 12
Dwyer, Michael 38
Dysart 41

East India Company, English 44, 82,
    104, 112, 119, 123, 131–5, 166,
    275–6, 279, 285, 292
East Indies 98, 112, 115, 263
Edinburgh 13, 16, 26–7, 293
Egypt 40, 193, 218–20, 225, 244, 251–2,
    263, 283, 289, 290–1, 293
Eliott, Lieutenant General George 182
Elliot, Gilbert 264, 293
Elliot, Captain John 35
Elphinstone, Rear-Admiral George
    244–5
Emden 71–2
Ems, river 109
Essex 111
Eugene, Prince 49–50, 52–5, 59, 69
Excise Crisis 2

Falkland Islands 95, 112, 163–4, 287
Fawcett, Sir William 200
Ferdinand, Prince Ferdinand of 72–3, 77
Ferguson, Major Patrick 169
Ferrol 193, 197, 213, 229, 289
finances 47–8, 58, 82, 267–9
Finland 31, 233
Fitzgerald, Lord Edward 37
flintlocks 13, 17, 59–60, 160, 181, 213,
    268
Florida 120, 126, 180, 182, 189, 282
Flushing 203–4
Folliott, Captain Fraser 76
Forbes, Brigadier-General John 140–1
Forbin, Antoine, Chevalier de 21
Forde, Francis 148
Forster, Thomas 23
fortifications 16, 35, 119, 126, 129, 131,
    157, 159, 162
Fort Albany 117
Fort Amherst 141
Fort Beauséjour 137
Fort Duquesne 137–40, 142
Fort Frontenac 141–2
Fort Gaspereau 137

Fort George 139
Fort Lévis 144
Fort Ligonier 157, 159
Fort Littleton 156
Fort Loudoun 145
Fort Loyal 117
Fort McHenry 254
Fort Massachusetts 129
Fort Michilimackinac 156
Fort Moro 149
Fort Necessity 136
Fort Niagara 143, 157, 253
Fort Ontario 139
Fort Philip 32
Fort Pitt 156–7
Fort Prince George 136
Fort Rupert 117
Fort St David 132, 147
Fort St Frédéric 129, 139
Fort St George 131, 148, 191
Fort St Jean 135, 165, 166
Fort St Louis 146
Fort Sandusky 156
Fort Washington 172
Fort William 30, 132–3
Fort William Henry 118, 139–40
Forth, Firth of 22
Fox, Charles James 178
Fox (Native Americans) 125
Fraser, Major-General Alexander 251–2
Frederick the Great, of Prussia 31, 45,
    54, 62, 71–2, 102–3, 105, 212,
    279–80, 290
Freemantle, Vice-Admiral Thomas 237
French Revolutionary War 193–200,
    221–8, 274, 280–1
frigates 107
Fullarton, Colonel 188
Fulton, Robert 283
Furnes 66

Gabarus Bay 129
Gaeta 227
Gage, General Thomas 138, 164–5
Galle 244
Galway 19–20
Galway, Henry, Earl of 56–7
Gambier, Admiral James 231, 237
Gaspé Peninsula 142
Gates, General Horatio 169
Gell, Rear-Admiral John 225
Genoa 89, 217, 228
George I 21, 61, 87–8, 90
George II 3, 16, 25, 29, 61–2, 65, 70,
    88–9, 277, 280
George III 38–9, 68, 74, 153, 163

Georgia 126, 174
Ghent, Peace of 255
Ghent, Treaty of (1814) 238
Gheria 123, 132
Gibbon, Edward 30, 32
Gibraltar 32, 55–6, 60, 84, 88, 95, 108,
    112, 177–8, 180–3, 189–90, 193,
    197, 218
Gillespie, Brigadier-General Robert 263
Ginkel, Godard van Reede van 19
Glorious Revolution (1688–9) vii, 1, 12,
    21, 267, 270–1, 282
Goddard, Colonel Thomas 162, 185–6
Gordon, George, 1st Duke of 13
Gordon Riots 43
Gorée 146, 152, 183, 244, 248
Graham, Lieutenant-General Thomas
    211
Granby, Lieutenant-General John
    Manners, Marquis of 45, 73, 242
Grant, Major James 145
Graves, Admiral Thomas 180
Great Lakes 125, 128, 156, 238
Greene, General Nathanael 169, 171, 264
Grenada 147, 180, 182, 242
Grey, Lieutenant-General Sir Charles
    242–3, 248
Guadeloupe 85, 119–20, 146–7, 151, 242,
    277
Guatemala 128
guerre de course 82
guerrillas 39–40, 212
Gurkhas 264, 283
Gurrumcondah 259
Gwalior 186–7

Haidar Ali, of Mysore 9, 161, 163, 183,
    186–91, 243
Haiti 242
Halifax 110, 130, 136, 139, 142, 151,
    174, 236
Hamilton, William, 2nd Duke of 23
Hanover 68, 71–2, 103–5
Hardy, Admiral Charles 180
Harris, Major-General George 259
Harrison, John 163
Harvey, Rear-Admiral Henry 243
Hastings, Francis 264
Hastings, Warren 186–7, 189
Hatton, Michael 71–2
Havana 98, 149, 151, 234
Haviland, Colonel William 143
Hawaii 163
Hawke, Admiral Edward 40, 97–8, 107,
    109, 111
Helder, Den 193, 196

Herbert, Admiral Arthur, Earl of Torrington 80
Hervey, Captain Augustus 147, 151
Hessians 167, 171, 189, 276
Hewes, John Oldershaw 232–3
Hexham 23
Highland charge 13, 25–6, 28
Highlands, Scottish 13–14, 25
Hill, Brigadier-General John 121
Hill, Captain John 199–200, 208, 291–2
Hispaniola 86
Hodgson, Major-General Studholme 74–5, 152, 278, 286
Holburne, Admiral Francis 105, 109
Holdernesse, Robert 4th Earl of 101, 105–6
Holkar 262, 264
Holmes, Commodore Charles 109
Hood, Admiral Lord 195
Hooghly 117
Hopson, Major-General Peregrine 147
Hopsonn, Vice-Admiral Thomas 21
Hosier, Vice-Admiral Francis 89
Hoste, Captain William 234, 237
Hotham, Sir Charles 61
Hotham, Vice-Admiral William 217, 223
Houghers 41
Howe, Admiral Richard Lord 109, 171, 178, 222
Howe, General William 166–8, 171, 174
Hudson Bay 115, 116, 122, 130, 136, 180
Hudson valley 129, 140, 142, 167, 172, 184, 270
Hughes, Vice-Admiral Sir Edward 183
Huguenots 15
Hull 12
Humbert, General Jean 38
Huron 130
Huy 47, 49, 51
Hyderabad 132, 148, 161, 255, 259–60, 263

Ibizi 84
income tax 2, 200
India 32, 123, 130–5, 147–9, 160–4, 183, 222, 243–4, 248, 255–67, 283, 291–2
Inverness 22, 25, 28
Ionian Islands 202, 204, 223, 231
Ireland 14–20, 34–40, 49, 61, 80, 82, 96, 111, 119, 180, 221, 235, 243, 277, 284, 286–7
Irish Legion 39
Ironside, Gilbert 134
Iroquois 118, 125, 128–9
Ischia 204, 227
Italy 31

Jackson, Andrew 254
Jacobites 3, 11–34, 44, 68, 90–1, 129, 147, 171, 173
Jaffna 244
Jamaica 5, 95–6, 98, 116, 120, 122, 151, 159, 180, 189, 242, 276
James II 1, 9, 11–12, 14–17, 19–20, 30, 44, 47–9
'James III' 20–2, 24, 26, 48, 57, 89
James Bay 117
Jamestown 117
Jenkins, Captain Robert 125
Jenkins' Ear, War of (1739–48) 60, 92, 125–8
Jenkinson, Charles 272
Jennings, Admiral Sir John 84, 90
Jervis, Rear-Admiral Sir John 223–4, 239, 243
Johnson, William 129, 139
Joseph Bonaparte 46, 213

Kajor 146
Kalpi 148
Karikal 148
Kassel 73
Keith, George Admiral Lord 224, 228
Keith, George, 10th Earl Marischal 24–5
Kelso 23
Kempenfelt, Admiral Richard 150
Keppel, Admiral Augustus 112, 152, 178–9
Khanderi 123
Kingston 238, 254
Kinsale 14–15, 17–19, 82
Knowles, Admiral Charles 98, 128

L'Etanduère, Marquis de 97
La Bourdonnais 130–1
La Galissonière, Marquis de 108
Lake Champlain 121, 129, 135, 139, 143, 165, 167, 254–5, 270
Lake, General, Gerard 38, 194, 261–2, 264
Lake George 118, 140
Lally, Thomas, Count of 144, 147–9
Lancashire 23
Lancaster 27
Lawrence, Stringer 132, 148
Le Havre 111, 234, 237
Le Marchant, Lieutenant-Colonel John 200, 209
Leake, Vice Admiral Sir John 84, 87
Leeward Islands 119, 129
Légion Noir 36
Leinster 37
Lestock, Vice-Admiral Richard 94

Lexington 164
Lezo, Don Blas de 127
Liège 49
light infantry 138, 198, 200–1
Lille 31, 53–5, 66
Limerick 16–20, 82
Lindisfarne 23
Lindsay, Commodore Sir John 108
Lisbon 83, 89, 208
Livorno 223, 227, 235
logistics 24, 49–50, 52, 57, 71–2, 75–6, 100, 119–20, 184, 187, 210, 212, 256–7, 257, 278
London 27, 40, 43, 47, 293
Londonderry 15–16, 20, 82
Lorient 73, 75, 129, 225
Loring, Captain John 237
Lorraine 65
Loudoun, John 4th Earl of 139–40
Louis XIV 12, 19–21, 46–58, 84, 119
Louis XV 66
Louisbourg 8, 96, 98, 109–10, 129–30, 136–7, 139–42, 152
Louisiana 109, 116, 129
Lowe, Colonel Hudson 203, 217–18, 246
Loyalists 34, 172, 174, 189
Luddites 43, 284
Luxembourg, François, Duke of 46, 58
Lyttleton, William 145

Maastricht 69
Macao 293
Macartney, George, Lord 188, 257
Mackay, Hugh 13–14
Madras 117, 130–2, 135, 147–9, 161, 183, 187, 189, 191, 239, 259, 267, 286, 287
Madrid 56–7, 206, 209
Madurai 160–1
Mahé 183, 186
Maine 121, 125, 165
Maitland, Brigadier-General Thomas 243
Majorca 84
Malacca 82, 98, 244
Malcolm, Brigadier-General Sir John 265
Malta 212, 227–8, 239, 247, 281
Manchester 27
Mangalore 189, 191
Mangalore, Treaty of (1784) 189
Manila 149–50, 161, 275
Manila Galleon 1, 98
Mar, John, 11th Earl of 22–3, 57
Marathas 123, 133, 184–6, 255–6, 260–7
Marlborough, John, 1st Duke of 3, 18, 45, 49–60, 65, 69, 73, 82, 121–2, 272–3, 278–9, 289

Marlborough, Charles, 3rd Duke of 71, 75
Maroons 122, 159, 242, 276
Marseilles 7
martello towers 201
Martin, Vice-Admiral William 94, 96
Martinique 85, 100, 146–7, 152, 229, 248, 277
Massachusetts 4, 117–18, 121, 125, 129, 136, 283
Masséna, Marshal André 46, 207–8, 212–13
Massey, Colonel William 143
Mathews, Admiral Thomas 94
Mauritius 130–1, 183, 249–50, 263
Maynard, Lieutenant 43
Mediterranean 82–5, 87–8, 92, 94, 102, 105–6, 108–9, 111–12, 119–20, 223, 231, 236, 280
Medows, General Sir William 256, 258–9
Menin 52, 66
Meuse, river 49, 51, 68
Miami (Native Americans) 125, 130, 135, 156
Middleton, Admiral Charles 181, 239
Middleton, Captain Christopher 130
militia 36, 39, 43–4, 117, 121–2, 124, 137–8, 159, 164, 176, 276–8
Minden 73
Minorca 32–3, 56, 61, 84, 88, 96, 102, 108, 180, 183, 189–90, 196, 218, 227–8, 270, 281
Minto, Gilbert, Lord 293
Miquelon 248
Mir Jaffir 123–4
Mir Qasim 134–5
Mississippi, river 128
Mitchell, Vice-Admiral Andrew 196
Mobile 120, 182, 254
Mohawks 118, 129
Mohicans 118
Monckton, Lieutenant-Colonel Robert 137, 147
Monmouth, James, Duke of 21, 30, 32, 49
Monongahela, river 136
Mons 46, 53–4, 68
Montcalm, Louis Joseph, Marquis of 139–40, 142–3
Montevideo 250–1, 291
Montgomery, Colonel Archibald 145
Montgomery, Richard 165–6
Montréal 118, 122, 135, 137–80, 144–5, 158, 165, 253
Montrose 24
Montserrat 182

Moore, Governor James 120, 124
Moore, General Sir John 195, 198,
    200–1, 203, 206–7, 220, 247
Mordaunt, Sir John 74
Mosquito Coast 126, 128, 286
Moyry Pass 17
Mughals 8, 117, 134, 186
Mull 14
multiple capability 284
Munro, Sir Hector 135, 187, 192
Münster 73
Murray, Brigadier James 144
Murray, Lieutenant-General Sir John
    211–12
Mysore viii, 8, 112, 186–9

Namur 46, 51, 54, 68
Naples 85, 106, 202
Napoleon 195–6, 201–2, 204, 206–23,
    244–5, 247, 253, 255, 269, 272, 287,
    288, 290–1
Nassau 182
Native Americans 109, 115–17, 120–1,
    124–6, 135–9, 155–9
Ne Plus Ultra 54
Nelson, Admiral Lord 9, 182, 223,
    225–30, 234, 237, 245, 293
Nepal 264–5, 289
Neville, Vice-Admiral 83
Nevis 116, 120, 182
New Caledonia 163
New England 96, 116–18, 120–3,
    128–30, 164–5, 168, 173
New Jersey 167, 169, 172, 191
New Orleans 99, 116, 125, 129, 136,
    147, 167, 169–70, 174, 191, 275
New Ross 37
New York 285
New Zealand 162
Newcastle 23, 27
Newcastle, Thomas, 1st Duke of 3, 90,
    93–5, 97–8, 101, 104–5, 136, 152
Newfoundland 83, 87, 96, 112, 118, 120,
    122, 151, 282
Newport 167, 175
Niagara 119, 143, 253–4
Nicaragua 126, 128
Nijmegen 195
Nine Years' War 9, 45–7, 79–83, 86,
    103, 117–20
Normandy 92
North Carolina 43, 124, 174
North, Frederick, Lord 170–1
North Sea 68
Northumberland 23
Northwest Passage 130

Nottingham 12
Nottinghamshire 43
Nova Scotia (Acadia) 96, 122, 136–7,
    152, 173, 282

Oakboys 35
Ochakov crisis 89, 107
Ochterlony, Major-General David 264
Ogle, Rear-Admiral Sir Chaloner 43, 127
Oglethorpe, Colonel James 126
Ohio Valley 125, 130, 135–7, 141
Oman, Sir John 202
Oneida 118
Ontario 125
Oporto 75, 206–7
Ordnance, Board of 47, 62, 74, 152, 268,
    278
Ormonde, James, 2nd Duke of 24–5, 55
Osborne, Admiral Henry 109
Ostend 33, 52, 68, 89, 93–4, 196
Oswego 125, 139
Oudenaarde 52, 68
Oudh 135, 161–2, 187

Pacific Ocean 1, 130, 142, 150, 162–3
Padang 244
Pakenham, Major-General Sir Edward
    254
Palembang 263
Palmer, Colonel John 120
Palmerston, Henry, Viscount 269
Panama 127–8
Paris, Peace of (1763) 153, 155
Parker, Admiral Sir Hyde 181, 228
Parliament 1–4, 27, 39–40, 48, 79,
    268–9, 271–2
Parma 91
Pasajres 210
Paterson, George 108–9, 162
Pelham, Henry 69
Pellew, Edward 224, 236
Peninsular War 194, 205–15, 218–20,
    238, 268, 288, 290
Pennsylvania 141
Penrith 27
Pensacola 120, 182
Pepperell, William 129
Perak 244
Persian Gulf 285
Perth 13–14, 22, 24, 26
Perumbakam 187–8
Peter the Great, of Russia 59, 87–8, 103,
    107
Peterhead 24
Peyton, Commodore Edward 98, 131
Philadelphia 100, 167–8, 172, 191

Philip V, of Spain 24, 47–8, 55–6, 88, 128
Philippines 6, 98, 149–51, 285
Phillips, William 72–3
Phips, Sir William 117–18
Pickawillany 135
pikes 39, 47, 60, 283
piracy 42–3, 123
Pitt, William, the Elder 3, 74, 140, 158
Pitt, William, the Younger 199, 281
Pittsburg 136
Plattsburg 254
Plymouth 68, 82–3, 95, 146, 199
Pocock, Commodore George 100, 107, 109, 149
Poland 107
Polish Succession, War of the (1733–5) 2, 61–2, 69, 88
Pondicherry 131–2, 147–9, 152, 183, 192, 222, 244, 277
Pontiac's War 155–9, 161, 286
Popham, Captain William 186
Port Royal 118, 121–2, 129
Porto Bello 127–8
Porto Novo 191
Portsmouth 68, 80, 82–3, 111, 199, 239
Portugal 56–7, 71, 75–7, 82–3, 89, 112, 115, 126, 159, 205, 218, 268
Prague 31, 33
Preston 27
Prideaux, Brigadier-General John 143
Prince Edward Island 141–2
privateering, British 7, 100
privateering, French 7, 82, 84, 93, 100, 102, 118, 120, 231
Procida 204, 227
Provence 84
Prussia 5, 45, 62, 76–8, 104–5, 194, 198, 215, 272
Puerto Rico 90, 243
Pulicat 149, 183
Pune (Poona) 184, 260
Pym, Captain Samuel 249–50

Quadruple Alliance, War of (1718–20) 60, 106
Québec 45, 76, 87, 118–19, 121–2, 133, 138–9, 142, 152, 165–6, 174–5, 190–1, 277, 285
Queenston 253
Quiberon Bay 36

Rainier, Commodore Peter 244
recruitment 272–8
Red Sea 245, 247
Rhode Island 4, 167, 172

Richelieu, Louis-François-Armand, Duke of 33, 87, 102
rifles 214
Riga 31, 106
Rightboys 35
Rijnberk 49
Rijswijk, Treaty of 21, 47
Riot Act (1715) 43
riots 41–3, 284
Rivers, Lieutenant-Colonel 120
Roberts, Bartholomew 43
Robin, Benjamin 69
Rochefort 74–5, 80, 109, 112, 142, 152, 229, 234–5
Rodney, Admiral George 107, 111, 169, 180–2, 191
Roermond 49
Rogers, Major Robert 145
Rollo, Andrew, 5th Lord 147
Rooke, Admiral George 82–3, 85
Ross, Major-General Robert 254
Russell, Admiral Edward 80–3, 91
Russia 70, 87–9, 102–3, 105, 111, 271–2, 279–80, 288–9

Sackville, Major-General Lord George 72, 138, 177
Sadras 183
St Augustine 120, 126, 128
St Barthélemy 243
St Cast 74
St Croix 248
St Eustatius 182, 249
St Helena 217–18
St John's Newfoundland 112, 118, 151
St Kitts 86, 116, 119–20, 182
St Lawrence 117–19, 122, 129–30, 136–7, 142, 144, 165–6, 248, 253
St Lucia 147, 182, 193, 242, 248
St Malo 7, 74–5, 82–3, 95, 109
St Martin 243, 249
St Pierre 248
St Ruth, Marquis de 19
St Vincent 147, 159–60, 182, 242
Saint-Domingue 128, 147, 234, 242, 248
Saint-Venant 54–5
Saintes 84
Salbai, Treaty of (1782) 186, 189
Saldanha Bay 183
Salisbury 12
Saltonstall, Dudley 176
San Sebastian 60, 210
Sandwich, John, 4th Earl of 98, 177
Santiago de Cuba 127–8
Saratoga 129
Sardinia, island of 84

Sarsfield, Patrick 18–19
Saumarez, Vice-Admiral Sir James 224, 233, 235
Savannah 33, 168, 170, 175, 238
Savona 228
Savoy 84
Saxe, Marshal Maurice de 25, 31, 46, 66–9, 69, 73, 102
Saxony 31
Schenectady 117
Schomberg, Marshall Herman von 15–16
Scone 24
Scotland 11, 13–14, 21–34, 39, 44, 111, 115, 277, 284
Sekondi 122
Senegal 189, 248
sepoys 132, 159, 190, 262–3, 265, 275
Seringapatam 257–9, 291
Seven Years' War (1756–63) 3, 5, 9, 34–5, 45, 70–8, 92, 101, 105–13, 127, 177, 190, 274, 278, 280, 286–7
Seychelles 244
Shannon, river 17–19
Sharp, Horatio 139
Shawnee 156–7, 160
Sheaffe, Major-General Roger 253
Sheerness 83
Shore, Sir John 256, 263
Shovell, Admiral Sir Cloudesley 84
Sicily 6, 24, 60, 87–8, 203–4, 211, 247
sieges 31–2
Sikhs 264–5
Silesia 31, 62, 70, 90
Siraj-ud-daula 132–3
Skelly, Major viii, 257–8, 291
Slade, Sir Thomas 107
slave trade 115–16
slaves 124, 159, 242
smallpox 124, 157, 249
Smith, Captain William Sidney 227
Smith, Major-General Joseph 161
smuggling 41–2, 284
Smyrna 82, 225
Soult, Marshal Nicolas 207–8, 210–11, 219
South Carolina 122, 124, 126, 136, 145, 168, 172, 174
Spain 39–40, 48, 56–60, 70, 75–6, 83, 85–92, 106, 108–9, 115, 119, 125–8, 149–53, 163, 177, 206–15, 221–3, 233, 286–7, 281, 286–8
Spanish Succession, War of the (1702–13) 6, 20–1, 45–60, 75, 83–7, 96, 103, 106, 126, 153, 272, 290
Spithead 90, 239
Sri Lanka 112, 183, 218, 244, 247, 263

Stair, John, 2nd Earl of 63, 65, 289–90
Stamp Act 3
Stanhope, James, Viscount 88
Stepney, George 84–5
Stewart, Colonel John 287
Stevens, Rear-Admiral Charles 149, 152
Stirling 16, 22
Stone, Andrew 94
Stono Ferry 175
Stono rising 122
Stornoway 24
Strachan, Captain Richard 224, 230
Stuart, Charles Edward 14, 16, 26–32, 44, 68, 95, 126, 267
Stuart, Major-General James 188
Stuart, Major-General John 202–4
subsidies 71
Suffren, Admiral Pierre André 183, 227
Sumatra 183, 244, 248, 263
Surat 185
Surinam 6, 202, 243
Sweden 83, 87–9, 102–3, 105, 111, 233, 279, 289
Swift, Jonathan 59

Tagus river 76, 207, 231
Tahiti 162
Talhahassee 120
Talmash, Lieutenant-General Thomas 46
Tangier 49
Tanjore 162
Tarleton, Colonel Banastre 169
Tate, William 36
taxation 3, 200, 268
teredo worm 181
Thurot, Commodore François 34–5
Ticonderoga 139–40, 142, 152, 167, 277
Tipu Sultan, of Mysore viii, 9, 188, 191, 255–9, 263
Tobago 182, 189, 242, 248
Tone, Wolfe 36, 224
Torbay 108, 111
Toronto 135, 217
Torres Vedras, Lines of 208
Toulon 80, 84–5, 88, 106, 109, 111, 177–8, 195–6, 218, 222, 225, 231, 234–6, 264
Tournai 53, 55, 66, 68, 195, 198
Tourville, Anne-Hilarion, Count of 80, 82
Townshend, Charles MP 136
Townshend, Charles 2nd Viscount 89–90
Townshend, George 4th Viscount 35
Traben-Tarbach 51

Trelawny, Edward 122, 128
Trevadi 132
Trichinopoly 131–2, 188
Trieste 237
Trincomalee 183, 190, 192, 239, 244
Trinidad 243, 244
Trois-Rivières 144
Troubridge, Captain Thomas 227, 234
Troyes, Pierre de 117
Tyler, Vice-Admiral Charles 42
Tyrconnel, Richard, Duke of 15

Ulm 50
Ulster 14–15, 20, 35, 37–8
Union of 1707 21–2
United Irishmen 35–8, 41
United Provinces, Dutch 4, 49, 51,
    65–6, 68, 70, 79–80, 83, 90, 101,
    107, 112, 115, 148, 177, 183, 194,
    176–7, 205, 219, 243, 272, 277,
    280–1, 286, 289
Ushant 97, 224
Utrecht, Treaty of (1713) 55, 88, 122,
    125

Valencia 56
Valenciennes 194
Vaudreuil, Marquis de 144
Vellore 265
Vermont 120, 124, 128–9
Vernon, Sir Edward 192
Vernon, Admiral Edward 94–5, 104,
    127–8
Versailles, Peace of (1783) 189
Victor Amadeus II 84
Vienna 33
Vigo 60, 83, 85, 197, 229, 231
Villaret-Joyeuse, Louis Thomas 222
Villars, Claude, Duke of 51, 53–5
Virginia 116, 124, 136, 138, 151, 160,
    169, 172, 288
Voltaire 108, 149
Volunteers 43–4, 201–2, 276–8

Wade, Field Marshal George 27, 44, 60,
    65–6
Wager, Admiral Charles 86–7, 89–90
Walcheren 9, 193, 203–4, 212, 220, 231
Wales 27, 32, 36, 40, 221
Walker, Rear-Admiral Sir Hovenden 121
Wallis, Samuel 162
Walpole, Horatio 275
Walpole, Sir Robert 2–3, 61, 92, 98, 127
War of 1812 215, 238, 251, 253–5, 284,
    287

War of the Austrian Succession (1740–8)
    see Austrian Succession, War of the
War of the Spanish Succession (1702–13)
    see Spanish Succession, War of the
War Office 269, 278
Warren, Admiral Sir Peter 96, 98–9, 129
Washington 238, 254
Washington, George 38, 136, 167–72, 176
Watson, Rear-Admiral Charles 132–3
Wauchope, Major-General Peter 252
weather 36, 71–2, 75
Wellesley, Arthur, 1st Duke of
    Wellington 8, 40, 45, 58, 73, 134,
    198, 203, 205–20, 236, 260–1,
    264–5, 268–9, 277, 283, 286, 289–91
Wentworth, Brigadier-General Thomas
    127
Weser, river 72
West Africa 43, 48, 115–16, 122–3, 146,
    189, 248
West Indies 37, 85–7, 89–92, 97, 99–100,
    112, 117–19, 146–7, 159, 180–2, 190,
    193, 198, 225, 236, 241–4, 247–9,
    287
Weston, Stephen 94–6
Westphalia 72–3
Wexford 37–8
Wheeler, Private William 209
Wheler, Rear-Admiral, Sir Francis
    118–19
Whitelocke, Lieutenant-General John
    250–1
Wightman, Major-General 25
"Wild Geese" 19
William III 1, 12–21, 30, 45–51, 118, 271
William V of Orange 244
Wills, Major-General Charles 23
Wilmot, Commodore Robert 119
Winthrop, Colonel 118
Wolfe, General James 45, 76, 140, 142–5,
    152, 275, 278
Woolwich 62, 77, 83
Wrenn, Commodore Ralph 119
Wright, Commodore Lawrence 119

Yamasee 120, 124
yellow fever 118, 243–4
Yeomanry 36
York 12, 118, 180
York, Frederick, Duke of 45, 158,
    194–5, 198, 200–1, 244, 253, 289
Yorkshire 27
Young, Vice-Admiral William 197
Ypres 66
Yusuf Khan 160–1